Writing Women in Modern China

WEATHERHEAD BOOKS ON ASIA

Weatherhead Books on Asia
COLUMBIA UNIVERSITY

LITERATURE

David Der-wei Wang, Editor

Ye Zhaoyan, *Nanjing 1937: A Love Story*, translated by Michael Berry

Makoto Oda, *The Breaking Jewel*, translated by Donald Keene

Han Shaogong, *A Dictionary of Maqiao*, translated by Julia Lovell

Takahashi Takako, *Lonely Woman*, translated by Maryellen Toman Mori

Chen Ran, *A Private Life*, translated by John Howard-Gibbon

Takeuchi Yoshimi, *What Is Modernity? Writings of Takeuchi Yoshimi*, translated by Richard Calichman

Eileen Chang, *Written on Water*, translated by Andrew F. Jones

David McCann, editor, *The Columbia Anthology of Modern Korean Poetry*

HISTORY, SOCIETY, AND CULTURE

Carol Gluck, Editor

Richard Calichman, editor, *Contemporary Japanese Thought*

Writing Women
in Modern China

THE REVOLUTIONARY YEARS, 1936–1976

EDITED BY

Amy D. Dooling

Columbia University Press New York

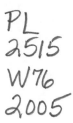
This publication has been supported by the Richard W. Weatherhead Publication Fund
of the East Asian Institute, Columbia University.

COLUMBIA UNIVERSITY PRESS
Publishers Since 1893
New York   Chichester, West Sussex
Copyright © 2005 Columbia University Press
All rights reserved
Library of Congress Cataloging-in-Publication Data
Writing women in modern China : the revolutionary years, 1936–1976 / edited
by Amy D. Dooling.
p.   cm. — (Weatherhead books on Asia)
Includes bibliographical references.
ISBN 0–231–13216–6 (cloth) — ISBN 0–231–13217–4 (pbk.)
1. Chinese literature—Women authors. 2. Chinese literature—20th century—
Translations into English. 3. Women and literature—China. I. Dooling, Amy D.
II. Series.
PL2515.W76   2004
895.1'0809287'0904—dc22
2004058206

∞

Columbia University Press books are printed on permanent
and durable acid-free paper.

Designed by Lisa Hamm
Printed in the United States of America
c 10 9 8 7 6 5 4 3 2 1
p 10 9 8 7 6 5 4 3 2 1

Lovingly dedicated to my mother,

Margaret D. McLaughlin

Contents

Acknowledgments

The second volume of *Writing Women in Modern China* was made possible by the solid support and assistance of a great many people. To them all, I owe a huge debt of gratitude. My esteemed colleagues Hu Mingliang and Tek-wah King offered rapid and always thoughtful responses to my countless translation questions. Shu Yunzhong generously read and checked drafts, and Rachel Wang helped immensely in improving the language of key passages. Charlotte Dooling allowed me once again to draw on her expertise in drama to help polish the Yang Jiang play.

Jeffrey Kinkley provided continuing encouragement on the project as a whole and in addition helped me locate a photograph of Chen Xuezhao. Steve MacKinnon offered useful details from his own research for the biography on Yang Gang. Lily-Chia Brissman and Barry Brissman generously shared their family photographs of Xie Bingying, as well as valuable biographical information. The eminent translator Sidney Shapiro provided immeasurable help on the biography of his late wife Fengzi, as well as a lovely photograph. And, finally, the staff at the Museum of Modern Chinese Literature in Beijing supplied important bibliographic material for several of the author profiles.

Thanks also go to Geremie Barmé, for permission to reprint his translation of the Zong Pu story, and to Howard Goldblatt and Indiana University Press, for permission to reprint the Chen Ruoxi story. The long process of hunting down the rare revolutionary papercut used for the cover art was finally brought to an end with the collective help of Charles Laughlin (in Beijing), Stephan Landsberger (in the Netherlands), and Justin G. Schiller (in Vermont).

And, of course, thanks to my adept translators, Hu Mingliang, Ann Huss, Sabina Knight, Shu Yunzhong, Cathy Silber, and Robin Visser, who never once complained about the tight deadlines I imposed. I am most grateful for their contributions to this volume.

Finally, special thanks are also due to the Chiang Ching-kuo Foundation, which provided an invaluable postdoctoral research award that allowed me to begin work on this project; to Kristina Torgeson for giving me the confidence that I could do the volume solo; to Bruce Branchini, whose generous grant to the Connecticut College Faculty Development Fund spurred me on to complete the project; to the Department of East Asian Languages and Cultures at Connecticut College; and to Jennifer Crewe, Leslie Kriesel, and the anonymous readers for Columbia University Press for supporting the sequel volume. Most of all, thanks to Peter Hitchcock for his steadfast encouragement and brilliant suggestions, and, as always, for keeping life in perspective.

Introduction

"Women and revolution! What tragic, unsung epics of courage lie silent in the world's history!" Thus muses the narrator of a 1936 short story by the writer Yang Gang (1905–1957). On the run from the authorities and with her comrade-lover imprisoned, this female political activist faces the devastating prospect of terminating an unplanned pregnancy, alone, at a moment of great national upheaval. The decision resonates on deeply personal and political, physical, and psychological levels, yet she seems oddly resigned to the fact that her struggle will not figure into the story of revolution, even as she takes pains to inscribe the experience in her diary. Reading this text today, one might be struck by how this paradoxical attitude relates to the predicament of the woman writer at that defining moment of modern Chinese history. On the one hand, Yang Gang's steady literary output as an acclaimed journalist, newspaper editor, poet, translator, and novelist, along with that of her many female contemporaries, strongly belies the notion that women's voices were somehow muted in the post–May Fourth era. For all the historical challenges brought on by war, foreign occupation, and revolution, not to mention the advent of Mao's socialist state, a good number of female writers committed to imagining and inscribing new meanings of Chinese womanhood continued to compose and to publish in the middle decades of the twentieth century, often—not unlike Yang Gang's narrator—under difficult circumstances and at some personal risk. On the other hand, however, it is still difficult to find references to, let alone serious analyses of, many such writers in mainstream literary studies and cultural histories. Indeed, notable exceptions notwithstanding, it is commonly suggested that the tumultuous mid-century decades all but stifled the nascent gendered expression nurtured by the previous generations and that only with the sweeping political reforms beginning in the late 1970s was such a tradition revived in women's literature. In other words, between the extraordinary bursts of female literary activity in the May Fourth and post–Mao eras is said to lie a long stretch of revolutionary history representing a protracted interlude in the project of "writing women in modern China."

The ideological and institutional reasons for this erasure, and how mytholo-gies of female silence are maintained and reproduced in mainstream Chinese literary studies today, are multifaceted problems that warrant a study of their own. Meanwhile, important efforts are under way in the field to remedy this gap.[1] This second volume of *Writing Women in Modern China* foregrounds the work of twelve authors active in the period from 1936 to 1976, aiming to foster further discussion about the diverse ways women's cultural responses to this complex era were informed by their gendered positions and perspectives, and how in turn they helped rearticulate the narratives of nation and revolution. Women's texts from the revolutionary period are neither necessarily tragic nor epic: the selections featured here include succinct journalistic forms that strive to capture snapshots of contemporary historical circumstances, deliberately comic accounts of the politics and culture of twentieth-century urban exis-tence, and carefully stylized, modernist experiments in fiction. And they do not articulate the relationship between women and revolution from any one ideological vantage point. Even within the left wing, women writers took a variety of stands on the Communist Party's radical agenda, while some of the most outstanding writers of the period bracketed topical political themes in their creative work altogether.

✻ ✻ ✻ ✻ ✻

TO HELP SITUATE the translations selected for the present volume within their historical and cultural milieu, this introduction provides a brief overview of some of the key contexts and trends in Chinese women's writing during the decades leading up to and following the founding of the People's Republic of China (PRC) in 1949 (1930s–1970s). As a whole, this body of work owes an unmistakable debt to the fundamental reconfiguration of women's social, po-litical, and cultural roles under way since the turn of the century. As described in the first volume of *Writing Women in Modern China,* the achievement of greater educational opportunities for women, demands for freedom of literary and political expression, and the quest for economic and sexual autonomy were embedded in the larger context of the national salvation movement, which continued to shape women's literary production throughout the thir-ties and forties. I begin with the palpable political turn Chinese literature in general took in the mid–1930s as writers, a good many women in their ranks, gravitated toward the leftist cause and devoted themselves to political advo-cacy. In addition to critical realist fiction, first popularized in the May Fourth era, literary reportage emerged as a key genre for writers who embraced a conception of literature as a tool for national resistance and class struggle. Next, I examine the ways in which women's writing of the period achieved new levels of technical mastery—most evident in the work of urban writers of occupied Shanghai and Beijing of the forties, who employ highly sophisticated descriptive techniques and narrative perspectives in their fiction, drama, and autobiography. And finally, I touch on the conflicts and challenges writers, male and female alike, faced as they coped with concerted state intervention in literary culture and the successive ideological campaigns of the Maoist regime after the founding of the People's Republic in 1949. The location of Chinese women's writing underwent major shifts in this period: whereas May Fourth literary production had emanated almost entirely from the semicolonial cities of Shanghai and Beijing, the historical conditions from the 1930s to the 1970s radically redrew the map of literary culture. Even before full-scale war broke out in 1937, some writers had uprooted themselves to avoid the political persecution of the Nationalist regime, leaving the country altogether—like Hu Lanqi (1901–1994), Chen Xuezhao (1906–1991), and Lu Jingqing (1907–1993)—or making their way out to Yan'an in northwest China—as did Ding Ling (1904–1986) and Chen Bo'er (1910–1951). After the onset of hostilities with Japan, many other established female intellectuals and writers—Bai Wei (1894–1987), Yuan Changying (1894–1973), Su Xuelin (1896–1999), Ling Shuhua (1900–1990), and Zhao Qingge (b. 1914), to name a few—joined the exodus of educated urban citizens to the Chinese interior to continue their work. No longer the center of the nation's cultural life, occupied Shanghai and, to a somewhat lesser degree, Beijing would nevertheless reemerge as vibrant enclaves of literary production during the war, for in the place of those who left sprung a new crop of women writers, including Su Qing (1917–1982), Yang Jiang (b. 1911), Zhang Ailing (1920–1995), and Mei Niang (b. 1920), who brought both a distinct sensibility and a unique style to their treatment of gender-specific issues.[2] Finally, in the period leading up to the Communist victory and subsequently, authors were explicitly urged to turn their focus away from privileged metropolitan settings to the rural landscape so that literature, in accordance with Maoist doctrine, would better reflect the lives of its intended mass audience. To accelerate this reorientation, in many cases creative writers themselves physically relocated, voluntarily or not, down to the countryside (or *xiafang*) to get to know firsthand the everyday realities of peasant life.

Women and the 1930s Literary Left

A PROGRESSIVE IMPULSE clearly underpins women's modern literary production of the early twentieth century, but what distinguishes the mid-thirties is the extent to which socially conscious women authors gravitated toward the leftist cultural groups that organized in response to the political and economic crisis gripping the Chinese nation. Apart from their active involvement with the League of Left-Wing Writers, a radical organization formed in 1930 with the express purpose of promoting proletarian culture, some joined propaganda teams that toured villages and small towns to raise public consciousness about the war effort, while others signed up with troupes of traveling performing artists. In a certain number of cases, such individuals were (or were soon to become) members of the Chinese Communist Party (CCP) (f. 1921). Among the women writers whose names began to appear in association with the activities of the progressive intelligentsia were Ding Ling, Bai Wei, Guan Lu (1907–1982), Chen Xuezhao, Xie Bingying (1906–2000), Yang Gang, and Luo Shu (1903–1938), all of whose publications dating from this period evinced heightened interest in the possibilities of politically engaged art, and the relationship of the writer/intellectual to processes of revolutionary change. In terms of specific thematic substance, one finds in their work resolute opposition to Japanese imperialism and impassioned pleas for support of the emergent peasant and working-class struggles. An increasing number of radical women writers also took it upon themselves to recast the politics of nation and class as an integral dimension of women's fight for socioeconomic justice. Such connections were hardly new to Chinese feminist literary discourse, but, as contemporary scholars have observed, the conditions of national emergency on the eve of World War II seemed to work against the "gendered" writing that had flourished earlier in the twentieth century. Wendy Larson, for instance, has cogently shown that as liberal and leftist critics began to call with greater urgency for an alternative literary practice more attuned to the social realities of the day, they often singled out contemporary women writers for their alleged "individualism, an excessive narrow scope and framework, a mystifying approach to experience, a lack of social knowledge and awareness, extreme emotionalism, pessimism and doubt, escapism, a poetic and romantic mentality, decadence, emphasis on individual (and especially female) psychology and on various kinds of love and love conflicts."[3] Yet, in spite of the relatively hostile critical climate, female literary radicals did not automatically abandon their feminist agenda, and quite a few continued publishing work that dealt explicitly with such issues as sexual freedom, domesticity, and the path to socioeconomic equality. The neglect this work has subsequently suffered, however, bespeaks the ongoing need for a revised understanding of the history of women's literary radicalism of this period.

Consider, for instance, the writer Bai Wei, a prominent member of the cultural left who contributed regularly to progressive literary journals in Shanghai, like Lu Xun's magazine *Torrents* and *Big Dipper,* the periodical Ding Ling edited for the League of Left-Wing Writers. In the wake of the September 18th incident, when the Japanese launched their military campaign in northeast China, she had been among the first to publish works protesting Japanese aggression, such as her 1932 play *A Certain Stop on Beining Road.* Bai Wei also played an instrumental role in mobilizing writers and artists in Shanghai as the anti-imperialist movement heated up, working tirelessly in progressive drama and film circles.[4] By the mid-thirties, however, she had grown frustrated by what she perceived as a marginalization of the cause of women's emancipation within leftist circles and accordingly published a series of works that challenged not only the dichotomies between self and society, personal and political, private and public that were coming to regulate the leftist discourse on revolutionary writing of the 1930s but also, more specifically, the ways those dichotomies threatened to contain gender issues. As she commented in defense of her writing at the time:

> A few years ago, revolutionary literature was all the rage in China; everyone devoted themselves to decrying the plight of the working class, though few paid attention to the far worse plight of women. Right now, the wheels of history are turning backward: the women who lifted their heads after the May Fourth movement are being forced back into the home, into that tomb, by the dark hands of the era. At the same time, the corrupt feudal patriarchy has reasserted itself within that tomb, demonstrating its force, wreaking havoc. . . . I wanted to use the opportunity to highlight as well as I could some of the innermost sufferings of women.[5]

Her 1935 short story "Suffering Women,"[6] for example, juxtaposes the plight of two embattled women in Shanghai, a poverty-stricken intellectual in poor physical health and a destitute refugee from the northeastern countryside now in her employ, to explore the classed nature of women's oppression. Similarly, her "Third-Class Hospital Ward," the series of reportage sketches translated here, seizes on the trope of illness to examine the ways poverty compounds female subjugation. No longer the figurative marker of modern romantic subjectivity, as exemplified by Ding Ling's memorable heroine Sophie, the afflicted female bodies that the I-narrator observes during her hospitalization—bodies ravaged by male brutality, economic deprivation, and sexually transmitted diseases—bear witness to the grim material realities that condition the lives of the female urban poor; they are, as the narrator aptly envisages them, "warriors," injured and maimed by the battles of daily life in a class society.

Literary activists like Bai Wei also grappled with the specific challenges facing the female revolutionary who rejects prescribed gender roles to work for a better future for society as a whole. *My Tragic Life* (1936), for example, her most ambitious creative work from these years, is a harrowing autobiographical novel tracing the vicissitudes of a young female radical entangled in an abusive romantic relationship that leaves her with a severe case of venereal disease.[7] Unlike many well-known examples of left-wing fiction and film of the 1930s, the novel does not dismiss romantic love and sexuality as obsolete middle-class issues antithetical to revolutionary endeavors; rather, they are shown to inform, for better or worse, the relationships of the men and women who pursue such endeavors.[8] The travails of female activists caught up in sociopolitical movements seemingly insensitive—if not altogether indifferent—to their concerns took other forms as well. Works of short fiction tracing the trauma of unwanted pregnancy or the complex impact of motherhood on political commitments and party work, for instance, implicitly interrogate the separation of private and public experience and problematize the revolutionary narrative in which female desire is mobilized on behalf of national salvation.[9] Yang Gang's 1936 work "Fragment from a Lost Diary," included in this volume, is one of several stories by women on this particular theme. A founding member of the Beijing Branch of the League of Left-Wing Writers and an early member of the Chinese Communist Party, Yang Gang originally composed the story for Edgar Snow's collection of contemporary fiction *Living China*. The author recycles the hugely popular fictionalized diary format to capture the intense mental, moral, and emotional anguish that engulf a woman radical as she contemplates the meaning of reproduction and motherhood amid the perilous throes of revolutionary change. For this writer, clearly, meaningful change in the contemporary social order was not to be achieved by transcending gendered subjectivity but instead by transforming it. More pointedly perhaps, the story makes the compelling case that the specific adversities women activists often encounter at times of great social upheaval need to be recognized as forms of struggle in their own right. Thus, in the very act of telling this story, Yang Gang implicitly takes issue with the lament of her lead character that women's participation in the fight for social change is doomed to be written out of history.

If leftist literary culture in China can be faulted for having granted insufficient space to feminist voices, socially conscious women writers nevertheless helped to shape a revolutionary discourse on gender emancipation by contributing to the many liberal-leftist publications of the day. In such literary journals as *Literature Monthly* and *Big Dipper*, both overseen by the League of Left-Wing Writers, for instance, readers often found featured works by Bai Wei, Yang Gang, and Ding Ling, among others. One of the most influential venues for feminist writing at the time, however, was the Shanghai-based *Women's Life* magazine, edited by the feminist social activist Shen Zijiu (1898–1989). Regular contributors included Luo Qiong, Hu Lanqi, Xie Bingying, Bai Wei, and Peng Zigang (1914–1988), as well as such prominent male leftists as Mao Dun, Xia Yan, and Jin Zhonghua.[10] The journal, financed by the progressive Shenghuo bookstore, was launched in 1935, and regularly published criticism of Kuomintang (KMT) policies and the looming threat of Japanese aggression meant to rouse readers to action. In addition, it gave extensive coverage to women's revolutionary participation in China and in progressive social movements abroad, with frequent investigative reports on Soviet women and female labor unions in the United States and biographical sketches of prominent political activists such as the German socialist-democrat Clara Zetkin and Alexandra Kollontai. Shen Zijiu apparently had no qualms about putting the journal to use for more practical and immediate ends as well, including assisting radical women in need: in 1937, for instance, in response to the outpouring of sympathy sparked by the publication of Bai Wei's *My Tragic Life,* she spearheaded a fund-raising campaign to cover the author's mounting medical bills for the treatment of her condition. The public appeal Shen issued in the magazine gathered signatures from many of the leading female artists and writers on the cultural left, including Chen Bo'er, a socialist involved in the Shanghai theater and film scene; Wang Ying (1915–1974), a progressive writer and actress who starred in several successful left-wing films in the thirties, including *The Goddess of Liberty* and *Women's Cries;* poet and novelist Guan Lu; and Du Junhui (1904–1981), the feminist activist, essayist, and translator who had helped Shen Zijiu launch *Women's Life* in 1935. After war broke out, the journal relocated to Wuhan, where it continued publication under the able editorship of Ji Hong (b. 1913) until it was finally closed down by the KMT in 1941.

These were years when a feminist defense of women's interests was more urgent than ever. Marking a sharp ideological reversal from the May Fourth celebration of the independent New Woman's bold entrance into the public world of politics and professional careers, beginning in the early thirties, urban China witnessed the resurgence of neoconservative ideals of domestic womanhood that underwrote an agenda of sending China's newly emancipated women back home. The years 1934–35 even saw a flurry of heated debate in the press about the prototypical New Woman "Nora," with many critics now vociferously condemning her ostensible abandonment of domestic responsibilities to her husband and children.[11] Ironically, this conservative gender discourse was partly fueled by the KMT's ratification in 1930 of the new Civil Code (and its legal provisions ostensibly protecting women's marital and property rights), which some viewed as marking the culminating achievement of feminism's political struggle. For proponents of Chiang Kai-shek's New Life campaign (*xin shenghuo yundong*), now that their "rights" had been "won," women's most fundamental (and lofty) duties were to be found in their traditional roles as wives and mothers.[12] The print media, public lectures, training programs, even the invention of "Good Mother's Day" all were marshaled in a nationwide movement to persuade the public that the domestic sphere was not only where women naturally belonged but also where they could most effectively serve society and the nation.[13] At a roundtable discussion sponsored by *Women's Life* magazine in 1936, a group of leading female intellectuals added their voices to the public debate, mounting a spirited defense of the modern women who had broken away from orthodox roles of daughter, wife, and mother. To those who now insisted that "women ought to return to their husbands as before," the panel posed the questions, "In reality, where are China's Noras today? And in what manner are they fighting back?"[14] Participants included prominent women leftists who regularly contributed to the magazine, like Bai Wei, Luo Qiong, and Shen Zijiu, all of whom, notably, had left behind conventional families and marriages to pursue independent careers and participate in the political arena.

But feminist discourse of the 1930s had a more expansive purview than the various obstacles confronting educated, middle-class Noras in their individual searches for economic and sexual autonomy. In an important sense, renewed concern about the need for revolutionary change brought radical intellectuals and writers of the 1930s more in line with authors like Qiu Jin (1875–1907) and other late Qing foremothers who had advanced in their writing a vision of total social transformation.[15] And in this view, the feminist agenda was understood not as a discrete politics of gender, stemming from a singular critical awareness of sexual discrimination and difference, but in terms of the ways the advancement of women's roles intersected with the project of sociopolitical transformation in general.[16] If their responses varied according to changing diagnoses of China's national malaise, Chinese feminists at both historical turning points envisaged the eradication of female oppression as encompassing struggle against both traditional forms of male domination and the other forms of domination suppressing Chinese women. Thus, in the words of veteran liberal activist Liu-Wang Liming, who published a highly informative insider's account of the urban women's movement in 1934, the overarching goal of Chinese feminism was to achieve human rights for women *and,* simultaneously, to empower them to create a more just society: "We don't simply want to emancipate 200 million women, we also want to join hands with awakened men and strive toward a happier world."[17]

The special affinity between leftist writers of the 1930s and the pioneer generation of feminists in the late Qing is further underscored by the way certain authors gaze back to the prior historical moment in narratives that recast the problem of gender oppression in terms of China's larger sociopolitical crisis. In her novel *Mother* (1933), for example, Ding Ling invokes her mother's generation to construct what Tani Barlow has described as a new "prototype for the female sister in revolution," while the younger author Yu Ru's heroine Luo Weina in *Remote Love* (1942) not only finds inspiration in Qiu Jin's poetry but also comes from a late Qing lineage as the daughter of revolutionaries.[18] Weina's political activism in the Women's Work Corps and as a Communist guerrilla fighter, moreover, is driven by a desire to fulfill her *mother's* dreams, a point spelled out when the heroine announces at a climactic moment, "I am my mother's daughter." The reimagining of the maternal figure as a source of ideological inspiration—in sharp contrast to the grim inscription of the mother-daughter relationship in earlier May Fourth women's writing as a site of confrontation and rupture—may well be indicative of the overall view promoted by this literature that transformation for women is a historical, not merely personal, process.

Picking up once again on the theme that women's destiny is intertwined with the political transformation of society as a whole, leftist women writers of the 1930s nevertheless departed from their late Qing foremothers in certain key respects. For one thing, with the rising influence of Marxist ideology, writers consciously extended their critique to the class dimensions of women's subjugation. Fiction by Luo Shu and Xiao Hong, for example, foregrounds the vicissitudes of poor women to show how economic factors compound their exploitation.[19] Others such as Feng Keng (1907–1931) and Guan Lu, both literary activists based in Shanghai, published short stories exposing women's sexual objectification as a function of capitalism.[20] Rather than imagining utopian resolutions to the plight of women (which was often the case in late Qing feminist fiction), moreover, such writers tended to adopt a critical realist approach, generating desire for an alternative social order by disclosing the imperfect realities of the status quo. Still other writers, like Xie Bingying and Bai Wei, sought to elucidate the intricate linkages between personal and political change for women, showing, for example, how political activism itself could provide meaningful opportunities beyond normative feminine roles or how domesticity (in both "traditional" and "modern" guises) remained a devastating site of imprisonment for women of all classes. In their most acclaimed works of this decade, *A Woman Soldier's Own Story* and *My Tragic Life* respectively, both authors turned to autobiographical genres, which might seem incompatible with the leftist mission of *engagé* writing but are nevertheless deployed to great effect to explore burning feminist issues. But these texts too depart from the earlier utopian vision of a revolutionary alliance between women (and women's interests) and other broad forces of social change: drawing upon their own life experiences, both Bai Wei and Xie Bingying represent the overwhelming personal obstacles women faced in becoming political activists, and impart powerful testimony of the immense difficulties of effecting social change in general.

With the full-scale outbreak of the Sino-Japanese War in 1937 and the ushering in of the second United Front between the KMT and the CCP, the cultural left toned down its radical rhetoric and shifted emphasis from class struggle to national resistance. The League of Left-Wing Writers had been formally dissolved in the spring of 1936 and replaced by less partisan coalitions dedicated to promoting patriotic culture and propaganda to serve the war effort. In 1938, the Chinese Writers' Antiaggression Association was founded in Hankou (subsequently relocating to the wartime capital of Chongqing) under the able leadership of veteran novelist Lao She. Many of the women writers who took refuge in the cities of the KMT-controlled interior—Chongqing, Kunming, Chengdu, and Guilin in particular—and in the British-held colony of Hong Kong lent their support during the course of the war and rallied to produce patriotic literature to raise public consciousness about the national calamity. Among the better-known female authors associated with the organization were Bai Wei, Ding Ling, Xie Bingying, Lu Jingqing, Zhao Qingge, and Bai Lang. The controversy over whether the Chinese New Women ought to "go back home" or not, interestingly, continued to simmer in the major newspapers and the numerous women's magazines that had mushroomed in the interior, becoming especially heated when the KMT announced its controversial policy of restricting female employment in certain government sectors on both ideological and economic grounds. As one incensed reader, a Wuhan University student, wrote to a contemporary magazine:

> My generation of women are truly like captive birds just freed from their cages, and the weaknesses that come from being shackled for thousands of years are difficult to eradicate. But today, we find doors slammed in our faces everywhere, and we are deprived of opportunities to stand on our own and make a fresh start.

This is the antithesis of shaking off feudal shackles, and it adds a new yoke that goes against the times. Moreover, in the past, because women were unenlightened, even though they were mistreated they were still content and found no shame in it. But today, with the development of human rights, the progress of civilization, and the continual raising of people's consciousness, the principles of freedom and self-respect grow by the day and no woman with even the slightest aspiration approves of a dependent, submissive life. The nation has conferred upon women the opportunity for equal education, yet they are still not independent in life. Even men regard this as shameful.[21]

Meanwhile, quite a few educated middle-class women, including established women writers, were increasingly active in the scores of women's organizations that sprang up across the country in response to Japanese military aggression: to cite just a few examples, novelist Yang Mo served as director of the National Salvation League in Hebei province; Xie Bingying took the lead in organizing the Hunan Women's War Zone Service Corps; Su Xuelin and Ling Shuhua, both of whom settled in Sichuan, joined Wuhan University's Wartime Service Women's Work Team.

Engagé Women's Writing During the War

AS THE LIFE of the nation grew ever more volatile in the late 1930s, and especially with the outbreak of war, the conception of literature as a tool of social struggle and national salvation, as opposed to a more or less autonomous aesthetic activity, came to hold greater sway among Chinese writers. Even those without formal leftist allegiances expressed a heightened sense of public purpose and responsibility in their literary output. One major artistic genre that emerged in this context was literary reportage (*baogao wenxue*), and women writers/journalists were to play a significant role in its development and practice.[22] Reportage had already gained a certain currency within the cultural left, with works such as Xie Bingying's *War Diary* (1928) garnering high critical acclaim, and the League of Left-Wing Writers promoted it in the early thirties as a genre particularly well suited to capturing the unfolding of China's national history. The form Bai Wei employs in "Third-Class Hospital Ward," introduced above, is an example of *texie,* or sketch, one of several emergent forms with which leftist women writers experimented to narrate the embattled urban landscape of the early to mid–1930s. Whether zeroing in on the dire conditions under which female factory workers toiled (Peng Zigang and Ji Hong) or giving readers eyewitness accounts of mass public protests

(Ding Ling), early female practitioners of reportage often offered a distinctly gendered vision of the historical crises sweeping urban China.[23] Now writers were drawn to the form as a medium for investigating and reporting on war-torn China, documenting the massive devastation but also the extraordinary acts of resistance and self-sacrifice on the part of ordinary Chinese people.

Reportage, with its predilection for observation and trademark journalistic style, might appear to offer the perfect medium for documenting the objective facts of current history, although few practitioners disguised their partisan views: indeed, situated somewhere between literature and journalism, the genre was embraced precisely because it enabled writers to probe beneath the surface of reality, and in so doing to shape the way their readers interpreted the contemporary world. When Chen Xuezhao, for instance, accepted an assignment from *National Dispatch* to investigate conditions and conduct interviews at Yan'an in 1938, she almost immediately found herself drawn to the revolutionaries she encountered and was stunned by the contrast in the atmosphere to that of the wartime capital of Chongqing, where she had resided for the previous two years. Thus, while she did not gloss over the primitive infrastructure at the Communist base camp in her resulting book, *Interviews at Yan'an* (1940), she did not hold back the reasons she was so favorably impressed by what she saw. In the essay from this collection translated here, the author candidly details the material deprivations Yan'an residents endured, only to reaffirm the powerful appeal of the camaraderie, *esprit de corps,* and political integrity that nevertheless prevailed.[24] Two years later, Chen Xuezhao would head back to Yan'an as a convert, having earnestly embraced the egalitarian ideals of the Chinese Communist movement and determined to overcome what she had now come to view as her elitist middle-class prejudices by throwing herself wholeheartedly into the process of thought reform. Her second major collection of reportage, *Wandering Through the Liberated Zones,* published on the eve of liberation in 1949, illuminates even further the author's ideological metamorphosis and her growing optimism vis-à-vis China's future under the Communist Party, though she still insists on anchoring her observations in subjective impressions and personal reflections on the nitty-gritty aspects of everyday life as she journeyed through the war-ravaged countryside of northern China and Manchuria.

Chen Xuezhao was one of a host of woman writers to publish reportage on wartime China and, in so doing, to help carve out new imaginative terrain for modern Chinese women's writing. In addition to the stifling patriarchal households and intricate mindscapes of the *xin nüxing* (New Woman) brought into focus by the previous generation of May Fourth authors, readers of women's literature were now afforded glimpses into life in remote rural villages, prison cells, guerrilla territory, and battle zones. However, what is perhaps more significant about such writing from the point of view of feminist literary historiography is the way it so powerfully articulates a sense of women engaging on the front lines of national history. If May Fourth authors helped to construct a literary image of the complex interior realities of modern Chinese womanhood, wartime writing presented a distinct—but no less important—vision of women as active participants in the collective pursuit of alternative historical possibilities. Whether giving voice to their first-hand experiences as revolutionaries in the Communist stronghold at Yan'an, as fearless volunteers on the battlefield, or as political activists working for progressive movements abroad, *engagé* writers affirmed women's legitimacy as agents in current events and their capacity to assist in the creation of a new social and political order. While "woman" continued to function as one of the most salient motifs of national calamity and social injustice in creative literature and film throughout these decades, in works by Chen Xuezhao and many other female authors, women emerge as concrete historical subjects who observe; engage in polemic, debate, and negotiation; and, more often than not, take active part in specific historical events and causes. Though not included in the present volume, many noteworthy examples can be cited: Xie Bingying published her *New War Diary* in 1940, detailing her experiences organizing the Hunan Women's War Zone Services Corps and their work at a field hospital near Shanghai in the early days of the war; Dong Su (b. 1918) published in the Communist *Liberation Daily* at Yan'an; Peng Zigang's pieces appeared in the influential newspaper *L'Impartial*; while Bai Lang (b. 1912) authored an extraordinary account of propaganda work on the front lines, *The Fourteen of Us*. It chronicles the expedition of the War Zone Interview Group, a team of writers organized by the Writers' Antiaggression Association to document the experiences of ordinary civilians and soldiers as well as their own efforts as cultural activists.

Other leftist women writers active during the 1930s and 1940s brought readers a distinctly more internationalist outlook on their contemporary moment with eyewitness accounts of the radical political and social movements unfolding in Europe and the United States. They placed China's struggles within a broader global framework of movements for social justice including, for example, the fights against fascism, racial discrimination, and colonial rule. Such accounts—often in the form of reportage, but also in memoirs and essays—opened up new social and political terrain across national boundaries, so that readers were encouraged to think beyond the specific Chinese context and develop political sensibilities that transcended a nationalistic logic. Hu Lanqi, a feisty intellectual and activist originally from Sichuan province (and the alleged inspiration for Mao Dun's New Woman heroine Mei in his acclaimed novel *Rainbow*), for instance, gained international attention after being detained for leftist activities in Berlin in the mid-thirties. Like quite a few of her contemporaries, including fellow writers Lu Jingqing and Chen Xuezhao, she had earlier fled to Europe in the wake of the Nationalist crackdown on radical elements in the late 1920s, and had quickly joined the Chinese-speaking group of the German Communist Party. Her widely read memoir of the experience, *In a German Women's Prison,* offered a forceful indictment of the Nazi movement. But the account, which appeared in various foreign language editions as well as in Chinese, also vividly conveys the author's sense of allegiance to her fellow inmates and thus reflects one of the defining themes of radical women's writing of this period: the conditions of female political solidarity.

From its inception, Chinese feminist literature had sought to imagine women's political unity across various lines of difference, though the early formulations tend to have the feel of overly abstract and sometimes superficial ideological musings. In work by radical women writers from the thirties and forties there is often still an uncomfortable distance between the author and her subject, but the gap appears to have narrowed somewhat as the focus shifted from a sentimental rendering of the embattled female other to more self-conscious representations of the origins and nature of social privilege and injustice. At least two thematic features stand out in the work informed by revolutionary ideals from these decades: emphasis on the devastating impact of structural inequalities on entire communities, rather than on individual victims of oppression, and the purposeful depiction of acts of resistance. In the selection here by Hu Lanqi, for instance, the author alludes to the way Hitler's repressive regime criminalized women whose behavior deviated from the prescribed domestic roles and consciously pitted inmates—common law prisoners and political detainees—against one another; at the same time, however, she takes care to balance this grim assessment with small but powerful acts of resistance to prison authorities on the part of female inmates, as if to make sure readers take away an uplifting message of the resilience of the human spirit and its determination to oppose injustice and challenge the status quo, even in the face of tremendous hardship.

Hu Lanqi's memoir exhibits the discernible autobiographical impulse that can be traced throughout the literary production of twentieth-century women authors as they strove to inscribe themselves into the discourses of Chinese modernity.[25] Besides the various lyrical forms (for example, the familiar essay, or *xiaopin wen,* and letters) and short fiction that had been popular since the

May Fourth era, from the 1930s on there was also a steady stream of full-length personal narratives in the form of autobiographies and memoirs, indicating the continuing presence of a robust audience for this mode of writing. Important full-length autobiographies or memoirs from the 1930s through the 1950s include Lu Yin's *Autobiography of Lu Yin* (1934); Xiao Hong's *Market Street* (1936); Bai Wei's *My Tragic Life* (1936); Xie Bingying's *A Woman Soldier's Own Story, Volume One* (1936) and *Volume Two* (1946); and Ling Shuhua's *Ancient Melodies* (1953).[26] But in Hu Lanqi's case, we find a particularly explicit harnessing of memoir as a political genre. *In a German Women's Prison* centers on the author's compelling personal saga, to be sure, but the message she seeks to convey has remarkably little to do with the merits or uniqueness of her own individual life; rather, she aims to explain her prison experience in the context of a broader sociopolitical struggle. The work shares much in common in this respect with the genre of prison memoir analyzed by literary scholar Barbara Harlow. According to Harlow, the prison memoir actually constitutes a prevalent genre within progressive literary movements worldwide, and typically features narratives that "are actively engaged in a redefinition of the self and the individual in terms of a collective enterprise and struggle. The prison memoirs of political detainees are not written for the sake of a 'book of one's own,' rather they are collective documents, testimonies written by individuals to their common struggle."[27] As Hu Lanqi herself would recall in a memoir published in the post–Mao period, "A lot of Chinese luminaries who passed through Paris, like the great patriot Zou Taofen, General Zhang Fakui and his wife, philosophy professor Feng Youlan, and the woman poet Feng Yuanjun, came to visit me as though I were someone famous. All I had done was faithfully record the atrocities of the German fascists in suppressing the revolutionary masses and shared it with the world."[28]

Hu Lanqi's contemporary Yang Gang was another writer who highlighted themes of generating solidarity and building coalitions of opposition between variously oppressed individuals and groups. An accomplished leftist fiction writer, poet, translator, and journalist who spent the latter years of the Second World War and the immediate postwar period in the United States, she penned a scathing collection of reportage narratives on topics ranging from white supremacy to capitalism in American society. Yang Gang had already published a collection of war dispatches from the front line (*Southeast Travels,* 1943) for the liberal *L'Impartial,* and the newspaper commissioned her to write about life abroad. Her essays on modern American life, later to appear in a single volume under the title *Notes from America,* gave readers a glimpse of some of the most pressing social and economic problems plaguing that country. In the selection translated here, "The American South," the author takes up the politics of race in the United States, recounting instances of both blatant racial discrimination and efforts by activists in the civil rights movement to build antiracist alliances, observed firsthand on a trip to the Deep South. The collection as a whole can be read as a fascinating response to the voluminous reportage about contemporary China by American writers in the thirties and forties. In particular, Yang's work invites comparison with that of American radical Agnes Smedley, a writer known for her advocacy journalism on the Chinese Revolution in the thirties, whom Yang Gang first got to know in progressive circles in Shanghai.[29]

And of course there was Xie Bingying, who, in addition to turning out patriotic reportage accounts from the front lines during the War of Resistance, also authored a prison memoir called *In a Japanese Prison* (1940), about her brief detainment in Tokyo when she was studying at Waseda University prior to the war. The book, whose title distinctly echoes Hu Lanqi's popular account, recalls how Xie was arrested by Japanese authorities for boycotting a welcome rally for Puyi, the former Qing emperor whom the Japanese government had installed as ruler of their puppet state Manchukuo. Despite what was clearly a traumatic personal ordeal, not least because of the brutal interrogation sessions she reportedly underwent, Xie Bingying remained sympathetic to ordinary Japanese citizens. The selection included in this volume is an unusual short story set during World War II, in which the author imagines the rise of Japanese militarism from the vantage point of a Japanese "prostitute" in China.[30] Euphemistically known as "comfort women," individuals like the protagonist Umeko were conscripted, abducted, or, as in Umeko's case, recruited under false pretenses for the purpose of servicing soldiers in the Japanese military at designated "comfort houses."[31] The appalling sexual slavery that these women endured is downplayed in Xie's narrative in favor of a romance between Umeko and a young pilot who secretly shares her pacifist views, but by choosing Umeko as her protagonist the author accentuates the grim truth that the violence of war also takes the form of sexual violence against women.

Urban Cosmopolitanism: Shanghai Writers During and After Occupation

WHILE THE POLITICIZATION of aesthetic practice marked a distinctive feature of Chinese women's writing from the thirties onward, it was not the only significant development in this literary tradition. New levels of technical mastery are also increasingly evident, beginning in the 1930s. In part this may be attributed to the fact that the written vernacular, or *baihua,* was by this point more fully developed as a modern literary language; many women actively publishing were also more seasoned writers. But the formal sophistication of much of the women's literature that came into print at the time perhaps also sprang from the experience of urban modernity itself, as writers at once were shaped by and helped to shape the modern city.

By 1930, Shanghai easily rivaled other modern cities of the world. In addition to the imposing colonial architecture along the famed Bund, there were now also new art deco theaters, jazz clubs, cinemas, luxury hotels, and department stores.[32] Magazines on the newsstands of New York City and London were also readily available in Shanghai, as were first-run Hollywood films, and foreign books could be purchased at the many western bookstores doing business in the city's international settlements. Domestic literary journals such as *Les Contemporains* kept readers up to date on the latest European, American, and Japanese modernist trends, with reviews, articles, and translations of such writers as T. S. Eliot, John Dos Passos, James Joyce, Gertrude Stein, and Yokomitsu Riichi. All this made for a cultural ambience that, as Leo Ou-fan Lee and others have recently observed, exerted a discernible impact on print and visual culture including, crucially, the depiction of Chinese urban modernity itself. Indeed, while the fictional landscape of leftist works was increasingly dominated by rustic villages and towns, it is important not to overlook the dazzling urban settings that come to life on the pages by cosmopolitan writers of this generation.

With the Japanese occupation of Shanghai and Beijing (1937–1945), which temporarily cut both cities off from the rest of the nation, these cultural trends appear to have intensified, and some of the most formally sophisticated women writers of the twentieth century were to emerge in that context. The brilliant literary stylist Zhang Ailing is undoubtedly the most famous product of this urban milieu, but others deserve attention as well.[33] Indeed, according to Meng Yue and Dai Jinhua in their survey of women's writing in twentieth-century China, the Shanghai occupation period marked one of the high points of the modern female literary tradition; a primary reason was the unique "discursive space" (*huayu kongxi*) that opened up to women during the war.[34] Notwithstanding the horror and turmoil imposed on Shanghai (not to mention the rest of the nation), the Japanese occupation ushered in a temporary suspension of the male-centered discourses of national salvation and revolution that had so often worked against the gendered discourse of feminist writers. This may help account for the significant output of Shanghai women writers during this era: in addition to Su Qing and Yang Jiang, whose work is represented in the present volume, others who made a name for themselves at the time and whose work reveals a distinct continuity with feminist literary discourse from the prewar era include Guan Lu (1907–1982), Shi Jimei (1920–1968), and Wu Guifang (1915–1990).

Su Qing, whose popularity easily rivaled that of Zhang Ailing in the 1940s, was an established essayist by the time the war broke out. Her earliest writing had been encouraged by Lin Yutang, but her success can largely be attributed to personal ambition, fueled by the practical necessity of making a living following a bitter divorce from her husband. When the exodus of intellectuals, writers, and publishers from Shanghai in the wake of the Japanese military invasion left a significant void and changed the atmosphere in the cultural establishment, Su Qing seized the opportunity to carve out a place of her own in modern Chinese literature, eventually launching *Heaven and Earth* magazine (1943). It was an enormous success, and Su Qing used the venue not only to showcase writing by up-and-coming young authors like Zhang Ailing but also to promote her own work, including her irreverent feminist novel *Ten Years of Marriage*,[35] which quickly became one of the best-selling fiction works of the day. By Su Qing's own patently understated account, however, she became a writer out of sheer boredom. Asked at a roundtable of women authors in 1944 about how she embarked on her literary career, she casually replied:

> At the time my family was giving me a hard time because I had given birth to a baby girl, whom none of them liked, so I wasn't speaking with them much. I would hide away in my room carrying the baby, and after she fell asleep I'd read a bit. I did this as a diversion and all I read were things like novels and plays. The only magazine subscriptions we had were *Analects,* which I was especially fond of, and *This Human World.* One day I suddenly got the urge to give it a go myself, so I wrote the essay "Giving Birth to a Girl" and sent the manuscript off to *Analects.* . . . It appeared in Issue 64, which was published on June 16, 1935. I earned exactly five *yuan* for it.[36]

Su Qing's image of herself as a writer in this passage is characteristic of her self-image in general as it emerged in her work from this period. Insofar as her writing evinces intense interest in modern female selfhood, Su Qing can be said to have inherited the May Fourth feminist tradition, yet she herself expressed a distinct disdain for the sentimentality of the previous generation of women writers. Literary scholar Edward Gunn affirms this striking difference in the tenor of Su Qing's writing in his comparison of the mildly satiric self-portrait she crafts in her long autobiographical essay "Waves" (1945), which has been translated for this volume, with the far more romantic inclinations of a May Fourth–generation writer like Xie Bingying. While the actual content of their life stories overlaps to a significant degree, Su Qing spurns the "romantic gestures" and "iconoclastic egotism" that characterize Xie's earnest account of feminist awakening and rebellion.[37] Instead, in "Waves" she gives a humorous account of coming of age amid the topsy-turvy world of politics and unevenly shifting social mores of the late 1920s, sparing few aspects of the New Culture, as it played out in the girl's school she attended, from her comic derision. Ultimately, the essay can be read not so much as a critique of May Fourth ideological principles per se but as a cynical appraisal of the shortfalls of the movement: through amused detachment, the author discloses that behind the highfalutin' façade of the New Youth's gender and political emancipation lie half-digested political ideas, petty self-interests, and typical teenage angst.

Su Qing was not the only Shanghai writer active during the occupation period to bring a burgeoning comic sensibility to the treatment of gender-related themes. A graduate of the foreign literature department of Qinghua University who later trained in Europe, Yang Jiang emulated the style of Oscar Wilde in the comedies she wrote about the urban bourgeoisie in Shanghai during the war. Witty repartee, cleverly structured plots with unexpected twists and turns, and colorful casts of contemporary characters helped make her plays box-office successes when they were produced for the stage in the mid-forties. Like Su Qing, Yang was primarily concerned with what one might argue were the by now familiar themes of modern Chinese literature: criticism of the patriarchal family system, the dilemmas middle-class women encountered in marriage and divorce, and obstacles to female employment and economic autonomy. What sets her work apart from previous treatments of such themes, however, is the subversive humor that so often underlies her narrative stance. Neither emotional in its engagement with women's suffering, like typical May Fourth fiction, nor marked by the urgent tone or pedagogical thrust of contemporary leftist works, Yang Jiang's writing presents a cynical comic vision and a playful approach that foregrounds not the unrelenting power of patriarchy but its hopeless absurdity.

In this regard, both authors exemplify the "antiromantic" trend Edward Gunn has traced in Shanghai literary culture as a whole during the war. Gunn attributes the trend to the convergence of a number of historical factors— above all, the deepening political skepticism of a disillusioned and war-fatigued public, the commercialization of urban culture, and the constant pressures of political censorship. All are similarly relevant in elucidating the forms feminist literary expression took at the time, though to this list one might propose adding another lens through which they might be seen: a heightened self-consciousness about modern gender rhetoric that prompted a new response to patriarchy. For both these writers, it was almost as though the language of emancipation had become an all too predictable, even cliché-ridden, feature of both political and cultural discourse. To write about the plight of women in these terms would not only have come across as naïve but also have risked eliding the engagement of a potentially large and generally receptive public audience.

The parodies of sexual stereotypes that appear in Yang Jiang's 1944 contemporary comedy of manners, *Forging the Truth,* translated here, and the self-deflating stance of the I-narrator in Su Qing's autobiographical essay "Waves" both show such self-reflexivity, by calling attention less to the social "realities" of gender relations than to the ways patriarchal culture has imagined itself in fiction. The world depicted is still very much a masculine domain, but the men who populate it have been demoted from their tyrannical stature as villains who control women's lives to self-deluding buffoons whose authority is often more illusory than real. Joining the gallery of twentieth-century female character types is a new laughing heroine: neither downtrodden victim nor visionary revolutionary, she mischievously disrupts the rules of patriarchal culture by playing its games to her own advantage, mimicking feminine stereotypes to outwit her would-be oppressors. On the other hand, critics may also detect in these ambivalent depictions of patriarchy a contradictory retreat from politics at the very moment when self-consciousness would seem to urge the opposite. In this sense, Su Qing's and Yang Jiang's work might be said to lack the feminist political edge evinced by other Chinese women writers, by eschewing any explicit vision of the possibility of resistance to the dominant social order or the need for collective change.

In the immediate postoccupation years, many of the intellectuals, artists, and writers displaced by war migrated back to Shanghai from the interior, bringing with them magazines, film studios, and publishing houses. Much of their writing still strongly emphasized literary technique coupled with a certain detachment from overt political stances, even if in urban women's writing one hardly ever finds the pure primacy of technique Shu-mei Shih discerns in the Chinese modernist tradition. Fengzi (1912–1996), the progressive stage actress-turned-journalist and novelist, resurfaced in Shanghai after the Japanese surrender, having spent much of the war working in the performing arts circles of Chongqing and Kunming and as a special war correspondent for *New People's Herald.* Back in Shanghai, she assumed the editorship of *In the*

World, a left-wing magazine with underground ties to the Chinese Communist Party. Unlike her pointed attacks on government corruption and graft in essays published during the war, in her creative writing from the immediate postwar period, including a full-length novel entitled *The Silent Singing Girl* (1946), the political message emerges naturally through the narrative rather than as a result of didactic commentary or other heavy-handed rhetorical devices. In her short story "The Portrait," translated here, she uses a tone of mystery and intrigue to narrate the tale of a young woman's sudden desertion of her middle-class marriage. In important respects, the story can be read as a subtle rearticulation of the Nora narrative from the angle of the men left behind. Earlier writers, taking their cue from Lu Xun, likewise often focused on the aftermath of the New Woman's rebellious act, almost always painting a bleak portrait of the enormous, at times fatal, impediments the Chinese Nora found herself up against.[38] Here, Fengzi cleverly turns the lens of analysis on *the men* whose lives are turned upside down by this bold act of female defiance. And she reveals an unflattering picture of psychological stagnation and degeneracy: whereas the female protagonist Li Ziwei, as the reader ultimately learns, has gone on to a fulfilling career in public service, her male counterparts have remained hopelessly obsessed with an idealized memory of her and are apparently unable to even begin to fathom the new life and future she has chosen for herself.

Fengzi's story was specially commissioned for publication by Zhao Qingge, who had taken it upon herself to edit what would become one of the most important postwar collections of women's writing, *Untitled* (1947).[39] Another contributor to the volume was Lu Xiaoman (1903–1965), widow of acclaimed romantic poet Xu Zhimo, who had remained in Shanghai but withdrawn from literary culture after the Japanese invasion. Employing a cinematic approach, her visually evocative "The Imperial Hotel" features a female protagonist who perceives the glitzy nightlife of a deluxe Shanghai hotel where she works and its glamorous clientele as a dazzling, but also decadent and highly alienating, spectacle. The fast-paced sequence of vivid scenes spotlights self-assured socialites who seduce men in order to support expensive urban lifestyles; innocent schoolgirls forced to prostitute themselves due to the hardships of the war; and fashion-conscious New Women who flaunt chic outfits and smoke cigarettes in public. Yet Lu manages to fuse attention to style with subtle social commentary: rather than overtly condemning capitalist urban culture, the story powerfully conjures up the material splendor—and deep inequities—of the cityscape through snippets of overheard conversation and descriptions of the well-heeled patrons who come and go in the ladies' lounge of the fancy establishment. Above all, the jarring contrast between the protagonist's financial desperation and the conspicuous consumption around her offers a refreshing aesthetic approach and poignancy to the themes of social injustice and the corrupting effects of material wealth.

Building Socialism, Building a New Literature, 1949–1976

THE FOUNDING OF the People's Republic of China on October 1, 1949 ushered in a sweeping reorganization of the nation's political and cultural life. The Yan'an experiment of reorienting literature and the arts to cater more directly to the needs and tastes of the mass audience of workers, peasants, and soldiers, or *gongnongbing* as they were becoming known, was instituted as national policy.[40] Also, with the exception of those who opted to follow the Nationalist government's retreat to Taiwan or emigrated to the west, all Chinese writers were organized into national literary unions such as the All-China Writers' Federation. The rationale for this major overhaul of the literary establishment was that as "workers" who were to perform vital intellectual or ideological service to the new socialist state, writers deserved material support. At the same time, needless to say, this move did much to solidify the CCP's authority over cultural production: besides creating a bureaucratic infrastructure to oversee writers, such organizations trained a new cohort of younger peasant and working-class authors, and to this day a great many professional writers remain affiliated with such state organs.

Women writers were among those who initially seemed poised to benefit from such institutions. Unlike the precarious literary careers embarked upon by their May Fourth foremothers, most of whom were barely able to eke out a living by submitting manuscripts to newspapers and modern literary magazines, for at least a small handful of professional writers in the early 1950s, the future seemed to hold immense promise with the hope of job security. Thirteen women belonged to the All-China Writers' Federation at the time of its creation, a number that more than quadrupled by 1966.[41] Veteran women cultural activists were assigned key official positions within the new cultural bureaucracy: most famous, of course, was Ding Ling, who, having transformed herself from New Woman author to guerrilla propagandist at Yan'an, now enjoyed a significant measure of power and status as an appointed member of the standing committee of the All-China Federation of Literary and Art Circles, and as vice-chair of the All-China Union of Literary Workers and editor of the federation's influential *Literary Gazette*. Shen Zijiu, who had been an affiliate of the Shanghai-based Women's Bookstore back in the 1930s as well as the founding editor of *Women's Life* magazine, was recruited to direct the Propaganda and Education section of the newly established All-China Women's Federation, or *Fulian*, the CCP's mass organization for women.[42] In this capacity, she was to serve simultaneously as editor-in-chief of the organization's central mouthpiece, *Women of New China*, from 1949 to 1956.[43] And Chen Xuezhao, along with quite a few other prominent women authors active before the revolution, was accorded the status of professional writer, which enabled her for the first time to draw a steady income while working full-time on her novels.

Yet, the sad irony was that at a moment when women writers stood to gain the most from the creation of such new literary/cultural institutions, there was arguably less opportunity to produce gender-specific writing in the post–1949 era than at any other point in the century. Indeed, contemporary scholars more or less agree that the nascent feminist literary perspective that had begun to animate the public cultural arena in the first half of the twentieth century languished with the advent and consolidation of Communist rule. Whereas women's writing had once served as a key medium for critiquing the condition of women in Chinese society, socialist literary doctrine rendered this vital function more or less obsolete after 1949. Thus the highly contradictory demands that the women of "New China" faced and the stubborn tenacity of patriarchal practices and attitudes in the postliberation era often tended to be concealed beneath the emergent socialist iconography of muscular iron maidens (*tie guniang*) and happy peasant women. Within the Chinese Marxist discourse that held sway, "liberation" (*jiefang*) was generally assumed to have triumphantly brought an end to patriarchy: in 1950 the sweeping Marriage Law was enacted, formally abolishing the customary social practices deemed most detrimental to women (including arranged marriage, polygamy, and the selling of child brides), and in 1957 the new regime publicly declared women emancipated! Under these circumstances, it became increasingly challenging and ideologically suspect to openly criticize or even represent contemporary gender discrimination, since to depict women's ongoing subordination was seemingly to dissent from the party line. The prominent example of Ding Ling, who had already been publicly rebuked prior to 1949 for her controversial critique of sexist attitudes at Yan'an in her controversial essay "Thoughts on March Eighth" (1942) was proof enough of that. Among the evidence of her "crimes" cited during the Antirightist drive of 1957 (which resulted in her expulsion from the party and exile to the remote province of Heilongjiang for the next twelve years) was this very essay, which was conspicuously reprinted along with a barrage of criticism denouncing its alleged misguided sentiments in *Literary Gazette*.[44]

Indeed, another reason gender critique failed to thrive in the Maoist period has to do with the tense ideological atmosphere that took hold during the "transition to socialism" from the mid–1950s on. As all writers struggled to weather successive ideological campaigns, "dissident" intellectual and creative voices who might have ventured notions of womanhood, sexuality, or a gendered modernity that deviated from the prescribed socialist ideal were discouraged, if not altogether silenced, by the newly installed government. Not surprisingly, quite a few of the authors represented here (Yang Gang, Chen Xuezhao, Hu Lanqi, and Zong Pu) fell victim to the Antirightist movement, when Mao purged intellectuals deemed disloyal to the CCP. Many of the charges ultimately proved bogus, of course, while in other cases the fate of writers seemed thoroughly arbitrary (one wonders, for instance, why the author Ru Zhijuan was spared, despite having published a high-profile story that easily might have been interpreted as inappropriately suggesting sexual attraction between a People's Liberation Army soldier and a local newlywed). Others managed to get through the Antirightist campaign relatively unscathed, only to subsequently find themselves caught up in the violent chaos unleashed by the Cultural Revolution (1965–1976): among the authors in this volume, Bai Wei and Yang Jiang, in particular, withstood the most cruel and humiliating attacks at the hands of Red Guards. In short, it is hardly surprising that in many cases women writers active before 1949 turned away from creative writing or took up scholarly research. Veteran May Fourth writer Feng Yuanjun, who had already stopped writing fiction to conduct research on traditional Chinese literature, devoted herself to teaching at Shandong University after 1949. Similarly, after returning from a journalistic assignment in Europe in 1948, Lu Jingqing took a position in the Chinese department at Jinnan University. Yang Jiang, who, along with her husband Qian Zhongshu, turned down several offers to teach overseas in order to remain in mainland China, took refuge in translation work while on the faculty of Qinghua University—among other projects, she immersed herself in improving her Spanish in order to translate the picaresque novels *La Vida de Lazarillo de Tormes* and *Don Quixote*. Despite Yang Jiang's self-censorship and her efforts to steer clear of potentially sensitive intellectual and literary projects, she was still not immune from political persecution. In 1958, she was forced to undergo a brief "reeducation" program outside of Beijing, and she was again persecuted during the Cultural Revolution. Between 1969 and 1972, she was sent to a so-called "cadre school" in the Henan countryside. Yang has since resumed creative writing, producing, among other works, *Taking a Bath,* a well-crafted satirical novel about literary intellectuals in the 1950s, as well as a poignant memoir of her rural experience during the Cultural Revolution (*Six Chapters from My Life Down Under*), but gender relations no longer figure among her primary concerns.

Others continued turning out creative literature in the early postliberation years but conspicuously reined in the feminist themes that had once driven their work. Su Qing, for instance, got involved in the performing arts, writing and publishing numerous scripts (including a great many adaptations of works of classical Chinese drama) in the early 1950s. Although she reportedly joined two of the newly established CCP women's organizations in Shanghai after 1949, her later writing does not sustain the gender critique that distinguished her wartime fiction and essays.[45] Su Qing made the mistake of publishing several essays in the *Shanghai Daily*, a Hong Kong–based newspaper, that were openly critical of the Communist regime. This, and lingering suspicions about her activities during the Japanese occupation of Shanghai, led to her arrest in 1955 by the Shanghai Public Security Bureau on counterrevolutionary charges. She was released from jail in June 1957. Su Qing died in relative obscurity in Shanghai in 1982, and it was not until two years later that her name was officially cleared.

Yet, without downplaying the pressures and personal traumas many writers and feminists faced after 1949, we may also note that gender did not simply disappear from the literary imaginary of postrevolutionary China. The dual image of oppressed/liberated woman so prevalent in May Fourth fiction remains in evidence in Maoist culture, albeit with new symbolic meaning as a consolidator of party authority. For instance, feminist literary critic Tonglin Lu has identified the recurrence of an overtly gendered "salvation" narrative in socialist realist literature that inscribes "women's emancipation [as] a gift imposed by the Communist Party."[46] The salvation plot often structures stories set in the recent past, revolving around a victimized peasant girl who is rescued by the CCP, such as Xi'er in Tian Han's popular opera *The White-Haired Girl*. Another classic example critics often cite is the model opera *The Red Detachment of Women*, in which a peasant girl abused by her landlord master finds empowerment upon joining the Red Army. In both examples, the ideological function of the female figure can be understood as not so much promoting awareness of present gender inequities than as bolstering the image and authority of the party.

On the other hand, the figure of the liberated woman, reincarnated now in the form of robust female workers, peasants, and soldiers, also abounds in Maoist literary culture. Physically impressive and undaunted by the tasks traditionally performed by men, such characters have been described by some critics as "masculinized" women whose sexual difference has been all but erased. Unlike the defiant modern heroines of earlier twentieth-century fiction, it is argued, such figures no longer represent women's personal or political triumph over patriarchy but rather primarily work to articulate loyalty to the newly founded state. Moreover, whereas the New Woman often tended to function specifically as the embodiment of sexual liberation in pre–1949 texts, the narrative quest for romantic love and the fulfillment of female sexual desire is overtly replaced by love-of-labor stories in the Chinese socialist literary canon. The priority accorded to the heroine's class status *over* her sexuality (through her strong class identification or struggles specifically relating to class difference) seems to indicate the overall downgrading of gender politics within Chinese socialism after 1949. Examples of this ideological hierarchy can be found in the host of fiction and nonfiction narratives that appeared in the 1950s, celebrating women who earn the respect of their men through selfless dedication to production or (in the following decade) to the commune.[47]

Yet if the formation of the CCP propaganda machine inevitably altered both the quality and the quantity of women's literary output, 1949 does not mark an absolute dividing line from the previous half century, nor should the Maoist period be characterized as a cultural desert in any simplistic sense. Female intellectuals and authors in the early years, in particular, grappled with contemporary issues, including gender issues, and in ways that at times deviated from the official party line. Indeed, even *Women of New China,* the formal mouthpiece of the All-China Women's Federation (edited by veteran activist Shen Zijiu), in the early 1950s seemed to take issue with the triumphant public declaration that the revolution had liberated Chinese womanhood.[48] Articles featured in the magazine noted the lingering influence of conventional patriarchal practices and attitudes and, sounding the mantra of earlier generations of Chinese feminists, called on women to assert their own agency in making the promised egalitarianism of the new order a social reality. Another compelling topic raised in this magazine, as well as in fiction of the time, was the role Chinese women had played in the revolutionary politics paving the way for the People's Republic. Yang Mo's widely read novel *Song of Youth* (1958), for instance, treats the experience of a young woman radicalized during the student movements of the 1930s. Other authors, including Chen Xuezhao, Wang Ying, and Yang Gang, all veteran literary intellectuals who had personally been involved in Communist Party activities prior to 1949, similarly sought to engender the narrative of recent CCP history by representing the formation of female revolutionary consciousness as an integral part of that history in their fiction.

The two stories from the late 1950s translated here, both by younger authors who began publishing after the Communist victory, narrate socialist woman-hood in ways that affirm the sense of enormous change taking place within the gender status quo in the early People's Republic but depart from the Communist state's official rhetoric on female liberation in subtle and interesting aspects. The first, by the niece of the renowned May Fourth fiction writer Feng Yuanjun, Zong Pu, was a product of the Hundred Flowers Campaign in 1956, a brief cultural thaw during which writers were ostensibly granted a greater measure of autonomy from party control over artistic and intellectual production. Not surprisingly, quite a few of the works that made it into print during the short-lived campaign offered a more critical assessment of women's lives in the PRC than would subsequently be possible.[49] At the same time, moreover, their staunch feminist stance distinguishes them from the uncritical endorsement of subordinated female roles that had begun to creep back into male-authored Communist novels such as those surveyed by Irene Eber.[50] Told from the retrospective viewpoint of the central protagonist, Zong Pu's "Red Beans" (1957) broaches the taboo topic of desire and love under socialism by tracing the growing tension between private and public loyalties in the context of the massive sociopolitical flux and civil war of the late 1940s. In the end, but not without a certain lingering ambivalence, the heroine breaks off her relationship with her college sweetheart in order to be true to her political convictions and participate in the building of a new social order. What makes the story interesting (but, in the eyes of critics who condemned it in 1958 for its so-called "rightist" qualities, ideologically suspect) is that emotional struggle would appear to supersede class/national struggle, insofar as the narrative dwells overwhelmingly on the conflicted private feelings of the heroine as opposed to the sociopolitical enterprise in which she is engaged. The heroine is attracted to the romantic aura of her artistically inclined lover, but she is more than a little troubled by the chauvinistic behavior he occasionally exhibits, not to mention by his indifference to national politics. When he leaves for America, she reluctantly declines his invitation to go along. To the extent that the narrative unfolds as an extended memory, sparked by the heroine's return to her alma mater after 1949, it is suffused with a wistful longing for the emotional intensity of her romantic youth. Thus, while there is little doubt that the heroine now enjoys a certain degree of personal and political emancipation (indeed, she returns to the school in a position of authority as a party cadre), the quest for sexual liberation alluded to is not resolved. The heroine may have resisted the trap of patriarchal romance, but there is little sense of an alternative on the horizon. Has the new society reconciled romance and revolution? This is the provocative rhetorical question the story raises.

Another take on the conventional formula of romance and revolution is presented in the story "Warmth of Spring," by Zong Pu's contemporary Ru Zhijuan (b. 1925). While the rather puritanical representation of the relationship of the married couple shares much with other contemporary socialist realist literature, romance and sexual desire are not merely sublimated by the revolutionary pursuit of labor; rather, they are shown to be sustained by it. The newfound sense of purpose and enthusiasm that the protagonist Jinglan acquires by taking part in a neighborhood production campaign turns out to be the very spark she has needed to reignite her workaholic husband's affections. In the end it is plain that the tender gestures between the couple are very much a function of the comradely identification they have (re)established. Throughout the story, the author's central focus is the female protagonist, whose experience is used to raise a series of highly topical and significant questions urban Chinese women faced in the 1950s: What is the value of household labor under socialism? How do women's perceptions of marriage and motherhood evolve when they are relieved of their daily duties as primary caretakers of husbands and kids? And what material conditions must obtain in order to allow women like the heroine to reallocate their labor to the public sector? On this last issue, the repeated references to domestic details in the story clearly indicate such a reallocation depends not only on an open-minded husband who helps out with domestic chores but also on a certain socialization of domestic housework (in the form of the local canteen that provides meals for the family, for instance). In other words, the story implicitly reminds the reader that it would take concrete measures, not just inspiring emancipatory rhetoric, to enable women of New China to move beyond their traditional subordination and perform the public roles now expected of them.

The accomplishments of state feminism under Mao remain a matter of heated debate today. While some scholars point to the Marriage Law of 1950 as a crucial legislative victory that helped weaken traditional patriarchy and improve marital arrangements in the early years of the People's Republic, others emphasize the contradictions of the state-sanctioned discourse of gender equality. In the latter view, the public egalitarianism of the Maoist years not only papered over conventional discriminatory practices and attitudes toward women in everyday life but also legitimized party interference in the private lives of individuals. In the final selection of this volume, "Residency Check" (1976), author Chen Ruoxi examines the persistence of traditional gender attitudes, specifically the disdain and distrust of female sexuality, in the post–1949 era. A Taiwanese-born writer who repatriated to the People's Republic in the mid–1960s, Chen brought fresh eyes to the ostensibly "new" social order that had emerged in China under socialism. Set during the Cultural Revolution, the story centers on a former model worker whose physical attractiveness arouses the jealousy and ire of the ladies in the neighborhood committee, who take it upon themselves to police her sex life. Whether or not Peng Yulian is actually carrying on an extramarital affair as the local busybodies maintain or, as the narrator seems to hint, has taken matters into her own hands to secure her husband's release from detention at a May Seventh cadre school, the narrative discloses the alarming and unprecedented level of state involvement in personal life and family relations under the Communist regime.[51]

* * * * *

CHEN RUOXI PUBLISHED her story in 1976, the same year Chairman Mao died and the infamous Gang of Four was arrested and tried for the atrocities of the Cultural Revolution. In the nearly three decades since, the People's Republic of China has experienced phenomenal change as the country transitions to a global market economy; begins to dismantle socialist state institutions, including the institutions of state feminism; and makes painful strides toward greater democratization, all of which naturally have presented considerable opportunities as well as challenges to women and to women writers of this generation. Because the post–Mao era marks a whole new chapter in China's modern cultural history in so many respects, examples of the vibrant women's literary culture that has flourished in this context have not been included in the present volume; it is my hope, however, that the texts featured here will provide readers with a deeper appreciation of the historical legacy inherited by contemporary female authors active in China today and a better understanding of their important literary foremothers.

Notes

1. Noteworthy recent publications include Liu Jianmei, *Revolution Plus Love: Literary History, Women's Bodies, and Thematic Repetition in Twentieth-Century Chinese Fiction* (Honolulu: University of Hawaii Press, 2003), and Tze-lan D. Sang, *The Emerging Lesbian: Female Same-Sex Desire in Modern Chinese Literature and Culture.* Chicago (Chicago: University of Chicago Press, 2002). See also Megan Ferry, *Chinese Women Writers of the 1930s and Their Critical Reception* (Ph.D diss., Washington University, St. Louis, 1998), and Nicole Huang, *Written in the Ruins: War and Domesticity in Shanghai Literature of the 1940s* (Ph.D. diss., UCLA, 1998).
2. There appear to be multiple reasons certain intellectuals and writers chose to remain in the occupied areas during the war. Often, as the case of Yang Jiang, who returned

to Shanghai to care for an elderly parent, it was a matter of personal circumstances rather than a political decision.

3. Wendy Larson, "The End of 'Funü Wenxue': Women's Literature from 1925–1935," *Modern Chinese Literature* 4 (1988): 50.

4. Yang Hansheng remembers her as the most prominent woman in leftist cultural circles, along with Ding Ling. See Bai Shurong and He You, *Bai Wei pingzhuan* (A critical biography of Bai Wei) (Changsha: Hunan Renmin chubanshe, 1982).

5. Quoted in *Sanshi niandai zai Shanghai de "zuolian" zuojia* (Leftist writers in Shanghai in the thirties)(Shanghai: Shanghai shehui kexueyuan chubanshe, 1988), 396. Originally from Bai Wei's essay, "My Motives for Writing It," published in *Women's Life* 2 (2) (1935).

6. First published in *Wenyi huabao* 1 (4) (1935). Reprinted in *Bai Wei zuopinxuan* (Changsha: Hunan renmin chubanshe, 1985), 226–238.

7. *Beiju shengya* (Shanghai: Shenghuo shudian, 1936).

8. For a nuanced discussion of the representation of sex and romance in left-wing cinema of the 1930s that has much to offer for understanding leftist literary discourse at the time, see Laikwan Pang, *Building a New China in Cinema: The Chinese Left-Wing Cinema Movement, 1932–1937* (Lanham, MD: Rowman and Littlefield, 2002).

9. Sally Lieberman offers an insightful analysis of this theme in her study *The Mother and Narrative Politics in Modern China* (Charlottesville: University Press of Virginia, 1998).

10. For more see Dong Bian, ed., *Nüjie wenhua zhanshi Shen Zijiu* (Beijing: Zhongguo funü chubanshe, 1991).

11. Nora, modeled after Norwegian playwright Henrik Ibsen's character, was a feminist icon popularized in the May Fourth press. For more, see Elisabeth Eide, *China's Ibsen* (London: Curzon Press, 1987).

12. They included many prominent women. Song Meiling, Chiang Kai-shek's wife, for example, assumed a leading role in promoting the policies targeting women as part of the New Life movement.

13. Elisabeth Croll, *Feminism and Socialism in China* (New York: Schocken, 1978), 153–184.

14. "Nala zuotan," *Funü shenghuo* 2 (1) (1936): 104–120.

15. Several examples of late Qing women's writing are featured in the first volume of *Writing Women in Modern China* (New York: Columbia University Press, 1998).

16. The appearance of liberal feminist groups that, like their early western counterparts, were chiefly devoted to achieving legal equality with men, was the exception.

17. Liu-Wang Liming, *Zhongguo funü yundong* (Shanghai: Shanghai Commercial Press, 1934), 156.

18. Tani Barlow, "Gender and Identity in Ding Ling's *Mother*," in Michael S. Duke, ed., *Modern Chinese Women Writers: Critical Appraisals* (Armonk, NY: M. E. Sharpe, 1989), 19.

19. See, for instance, Luo Shu's "Another Man's Wife" and Xiao Hong's *Field of Life and Death*. Both are available in English translation.

20. See, for example, Feng Keng's "A Piece of Flesh" (1930) and Guan Lu's "Diary of a Concubine" (1935). Guan Lu's decision to remain in Shanghai during the occupation and work for a Japanese-backed magazine raised some suspicions about her political allegiances, though the CCP confirmed in 1982 that she been on assignment doing underground party work.

21. "Wuhan daxue nüsheng zhi nücanzhengyuan shu" in *Women's Echoes* 11 (2) (April 1942). As quoted in Lu Fangshang, "Kangzhan shiqi nüquan lunbian," *Jindai zhongguo funüshi yanjiu* (June 1994).

22. For a thorough analysis of the development of reportage as a literary genre in modern China, see Charles A. Laughlin, *Chinese Reportage: The Aesthetics of Historical Experience* (Durham: Duke University Press, 2002).

23. Reportage works by Peng Zigang and Ji Hong frequently appeared in *Women's Life* magazine.

24. For a detailed account in English of this period in Chen's life, see Jeffrey Kinkley's informative introduction to her memoir of the Maoist era, *Surviving the Storm* (Armonk, NY: M. E. Sharpe, 1990).

25. For an excellent new collection of translations of autobiographical writings by Chinese women authors, see Jing M. Wang, *Jumping Through Hoops: Autobiographical Stories by Modern Chinese Women Writers* (Hong Kong: Hong Kong University Press, 2003).

26. Autobiographical novels also begin to appear from the 1930s onward and include Bai Wei's *My Tragic Life* (1936), Guan Lu's *Era of the Old and New* (1940), Chen Xuezhao's *To Be Working Is Beautiful* (1949), and Wang Ying's *Child Bride* (1954).

27. Barbara Harlow, *Resistance Literature* (London: Methuen, 1987), 120. See also her *Barred: Women, Writing, and Political Detention* (Hanover, NH: University Press of New England, 1992).

28. *Hu Lanqi huiyi lu, 1901–1936* (Chengdu: Sichuan renmin chubanshe, 1985), 267.

29. See Janice and Stephen MacKinnon, *Agnes Smedley: The Life and Times of an American Radical* (Berkeley: University of California Press, 1988).

30. The story was the title piece in a collection of short stories published in 1940 by the Xin Zhongguo wenhua publishing company in Xi'an.

31. See Yoshimi Yoshiaki, *Comfort Women: Sexual Slavery in the Japanese Military During World War II* (New York: Columbia University Press, 2000).

32. For more on the formation of Chinese urban modernism, see Leo Ou-fan Lee, *Shanghai Modern: The Flowering of a New Urban Culture In China, 1930–1945* (Cambridge: Harvard University Press, 1999), and Shu-Mei Shih, *The Lure of the Modern: Writing Modernism in Semicolonial China, 1917–1937* (Berkeley: University of California Press, 2001).

33. Zhang Ailing's work is readily available in English translation.

34. Meng Yue and Dai Jinhua, *Fuchu lishi dibiao* (Emerging from the horizon of history) (Taibei: Shibao wenhua chubanshe, 1993), 292.

35. In 1944, Heaven and Earth Press issued a book version of the novel, which had received an enthusiastic response from readers during its serialization the previous year in the magazine *Talks Amid Hardship*.

36. "Nüzuojia jutanhui," *Zazhi* (April 1944):50.

37. Edward Gunn, *Unwelcome Muse: Chinese Literature in Shanghai and Peking, 1937–1945* (New York: Columbia University Press, 1980), 73.

38. Lu Xun helped frame the May Fourth debate with his 1923 speech (which subsequently appeared in print), "What Happens When Nora Leaves?"

39. The collection features new work by many of the established women writers who had made names for themselves in the May Fourth era, including Bing Xin, Yuan Changying, Feng Yuanjun, Su Xuelin, Lu Jingqing, and Chen Ying. Two other important collections of women's writing published at the time were Tan Zhengbi's 1944 collection *Contemporary Women's Fiction*, which introduced many young new writers from this period, and *Selected Autobiographies of Women Writers*, edited by Xie Bingying.

40. This doctrine was articulated most famously by Mao Zedong at the 1942 "Yan'an Forum on Literature and Art."

41. Ravni Thakur, *Rewriting Gender: Reading Contemporary Chinese Women* (London: Zed Press, 1997), 88.

42. Luo Qiong (b. 1911) was a contributor to *Funü shenghuo* in the 1930s, and had collaborated with Shen on a translation of Alexandra Kollontai's *Novayia zhenshchina*. After going to Yan'an in 1940, she became the editor of the "Chinese Women" supplement to *Liberation Daily*.

43. In 1956 this magazine was renamed *Zhongguo funü*.

44. Merle Goldman, *Literary Dissent in Communist China* (Cambridge: Harvard University Press, 1967), 230.

45. According to her biographer Wang Yixin, this was primarily an expedient measure to ensure a salary. *Su Qing zhuan* (Shanghai: Xuelin chubanshe, 1999), 250.

46. Lu Tonglin, ed., *Gender and Sexuality in Twentieth-Century Chinese Literature and Society* (Albany: SUNY Press, 1993), 7.

47. Li Jun's "The Story of Li Shuangshuang," later adapted as a popular film, is one example critics often cite to illustrate this ideological trend.

48. This magazine was eventually shut down at the beginning of the Cultural Revolution for having promoted a supposedly narrow, bourgeois feminist platform.

49. Another example is Wei Junyi (b. 1917)'s short story "Women" (1956), which portrays the mounting frustrations of the central female protagonist, who feels that her co-workers see her merely as the wife of a high-ranking cadre rather than as the dedicated and seasoned comrade she in fact has become.

50. See her "Social Harmony, Family and Women in Chinese Novels, 1948–1958" in *China Quarterly* 117 (March 1989).

51. May Seventh Cadre schools (Wuqi ganxiao) were rural reeducation camps, mostly located in poor, remote areas, to which denounced intellectuals and cadres were sent during the Cultural Revolution. The goal (formalized in a directive Mao issued in 1968) was to reform such individuals through manual labor.

1
Yang Gang
(1905–1957)

*B*orn in Jiangxi province in 1905, Yang Gang grew up in an afflu-
ent household dominated by her father, a strong-willed provincial official who had worked his way up through the traditional
examination system. Her birth was overshadowed by the death of an
infant stepbrother, born to one of her father's concubines. After being
schooled in the classics by private tutors at home, she was sent to the
Baldwin School for Girls in Nanchang. According to her autobiographical novel *Daughter,* it was at this private boarding school, where many of
her classmates were work-study pupils, that she first became conscious of
the social privileges of wealthy families like her own. A student activist at
Yanjing University, where she majored in English, Yang Gang joined the
CCP in 1928 and was soon taking part in radical causes in Beijing. She
was arrested and jailed briefly in 1931 for demonstrating on International
Workers' Day, and upon her release she became a founding member of
the Beijing Branch of the League of Left-Wing Writers. During this period she became acquainted with the American journalist and activist
Agnes Smedley, who would become a lifelong friend, and she used her
fluency in English to assist Edgar Snow on the translations for his collection of contemporary Chinese fiction, *Living China* (1936). Her own
anonymous contribution to the volume, "Fragment from a Lost Diary,"
was composed in English but later also appeared in Chinese. This story,
reprinted here, vividly captures the complex emotional and physical ordeal of a pregnant female revolutionary, providing a uniquely gendered
lens through which to examine the turbulence of early twentieth-century
Chinese history. Yang Gang experimented with multiple literary genres
throughout her career as a writer, and examples of her fiction, poetry, essays, and translations (including a full-length translation of Jane Austen's
Pride and Prejudice, which she published under a pseudonym in 1935) can
be found in newspapers and periodicals from the time.

After the outbreak of full-scale hostilities with Japan in 1937, Yang
Gang moved to Shanghai, where she quickly rose to prominence as a

journalist for the newspaper *L'Impartial.* She followed the staff of the paper to Hong Kong in 1939 and eventually succeeded Xiao Qian as editor of its famed literary supplement. In Hong Kong she was involved in the anti-Japanese resistance. Her publications from those years include a full-length historical novel, *Gongsun Yang: A Statesman* (1939); a collection of essays about occupied Shanghai, *Raging Dreams* (1939); and a volume with two novellas, *An Unofficial Biography of Huan Xiu* (1941). In 1942, she accompanied the Australian reporter Wilfred Burchett as a special war correspondent for *L'Impartial.* A collection of her dispatches from the war zone were published under the title *Travels in the Southeast* in 1943. Yang Gang's style in this volume and her other wartime writing has won critical acclaim for its merging of journalistic precision and a lyrical sensibility.

From 1944 to 1948, Yang Gang was in the United States on a Radcliffe fellowship to study literature. During this period she began work on a major autobiographical novel in English. Entitled *Daughter,* the novel bears an interesting resemblance to Smedley's *Daughter of Earth* (1929). As Smedley does, Yang Gang employs a fictionalized autobiographical protagonist to chronicle a young woman's struggle against the dominant sexual and class politics of the society she inhabits. Whether because of the unfavorable political and cultural climate of the early 1950s or simply because she was absorbed in other projects at the time, Yang Gang did not pursue publication, even though the manuscript seems to have been more or less finished by the time she returned to China. Only decades later, in the post–Mao era, did the novel finally make its way into print (in both English-language and Chinese editions). Throughout her sojourn in the United States, Yang Gang continued writing for the Chinese press, sending home articles based on personal observations and critical analyses of contemporary American society. The best of these were assembled and eventually published in *Notes from America* (1951), a fascinating collection of incisive reportage pieces on topics ranging from racial injustice to McCarthyism. The second selection here is a short but powerful essay from that volume, in which the author documents her eye-opening journey to the Deep South with a white civil rights activist.

Upon her return to the People's Republic of China, Yang Gang worked as a deputy editor for *L'Impartial* (now renamed *The Progressive Daily*) in Tianjin, and later for the *People's Daily.* She also held posts in the Ministry of Foreign Affairs and the Ministry of Propaganda until her suicide in 1957. The reasons she took her life remain unclear, though her friend the late sinologist John Fairbank speculates that she did so after sustaining serious physical injuries in a car accident and not, as one might assume from the timing of her death, because of the adversities she encountered during the Antirightist campaign.

Fragment from a Lost Diary
(1936)

May 24, Windy

THE HEAVINESS OF this long May day nearly suffocates me. Endless hunger, endless nausea, endless doubt and anxiety. I move from my side to my back and then to my side again. The wooden planks of the bed are harder than stone. Hard, hard. It is impossible to get any rest! It is impossible for one moment to relieve the constant throbbing pain in my body, however I turn and toss. I cannot read. Only writing—since there is no one to talk with—seems to take my mind out of itself, as small idle occupations do.

Jing's forehead has become noticeably more lined since he learned the reason of my illness. Often he stares at me with wide eyes, saying nothing. When I ask why it is he looks at me like that he answers vaguely, "Nothing, nothing. Rest and get well quickly, that's all."

Meaningless words! I know well enough how inconvenient a thing I am. What small regard the female womb has for the "historic necessities"! It is its own history and its own necessity! It is the dialectic reduced to its simplest statement. What generosity of nature to make me this gift of the "illness of the rich" at just such a time!

I can't even enjoy being heroic in bearing my personal discomfort. With the tyranny of helplessness I must drag the whole of our close-knit organization into this trouble. When conditions are critical, and the situation everywhere is hostile, the individual burden unavoidably becomes the group burden. It isn't that my own small *role* remains unfulfilled. It's that my incapacity causes interruptions and irregularities for everyone. Most of all for Jing. He has become the slave at a sick-bed. He is *amah*, nurse, cook, errand-boy—and beggar. His work is neglected, badly done, and he goes about his duties with an absentmindedness born of fatigue. This in turn means confusion in the organization, and all because of my demands. It is so terribly important that all our plans at this time should be unfailingly sure, so much more important than this struggling life inside of me. Jing never complains of this added worry and responsibility, but I know how greatly it weighs upon him.

Now that the Thirtieth of May is approaching he drags himself out every morning at six and cannot return until late at night. Out of this precious day he must steal time for me—begging a few coppers from friend to friend to buy the small indispensable things for me, the invalid. I know this, and I know too how it troubles him to be away from me. Yet, under this unendurable sickness, I forget and quarrel with him again and again for his negligence!

Our house is like all the rest of the *gongyu*[1] along Shatan. Our room is the middle one of three facing south. There is no window in it. The only opening is the door. When that is closed no air or sunshine can stir within. The room itself is very narrow, with space only for a bed and table and a small bench. I can reach over to the table from my bed. That at least is a convenience.

The boy hasn't cleaned our room for several days. Probably this is because we haven't paid the rent (four dollars a month!) since March. The wall-paper is cracked, and a corner of it hangs from the ceiling. Dust and cobwebs drop from it. Rats run back and forth in the bamboo rafters. Sometimes one of them, in a fight, tumbles down to the earthen floor. It has to lie there till Jing returns. I myself cannot get up, however nauseating the sight and smell of the creature may be.

Everything in the room is covered with dust, blown in through the open door—open to anyone who wants to gape in from the courtyard. Spiders work back and forth. I look at them, entranced, as they crawl even up to my bed, and spin their silvery threads in the sunlight. They are at least *alive*. They are the only companions I have. They help me to forget the oppressive loneliness and agony of this dreary May day.

Our neighbor on the left is evidently a student at Beida.[2] He seems to be in some way related to the landlord, and for that reason hasn't paid his rent for months. The landlord has now begun to seize his mail, however, even registered letters containing money. The student doesn't complain about it. What is money to him? His fat red face radiates peace and serenity. When he needs money he tries to beg it from the landlord. If successful he goes out with a handful of coppers, and soon returns with a bottle of *baigan* and a piece of

---

[1] A *gongyu* is a lodging house. Many were used as dormitories for men and women students in Beijing. Shatan is an eastern district where Beijing University was formerly located.
[2] Beijing University.

roast chicken. Locking himself up inside, he proceeds to drink for the rest of the day, clucking and imitating the opera stars in an impossible falsetto. When the last drop is gone he gives a loud slap on his thigh, rolls over, and is soon thunderously snoring in deep contentment. Sometimes he cannot squeeze a single cent out of his relative, but receives instead a large piece of harsh criticism or advice. On these occasions he returns to his room very depressed. "Ah! . . . Sh! . . . Ha! . . ." Is he actually planning to commit suicide? Nobody worries about it, least of all the landlord.

On the other side there is a dramatist, also a student of Beida. He is often away for a whole day, for which I offer thanks. When he stays at home he practices his chosen profession, and this is very tiresome indeed. He sings like a Great Painted Face of the theater, in a froglike voice. Sometimes he attempts the lines of the Bearded Face, with his voice ranging in all dimensions. But the most unbearable of all is the sound resulting when he lifts his throat to a shrill soprano and shrieks in imitation of the female lead. One can picture him twisting his waist and swinging his hips in rhythm with the singing. He frequently asks the landlord in for a chat and "refreshments." At such times he joins the villain in cursing the other lodgers.

"*Aiya*," he exclaims, "it's time even for me to pay the rent. Only this morning I reminded myself to go to the bank, but my wasteful memory has again failed me. Look, here's the account book in my pocket. You see I really intended to go there!"

This fellow looks after the house servant too. Bribing him with a handful of peanuts he collects all the gossip he can. How much money has the rickshaw man's wife—she in the corner on the western wing—squeezed behind her husband's back? With whom has the actress been copulating? What dress did she wear? And so on. Between them a most provoking conversation ensues, evidently to the interest and high satisfaction of both. It never occurs to him to give me any consideration. Yet when I am retching with anguish he heaves audible sighs. "How unendurable! How much better off dead!" Not content with exaggerated groans to himself, he sometimes ventures to tap the thin wall and whisper through the chinks in a soft, sympathetic voice: "Madam, sister, would you bring peace to my heart by permitting me to assist you? Ah, it is bitterly painful to me, painful!"

However great my contempt of him I am helpless. I say nothing. My very silence provokes him to actual savage scolding and cursing. I am a pestilence to him! We paste up the chinks in the wall, but he slits them open again with a knife. Sweet are one's neighbors, unto whom one should do as unto oneself.

The whole courtyard is crowded with quarrelsome voices. Women curse and scold and beat. There is a droning voice somewhere forever mechanically reading the old Four Books and classical poetry. Eight different families, living in a twelve-*jian* house, and each one rivaling the other to produce the loudest noise and create the greatest possible friction! The whole day long this courtyard boils and seethes, and only my damp, suffocating little room contributes nothing. Perfect Confucian harmony: *li, yi, lian, chi.*[3] I am seized alternately with chills and fever. All the time I am half-famished. The hungrier I am the more I want to vomit. But not a crumb to feed that twin torment, either the hunger or the physical need for expelling food. And all this suffering utterly without significance! That I can have actually endured it for over two months! That I should think, even now, of wanting to continue to exist only as the vessel of a chemical experiment heartlessly, inexorably formulating itself within me! And against my will!

Am I insane to think of *that* way out? But it is obviously the solution. Still, I won't consider it again today.

May 25

JING RETURNED LAST night looking like a mask of himself. He fell on the bed almost as soon as he entered the door. He was very gaunt, terribly thin, and his dark eyes opened to show frightening depths, cavernous like wells and full of foreboding.

He looked vacantly at me, while I asked him what he had eaten. He admitted having had nothing since noon, when he had bought six dry cakes from a street vendor.

At last he pulled himself from the bed and turned to cook the little tubes of wheat rolls he had brought home with him. He lit the tiny flame under the oil lamp on the table. When the water boiled over it he put the rolls into the pan. He did not speak until then. Going to the thin panels of the wall he pressed his ear close, listening on both sides to make certain our neighbors were asleep.

"I'm afraid we'll have to leave here soon," he whispered to me. "It's unthinkable while you're so ill; and yet . . ."

He looked questioningly at me, but I simply signaled that I wanted to hear the inner truth of it.

---

[3]Propriety, righteousness, honesty, and humility, the "pillars of Confucian culture," which Generalissimo Chiang Kai-shek's New Life movement attempted to revive in 1934.

"It's the landlord. The rent. He kicked up another storm about it. Threatened to call in the police if we don't pay or get out."

I did not say anything. There was nothing to be said. I knew quite well that Jing had not told me the whole story. The rent problem can't have reached a crisis; it has already been at that stage for weeks. This alone wouldn't alarm him. He wouldn't at any rate speak so seriously about it were this not merely a screen hiding the real facts. I didn't question him further. No doubt he knows what is best for me to hear.

And yet to move! How? First of all money is needed, and after that my health has to be mentioned.

"Can't we stay a few days longer?" I finally asked him.

"Certainly—a few days. Only we *must* be out before May Thirtieth. Don't worry about it, anyway. I simply told you so that you won't be surprised when the time comes. It isn't a serious matter. I will have money very soon." He smiled a little wan smile with his mouth, but his eyes did not change at all. The effect was somehow terrifying. "It will do you good to get a change of atmosphere, eh?"

He blew out the flame and drew forth some of the boiled rolls. Sitting on the bed he helped me eat. Before we had finished half the food my stomach rebelled, and up it all came. Not only the miserable food! It seemed to me that a violent internal explosion was taking place, forcing up my very soul! My eyes felt like gates being hammered at by battering-rams inside. My whole head burned as if afire. I couldn't control myself at all. Even while my body was bathed in sweat it also felt cold, and I shook all over.

Jing wasn't suffering much less. He jumped about excitedly, in a rage because he was so helpless to ease my pain. He tried to hold me up. He rinsed my mouth and nose, and bathed my eyes. He soaked towels in the hot water and put them on my forehead. He got his four limbs mixed up trying to do everything at once.

I didn't sleep all night. I could not even keep my eyes closed. After this performance I kept thinking of that hope, and it seemed to me the only way to freedom. I must have been very delirious. I remember pinching and pressing and even sharply striking my womb. How I wanted the little creature to die! And yet at the same time my heart seemed to be protesting with all the vigor left in me, responding with a blow at *me* for every one I struck at *it*! With the conflicting instincts—the one selfish, for the preservation of my child, the other unselfish, for the preservation of my usefulness—I felt for a while that only through a double death could any solution be cleanly achieved. Traitorous thought!

And yet I love this little life! With all the pain of it, I long for the wonderful thing to happen, for a tiny human creature to spring from between my limbs bravely out into the world. I need it, just as a true poet *needs* to create a great undying work. No, more than that; for my little one shall be the instrument of Mother Nature to change nature. Of that I am certain, just as I am certain even now that it is already shaping into a—human being! That little fellow, at first so helpless, so full of a need of me, curious with the curiosity of little eyes slowly opening, that little man will later on stand up and assert, with his great beauty and his great power, such fine true things about men and nature that all the authorities, all the rulers of heaven and earth, cannot but bow down to his will!

Ever since my lunar pause, ever since the first quivering in my womb, my heart has been unspeakably shaken with the wonder of this knowledge. My throat has ached to proclaim it to the whole world. Despite his purity and his splendor, it would actually be upon me whom this young man would bestow his first smile! It would be me whom he would call mother! Ah, yes, all that I've thought about, and of all that known the joy and the power and the longing!

Where is the woman strong enough alone not to dream such dreams? No, there is not one, and certainly not I. Not one—and yet perhaps many, thousands, millions of us together! Cannot the essential spirit of mother-hood, strengthened in the unity of many women, reject its selfish little in-dividual rights? Can't we become for once *conscious* in travail, dedicate that priceless fertility to the nourishment of a vast physiological act of Mother Nature herself, greatening her womb in our own time with a new *kind* of human being?

I believe we can. Yet turning an abstract philosophy into a poisoned needle to thrust into my own womb, that is a different thing! I am full of the distress of mental and physical torment as these emotions battle ceaselessly. Still, I am determined. I am awake at last, after years of bovine slumber. I am more fully awake than when I first made up my mind to join the Revolution. Only when the beat of life is lifted to this pitch, this fury, and this danger, only when des-tiny (here in my case it is but a wayward sperm carrying its implacable micro-scopic chromosomes, but nevertheless it is a form of destiny!) poses the choice between irreconcilable desires at a given moment, only when a human being feels the necessity of ignoring personal feeling in the decision taken—only then can one talk of a revolutionary awakening!

Well, all that is to say that for the pauperized millions to bear children in society as at present disorganized is simply to increase the number of those living in hopeless misery. Every child thrust from the womb of a sick, under-fed, unattended mother just so much further degrades the disinherited. For the child of poverty there lies ahead nothing but hunger, insults, ignorance, abuse, bitterness, and no hint of the spiritual exaltation that divides men from beasts of the jungle. For us the problem of new life is the problem of life as we know it now, ourselves, and this we cannot unconscionably impose upon the unborn.

And yet I still fondly amuse myself with maternal fancies! I still now and then dream of freeing my own life by projecting another one into the world!

Jing will meet a Korean friend today. With the help of this fellow I may bring my plan to a practical conclusion. I told Jing to seek out this man. It never occurred to me that he would be shocked, and his curious stare and his silence dismayed me. He just stood still for a while, with his hands thrust deep in his pockets. Then he turned his head, and ground out, in a decisive tone:

"Abortion! It isn't to be thought of! It's impossible."

"Abortion, on the contrary, is the only way. It is settled!"

He turned and looked at me with a strange look, as if he had been struck. He sat down on the bed and took my hands in his. His expressive eyes spoke half of compassion, half of remonstrance. I began to explain to him how I had reached the decision.

"We cannot," he broke in, and covered my mouth with his hands. Lowering his lips to my ear he whispered: "I understand, dear. I know everything you feel, but later on you will regret it. And it is dangerous, by such means—" He shook his head and for a while said nothing. I felt suddenly sick and lay back, silent too.

After a long while he whispered again: "However great the pain—two kinds of pain, I understand—it isn't so serious as this step. You do not know how dangerous it is—dangerous first for Li, and then it is an attack on your very life. Besides we haven't time. We must move . . ." He choked and did not fin-ish. We both sat staring at each other, profoundly miserable.

Just then we heard a scratching sound on one of the walls. Jing looked sig-nificantly at the slit cut open between the paneling, and then got up, gently stroking my arm.

May 26

CAN JING ACTUALLY not have returned once during the entire night? Do I de-serve to be forsaken? What have I done that I must lie here in torn anguish, helpless, uncomforted, hungry, with nothing to break the horrible monotony of these surroundings—that old broken washstand, the stained wrappings of food, stale spinach, and the ceiling webbed with the spider's spinnings, somehow making the room seem like a place where only discarded things should be?

Laid away like this, a dead one, is it possible for me to feel the same sense of value, to believe in my own significance as a social being, as I do when living with the working masses?

Ordinarily, even when busiest, Jing never fails to get back sometime during the night. What can have happened?

I waited last night, as usual, for the sound of his footsteps. I kept my eyes on the door steadily after the landlord's clock struck eleven. I heard every sound it made after that: half-past eleven, twelve, half-past twelve, and then just as regularly one, half-past, two, half-past, three, and so on till after dawn. Every boom of the clock deepened my own anxiety; and, as sometimes happens to one, I became intensely aware of the irredeemable loss of each of those hours, aware of time actively destroying me.

It was quite unnecessary for me to torture my mind worrying about ordinary accidents, such as Jing being struck by a motorcar, or falling dead from exhaustion, or being bitten by a mad dog. And yet I did so. I even hoped that it was something like that. I invented several highly improbable situations to account for his absence. I refused to think about that most dreadful—and yet most likely—possibility.

Just now I would welcome even the arrival of some spies or *gendarmes*. I cannot stand the suspense any longer. Even to know that he is in police hands is better than this hovering dread, this awful uncertainty! It seems to me that I cannot breathe for another hour! What the devil is going to happen to me? It is perhaps preferable even to be in jail than to be an abandoned lump lying lifelessly here. . . .

Later

LAO LI[4] HAS been here and has brought news of Jing! It is, of course, as I feared.

His thick brows were locked under his broad forehead, and I knew before he spoke what had happened. He came in, nodded his head in greeting, and simply said, "*En!*"

---

[4]Here "Lao" is not part of the name, but an honorific. Literally "old," though Li is still young.

"What is it?"

"Jing has been arrested."

May 27

I WON'T DIE! I thought of it last night, the easiest way being simply to languish in the *gongyu,* where nobody would lift a rice bowl to save my life. But I won't die. Lao Li gave me some encouragement. He advised me to move to his house, where his wife, a doctor, can help me. This good news, now that Jing has already lost his freedom, is perhaps the only thing that made me want to live.

Li helped me to move. I am lying now in a bed placed in one of their two small rooms, which they rent from a Korean landlord. He is a sympathetic fellow, and lives in the other part of the house himself.

Lao Li's Korean wife seems to me rather quaint in appearance, with a grey-tinted yellow face, greyish-brown eyes (very narrow), and thick lips. She is quite fat, a distinct contrast to the sharp, straight architecture of her husband's body. She has not been long in China, and has to dig for words to express herself, and often, failing to find them, she fills in the blanks with an embarrassed smile.

She was very moved when I told her what I wanted. At first she was speechless, and only shook her head violently. Then from her little eyes tears began to sprinkle her piteous face, and she jumped up impetuously and came to my bed. She held me close to her fat breasts while she shook with convulsive sobs. Almost hysterically she cried, "No, no, no! You shall not!" Her obviously deep emotion rather surprised me.

Lao Li pulled her up gently and spoke to her in Korean. I couldn't understand. She kept sobbing, as pathetically as if she were a small orphan girl. Gradually she grew quiet, under her husband's persuasion, and at last came to say that she would help me.

There is only one bed in the rooms, and last night Li and his wife had to sleep on stools set before me. During the evening Li *taitai* told me something of her life.

She is now thirty-nine years of age, but she has no children. She has, however, constantly longed for a son, but each time this desire seemed about to be fulfilled she was frustrated.

Li *taitai*'s family were Christians and furious when she married her revolutionary husband. They disowned her. What annoyed them particularly was that, after they had spent so much money educating her and getting her medical degree, she had turned it to the service of such a worthless cause. They refused to extend to her even a copper of help.

Lao Li, extremely busy in revolutionary work, rarely had any money. Often he was compelled to go into hiding for weeks or even months, leaving his wife alone. Each time she was with child it happened that Lao Li was in danger, and she had to suffer the shock, worry, and nervous tension of this knowledge as well as being left with inadequate funds for either proper care or nourishment. Seven times she lost her unborn child!

Seven! Is it possible for a woman to go through this horror seven times? Women and revolution! What tragic, unsung epics of courage lie silent in the world's history!

At the time of his wife's eighth pregnancy Lao Li, in desperation, arranged to get leave for a while, borrowed some money, and took her to the seashore. He provided her with such material comforts as he could and bent every effort towards protecting her against disturbance. The result was that at last her son was born. It grew into a beautiful, healthy child, and by the time it was seven months old delighted its parents by the long and fascinating conversations carried on by the changing expressions of its face and by its adorable infant chuckling and babbling. Needless to say, the parents were enchanted with their precious possession.

At this time both Lao Li and his wife were suddenly arrested and thrown into prison, their baby with them. Ten days of that is sufficient to kill any child. Theirs died.

As the unfortunate woman talked on she wept freely. Her husband, sitting beside her, patted her gently and spoke to her in the most compassionate way. He was evidently glad that she had taken this chance to give expression to the repressed misery burning within her. Hardly less moved himself, he even reminded her of details she had forgotten and helped provide her inadequate Chinese with words and phrases whenever she paused.

This morning I took an enormous capsule, administered by Dr. Li. She promises that one of these is sufficient to abort a fetus one month old, and three are enough to expel one gone three months. Three days after taking this medicine one can hope for the best.

Afternoon

THE STORMY MAY wind, carrying down tons of Gobi dust, seems to set fire to your eyes and nose and throat. It is enough in itself to make most people a little ill. Now, as it howls outside, and the fine yellow silt drifts in and covers everything, I take a savage delight in describing my own feelings! Perhaps it will be instructive to read later on. . . .

Well, then, I feel exactly as if there were dozens of repulsive hairy worms crawling back and forth in all my joints! It seems to me that if these worms managed to get out they would take with them the basic tincture of my life-blood! Ugh!

Later

I JUST SAW Jing being tortured! An old man with red, blinking eyes bent over him, holding a huge kettle with a tiny spout, out of which he poured "pepper water" into Jing's nose. "Among means for the regeneration of Mankind," old red-eyes quoted Confucius, "those made with great demonstrations are of least importance."

Jing struggled to free himself, and let out blood-drying groans. He tried to turn his face, but that tore his lips on the rope binding him across the mouth to the floor. The water poured from his nose, his mouth, and his eyes, several times he fainted. The torturers revived him by turning him over and emptying him of water.

More than forty kettles had been poured into him!

Now and then the torture would cease while Jing was cross-examined. All the time I stood by, helplessly watching his agony. It seemed that already I had been shoved in front of him, and whipped on my bare back. They had demanded that I ask him to talk, to tell his address. It seemed also that my lips had already been burned by incense because I had refused to speak.

Apparently Jing did not recognize me. It may be that he could not see. His face was mottled with red, blue, purple, and greenish bruises. Blood clung to his hair. He looked dumbly at me without any comprehension in his eyes at all.

Since they already had me in custody, what was the object of torturing Jing for this information? Had he another address that they wanted? Having changed him into a different creature, why did they continue with this bestial abuse? Did they hope to break his spirit by making him confess to the fact that he was under arrest? I did not understand it. I wanted to scream. They came towards me, tore off my jacket, and prepared to whip my back and breasts in front of him. Then I did scream.

Opening my eyes I looked into the face of Li *taitai,* who had her arms around me. She held her narrow eyes close to mine, and they were as wide open as she could get them, full of fright and astonishment. "What is it?" she demanded. "What?"

The tortures of which I had dreamed were exactly like those used on Y—

and P——. But the significance of Jing's refusal to divulge his address? What was it? Obviously it betrayed my anxiety that Jing, thinking me still helpless in the *gongyu*, was submitting to some ghastly inquisition rather than give the KMT his address.

May 28, Windy

WINDY INDEED!

As the wind rises my fever rises, and as it dies I am shaken with chills. All the paper panes in the windows have been burst open by the storm. The wind screams like a woman, like a woman in torture and travail. It shows its torn face through the window—but am I still delirious?

Because of my fever Dr. Li refused to give me another capsule today. I pleaded with her. I insisted. Now that this is begun I want it finished quickly. I am impatient to get into the world again, to carry on Jing's work and my own. Then, too, I cannot waste any more of the Lis' energy or money than is absolutely necessary—on this useless, pointless enterprise.

I swallowed two of those great cylindrical pills at once!

Midnight

SHAO FENG JUST ran in breathlessly. His face lengthened when he saw me here. He had come to warn the Lis to move immediately. At the same time he wanted his wounds dressed by Dr. Li.

The day before yesterday Shao Feng was carrying some things on a bicycle. As he was going along Beiheyan another bicycle suddenly dashed against him. A spy jumped out, grabbed him, and yelled as loudly as possible for the police. Shao Feng succeeded in tripping the man over the rickshaw, and escaped by running down small lanes, jumping some walls, and crossing several low roofs. He tore his left arm, and it was swollen with neglect and covered with ugly dark blood. Dr. Li dressed his wound, and he left immediately, giving an anxious glance at me.

"Move at once!" What mockery to me lying here, a helpless burden, endangering the lives of my friends! Tomorrow is May Thirtieth,[5] day of awakening for China, day on which the masses everywhere rise up to show their growing

---

[5]May 30, 1925, was the day on which foreign police in Shanghai killed many students and workers in a demonstration, an incident that inflamed the whole nation to anger.

strength and unity. Tomorrow over the whole nation resolute young men and women will march forth, defiantly, and some of them will be killed—and from their deaths new strength will arise. But I—weighed down by a stone! Women and revolution—strange pair!

Today they will spare no search to get our people imprisoned before the demonstration. . . . The Lis are talking together in Korean. I want to tell them that they must go, that I don't want them here with me, that they must leave me! But on my lips there is only a silent scream which will tell them that suddenly my womb feels as though pierced with ten thousand hot needles. I want to keep on writing this, to hide that scream that will betray me. . . . My whole flesh itches and stings and burns. My entire body pulses as if with anchored lightning. Everything around me is poisonous, sickening. There is that hot stone ready to burst from within me at any moment—and another ready to burst from my head.

[*Here the diary ends.*]

The American South

(1951)

ONE SPRING AN American friend and I toured the American South. Our goal was to pass through every state in the Deep South on the way to California. We heard that the best season to travel this route was spring, when the lush subtropical climate fills the senses without being unbearably hot. By the time summer arrived and the South got too hot, we would have left it behind for golden, glittering California.

My friend is of Northern European stock, with light brown hair and tiny yellow freckles on her white skin. Her sharp, small brown eyes flit back and forth, giving the impression that she is bright and competent, albeit occasionally lacking in composure. Her name is Erja. We decided to travel together to attend several lectures down south. Erja belongs to an organization fighting racial discrimination, so she takes part in these lectures.

I have to admit that I was already biased against the American South because the region is notorious for its discrimination against blacks. I remember on my voyage to America there was a waiter on board the ship who told me that he simply did not feel American. (The reader should forgive me for not having noted the color of his skin. Think about it. Which waiters serving

Chinese passengers on American ships are not black?) In New York, that so-called "city of freedom" with the Statue of Liberty ensconced at its head, I repeatedly heard references to Harlem, a part of town that white folk fear to enter, shunning it as if it were a leper colony. Actually, the place is nothing but a black community deliberately established by white capitalists. In fact, the "black problem" seems to be synonymous with America. It also seems to be a large pustule growing on America's nose, clearly evident, with a stench palpable far out at sea. Thus I felt fully prepared for the pus-filled region of the South, and was not expecting a wonderland. Nonetheless, as the train passed through Washington, D.C. I felt I had entered a barbaric world. The railroad cars were still very attractive. The whites still buttoned their collars neatly, their chins cleanly shaven like red persimmons, while blacks in white aprons served them. The dining cars still used shiny silverware and porcelain dishes, and the glistening yellow chicken was elegantly prepared with a side of fragrant green vegetables. The whole car was filled with outwardly clean, attractive people, meeting the highest standard of western civilization. Yet amid this civilized world I had a shameful feeling of savagery. Our car originally had two black passengers who were now nowhere to be seen. Perhaps they had disembarked at their stop. Nor were there any blacks in the dining car. A thick woolen curtain had been draped heavily across the front end of the dining car, tightly covering that constricted space, as if concealing something unfit for human eyes. Occasionally the curtain would be lifted and a bald, white-frocked black waiter emerged with a tray of food held high. I caught a fleeting glimpse inside, and saw nothing but black faces and black heads squirming in a tightly packed space like a forest thicket. But this was only for a brief instant; the curtain was immediately drawn shut once again. The car was once again dazzling bright, with dazzling bright white folk chatting casually as before.

This shocked me enormously. I must have stopped eating to stare at that peculiar curtain, because Erja nudged me and said in disgust, "What are you looking at? Black people eat in there. That's precisely how they're discriminated against." She turned her fork over and stabbed a piece of chicken, continuing to caution me in her worldly-wise way that I should stop staring, lest the mistreated blacks notice and take offense.

After our meal, driven by curiosity, I decided to walk the length of the train to see what this racism was all about. To be honest, even though I was born in multiethnic China, I had never seen one ethnic group command another to do all of its menial labor. It seemed to be behavior out of the caveman era, completely incommensurate with the dazzling bright, so-called western civilization before me. I set out on my inspection tour without saying anything to

Erja. I wanted to see the rail car reserved for blacks, and above all to locate the two black passengers who had shared my car. The woman in particular had large, expressive eyes that I found beautiful.

Once we passed D.C. there seemed to be fewer passengers, and some cars were virtually empty. I quickly passed through seven or eight cars that hardly contained any passengers at all, let alone black passengers. I was a little disappointed and was about to turn back, when I came upon a car that was separated into two parts: one section was comparatively long, for whites, and the other shorter, filled with blacks piled up like grain in a hopper. The black section seemed dark and dirty, probably because the car was too old, the light too dim, and the passengers too noisy and crowded. Suddenly I realized that every eye in this part of the car was fixed on me. And in the midst of these cold white eyes I saw a pair of large hateful eyes directed at me like two daggers. I was terrified, and quickly turned to leave. Even the woman who had shared a car with me was glaring at me with a hateful, poisonous expression.

After I returned to my compartment I didn't tell Erja about my encounter; I only looked out the window in anger. Erja stared at me in puzzlement for a long time, not knowing what the matter was but likewise remaining silent.

The farther south we traveled, the more often I had this type of unsettling experience. Because I was with a white person, I felt constantly under attack by blacks; I could not inhabit their space, nor could they inhabit mine. Even the streets were divided between black and white. As for restaurants, hotels, waiting rooms in train or bus stations, restrooms, trams, automobiles—white drivers did not transport blacks or enter black areas—anyplace people mixed was divided into two worlds of black and white. Whenever whites and blacks meet, murderous violence ensues, the one possible exception being when a white man rapes a black woman. A horrifying battle from prehistoric times is being waged in the belly of this superficially gleaming American civilization.

At first I tried to discuss these matters with Erja, but she was unwilling to talk at length, instead responding curtly, "This is precisely what we are struggling against!" She did not encourage me to pursue the topic further. She worried that if I were at an event with black progressives I would make an offhand comment and offend someone. That would complicate her work. Once when we were to attend a lecture in a black neighborhood, she insisted that we set out an hour ahead of time even though it was only half an hour away, saying it was better to wait for the speaker than to have the blacks think we were putting on white airs.

There was one, the fatherly New Orleans mayor, however, who refused to acknowledge such dynamics. As if he were a man of great vision, he was bent on enlightening me: "Don't believe what those Northern folk say. They don't live down South, so how can they understand our affairs? They don't understand blacks either. Blacks truly do not want to mix with whites, do they? We in America are free; individuals are free to live as they choose. Blacks like the South. They like to be with their own kind. It's not a matter of discrimination; they want to be separate from us. You need to understand America is the freest country in the world!"

This charlatan gave "Northern folk" too much credit. With the exception of the progressives, most Northerners share the same attitudes and deliver the same old spiel about blacks as Southerners. Thus I was scarcely surprised to hear him say this, but did not feel obliged to respond. The blacks themselves provide the real answers day after day.

We arrived in Texas, the largest state in the Union. Texans are renowned for their fierce bravery, and the state is also said to be the most liberal in the South. The University of Texas is located in Austin, the capital. The university had recently fired its president for endorsing Roosevelt's policies. When we arrived, the president had just been forced out by the board of trustees. The students were very sad to see him go, so they used the occasion of our arrival to organize a farewell party for the president while also welcoming us.

Before the event, I overheard Erja and the students discussing plans to invite representatives of several black youth organizations to the party. This was illegal; if the police found out, we could be incarcerated. But Erja and the students decided to take the unprecedented step of staging an assault on the laws of reactionary authorities, relying on the progressive atmosphere of the university and the relatively liberal reputation of the state.

The events that evening really were exciting. The students invited a military band, and erected the American and Chinese flags. The band played the two national anthems, with the tune of "The Volunteer Army Advances" as China's anthem. The president delivered a speech, and many other speakers followed. We sang and played games. Yet there was not a single black student representative present, not to mention performances by black organizations. I don't know how the others felt, but I was engulfed in a thick fog of gloom until the party ended.

As the party broke up, Erja immediately grabbed me, threaded her way through the crowd that had gathered around to sign the petition and jumped into a friend's car and urged the driver to get going. It seemed as if she were trying to make an escape or going on some secret mission. When I questioned her, she merely whispered a few indecipherable words in my ear. We didn't leave for some time, for the owner of the car seemed to be orchestrating some sort of activity outside. Gradually the small car was packed with four or five people speaking in hushed voices about going somewhere, while also laughing and urging the driver to hurry up, lest we be late. The car's owner warned us to keep quiet for fear the wrong people would overhear. Clearly we were not heading back home, but were about to embark on some risky venture.

And indeed, we arrived at a stranger's house late at night. The owner was a man with a dark face and tight, bristly black curls. His wife was lighter-skinned, with a thin nose and lips suggesting she was biracial, a mixture of Northern European and African descent. There were already a number of black men and women in their living room, so when the newly arrived whites entered it became the kind of mixed event at which police have the right to make arrests. I now understood why we had been so vigilant in coming. Here was concrete evidence of the American freedom to which the mayor of New Orleans had referred.

The meeting had been organized by Erja and her friends. Because the University of Texas administrators had not allowed blacks to attend the school party, they decided on this locale to hold a mixed meeting with progressive whites and blacks. Our host was Mr. Carlton, the pastor of a black church who was quite well known locally, especially among blacks, who regarded him as a man of great intellect. It goes without saying that there are not that many intellectuals in the black community. His wife was said to be a brilliant graduate from a prestigious black college in Tennessee, though at present she was not employed. The handful of other blacks in the room all occupied fairly high social positions in the black community—doctors, teachers, and so forth. Erja carefully and thoughtfully consulted with each one of them. She seemed to disparage the local whites with every remark she made, trying hard to make each person forget about her bland colorless skin and accept her as one of them so they would freely speak their minds.

Erja's approach worked. Each one of those blacks—the cream of Austin society—unburdened their tales of distress, turning the evening into a session of venting grievances. At first people reported what they had seen and heard, but after a while they got to talking about their own painful experiences. One told about having endured a tongue-lashing from a white man on the street because he failed to address him as "Sir." Another told of being tossed out of a restaurant up north because of his skin color. One recounted how he had so wanted to be addressed as "Mister," he paid a white prankster $200 to address him loudly as "Mister X."

"My very bones laughed with glee when I heard that white pig call me 'Mister.'" When the doctor finished his story, he shook his head in despair, saying, "It's horrible to be humiliated; those white pigs definitely want us to remember we were once slaves! They'll destroy us this way. What hope do we have? How much longer will this go on?"

"That good-for-nothing mayor of New Orleans went so far as to claim that this happens because you have freely chosen to live this way," I said.

Our host, the pastor, leaped off his seat, gnashing his teeth in anger, and practically shouted, "Free choice? What roads are open to us? What choices do we have? My wife couldn't even go to Chicago a few days ago. The train station refused to write 'Mrs. Carlton' down on her documents. They said, 'How can a Negro be called "Mrs."?' That's exactly what they said. I'm a pastor with a Ph.D., but what can I do? My ancestors were slaves, yet I am a free man and have attained a high social status; but my wife still can't have a formal title?"

"Forget it," said a young female teacher. "What's the point of trying to explain the logic behind all this? It's like the university party tonight. They said they were going to invite us even though we did not ask to go or even care to go. But did they end up inviting us?" she said, laughing scornfully. Erja listened in discomfort, as though she were being unjustly condemned. Actually, the blacks in the room all knew why they hadn't been able to attend the party. Several white students apologized to the young black teacher as they explained. The pastor also cut in, explaining that it was the university administration that disrupted the plan.

But the more she heard, the angrier the teacher seemed to get. As her brown face turned red, she stood up and said loudly, "I don't mean to offend anyone. I know that progressive whites oppose our oppression. But so what if they are opposed? And so what if they are not? Aren't they all in cahoots with the reactionaries? I say that what they really want to ensure is that we do not rise up. All white people are the same; they hate us. We are burdened and oppressed and lack self-respect; we trample on ourselves. We have become America's blight, the white man's burden. They hate us. They may say nice things to us, but they hide their consciences, secretly following the reactionaries. I hate them! I hate all white devils, especially progressives! As far as I'm concerned we should stop hoping for anything from whites, we have nothing to hope for!" Having said all this, the young teacher suddenly erupted like a kettle boiling over, and burst into tears.

Everyone in the room was upset by this angry outburst of despair. Some lowered their heads to wipe away their tears, others looked up to stare at the teacher, with expressions of pity mixed with anger. The pastor and his wife went over to the teacher and appeared to be holding her, patting her shoulders to calm her down. Erja's face had completely blanched, her brown eyebrows trembling above her small, sharp eyes. Throughout our trip the thing she had most worried about and dreaded was encountering among blacks this type of deep-rooted mistrust and hatred toward whites. For this would indicate that the problem exceeded white prejudice against blacks; it was also a matter of blacks deeply prejudiced against whites. Such attitudes presented a serious impediment to antiracist efforts, for they would be even more difficult to eradicate than the overt obstacles posed by the reactionary opposition, especially when they were expressed in mixed-group meetings like this one. The white youth in attendance had never encountered such sentiments before. What would their response be? Erja lowered her head, rubbing her palms tightly together, small beads of sweat forming on the tiny yellow freckles on her face.

The atmosphere in the room was tense; the teacher could not stop sobbing. "How can this be good? I'm afraid the only road for us is revolution!" someone said in a pained voice.

Erja seemed enlightened by the comment. She stood up and faced the teacher, mustering all her strength to say in a calm, bold voice, "Miss X, I am terribly sorry for upsetting you. But it is very good that you brought up this issue today and that you could express yourself so candidly. Otherwise we will fall prey to the cunning schemes of the reactionaries. Their true intention is to make us—blacks and whites who have been oppressed—look down on and despise each other. They intentionally turn class issues into race issues, to divide those who have been oppressed. If we don't unite, we will never be able to enact significant change in America, let alone make revolution. Now, it's better; what we were discussing was the poison fed us by the reactionary party, so we need to spit it out. That way we can unite even more closely and fight together to achieve our goals. Friends, in a system that oppresses people, the oppressed—blacks and whites—have no way forward. At present every path has been obstructed by Wall Street. The rulers of Wall Street want our labor, and they want our lives. We need to stand hand in hand to oppose them!"

"Exactly. They are all too happy to have us hate one another. But it is good to speak out." Many voices chimed in. The room grew more relaxed, and everyone started talking all at once. A black woman at Erja's side leaned over to quietly whisper in her ear, "If only we had united earlier the opposition would have toppled long ago. We need to do this now. We need to draw a clear line between our enemies and our allies, uniting regardless of skin color!"

2
Bai Wei

(1894–1987)

*B*ai Wei was born Huang Zhang in Zixing county, Hunan province in 1894 (she adopted the pen name Bai Wei after moving to Japan in 1918). As a young girl she attended the school run by her father, a keen supporter of the late Qing social reform movement. For all his enlightened views, however, he insisted that his daughter heed social convention, so in 1910 she was forced into an arranged marriage. Bai Wei endured the harsh tyranny of an abusive mother-in-law for six years before running away to enroll at the Third Normal School for Girls in Hengyang. Later, having been expelled for political activities, she transferred to the First Normal School for Girls in Changsha. In 1918, shortly before she was due to graduate, she outwitted her father and the school authorities by sneaking off the campus grounds via an old sewage duct, after which she made her way to Shanghai and bought passage to Japan. On her arrival, she was virtually penniless and had no choice but to take on menial work as a domestic servant in the home of British missionaries. Demeaning as she found this to be, the circumstances were nevertheless preferable to returning to live at her husband's house. Eventually she was awarded a scholarship at the Tokyo Higher Normal School for Women, where she would study biology. During this time she also became acquainted with the young playwright Tian Han (1898–1968), who tutored her in English and introduced her to the work of the Norwegian author Henrik Ibsen.

Bai Wei started writing while living in Japan in the early 1920s, with such dramas as *Sophie* and *Miss Linli*. The publication of the latter, a three-act romantic tragedy, by the Shanghai Commercial Press in 1925 won her wide critical acclaim back in China. A number of female authors in the May Fourth period had taken to experimenting with modern dramatic forms, but this work was hailed as an exceptional achievement. Critic Chen Xiying went so far as to rank it among the top creative masterpieces of modern Chinese literature, lavish praise that no doubt helped secure Bai Wei's reputation as one of the most prominent female literary figures of her day.

In 1926, with revolutionary fervor on the rise back home, Bai Wei gave up her fellowship for graduate study to return to China, where she took a position as a translator for the Wuhan Revolutionary Government while teaching part-time at Zhongshan University. This arrangement did not last long, however, and following the breakdown of the coalition between Nationalist and Communist forces, she moved in with the poet Yang Sao in Shanghai. That same year saw the publication of *Fighting out of the Dark Pagoda of Spirits,* a three-act play, as well as her first full-length novel, *A Bomb and an Expeditionary Bird,* both of which first appeared in serial form in *Torrents* magazine, the leftist journal edited by Lu Xun and Yu Dafu. Later they were issued as single volumes. Both works are set against the contemporary backdrop of national revolution and thematize the interconnectedness of women's domestic subjugation and China's social and economic turmoil. By the early 1930s, Bai Wei had emerged as an important figure in the literary left, joining the League of Left-Wing Writers and taking part in activist drama circles. She was among the first practitioners of the new resistance literature that emerged after the Mukden Incident on September 18, 1931, publishing such patriotic plays as *A Certain Stop on Beining Road* in *Big Dipper* magazine.

Quite aside from the brewing national crisis, these were not easy times for Bai Wei personally: she was not only financially strapped (so desperate, in fact, that despite their now deeply strained relationship, she and Yang Sao copublished a collection of love letters, *Last Night*) but also plagued by increasingly serious physical ailments stemming from a prolonged battle with venereal disease. The reportage sketches translated here, "Third-Class Hospital Ward" (1936), were composed during one of her many hospitalizations in this difficult stage of her life. The excerpts are drawn from a five-part series Bai Wei wrote for *Women's Life* magazine, and reveal the author's keen awareness of the complex intersection of poverty and sexual politics.

Disease figures prominently in Bai Wei's best-known literary project of the 1930s, her voluminous autobiographical novel *My Tragic Life,* which was published in 1936. Described in the foreword as a story about "Nora" after she leaves home, it spares no detail in candidly describing the devastation venereal disease has wrought on the heroine's body and her life. While some critics found the work overly self-absorbed, it evidently struck a powerful chord with contemporary female audiences. Shen Zijiu, editor of *Women's Life,* was inundated with letters of support from sympathetic readers after the novel's publication and consequently issued a public letter to solicit donations for Bai Wei's mounting medical bills. Money poured in from fans of her work inside and outside China, enabling her to pursue further treatment.

Despite her condition, Bai Wei journeyed to Wuhan to join the Chinese Writers' Antiaggression Association after the Japanese invasion and supported herself by working as a special correspondent for *Xinhua Daily.* Her requests to visit the Communist base at Yan'an were reportedly denied on grounds of her ill health, but she would show her support for the CCP by engaging in propaganda work for Communist guerrilla forces in the Jiangnan region during the civil war in the late forties.

In the postliberation era, Bai Wei joined the newly founded Chinese Writers' Association in Beijing but for all intents and purposes gave up creative writing. Instead, she volunteered for service in the Great Northern Wilderness (*Beidahuang*), and later worked in the remote northwestern province of Xinjiang. She returned to Beijing in the early sixties, at which time her formal application for party membership was rejected, despite her seemingly impeccable revolutionary credentials. Like many veteran intellectuals and artists, she was persecuted during the Cultural Revolution, and on one occasion was beaten so severely by Red Guards that she was left partially crippled. Besides a few poems, Bai Wei published little during the Maoist period. She died in 1987.

Third-Class Hospital Ward

(1936)

AFTER BEING SICK for two weeks, cradling my aching belly, in such pain I could barely breathe and bracing myself on the furniture as I inched along, I threw together a few simple belongings and had my new maid take me to the hospital.

I registered at Outpatient Services, as the sweltering September sun beat down on the patients waiting in the courtyard to go in to the doctor. When the nurse who came to take my temperature noticed I was in such agony that I couldn't even raise my head, she sighed with a look of sympathy on her face. "Ai, you always put it off until you're this sick before coming to see the doctor!"

I had come to this hospital for treatment on a number of occasions over the last few years, so she recognized me. She ushered me inside to a consulting room and cheerfully instructed me to undress.

The doctor knew me well too, as though I were an old patron, and seeing me shuffle in all hunched over, holding my stomach, he exclaimed in shock:

"Aiya! You can't even walk anymore?"

Once he had inquired about this, that, and the other, the upshot was that I was to be hospitalized. I showered in the steamy washroom, then followed a hospital attendant to the third-class medical ward.

"Oh, you're back!" a fat woman cried out in surprise from her bed, looking at me with a smile.

"I know, what rotten luck!" I replied as I walked over.

"There's no two ways about it, getting sick is awful! Last time we were both checked in here as patients, no sooner had I recovered and left the hospital than I got sick all over again," said the woman.

The nurse told me to take bed number one, so I bore the pain and had a few words with the fat woman in bed number two.

One hour, two hours, three hours, I dozed quietly in pain and unattended, the groans of the critically ill patients in the ward and the chatter and laughter of the not-so-sick droning on and on. . . .

The plump female doctor Dr. Yang came to examine me and inquired, "When were you admitted?"

"Eleven o'clock this morning."

"That was hours ago, and no one's been here to see you?"

"No."

"They must be out of their minds! Admitting a patient so long ago, and nobody even came to inform me!"

What Dr. Yang said made perfect sense to me: perfunctory is the only way to characterize how patients in the third-class medical ward are treated in big hospitals like this. But for someone with a serious illness, think how nerve-wracking the wait can be, and how much worse their condition gets in the meantime. After that doctors streamed in, one after the next, some really keen to treat me, others who simply regarded patients like me as objects to experiment on.

At dusk, the patient in bed number five got dressed to get ready to be discharged. Her husband hurried her along with a scowl on his face, but she wouldn't leave until the doctor came to have a word with her, so she dawdled over her clothes and her hair until he finally appeared, none too happy, and asked:

"You had something to say to me?"

"Doctor, I'm checking out. Is there anything I should avoid eating?"

The doctor feigned a serious expression and replied, "Anything's fine except opium."

The ward erupted in laughter.

"What a funny response." From all the laughter, I surmised that the woman had attempted suicide by swallowing opium, and when I looked back over, she was standing there woodenly, absolutely mortified. All eyes were fixed on her as if to say, "You fool!"

My condition got worse with each passing hour and day; it hurt so much that I tossed and turned in bed, sweating so profusely that I drenched several changes of clothing a day, but I bore the pain without so much as a moan or a whimper, so quiet it was as though I weren't sick at all. The groans and cries, the chatter and laughter in the ward; the various shapes and shadows of the doctors and nurses passing back and forth—it was as though my ears and eyes had been made just to take this all in. My senses, my intellect, my emotions had been deadened by the intense pain.

In the middle of the night, the insane patient in the next room kept screaming: "Ow . . . dear mother!"

And all throughout the night, the fat woman would groan, "Oh, how it hurts."

The buzzing of mosquitos, the batting of the fans, mingled with the faint groans and sighs, the agonizing wails of the dying tuberculosis patients, shouts for the attendant and the nurses, the sound of pissing, the summer breeze outside the window rustling through the leaves on the trees . . . not a single one of these sounds escaped my ears, and for four whole nights I couldn't sleep a wink, though I did not utter a sound.

The days sped by. I lost consciousness twice and I underwent an unsuccessful surgery. I was completely incapacitated and devoid of thought. All I had were my eyes and ears to take in the sights and sounds of the ward.

*****

HOSPITAL BEDS LINED both sides of the ward, their white curtains drawn back at right angles, forming three-dimensional squares like the stage for a puppet show.

The patients were like living puppets, moving simultaneously on display between the curtains. Some were stretched out on their backs; others lay on their sides; some sat up, with the faintest murmur of moans and groans, bodies either half stripped or stark naked, letting the attentive nurses bathe them.

In front of each bed was a washbasin filled halfway with water, and the nurses helped to wash and dry off the sick. Sounds of splashing water, *xi-xi sha-sha, dong-dong ding-ding*; white towels one after another scrubbing and scrubbing emaciated bodies, from the shoulders down to the feet; white sheets flying up and over, swift change of white clothing; nurses all in white, bustling about cheerfully with their altruistic spirits.

It was as intense as if a mobilization order had been issued, as disciplined as the military. Each patient, either by themselves or with the help of a nurse, would be sponged down and given fresh clothes, the sounds of splashing water mingling with moans and groans. Outside the window, the breeze, the birds chirping, the shade of the trees, and the palm leaves no longer entered the picture.

Dressed all in red, Miss Deng, from the ophthalmology ward, waltzed in with her chin up high and her chest out to visit her sick friend Miss Guo, and upon seeing this scene exclaimed:

"My, what a pity I am not an artist, otherwise I would paint this erotic picture!"

Together with the patient next to them, they turned their conversation about the sponge baths to the Imperial Concubine getting in the pool.[1] In my opinion, there was nothing picturesque about it, but it was a great image. Thus prompted, I felt there was much to write about the women's third-class ward, none of which could be separated from "women" and "class."

I. Beautiful Woman Born Under an Unlucky Star

AS I RECALL, she was the patient in bed number three. She had a beautiful face and a pointed nose, lovely brows and thin but curvy lips, an exquisite pale complexion, and a frail physique—these were her distinguishing features.

When a burly policeman came to deliver a message from her husband, it was obvious from her simple conversation with him that she was a gentle and well-mannered person. The attendant peered over at the beautiful woman with great admiration, hanging on every word she said. After the policeman left, waves of grief enveloped the woman as she covered her face with her hands and sobbed.

---

[1]Reference to the famous legend of the beautiful imperial concubine Yang Guifei and Emperor Xuanzong of the Tang dynasty (618–907).

The fat lady, the kindest soul on the ward, asked with a look of compassion, "Why are you crying?"

"They want me to go home tomorrow, but I am not well yet, and I'll have to face that brute every day again!"

She said this choking back her tears, and used the corner of her hospital gown to wipe them away, then sighed as though she had unknown worries.

"Don't be sad, stay here a few days longer until you feel better."

"How can I? My old man already sent someone here twice to fetch me, and he's set on having me go home tomorrow."

"But if you haven't fully recovered, how can he insist?"

"Oh, *nainai*, I'm not as fortunate as the rest of you! I am staying here for free. . . ."

Up until this point she had been sobbing, but suddenly she grew self-conscious and lowered her head, as though she feared to show her distress, and just sat there in embarrassed silence. The fat lady leaned over to console her.

"That doesn't matter, this hospital often does good deeds. Lots of folks get treated here free of charge. And the doctors here are excellent. You should talk to your husband and tell him to wait until you're all better."

"You don't understand, *nainai*, my old man works for the railroad, and the only reason I got hospitalized in the first place was because of help from my relatives who also work there. Now that my man had someone sent over to get me, how can I refuse? Still, going home in this condition is too much. Whenever my man gets a little cash in his pocket, all he does is go out boozing and gambling, and once he's liquored up and broke, he comes back home and takes it out on me. He's smacked me around me in broad daylight, at night, when I was pregnant, and after my delivery. We've been married eight years, and for eight years I've taken his beating."

"Oh my, you really have had it bad!"

"Poor me, ever since I married him, I haven't had more than three or four months of peaceful sleep in his bed—when he wants me he just yanks me over, and when he's had enough he just kicks me onto the floor . . . so I always sleep on two benches in the corner. After I had my baby I slept on a door plank that made my entire body sore. . . ."

Meanwhile, the tuberculosis patients across from them had been chattering away—how splendid it was to summer in Qingdao, how wonderful the cuisine was, how much Jesus loves mankind. And the arrogant obstetrics student in the bed opposite, a typical "modern" wife, was going on about the New Life movement. Somehow that poor woman and the fat lady digressed onto the topic of clothes, and the woman pulled out an article of clothing from the small cupboard at the head of the bed to show the fat lady.

"Just look at this, other people wouldn't even use it for rags. But these past years it's all I've had, summer, spring, fall, and winter. When I wash it I have nothing else to wear the next day, so I just put it on the stove to dry. My baby froze to death because it had nothing to wear. Once, I secretly got a job as a wet nurse so I could make some clothes for me and my baby, but my man wouldn't have it and came and dragged me home and gave me a beating.

"At home, I'm either starving or freezing cold. Just think, if this is what I wear when it's hot, you can imagine how unbearable it gets in the winter. Other people's maidservants dress better than this, so all these years I've wanted to find work as a maid, and once I even snuck out. But again he found me and gave me such a thrashing that a few days later I had a miscarriage, and I've been poorly ever since. But he still beats me, sometimes until I'm black and blue. Oh, what misery! How can I go on?"

She got so choked up she could hardly speak, and the fat lady didn't know what to do to console her.

The next day, just as the ward was abuzz with people getting ready to be discharged, the fellow who appeared to be a policeman returned. The clueless attendant threw admiring glances at the pair, and attentively went over to ask: "Are you being discharged? Do you want to settle your bill . . ."

Within a quarter of an hour, the man had returned from handling the bill, but the woman was still sitting there on the bed listlessly, without having gotten dressed. From outside came a gruff shout: "The car's here!"

Mortified to the point of tears, the woman took off her white hospital gown and with nimble fingers put on her own threadbare clothing, and with deeply furrowed brows slowly climbed down off the bed. A mean-looking fellow strode in and bellowed: "Get a move on!"

He didn't show her the slightest bit of affection or courtesy but instead just grabbed her belongings and left. Seeing the true nature of the couple, the attendant who had previously been so ingratiating now put on a contemptuous air and walked away.

"Hurry it up!" Again came a gruff shout from outside, and the one who looked like a policeman seemed afraid to accompany the woman, so he rushed out ahead of her, saying, "Hurry! At four-thirty the car has to be someplace else."

The woman left behind limped along unsteadily, her face in pain, and all eyes fixed on her as though she were an old beggar. Her yellowed shirt was patched in a dozen places, while her tattered black trousers, faded from washing, barely covered her knees, and you could see her toes poking through her worn-out shoes. Such beauty concealed beneath an outfit like this was as pathetic as a winter flower encased in ice and snow. She hobbled slowly across the ward, and only after quite some time did she reach the exit, where she steadied herself against the door and the wall, clearly unable to move any farther. She called out, "Attendant, please go outside and tell the car to pull up closer to the courtyard!"

The attendant glared at her with an arrogant, icy look, and replied disdainfully, "I'm busy."

With that, she strode by, assisting other patients with their belongings. The woman was like a squashed caterpillar, wounded; her neck recoiled and her face filled with humiliation and anguish as she slumped against the doorway, crestfallen. The nurses passing back and forth ignored her, and the attendant, all smiles, accepted tips from the other patients being discharged, and respectfully helped them out with their luggage. Tears glistened in the woman's eyes as she had no choice but again to call out, "Attendant, thank you kindly, while you are outside could you tell my car to pull up here?"

"Humph! Car! . . . I wouldn't know anything about that!"

With an especially sarcastic, disdainful tone of voice and a cross expression, she swaggered past. It was as though the woman's spirit had been crushed. Offended and indignant, she emerged from the corner of the ward. She inspected her own clothes and her toes poking through her shoes and sobbed with tears gushing, as all eyes, with looks of both contempt and pity, converged into one sharp angle onto her sad face.

Meanwhile, I was lying immobile in the bed by the entrance, gasping for breath. I found the scene incredibly upsetting, and in my heart I lamented, "Even in the third-class medical ward there are classes! And these are indeed classes within a class. . . ."

IV. Lost Youth

. . . SHE AND I had been acquainted for a couple of days. Ever since I'd been on the mend, I had taken to strolling up and down the corridor here, and on one occasion I sat down on a bench with her and we'd gotten to talking about all sorts of things. She was married to the manager of a steamboat company who in his earlier years had been a big shot in the business world.

The older woman beckoned her over, and she approached beaming, delicate and exquisite, just like an oriole flitting about in the trees. The married woman explained that I wanted to talk with her, so she was kind enough to sit down and we made some idle chitchat until we got on the subject of being ill.

"You've had three operations here?"

"Yes, unfortunately!"

"What is your condition?"

I knew what her ailment was, but I couldn't very well say it outright, so I asked her this way on purpose. She laughed and replied candidly, "Oh . . . how shall I put it? . . . You could call it a marital disease."

The rest of us started laughing.

"What are you laughing about?" Her eyes widened as she looked at the three of us nervously, then rapped the nurse on the shoulder with her fist and said, "If I hadn't gotten married, I never would have contracted a nasty disease like this."

I found her innocence and honesty far more appealing than the efforts the elder matron made to cover her condition up.

"Is it gonorrhea?

"Exactly. Advanced gonorrhea."

"Me too. The doctors have been advising me to have surgery for a long time now, so I thought I would ask you about your experience."

"Oh. Once you catch this wretched disease it ruins your reproductive organs, and it's agony whether you have the operation or not. Women really have the worst luck."

She sighed and looked at me sympathetically before continuing:

"Before I got married, I had lots of suitors and even fell in love a few times myself, though they were just youthful crushes. When it came to sex, I always felt that it was something that defiled a young woman's beauty. Who would have known that within a month of getting married I would start getting severe stomachaches? One day I had eaten some crabs, and that night I got this strange cramp. By daybreak it felt like my stomach was in knots. I was sweating and aching and had difficulty breathing, so at dawn I drove to Baolong Hospital, where they diagnosed it as acute appendicitis that had to be operated on immediately—"

"This time the doctors also told me it was chronic appendicitis, since my right side hurt," I interrupted.

"My right side really ached too, and after the operation I was in high spirits, but then to my surprise the doctors kept coming in one after the next, asking if I had gonorrhea. I said I did not, but they determined otherwise, and when my family consulted with the doctors they were told the strain was really virulent and had the doctors known this beforehand, they would not have performed the operation. I fainted from the shock. When I came to I asked my husband if he was infected, but he shook his head. At the time, my family and friends and his mother all heard him, and so they gave me strange looks as if I were a loose girl with no morals. I fainted out of anger and was unconscious for five or six days. On the seventh day, the incision split open and there was pus and blood, and the more they tried to fix it the more infected it got and my lower body hurt terribly; at the time, I just wanted to die. . . .

"After I was discharged from the hospital, the gynecologists I saw all said that the bacteria from the gonorrhea had damaged my ovaries, and that I would need surgery. But my mother and the rest of the family were opposed to me having another operation. After that I got pregnant, and throughout my entire pregnancy the ovaries on both sides hurt something awful. I also came to realize what a philanderer my husband really was. I was filled with such regret—a girl from a humble family like me should not have married a rich man. Later, when my baby was born, it was not just tiny but also blind in both eyes. And as for my husband, he would constantly flirt with my younger sister, and they were always doing all sorts of revolting things right in front of me. Once I got so mad I fainted. Even though they brought me back to life, that time I fell dangerously ill.

"My mother was afraid I wouldn't recover. For fear of losing her cash cow, she openly forced my sister to get involved with my husband and spend the night with him at a hotel, just waiting for me to die so she could marry my sister off to him."

Hearing this, we were all shocked, and the older married woman proclaimed loudly:

"Oh! . . . How could your own mother be so cruel?"

"My husband was really rich back then, and had I died, can you blame her for being reluctant to part with such a money tree?"

With indignation in our voices, we discussed this for quite a while; the young woman shook her charming head and body slightly and, as if reciting a lesson she knew by heart, went on talking of her disease:

"As a result of this, the shock was so great that I nearly went out of my mind, but I knew that I had to be completely cured of the disease or I'd never be free of this tragedy, so I made up my mind to have the operation. My husband discovered his conscience and admitted to me that he had suffered from the disease for many years. As a gesture of repentance, he agreed to give my sister ¥50,000 and end his relationship with her once I was completely cured. Luckily the first operation went smoothly, and the doctor said that since I was young he left in one ovary. However, that remaining ovary often troubled me and felt uncomfortable whenever it became inflamed. Whenever I got upset, I'd blow up and lose my temper. I also found out that while my husband had supposedly paid off my sister and severed relations with her, in fact they were still having an affair, and on top of that my sister was not only a tease but was also jealous and brazen, and regarded me with contempt. Finally I got so depressed that I was going insane, and the second time I came in for surgery everyone treated me like a madwoman.

"The truth was, I wasn't really insane at all; my mind was very lucid, though I did have a terrible temper and whenever my husband wasn't nice to me I would blow my top and have a spectacular row with him. Even I knew it wasn't appropriate. All I wanted was to suppress my temper and stop making everyone unhappy, but it was futile—as soon as the anger came, I would lose my resolve. I used to be gentle and mild-mannered, I didn't know how I got like this. Later I asked a doctor, who told me that generally hysteria is quite severe in women with diseased uteruses and ovaries. And in the worst cases, it can easily turn into mental disease. So the year before my second surgery, practically everyone thought I was insane, and on that pretext my husband wanted to leave me. Fortunately, the doctor said that I'd be better once I had the operation, so I had no choice but to come back to do it.

"During the second surgery do you know what they removed?"

"They took out the bad ovary."

"With both gone, isn't that tantamount to being neutered?"

"Exactly! Because I was still young, the doctors left a small section of the ovary so it would continue to function. But afterward it was worse than being crazy."

"How's that?" the married woman asked.

"For more than a year I felt no emotion; it was as though I were a wooden puppet. Whether it was a happy occasion or a sad occasion, nothing could excite me. Even when my husband was intimate with me, I felt like a stone; in short, I was completely frigid. Even if my beloved mother had died right in front of me, I would have been incapable of grieving or crying. At the time, I thought, what's the point of living like a block of wood? I was done! Done! I'd have been better off dead. . . ."

Brimming with emotion, she shook her head and leaned over as if she were seeing scenes of the past. It reminded me of something a friend had said to me few years back:

"In my opinion, you'd be better off having surgery. Even if ovaries are the treasure of female youth, now that they're unhealthy, there's no point leaving them inside your body. All your suffering is futile, for if they develop an infection that spreads to other parts of your body, you could get peritonitis, and that could be fatal. If you have them removed and forego your youth, you will have spared your life. And if your youth is gone and you can't do anything creative, you can always go work in a cotton mill, spinning year in and year out; you could spin your whole life and become a revolutionary woman through and through."

As I recalled the last few things she had said, I looked back over at the poor young woman and simply didn't know what else to say to her. I brooded over what my past had been like after I caught this wretched disease. As for my future, did it hold any more promise than hers?

The young woman unhurriedly spoke of her terrifying state of mind after losing her youth. Then she mentioned the infection that brought her here for surgery on this occasion. She looked over at the married woman with a gloomy expression and said:

"Perhaps this time I'll be like you and they'll take everything out—my ovaries, uterus, and fallopian tubes. Otherwise, why haven't the doctors told me what they're removing? Alas, I am only twenty-seven years old, and I'm not ready to turn into an old woman. Had I known it would be like this, I never would have gotten married! I hate my husband for giving me this deadly disease!"

As she sighed in sorrow, the tears glistening in her eyes reflected the rays of light from the sunset filtering through the trees. From a window in the corridor a nurse shouted out that it was time for our medication, so we each went back to our own wards.

* * * * *

MIDNIGHT. THE PATIENTS on the ward are deep in slumber; a still night, a forlorn heart. I hoped that my present illness was unrelated to that damned disease, otherwise I would soon become the third of them, a creature that was neither female nor male.

Farewell, third-class medical ward. I was again wheeled into the operating room. The doctors and nurses put me into the fetal position and administered a shot of anesthesia in my back, then straightened me out flat and made the first incision in my abdomen. Then came the clanging of forceps as each of the three doctors swiftly snipped and cut; ten minutes went by, and then they sewed me back up with great big stitches and the doctors left, leaving me on the operating table.

Half an hour later, they returned, made another quick and somewhat larger incision, with the rapid clinking of forceps and scalpels; they lifted out my intestines and guts, snipping, cutting, ripping, chopping, now so careful they held their breath, now chuckling away:

"Miss, you've got the most peculiar appendix, nothing like other peoples'."

"Ai, what a nuisance, this is really hard to cut."

"Are you married or single?"

"All that's over now, just call me by my first name."

"Your period must be very uncomfortable, no?"

"Oh . . ."

I felt as though I were being operated on without anesthesia, that's how much it hurt, and I couldn't answer anymore but just strained to breathe and bear the pain.

"Calm your breathing! Relax your stomach! Otherwise, we can't do our job!"

Scalpels quickened, prodding and pulling. I nearly fainted and moaned softly in agony.

"Hey, are you really in pain or are you just being a baby for our sakes?" the doctor teased me.

"Hurry up! If you're going to take your time like this, then remove this cover from my eyes and set up a reflector so I can see what you are operating on."

The anesthesia seemed to have worn off completely, but despite the pain I laughed and chatted as though nothing were happening. An hour later, they stitched me back up and wheeled me back to the third-class ward with the female workers with broken hands and cracked skulls, maids with opened bellies and throats, gunshot victims, and those wasting away from consumption.

These were warriors suffering from physical ailments: the critically ill who rarely uttered a sound; the mildly ill who clamored on; the missionary ladies like ants swarming around something rotten, encircling the patients, singing and preaching; the medicine cart rattling by; the cries and hollers when it came time to change bandages; the sloshing of bathwater being poured late at night before even the first light of dawn had spilled out; on one side, the clatter of eating utensils and glasses; on the other side, the whir of someone urinating.

The attendant still fawns all over those with money while ignoring the poor, and she even said to my maid, "Since she doesn't have a man, who in this hospital is going to pay her bill?"

There is still a great deal worth reporting about the third-class ward, but I have written too much and will stop here.

3
Hu Lanqi

(1901–1994)

idely believed to have been the real-life inspiration behind the paradigmatic New Woman heroine Mei in Mao Dun's *Rainbow*, Hu Lanqi was born in 1901 into a Sichuanese family who supported the movement to overthrow the Qing dynasty. Emboldened by the ideological currents of the May Fourth movement, she broke from an arranged marriage in 1921 and left Chengdu to teach briefly at a girl's school in Chongqing before enrolling in a teacher's college. There she joined a Marxist reading group and became active in the local women's movement. She was selected to represent the women of Sichuan province at the Sixth National Student Congress in Shanghai in 1926. Later that year, she journeyed south to take part in the revolutionary upsurge by the Nationalist–Communist alliance to reunify the nation by ridding China of warlordism and foreign imperialism. Together with a relatively small cohort of women recruits, including, most famously, Xie Bingying and Zhao Yiman, she had been accepted into the training program for female students at the Wuhan Central Military and Political Institute. After the program was dissolved due to the collapse of the United Front, she transferred to the Nationalist Central Women's Department under the leadership of He Xiangning (1878–1972) and helped unionize women workers in Wuhan. Before long, as the KMT purges of radical elements grew more intense, she was forced to flee with Lu Jingqing (1907–1993), who at the time was also on the staff of the Women's Department, to Wuchang and eventually Shanghai. In 1928, having been effectively blacklisted by the KMT, she left for Europe. In Berlin, she briefly shared a flat with He Xiangning and joined the Chinese-speaking group of the German Communist Party through the introduction of He's son Liao Chengzhi. Following the September 18th Incident in 1931, which transpired while Hu happened to be back in China on a brief visit, she returned to Germany and became involved in organizing overseas Chinese students into an anti-imperialist alliance. One of the highlights of this period, as she

would later recall, was meeting the prominent socialist-feminist leader
Clara Zetkin (1857–1933).

Hu was arrested and imprisoned for her left-wing activities in the spring
of 1933 for three months, and was released only after Song Qingling and
Lu Xun intervened by lodging a formal protest on her behalf with the
German consulate in Shanghai. Deported by the German authorities,
Hu settled briefly in France and then England. In 1934 she began writing
an account of her experience, excerpts of which appeared in the French
newspaper *Le Monde.* The work was so well received internationally that
it soon came out in English, German, Russian, and Spanish translations.
Upon Hu's return to China in 1936, the text was serialized in its entirety in the radical women's journal *Women's Life,* edited by Shen Zijiu.
The following year the text was published in book form under the title
In a German Women's Prison by the Shanghai Life Bookstore. It went
into multiple reprintings and was reportedly used as teaching material
at Yan'an. Now a celebrity, Hu Lanqi was invited to the Soviet Union as
a Chinese representative at the First Congress of Russian Writers, where
she is said to have been singled out for praise by the literary luminary
Maxim Gorky.

Between 1937 and 1940 Hu Lanqi worked alongside other well-known
female activists in Shanghai, including Chen Bo'er and Wang Liying, to
help found the Chinese Women's Wartime Relief Association, a United
Front organization aimed at mobilizing women to assist in the war effort.
As part of this project, she organized working-class women for service on
the front lines. Her wartime writings consisted primarily of reportage,
including personal accounts of her experiences traveling with a military
division. Many of these appeared in *Xinhua Daily* and *Women's Life,*
which had relocated to the interior when war broke out, as well as in
individual volumes. She also collaborated with Xie Bingying and Xia Yan
on a collection of essays on patriotic themes entitled *On the Songhu Battle
Line* (1938). After Japan's defeat, Hu Lanqi served as the chief editor of
Guizhou Daily. She eventually settled down in Beijing, where she taught
and, in her spare time, translated German children's literature. Like many
other veteran activists, Hu fell victim to the Antirightist Campaign in
1957 and was expelled from the party. In 1975 she finally returned to her
native Sichuan province, where she completed a memoir of her early
career as a political activist. Hu Lanqi died in Chengdu in 1994.

The excerpts here are from *In a German Women's Prison,* Hu Lanqi's
autobiographical account of her time in jail with female political detain-

ees as well as ordinary petty criminals. While the account as a whole is animated by mild humor as the author documents the everyday challenges of the ordeal of imprisonment, at the center of the text is the loftier political theme of female solidarity across lines of class and national identity.

In a German Women's Prison

(1936)

Chapter 6. A Piece of Chocolate

PEOPLE USUALLY THINK of Sunday as the happiest time of the week, but I spent my Sunday waiting in anxiety, anger, and depression, pacing back and forth in my small prison cell. Though I no longer felt the anxiety and fatigue of the previous day when I got up that morning, I still hated the iron barrel of a prison wall that sunlight could not even penetrate. It was a hot June day, but my hands and feet were stiff with cold and my nose was running. And I could not exercise to work up a sweat because the place was too narrow and there was nothing to do. If things went on like this, I knew I would get sick. No matter what, it was not worth getting sick on top of being imprisoned. Therefore, I had to consider my health. With that in mind, I would wash my face and brush my teeth with the water from the bucket as soon as I got up every morning. After that I would made good use of the tiny space to do some exercises. As long as I exercised, I would sweat a little bit.

After I drank my coffee, the woman guard opened the door so I could get some water to wash the floor. Ordinarily I liked washing the floor, but on this day I found it tedious. In a few minutes my mood was quite different from when I got up, so I did not work very hard. I did not feel like touching the bucket in front of me, nor did I make much of an effort as I dragged the mop across the floor. I mopped the same spot over and over again. In a word, I was overcome with boredom and did not put the kind of effort into my work that I usually did. But thinking about it again, I really had nothing to feel depressed about, and people would not have been able to find any disappointment or sadness in my words. Still, I felt rather unhappy on this day!

The gloomy morning passed, and after lunch the woman guard came to open the cell door as usual for our break in the yard. Out in the open, I felt relaxed at once and gave a deep sigh. Many of the women inmates looked at me with a smile when I joined their marching ranks. On their faces I could not detect any trace of anxiety. It had seemed that they were already my old friends upon our first encounter, and it was hard to tell which of them were close friends and which were strangers. Their eyes were filled with sympathy and warmth.

Mrs. Heinrich took out a paper packet from her pocket and quickly passed it to a lady behind her, murmuring something, which I could not hear because she was too far away and her whisper sounded like buzzing bees. Her eyes were fixed on the packet until it finally reached my hand, at which point a happy blush appeared on her face.

The lady who handed me the packet started to talk to me in a low and steady voice, "Comrade, you've got to eat! Don't let the potatoes upset your stomach!" I was dumbfounded, and only when I saw her passionate eyes looking at me did I grasp her words, which were so gentle, yet so powerful! The voice expressed the deep feeling of a loving mother toward her children. Hearing her words and seeing what the women had done, I was too moved to say anything, and tears kept rolling down my cheeks like pearls from a loosened necklace, pouring out all the sadness that had accumulated over the past few days. As it had never been easy to contain my sadness, I broke into sobs. The more they kindly comforted and coaxed me, the more sorrowfully I wept, until I was almost out of breath.

When the woman guard went to unlock the side gate, the young girl in a gray skirt, about seventeen or eighteen years old, tiptoed over to me like a waitress in a restaurant and put her hand on my shoulder. She said, "Be courageous! Don't cry! You must get through this!"

In spite of her encouragement, her own eyes were also moist. I did not explain anything to her but grasped her hands with tears flowing from my eyes like a bottomless spring.

My tears were not from cowardliness, nor from sadness, because I would never beg for their sympathy! I was bitterly crying because I was moved by their brave act and my tears were an expression of my gratitude. I did not think I was a coward.

The outdoor break, just like any other before, came to an end with the guards' pushing and pulling us back to the cells. In my cell, I opened the packet and inside saw a big piece of chocolate. I had already guessed that it was something to eat when Mrs. Heinrich passed it to me.

What's the value of a piece of chocolate? But if you knew that it was something given to me by a person who was also in prison and had no more freedom than myself, then what would you think? The women in this prison were all considered political prisoners by the German fascists, who had charted for women a road like this: "Go to church!" Go to the kitchen!" "Look after the children!" Or else, "Go to prison!"

The German working people were already in a wretched situation, and those sent to jail definitely suffered more in even worse conditions. It was not easy for female prisoners to get hold of even a little food. Considering their lack of money and the prison conditions, food was extremely rare and precious. Yet they gave up their chocolate that was so valuable and hard to come by and let me have it, urging me, "You've got to eat! Don't let the potatoes upset your stomach!"

Such words made me think: I was not the only one living on potatoes, for everyone here ate the same meals as I did. But why weren't they afraid of ruining their own health? Why did they worry about me? Why hadn't they saved the treat for themselves instead of giving it to me? Now I knew why. Although the chocolate was not worth a penny, it actually represented a friendship more valuable than anything in the world! Such friendship, such compassion, only existed in prison, only among revolutionaries and the oppressed. It could not be found among members of the leisure class, who hardly had any compassion at all. They would snatch a lifesaving crust of bread from the hands of a starving man and stash it away in their warehouses, and would certainly never give away any of their own food for no reason. Of course, they sometimes offer you a sweet in order to use you. Their ulterior motive is to make you repay with your whole life. Aren't such sweets more poisonous than arsenic? Yet they call them "mercy" and "charity." They calculate such favors very carefully and don't bestow them unless they can recoup more than they originally gave. Once you are no longer useful to them, they won't give you a penny. Oppressed people, however, know no such thing as "mercy." Nor do they have any of the shallow sentiments of the petite bourgeoisie. They have only passion. When Mrs. Heinrich gave me the chocolate, she did not expect any payback or gratitude from me, nor was she showing me pity. It was out of the true solidarity that exists among revolutionary comrades that she saved the valuable chocolate and gave it to me. And no, it was not limited to a piece of chocolate. Should it be necessary to help me, she would not hesitate to bestow things of even greater value. And it was not just Mrs. Heinrich. The girl in the gray skirt and the other women prisoners, especially the white-haired old lady, had all exuded very sincere and strong love. With their courageous actions and optimistic morale, they were sure to be able to carry the burden of a great cause.

With that thought, I was profoundly moved, and tears streamed down again as I held the chocolate in my hand. Although I was not weak and knew that my tears were out of gratitude for having received solace from a comrade, and although I did not want to cry, I could not hold back. Feeling the futility of crying, I tried hard to close my eyes, but the tears were like torrents breaking through a dam and I felt great pressure in my chest. So I had to let myself go and burst into a loud cry.

After a long spell of sadness, my bitter sobs broadened my mind and brightened my view. The loneliness and depression were whisked away from the bottom of my heart and I felt unusually peaceful and calm, as light as a bird flying in the sky.

The chocolate, like a dab of glue, bonded my heart and those of its original owners on the same battle front.

Night had gone. A thin slice of dawn crept up the iron window of the prison cell. As I woke up, the church bells in the distance played the rhythmic and sonorous tune for the hour and clanged four times. It was still too early to rise, but I quietly got out of bed and tiptoed to the door. Listening hard, I could not hear any snoring or other human sound; the whole place was as quiet as an ancient, lonely temple in the wilderness. I then went back to bed, rolled up the blanket, and gently put the small square desk on the bed and the stool on the desk. I took the chocolate, whose tinfoil wrapper was still shiny with white light, out of the drawer. As I thought of the friend who had given it to me, my heart started to pound so fast in excitement that I could hardly breathe. I opened the wrapper and brought the chocolate to my lips.

Mrs. Heinrich, I adore you! The white-haired old lady, I kiss you with all my heart! The girl in the gray skirt, a kiss to you. My sweetest kiss to you all, all the fighters in our struggle!

I climbed onto the desk, stepped on the stool, and, straining on my toes, with my left hand clinging to the wall, I used the chocolate to scratch this on the ceiling: "Oppressed classes and nations, unite to struggle for the happiness of working people all over the world!"

The chocolate was barely enough to complete those words, but the strokes were clearly visible and filled more than half of the ceiling. I returned the desk and stool to their original places and quickly made up the bed. Since it was still too early to be up, I crawled back under the covers and opened my eyes to gaze at the words on the ceiling, feeling so happy and excited. My heart was like a white cloud in an autumn sky that continuously sent out a passion to fight!

Chapter 19. A Huge Prison

THIS HUGE PRISON for women, when taking in a few hundred people, was like a big lion gobbling down a few steamed buns without showing any trace on its stomach. Tea for dinner was delivered to our wards in a huge iron urn on a cart, much bigger than the coffee urn used in the jail at the police station, although I had also been greatly shocked on seeing the coffee urn there.

One or two hundred prisoners were housed on each floor, and the women here would have made an excellent female army had they been able to undergo some military training! Of course, there would be trouble if such women ever rose in rebellion. Therefore, the ruling class would never teach them combat skills. Instead, they jail such women with iron locks and bars like birds in a cage, and don't release them until their limbs and nerves are numbed by prison and they are stripped of the desire to fly, even though they still see the vast sky.

My new prison cell was a square room smaller than the one at the police station. Besides the toilet at the head of the bed, there was also a washbasin hanging on the wall. Next to the washbasin was nailed a double-decked shelf, on which there was a crockery bowl and mug, a wooden board on which westerners cut sausage, a spoon, a fork, and a small knife. None of those had been allowed in the cell at the police station. Here I had more water, too, whereas in the first prison there had been only a small jar of it. In addition to a big jug of water for cleaning one's face and teeth and cleaning the dishes, there was also a large bucket of water for cleaning the desk, stool, shelves, and floor. The bedding, all white, also looked more decent. I did not see the blue-checkered sheets used at the police station. The bed was made of wire and a steel frame. Whereas in the first prison, the terrible iron window never showed the sky, here, because the roof was lower and the window much wider, the moonlight could shine in and the air in the room was much fresher. Over there, the electric lights were for decoration only and the guard would order lights out as early as six o'clock in the evening, even though it did not get dark until nine o'clock in the summer in Berlin. All in all, everything here seemed superior to the other place, not to mention the wooden plaques on the wall bearing various moral teachings, such as the sayings of Jesus: "If anyone strikes you on the right cheek, turn to him the other one also," and so on.

There's nothing comfortable about being in jail, but transferring from a bad prison to a better one can inspire fresh interests and ideas. Consequently, I had a hard time falling asleep the first night, and yet still woke up very early the next morning, feeling nervous inside, as if a new life had begun.

I was out of bed when it was barely daylight. I did some exercises on the floor till I was drenched in sweat. Then I bathed with the water from the bucket and afterward used the same water to mop the floor. Doing this reminded me of a story I had heard when I was a child. Because water was in such short supply in Gansu province in northwest China, people there would use a small bowl of water to wash first their face, then their feet, and then use the same water for other purposes. But now, in the more civilized Europe, who would expect that I would be doing just that!

By the time I had cleaned up the cell, it was broad daylight. I suddenly heard somebody talking but could not make out what the voice was saying. That was strange, because I had already heard people talking the day before. Why couldn't I now tell who was saying what, or where the voices were coming from? Sometimes the voices seemed to come from the sky, sometimes to pop up from under the floor, and sometimes they sounded as though they were right next to me. Finally, I could hear clearly. They were saying:

"Sixteen of them, and one Asian girl, but I don't know if she is Chinese or Japanese."

The words were not as noisy or confusing as the day before. It seemed that two or three people were talking. One was to my left, another seemed to be opposite, and the third seemed to be below me. *What is going on?* I wondered. I decided to investigate. Naturally, I had to use the desk and chair. First, I moved the desk to the window, then climbed on it with the help of the chair. I grasped the corner of the window attached to the roof by iron hooks to look out.

Oh, was I dreaming? How could this be? I thought. From this disgusting window, I could even see the sky. Oh, blue sky, with drifting white clouds! The morning air, cool and fresh, gently brushing against my face! I could hardly believe this was really happening. But through the rows of double-glazed windows, iron bars on the outside and wooden frames with glass panes on the inside, there were many people with their faces partially in view peering out just like I was. The voices I heard came from the mouths of those people looking through the windows. If I had not seen this so clearly or heard it so distinctly, and actually held onto the corner of the window with my own hands, I would have suspected it was all just a dream!

I was so happy that I forgot I was a detainee. I stood behind the window and greeted the others, nodding, talking, and in the meantime forgot about everything else. I did not even notice the woman guard who came to deliver breakfast until all of a sudden her rude shouting jolted me back to reality.

This guard was not as old as the head guard, nor as large as the fat guard, though she was fairly heavyset. Short in stature, she had a barrel for a belly, and not only were her body and face round, her hands and feet were too. When she cursed, she sounded like a barking dog.

Curse me though she did, she could not deprive me of my breakfast. But when the work woman handed me my coffee and bread, the guard glared at me with displeasure before slamming the door and locking it. At that moment I could not help thinking of the tall woman guard and my friend Anna. How I missed them!

Soon after finishing my coffee, I heard footsteps in the yard, the footsteps of many people. I used the same method, of course, of moving the desk to the window and stood on top of it to look out. I saw crowds of women wearing the same blue twill uniforms walking around in the yard. Because I was on the top floor and the window was too small, I could not make out their faces. Only by straining on my tiptoes with great effort and looking through a corner of the window could I see at an angle the faces of the people passing that spot. Among them was the work woman who had delivered my coffee and bread and whom I had not realized until now was also a prisoner. But she did not look like a political prisoner, and was probably somebody like Anna.

With the lesson learned earlier in the morning, this time I kept an eye on the door and listened for the guard's footsteps. I had experienced many times the guards' sneaky ways of always spying on us. That was their job.

When the guard came to unlock the doors to let us out for the break, I had already hopped down to the floor and moved the desk back to its place. I thought, *Let's see what you can say!* But she was so cunning that she found some other infraction and gave me another dressing down. Seeing that my water jug and iron bucket were still empty, she asked me whether I had the brains to know that I was supposed to take them out to get water when breakfast was served. What she said was right, but I did not like her stern, fat face!

Especially intolerably insulting were the crude, mean curses that she spat out of her thick lips. I was used to a life of freedom and felt great indignation at the way she treated me. However, under such intense pressure, what was I to do? I could do nothing but pretend to be deaf, as if not hearing what she said.

Out in the open, I immediately spotted the girl student named Sarah with brown eyes, black hair, thin lips, and good manners. We were already acquainted from school, and had lived on the same street. I had been told that she was a friend of Mr. Wei who had come to Germany from America. When we saw each other, we greeted each other with our eyes and walked together once we were outside in the yard.

The yard for our break was somewhere down below my window and, surrounded by buildings on all sides, seemed very small. Looking up at the sky, I felt myself trapped in a deep, square well. Still, with a green lawn in the center, it was better than the police station yard that was covered in horse dung.

While I walked with Sarah, my eyes searched the crowd and I spotted Anja, Maria, and Kate of the Socialist Party, but never found Mrs. Heinrich. Sarah was talking freely, as were many others. I was surprised by this and asked her, "Can people speak at will here?" Sarah, as if telling a story, said "Yes." She continued, "Here we are not considered prisoners but detainees. We are not civil or criminal offenders, we have never stolen anything, so we're treated better than the convicts here. For instance, they get only a half-hour break, but we get one hour. They cannot talk while walking outside, but we can say whatever we like, choose to walk with whomever we like, and change position in the line." Pointing to the huge building, she added, "Those on the first to fourth floors are not political prisoners. Though they are degenerate, they are very pitiable. Some of them hate us very much."

"Why should they hate us?" I did not understand and looked at her in puzzlement.

"The more people imprisoned here, the fewer rations they get. This prison does not have the budget for so many people, and now there's not enough food for all the inmates. You have to admit this is an excellent strategy on the part of the fascists: on the one hand, they can jail us, and on the other, they can make those ignorant women hate us. . . ."

Sarah's words sounded reasonable, but I still believed that this was just another stupid move by the fascists. It might work for a while, cheating the broad masses of laboring people who were blinded in the darkness of the old society. However, the new society had already showed its brilliant rays, and the dark mist of the old could not last much longer.

Maria had something different to say when she walked with me, maybe because she had had a different experience. She told me to keep an eye on the other inmates, and warned me that not all of them were revolutionaries and that some were spies. She said that I could be imprisoned longer now that I had been transferred here rather than released from the police station. She told me to write to the warden to petition for my release, or for deportation out of the country. A revolutionary, according to her, should be working on the outside, rather than kept in prison all the time. She was also quite confident in her own case and believed her sentence would for sure be overturned.

A bell somewhere clanged once, and Maria said we had used half of the break time and that the inmates could change positions in the line as they liked. Since Anja had indicated that she would like to walk with me, I parted company with Maria.

Anja and I walked side by side, her hand on my shoulder and my arm around her waist. We kept talking, and I asked her where Mrs. Heinrich had gone and why she was not here. She replied that Mrs. Heinrich had been separated from us and put in Ward 7, on the floor below us. We were in Ward 9, on the sixth floor.

She then asked me, "What do you think about this place?"

I said, "Better than the police station."

"No, no! This place may look more civilized from the outside, but actually it's very reactionary inside. Since yesterday afternoon, I have been scolded four times by the guard."

"Was it the fat, short woman guard?" I asked.

"Yes."

"Hmm, she has also yelled at me twice," I said. "She looks just like a bear."

"Ha! Ha! You are right." Anja completely agreed and could not help laughing heartily. "Let's call her Bear then!"

"Let's call her Bear then!" We both started laughing, as if we had done something very funny.

Our conversation flowed on and on like endless river waters just released from a dam. What was more important, we exchanged our cell addresses. She pointed out her cell for me, and I told her my location. Her window was on the north facing south, near the corner to the east. My window was on the west facing east, near a corner to the south. If we both stood at the window, we could partially see each other's face. Had we not been so far apart, we might have been able to stand at the windows to talk to each other, as an open secret.

We were deeply engrossed in our conversation, and I told her how the women inmates here hated us and how I saw the issue. She seemed greatly moved, saying, "The old society still exerts great influence! However, the creation of the new society is just like the sun over the ocean and will soon rise up in the sky!" Her eyes shone with indomitable enthusiasm.

4
Chen Xuezhao

(1906–1991)

*L*iving in France until the mid-1930s, veteran May Fourth writer Chen Xuezhao had solidified her reputation as an outspoken feminist in progressive literary and intellectual circles back in China through regular contributions to avant-garde journals, yet she had remained aloof from the leftist politics into which so many of her contemporaries were being drawn. It was not until her return to China in 1935, amid the deepening national crisis and under surveillance by KMT police, that her sympathies for the Communist Party began to grow. In 1938, she accepted a special reporting assignment from *National Dispatch* magazine and traveled with her young son and husband to the Communist base at Yan'an to gather material and conduct interviews for a collection of journalistic essays—what would eventually be published in Hong Kong under the title *Interviews at Yan'an* (1940). Other female reporters had preceded her, including the Americans Agnes Smedley and Nym Wales, but she would be the first Chinese woman writer to document life at the Communist guerrilla base. The first selection here, "The Essentials and Ambience of Life," is from that collection and focuses on the spartan material conditions of everyday life in Yan'an while evoking the unique *esprit de corps* that the author witnessed during her ten-month visit. In 1940, Chen returned to reside permanently in Yan'an as a committed member of the community, working alongside Ding Ling, Ai Siqi, Bai Lang, and others as an editor at the party newspaper, *Liberation Daily.* Her critically acclaimed autobiographical novel *To Be Working Is Beautiful* (1949) gives a moving account of the author's personal metamorphosis as she moved from the bohemian milieu she inhabited in the twenties in Shanghai and Paris to her idle days as a young doctor's wife in the KMT-controlled interior to her newfound political calling at Yan'an. The novel examines the autobiographical heroine's ideological transformation, including the profound impact of Mao's Rectification campaign in 1942, during which urban middle-class intellectuals and writers such as

Chen were enjoined to reevaluate their attitudes toward the public they allegedly served.

Chen was formally accepted into the Chinese Communist Party in 1945, and in the years leading up to liberation she completed several important literary projects, including a new reportage collection based on first-hand observations of the so-called liberated areas in northern China, *Wandering Through the Liberated Zones,* from which the second selection is drawn. Chen makes little attempt to disguise her partisan allegiance to the CCP here or elsewhere in the volume, but attention to the gritty details of everyday life among the ordinary rural folk she meets, along with the self-effacing anecdotes of her own mishaps and physical discomforts along the journey, helps to ground her account in a materiality that is characteristic of the best journalistic work of the period. This collection, along with her novel, was published on the eve of the Communist victory in 1949.

By her own account in her post–Mao memoir *Surviving the Storm,* Chen was eager to witness and write about the agrarian reform movement sweeping her native Zhejiang province in the immediate postliberation years, and thus specifically requested an assignment in the countryside. Her request was initially denied on grounds that her intellectual training better suited her to an academic post, and she was instead appointed as director of political study at Zhejiang University, where she also taught part time in the Chinese literature department. Chen's persistence eventually paid off, however, and she was permitted to move to a village in Haining county to begin research for a new novel. Around that time she was also accorded the status of professional writer by the Central Research Institute of Literature and thus assured a steady income. In 1953, in accordance with party directives, she published a slim novel entitled *The Land,* about the collaboration of a land reform brigade with members of a village peasant association to eradicate the lingering influence of reactionary local landowners. Although the novel provides a straightforward account of the process—complete with scenes of "speaking bitterness" sessions, public trials of landlords and unrepentant rich peasants, and the redistribution of property to the poor masses—neither the characters nor the plot are sufficiently developed, and the novel appears to have attracted little critical attention. More disappointing in terms of Chen's long-standing feminist concerns, the novel alludes to a number of topical gender issues (including the special challenges the female peasants mobilized by land reform faced) but leaves them unelaborated as themes.

The following year, Chen relocated to the Longjing Tea Plantation to begin research on tea cultivation, the basis of her next novel *Spring Camellias* (1957). Set in Lionridge Hamlet, on the outskirts of Hangzhou, the novel examines the collectivization process following land reform through a candid story of the conflict that arises between grassroots organizers and ignorant party bureaucrats. Chen may well have been emboldened to explore this theme in the context of the new freedoms ushered in by the Hundred Flowers campaign that briefly flourished in 1956–57. One of the more interesting subplots involves the budding romance between Yue-ying, daughter of an unenlightened peasant, and Shen Dada, the branch secretary, through which the author illustrates the new freedoms under the Marriage Law (1950).

Testimony to the high regard in which Chen was held by the new leadership in the early postliberation years is the fact that she was invited to join a high-level women's delegation headed by Xu Guangping on an official visit to the Soviet Union in 1953. And in 1955, she was asked to host Jean-Paul Sartre and Simone de Beauvoir when they toured China. Unfortunately, two of her articles on socialist-era labor relations published in *People's Daily* in 1957 were labeled "poisonous weeds," and Chen soon found herself branded a rightist and was stripped of party membership. What ensued in the course of the next two decades was a tragic, if not untypical, ordeal: she was subjected to public struggle sessions, demotion and loss of salary, and a series of humiliating work assignments (including the task of scrubbing the toilets at Zhejiang University during the Cultural Revolution). Chen's reputation was partially restored after Lu Xun's diaries, which contained positive references to her, were issued in a more complete edition in 1976, and by 1978 she had enough confidence to resume work on the sequels to *To Be Working Is Beautiful* and *Spring Camellias,* the drafts for which she somehow managed to protect from several raids on her house. She was officially rehabilitated in 1979. That year saw the reissue of *To Be Working Is Beautiful,* in a volume that also included the sequel. Interestingly, she made a number of revisions to the original novel, including an entirely new chapter that depicts in greater detail how the heroine benefits from party leadership in developing the correct revolutionary outlook. A collection of critical essays on Chen's work has been published in mainland China, but her voluminous output still remains largely unexamined by scholars abroad.

The Essentials and Ambience of Life

(1940)

HOW SHOULD ONE describe life in Yan'an? It seems to me only a few verses written in beautiful, solemn language could begin to do it justice. As an ungraceful writer, I can only let the poets in Yan'an realize this dream.

My dear friends far and wide, I do not have the ability to sit tight and offer a serious account, so please allow me to ramble on without following a fixed direction. I will talk about this today and about that tomorrow, in an unsystematic and subjective manner. You may say that what I talk about is nothing more than my own life.

As far as food, clothing, shelter, and transportation are concerned, life in Yan'an is, in itself, monotonous and boring. Take clothing, for example. With the exception of local civilians, those who serve in the Eighth Route Army or work in the offices of the border-area government all wear blue army uniforms, and things such as georgette are nowhere to be seen here. . . . In general, seasoned cadres in the Eighth Route Army wear clean and neat clothes, with puttees wrapped around their legs, typical of a military lifestyle. Of course, not every cadre is dressed that way. I have seen some with the fronts of their padded army uniforms covered in so much grease that you probably could stir-fry a few dishes with it. As for the student recruits, they wear army uniforms, but they do not look like soldiers the way the seasoned cadres do. In addition, their puttees are often sloppily wrapped and often look rather dirty. Some of them argue that, since they were used to wearing western-style clothes before coming here, they do not know how to put on an army uniform properly no matter how hard they try. They argue that, if it is really true that the right way to wear the uniform comes from experience, you cannot blame them for making such a mess of it. Indeed, it appears that there is no such thing as fashion here and people wear clothes solely to cover their bodies and to protect themselves from the cold. However, in my daily life I have seen some young people, particularly girls, tilt the visors of their hats slightly to the left or to the right, or push them upward or downward a little, just to show their individuality. If this were a one-time occurrence, you might think it was inadvertent. But when it happens every day, it must have something to do with the notion of beauty. For a while, many girls wore colorful silk scarves around their necks. Women are particularly keen on displaying their individuality, so the futurist painters think that someday women will carve words on their faces to show their uniqueness. Now, amid the hardships of the War of Resistance, we have to make do. In the future, when a new China is established and the government has the spare energy to develop a cosmetics industry, the market will be flooded with countless types of perfume and face powder, and young girls will be able to pick whatever they want to their hearts' content.

In my opinion, men should look a little homely in appearance. If a naturally handsome man gives himself all kinds of embellishments, he only deserves to go to Montmartre to become a plaything for women. He is by no means an enterprising man! For a naturally handsome man, only serious work and a serious character can round out his natural appeal. And the same thing goes for women too.

As for food, everyone outside Yan'an knows that millet is the staple for most people here. In the winter, cabbages, tofu, bean sprouts, red and white turnips, potatoes, and bean-starch noodles are the only vegetables available. Virtually the only meat to be had is pork and everything else that comes from pigs, since mutton, chicken, and beef are rarely for sale. Furthermore, the beef on sale comes from cows that die from disease. Eggs are nowhere to be found because the winter weather is too cold here for hens to lay eggs. At the moment, in this beautiful early spring, we only have spinach and no cabbage. The rest of our food is the same as what we ate in the winter. The only difference is that eggs have been added to the diet. Back in my hometown, plenty of seasonal vegetables will be on the market now, not to mention freshwater fish and seafood. One evening, as I sat in front of my cave dwelling and "enjoyed the natural scenery" (an expression some of my friends here like to use to tease me), I thought of the foodstuffs in the south. "How delicious the Hangzhou pork soup would be if you added spring bamboo shoots and extra condiments to it!" I said to a friend.

"Women like to eat!" my friend commented with a suggestive smile.

"Women appreciate fine food, whereas men just eat!" I retorted, smiling.

In Yan'an, you can do very little to vary your diet, since such a limited number of ingredients are rotated. In addition, food is prepared here in a way that is entirely different from the way homemade dishes or those offered in the restaurants in the south are prepared. Pepper, aniseed, scallions, and so on are often added in great quantities, making the food taste very spicy or very vinegary. Some people tell me this is typical army food. If that is true, I would never have known the characteristics of military food had I not come to Yan'an. Most of the cooks come from Sichuan. These people accustomed to eating sour, spicy, and strange-tasting food for so many years are among those I respect very much. But those suffering from digestive ailments find the food indescribably monotonous for their peculiar, pitiable, and delicate stomachs. In fact, in my opinion, I am not the only person concerned about food. As it is a necessity of life, people should do no more and no less than be frank about it. In Yan'an, when folks meet for the first time, the first question is "What kind of work do you do?" The second one is "Where do you live?" and the third is "What kind of food do you eat?" As far as staple food is concerned, I reckon steamed buns are the best, but on one condition: they mustn't contain so much baking soda that it leavens them. (All the buns made here are unleavened.) If you slice up a bun and toast the slices over the fire until they are browned, they taste like bread. Once a friend of mine gave me a pound of honey. It differed in color from the honey produced in the south and wasn't as fragrant, perhaps because of the poor raw materials. Other than certain wildflowers, there is little variety in flowers in the north. However, I suspected that either it was not pure honey or the merchant had mixed it with some powder before selling it. If you put a little honey on a toasted slice of bun, it tastes like jam. The border area supposedly produces suet, but it is not on the market in Yan'an. The second best thing to eat is rice. Since southerners are accustomed to rice while northerners are used to wheat, buns, no matter how tasty they may be, get boring for a southerner if he eats them all the time. The third best is rice cooked with millet. The fourth is porridge made with millet and red beans. The fifth is millet porridge and the sixth cooked millet. The ranking reflects my personal preferences.

There are only three things here to which I am not quite accustomed. The first, the matter of sugar and sweets, concerns food. The other two are privies and bathhouses. In Yan'an sugar is rarely for sale. Although restaurants and cooperative stores have it in stock, they are loathe to sell it because they want to use it to make sweets such as eight-treasure rice pudding, candied millet sticks, frosted spinach, etc. . . . In the shops run by the locals, sugar is in short supply, and it is also very dirty. Brown sugar is easier to buy, but it is horribly dirty. With no knack for shopping, I feel that the locals always overcharge me. Why? Is it because my clothing or my face looks different? I know a married woman, a frequent guest here, who goes shopping every day and spends all her time "getting something to eat." Knowing virtually every street and every store in Yan'an like the palm of her hand, she was able to buy a pound of sugar for just a dollar. During my two-week search, however, I was always snubbed. "A dime an ounce and I can sell you four ounces," a store owner replied to my inquiry as I approached his store with sugar on display. "You cannot even sell half a pound?" "No!" I got really mad. *What an outrage! I might as well go without sugar!* I thought to myself as I turned around and left. Eventually I got a tip from that woman, who told me about a shop where I was able to buy a pound of sugar for a dollar. It was foreign sugar, made in Japan. The shop looked very small, but it had plenty of foreign sugar. There were no posters advertising what was in stock on the front of the door. Even the shop sign was nowhere to be seen, whereas before the bombings every store had its own sign. The stores and stands on the streets of Yan'an carry lots of Japanese goods. Dare I say this? Last December, the supply of certain goods that were already low, such as enamel bowls, was suddenly cut off because of the fall of Hankou. Now the supply has suddenly increased and many items are available in complete sets. I think those matches with the words "Tianjin, Zhili Province" printed on their boxes are also Japanese goods. It is said that such items come from Taiyuan and the areas along the Yellow River. In that case, they are contraband. We have so many tough choices to make in the War of Resistance. In order to satisfy our needs, we are forced to use goods made by the enemy, and who knows how much money has flowed to them as a result? This proves that fighting without construction is insufficient. In my opinion, Yan'an can use "Boycott enemy goods" as a slogan to alert ordinary citizens. Under the current circumstances, it is true that we cannot but use certain enemy goods, but we should do our best to avoid it when possible. Last July, the market price for domestic sugar was twenty-five cents a pound in Chongqing. I wonder how much the price has gone up. But I do not think it could ever reach a dollar a pound under any circumstances. We should do our best to improve the transportation on the Sichuan–Shaanxi Highway. At the same time, we hope the border area will try its best to promote the production of basic consumer goods. That is precisely what it has been doing recently. An exhibition has been held here to stimulate the handicraft industry.

To tell the truth, I have consumed nearly thirty pounds of sugar in the nine months since I arrived in Yan'an. Before I came, a friend in Xi'an told me that I would need to bring some sugar, so I brought ten pounds with me. Later, a friend asked someone to bring me ten pounds of sugar and five pounds of toffees as gifts for the Mid-Autumn Festival. Then a friend here gave me another ten pounds of sugar. Having a sweet tooth is a bad habit and a weakness. But it is only fair that I defend myself. I do not smoke or drink tea. Nor do I eat peanuts. I just enjoy an occasional sweet. Isn't that forgivable? A person's desires can change with the environment. Now, with things such as toffees, fruit drops, and so forth out of reach, give me some sugar and I will be wild with joy.

Mentioning the privies in Yan'an, many people perhaps will frown. In fact, the more you travel in the northwest, the more you will find that all the privies in the region are similar. So Yan'an is not unique in this regard. Using the privy is the most unbearable aspect of my daily life.

I used to live near the Red Cross office, where there was a beautiful toilet for women. The pit was dug very deep and it had a wooden lid. Thanks to frequent scrubbing, it was also rather sanitary. Later I moved and had to bid a rueful farewell to the toilet. Things got really miserable from then on. Usually privies in Yan'an are not very deep. Some, those that might be considered among the best, are enclosed by dirt walls. Since they do not have partitions, men and women avail themselves of the same ones. As for the ordinary folks in northern Shaanxi, they couldn't care less about whether there is a privy or not. They simply squat down and drop their golden natural fertilizer everywhere. During the New Year in 1939, the Central Committee of the Chinese Communist Party treated some people from the cultural circles in Yan'an and some other guests to a banquet one evening. After the banquet, as I started to leave, a friend called me back and offered me a ride in a truck. I happened to notice that Mr. Mao Zedong and Mr. Wang Ming were seated in the same truck on their way to another party. En route, Mr. Mao Zedong joked with Mr. Wang Ming: "What does Yan'an have in abundance? Lots of snow, lots of mountains—"

"And lots of privies!" Mr. Wang Ming cut in. Many people could not help bursting into laughter. "How convenient! Elsewhere, sometimes you have to go quite a long way to find a privy. In Yan'an, you can find one whenever you need to go."

Mr. Mao Zedong and Mr. Wang Ming then talked about the good things about the north. Mr. Mao Zedong said, "Here the moon is clear. . . ."

"If this were Wuhan, Japanese bombers would be back on an evening with such a clear moon," Mr. Wang Ming said. "Then this is another good thing about Yan'an."

The climate in the north is dry and the moon is crystal clear. The sky is cloudless, particularly on snowy evenings when there is no wind. But the air is very cold. The reflection of the moonlight on the snow gives people a feeling of purity and tranquility. Riding on a sled and speeding across the snow under the moonlight would be an indescribable thrill.

Indeed, Yan'an has so far not suffered any night air attacks, and the air raid sirens have never been sounded even on those bright moonlit evenings. Is that because the weather is too cold, or the enemy thinks there is no need for night air attacks? Or because there are too many mountains here and an air attack at night would pose too great a danger to their bombers?

With regard to housing, everyone knows that most people here live in cave dwellings. The way those are built in such haste for the sake of saving money, I am afraid, is something brought by the Eighth Route Army. The cave dwellings are separate from each other, but sometimes they can be conjoined. Housing in Yan'an can be said to be a most interesting issue. Because this is a place with no superstition or theft, you could say life here is most carefree. I remember when I went back to my hometown I found that people were so deeply steeped in superstitions in their daily lives that, as soon as I got there, I felt as though a ghost were following on my heels. And in the past, I never wanted to stay in a hotel alone no matter where I was, for fear that the guest next door might turn out to be a murderer or a rapist. . . . Those gruesome incidents that I so often heard about made me nervous. Luckily, I rarely had to stay in hotels. Whenever I traveled somewhere unfamiliar, I would always be put up by a close friend's family. I was also most afraid of living in an unfamiliar place. Unsure what kind of neighbors I would have, I had a hard time making a decision anytime I tried to rent a place. I like to live a life that is all light and no darkness, a life that can be read like an open book. It's not that I am afraid of the dark aspects of society. It is just that I get sick to my stomach when I see something gruesome happen, as if I have run into something filthy. Around your cave dwelling in Yan'an, your neighbor might be a government worker with a peasant background or a revolutionary. When he talks, he might sometimes dot his remarks with "damn this" and "damn that." He might somewhat have the air of a country bumpkin. But he is bound to be very simple and honest, making you feel that he is what a human being should be, a Chinese with dignity and not someone to fear. You might even feel he is rather lovable. Sometimes you might have a neighbor who works as a cadre in charge of such and such an office or department, and you will see him busy with this and that all day long. Their life is so incredibly simple. And their diligence at once moves you and makes you feel ashamed of yourself.

In terms of travel, it is to be expected that, given the sheer size and sparse population of the border area, you can be on the road for five or ten miles without seeing a single house. Undulating mountains are everywhere and go on forever. I have tried to imagine what kind of transportation will be developed in this area once it becomes a base for heavy industry in a new China. Will the elevator or the mountain-climbing electric train be the common vehicle? At present, everyone has to walk. The northwest and the south are different in that, in the place where I come from, you will come to a village or a wayside pavilion every few miles where travelers can sit down and take a break. In summer the villagers there will make sure that tea is served. This kind of pavilion must be what is meant by the "post house," which is so frequently described in traditional poetry in expressions such as "a dim light in a post house by the water" and "people talking by a bridge next to a post house." Indeed water, bridges, and pavilions occupy an extremely important place in the daily lives of southerners. But these do not exist in the northwest. After traveling a long distance, you won't be able to buy any boiled water on the road, even in the middle of a sweltering summer day. Even if you can find a shop, there won't be any boiled water or tea for sale. The common mode of transportation is draft animals—horses, donkeys, and mules. It goes without saying that local residents excel at riding. What amazes me most is that seasoned cadres in the Eighth Route Army, both men and women, are also skilled riders. Among them are southerners who can ride. Although "southerners take boats while northerners ride horses" sums up the situation of transportation in ancient times, it appears that this expression still describes the northwest to a certain degree. The roads here are all made of yellow sandy dirt and, since no trees were planted in the past, there used to be no shade at all. This year, thanks to the production campaign, over a hundred thousand trees have been planted in the border area, adding to a comparable number planted last year. In several decades, these trees will provide shade along asphalt roads for travelers who will be able to take a rest on benches complete with seat backs. At present, people just enjoy the light and the unpretentious atmosphere in this area as they put up with the temporary imperfections.

Real life in Yan'an is more or less what I have described thus far. This area, which can be regarded as the poorest region in China, is nonetheless a place that makes one reluctant to leave. I believe that I will remember Yan'an after I depart. I am so fond of the ambience here. "Life in Yan'an is really gratifying, mentally gratifying!" some young people always say, but they cannot explain why. Of course, it is not exactly gratifying to eat cooked millet. Getting a monthly stipend of one or two dollars isn't bad, considering that the money is saved by the Eighth Route Army. But it is probably not very gratifying to use this amount of money, I am afraid. Then what is it that makes life so gratifying here? I have been pondering this question, but I am not quite sure that I have come up with the right answer, since I certainly have no political acumen to speak of. To me the most important reason, to borrow an expression used in my hometown, is the political integrity, given that everything is so clear and aboveboard, and good leadership. As for other reasons, I think they are the reflections of political integrity in social life. And social life here is so full of light, candor, and purity! Not to sound too disrespectful of menfolk, but there are no brothels, no teahouses, and no taverns here. A visitor who stays for two weeks or a month is only able to see certain aspects of Yan'an, such as people's intense work and study; their spartan clothing, food, and housing; their enthusiasm in the War of Resistance; and so on, but only those who have stayed here longer can feel the real greatness of Yan'an and what makes people reluctant to leave.

Living in the society of Yan'an marked by its light and purity makes me think of the dark social life Maupassant realistically described in his stories.[1] I believe back then Maupassant must have described those dark aspects with feelings of disappointment and disgust. People say that after he died someone found a Bible under his pillow. I wonder what kind of book Maupassant would put under his pillow if he were still alive now.

Crossing the Tong-Pu Railroad
(1949)

WE STAYED IN the Village XXX for two days, preparing to cross the Tong-Pu Railroad. During the anti-Japanese war, crossing this railroad was usually called "crossing the blockade line," since the enemy had dotted the whole railroad with fortresses. Blockhouses, equipped with troops and heavy weapons, had been built at one-and-a-half-mile intervals. Even though the enemy had by now already declared its surrender, since the Guomindang would not allow the Eighth Route Army to accept the surrender of Japanese troops and, moreover, since Yan Xishan, in collusion with the enemy, was using Japanese troops as the backbone of his anti-Communist operations, the fortresses along the Tong-Pu Railroad remained filled with enemy soldiers. Several of them had been fortified with even more troops than before the surrender. These enemy soldiers made forays everywhere and created havoc with their plundering.

When we reached the village, the scene could be described by the following lines: "Amid the surrounding mountain glow, a whip cracked in the setting sun." Here and there peasants were threshing grain. Though not a painter, I was moved by this lively scene of hard work that reminded me of Millet's oil painting *Autumn Harvest*.[2]

---

[1] Guy de Maupassant (1850–1893), a noted French realist writer.
[2] Jean-Francois Millet (1814–1875) was a French realist painter known for his depictions of rural life.

This area, including the county of Wuzhai, was not rich in agricultural products; it only produced hulled oats, sesame seeds, and potatoes. "Eating oatmeal and sleeping on warm brick beds" summed up the lives of ordinary people in northwestern Shanxi. When I saw hulled oats and oat flour for the first time, I did not know how to prepare them and had to ask the locals to cook them for us. In the house where I stayed, the two sisters-in-law gladly lent me a hand. Chatting with me as they prepared the oat dough, they found it funny that I had never seen hulled oats. A series of questions followed as they tried to imagine me, not as someone who knew nothing, but as someone who lived a life completely different from their own. After they kneaded the dough and rolled it into small rolls, they put them into a steamer, steamed them, and got them ready for serving. They told me that food made of oats would sit in the stomach for a long time so, according to local custom, one was supposed to eat such foods with vinegar or a broth of pickled vegetables. So every household in the area made its own pickled vegetables. They then sliced up some of their homemade pickled carrots, made some broth, and brought it over for me to drink. Though generally not particularly keen on pickled foods, I found the broth rather appetizing. Meanwhile, the freshly steamed oat rolls began to give off a delectable fragrance that smelled very much like the aroma of freshly baked bread. They told me that under the enemy occupation ordinary people in the area had nothing to eat. An acre of land could yield at most a little more than a hundred pounds of hulled oats, but the enemy would force people to hand over more than three hundred pounds. After handing in all the food they could collect from their houses, people had to live off the wild vegetables they scavenged. But now they had oats and potatoes to eat and, on top of that, they had several crocks of pickled vegetables in store.

In high spirits, they talked about what good the rent and interest reduction campaign had done: "Now that the rents have been reduced, even peasants have food to eat!"

Of course they supported the revolutionary regime. They also had a certain understanding of the Eighth Route Army as a revolutionary force, for they kept saying, "The Eighth Route Army does not take advantage of us ordinary people." Their household appeared to be a big, harmonious one, which was to be expected since the peasant family naturally becomes harmonious once its livelihood is protected. Things such as men beating and cursing women to vent their anger disappear. So without exception, every woman I met in the old and new liberated areas praised the Eighth Route Army. Indeed, immeasurable benefits had been brought to women by the revolutionary regime and the revolutionary armed force. Chinese women had always been doubly oppressed—by their fathers-in-law and their mothers-in-law. In this household the two sons had both gone out on business for a couple of days. With a high, wrinkled forehead, dark eyes, and a tall stature, the old man, close to sixty, appeared rather vigorous. Without saying a word, he would quietly slip past other members of his family as if to avoid displeasing anybody. I sensed he was an understanding, sensitive old peasant. After he got a saddle for me from his nephew, he fixed the leather straps with his shaky hands and told me the precautions I should take, and I was touched by his kindness. The attendant who had been traveling with me was an impatient, hot-tempered man. Whenever he waved his whip and yelled out "Giddyap" on the road, not only the donkey was scared to death; my heart almost jumped to my throat as well. Whenever I took a fall, I was afraid he might see and scold me as if I had made a mistake. I imagined that had this old man been my travel companion, he would certainly not have been unpleasant in the least. Youth is always appealing, but I love noble character and wisdom more.

As I sat in the warm sun on a pile of hulled-oat straw in the courtyard and jotted down some notes about my journey with a pencil, their oldest grandson, aged nine, snuggled up against my knees and watched me, despite the fact that the grownups kept urging him to go away and leave me alone. "Do you like to go to school?" I asked him.

"Yes," he said.

"How come you aren't in school now? Is there an elementary school here?"

"There was one before, but we did not want our kids to use the textbooks from Jap devils. They were filled with nonsense," the old man cut in as he walked by.

"In the future you can go to school and learn from our own textbooks, Chinese textbooks!" I stroked the child's head and said. "Did Jap devils ever come to your house?"

"Yes."

"Why did they come?"

"They came to our house and said they wanted to 'learn something.' Then they snatched the chickens from the coop, carried off our oats, and took away the eggs. They wanted everything, even my trousers," the child said. "They also took out their bayonets and asked my grandpa, 'What do you do for a living?' before shoving him down to the ground."

At this point the old man said emotionally, "I have suffered enough! I wish I were dead!"

"You shouldn't say things like that. You should live on so that we can show you a thriving new China and let you enjoy some happy days!" I said to him.

Having had our fill of food and water, humans and mounts alike, and a good rest to boot, we resumed our journey. At dusk, we got to a small village and stopped to take a break and have a drink of water. As I turned around I was, for a minute, stunned to find a man standing right beside me with a rifle over his shoulder. "What are you doing here?" I asked him.

"I am here to protect you," he said proudly.

"How old are you? And what is your name?"

"My name is Ma Sanxiao and I am twenty," he replied.

"When did you join the Eighth Route Army?"

"Four years ago. Tonight my assignment is to ensure that you cross the railroad safely."

Touched by the forthright, proud tone in his voice, I still felt somewhat offended and embarrassed that I required the protection of a young man who was barely twenty years old. On the other hand, I understood why the young soldier felt about himself the way he did, for he already had a four-year history of fighting at such a young age. How glorious and honorable it is to be a soldier in a revolutionary army! Even without my promotion or praise on their behalf, their own conduct is proof enough of that. The Eighth Route Army is such a fine army. With their strict discipline and their love for ordinary folk, these soldiers represent a whole generation of marvelous Chinese youths! And I respect them from the bottom of my heart. "Are you saying we have already entered the danger zone?" I asked.

"Not yet." His answer was firm and precise, without any undue brevity or verbiage.

Soon after we set out again we reached a river, which, unexpectedly, my donkey stubbornly refused to cross. It bolted here and there on the riverbank, as if spooked by something. I whipped it for all I was worth, but the whip, a willow branch, seemed to have no effect whatsoever. From the very beginning of the journey, before I got on the road each day I would have to get a branch to use as a whip. My travel companions all laughed at the embarrassing scenes I made. Luckily, with one shove from the butt of his rifle, Ma Sanxiao got my donkey to catch up with the others ahead. In order not to lag behind too much, I had to depend on the butt of his rifle the whole way that night. Knowing that this was not his responsibility, I felt rather bad. My donkey galloped on and on, across high mountain ridges and along gravel roads. It went so fast its legs seemed to have shortened so that its body was close to the ground. The surrounding area was quiet, and the only sound that could be heard was the hoofbeats skimming the ground monotonously. With Ma Sanxiao next to me the whole time, we crossed the Tong-Pu Railroad without incident other than hearing six explosions of grenades launched by grenade dischargers.

On the trip the travelers were tormented by either exhaustion or thirst. Most were weighed down by sleepiness; some even fell from their mounts as they dozed off. But I remained alert. Looking up at the Big Dipper glittering in the sky like sparkling eyes, I could not help wondering in a trance, *Is there any friend living far away who would, while working late tonight, be aware that someone is spending the night traveling on the road?*

When I took out two flat cakes from a pocket in my padded army uniform and tried to give one to Ma Sanxiao, I found he had already gone.

January 19, 1946

5
Xie Bingying
(1906–2000)

*T*he acclaimed author of *War Diaries* (1928), a stirring autobiographical account of her experience as a young female
soldier on the 1926–27 Northern Expedition, Xie Bingying
continued to combine her commitment to active public service and her
talents as a writer throughout the 1930s and '40s. In 1932, in the wake
of the Japanese occupation of Manchuria, Xie took on the editorship
of *Women's Light,* a weekly journal sponsored by the Women's National
Resistance and Salvation Alliance. And with the outbreak of the Sino-
Japanese War, she joined the national resistance cause in Changsha, organizing and leading the Hunan Women's War Zone Service Corps, a
volunteer brigade of nurses, to the front line. Sketches of this experience
and other eyewitness accounts of the battlefield appeared in her reportage collection, *New War Diary,* in 1938 and in the voluminous essays
she published throughout these tumultuous years. Patriotic themes also
dominate her 1940 memoir, *In a Japanese Prison.* The work describes
the author's harrowing ordeal in a Tokyo jail after being arrested for
refusing to join a welcome rally for Pu Yi as the chief executive of Manchukuo, when she was enrolled as a student at Waseda University in
the mid-thirties. During the latter part of the war, Xie Bingying helped
establish and then edit *Yellow River,* a literary magazine based in Xi'an.
After Japan's surrender, she served as the editor of *Peace Daily News*
in Hankou before moving to Beijing to take up a teaching position at
Beijing Normal University. In addition to the second volume of her
widely read 1936 autobiography, *A Woman Soldier's Own Story,* Xie's
postwar writing also includes several noteworthy works of fiction. Especially interesting is her mildly humorous first-person novella *Divorce,*
first published in Zhao Qingge's postwar collection of women's writing,
Untitled (1947). Set during the war, the story charts the rude awakening
of a naïve and overly adoring young wife who comes to realize that her
husband (Guoqiang or Nation Strengthener) is not the patriotic hero

she imagined him to be. Consistent with the antiromantic trend in occupation-period fiction, the story ends on the "triumphant" note of the heroine's divorce.

Shortly before the fall of the KMT in 1949, Xie Bingying departed abruptly for Taiwan with two of her children and her husband, Jia Yi-zhen. Over the next few years, she led a relatively quiet life teaching Chinese literature in Taiwan and Malaysia. She and her husband emigrated to the United States in 1974. Xie continued writing and publishing fiction, children's literature, essays, and travel writing until her death in 2000. Her 1936 autobiography, the work for which she is perhaps best remembered today, has remained in print in Taiwan and has recently appeared in a new English translation by her daughter and son-in-law.

In this unique patriotic work, "The Girl Umeko" (1941), Xie examines the anti-Japanese war from the point of view of a comfort woman conscripted to serve as a prostitute for Japanese soldiers during the war in China. Having spent time in Japan in the mid-thirties, Xie had developed close friendships with progressive Japanese scholars and writers, which may help account for the empathy she shows for ordinary Japanese citizens such as the characters in this story.

The Girl Umeko

(1941)

I

IT WAS DRIZZLING and the room was gloomy. Kieko was putting on make-up in front of the mirror. She had to paint her eyebrows herself because Umeko, who usually helped her, was ill today. Drawn with a pencil that was too dark and by a hand that had pressed too hard, her eyebrows looked as if they had been smeared with black ink.

"Umeko-san, how's my make-up?"

"You've got on so much lipstick that your mouth looks bloody. And your eyebrows are too dark. Kieko-san, you might as well wash it off. With your fair skin, you look more beautiful without make-up!" Umeko spoke with difficulty and made a few dry coughs.

"Umeko-san, if you can get up, I'd like you to paint my eyebrows. Oh, the trouble we go through to please men!" With that, Kieko thought, she could arouse Umeko's sympathy.

What she got instead was Umeko's disgusted reply, "To please men? Why should women be playthings for men? I have no objection if you wear make-up out of your own love of beauty. But if you paint and powder yourself to gratify men, this is simply an insult to us women. Don't you think?"

"What do you mean by insult? Aren't we already living the life of animals?" Midako, who was in the next room, interrupted them. "Who's that complaining again? It's getting really tedious. Serving with the Comfort Corps for the Imperial Army is an honor. What are you unhappy about?" She was a very flirtatious girl, who inevitably exasperated them whenever she opened her mouth to speak. However, nobody dared to offend her because she was a frequent guest at Commander Kawashima's place. As she spoke, a captain was still asleep on her lap, snoring thunderously like a fat pig. She might have intended her words for him rather than the other two girls. In any case, Kieko did not respond, but concentrated on manicuring her nails.

This was a group of military prostitutes, ninety-six of them all together, who had just come from Hankou to Shashi and were now stationed at the Fu'an Inn. Upon arriving in Shashi, Umeko had taken ill, coughing and running a high fever. She was depressed, having never expected such an ordeal after coming to China. She had assumed that all the Comfort Corps did was distribute the thousand-women-sewn cloth talismans,[1] flags, cans, handkerchiefs, care packages, and other such amenities to the soldiers. That was it. How could she have known that they would be organized into corps of prostitutes in Hankou to satisfy the sexual needs of the troops?

"Oh, I have been deceived. Deceived. How did I land in this tiger's den?" Whenever things got really bad, all Umeko could do was cover her head with the quilt and murmur this to herself.

Umeko was from Shirasato county on the island of Kogoshima. Her father, Kinjiro, a cobbler, had taken the family to Tokyo in 1931. To his chagrin, the ladies of Tokyo did not care for the style of shoes he made; moreover, being an honest peasant, he did not know the first thing about business. He suffered huge losses in three years. In view of his bad luck, Umeko's mother, a gentle and considerate woman, tried hard to save money and even scrimped on food. When her father was away during the day, her mother would take in

---

[1] *Qianrenzhen,* literally, "thousand-people-needle," a cloth talisman supposedly sewn by a thousand women to be carried by soldiers for protection in war.

laundry in the hope that she could help support the family with the money she earned. But Kinjiro was an honest and frank man and, seeing his seventy-year-old mother and his wife wasting away from malnutrition and having no money for his daughter's schooling, took his friends' advice and went to do business in Liaoning province in China. But only a year later, the September 18th Incident took place and he was drafted into the Japanese army, only to be killed two weeks later. Upon receiving the news, Umeko's mother fainted three times. And the grandmother contracted an eye disease due to her excessive weeping, and eventually went blind. Umeko was only ten years old at the time, and seeing her family in such misery, she could do nothing but cry with her mother.

God always seems to make things tough on the poor. Umeko's mother fell seriously ill with pulmonary tuberculosis the following year and passed away before too long. Umeko and her grandma depended on each other to survive for a short while before her uncle came and took her grandma back to the island of Kogoshima.

From that point on, as an orphan who had lost the love of her parents, she began her sad life as a wanderer.

II

UMEKO WORKED AS a waitress in a café, as a nurse, and as a dancing girl, and she also went through labor in a maternity hospital, although she was not to become a mother. That was her most depressing memory, and whenever she saw children or pregnant women, she would recall that sad chapter of her life.

It was a night with crystal-like moonlight shining down upon the Earth as she lay in Ward 34 of the maternity hospital, groaning in pain. The nurse came in and turned on the light, which momentarily stung Umeko's eyes like thousands of painful arrows.

"Miss Rinbu, is the doctor here yet? Please give me the operation or I will die of pain!" Umeko pleaded with the nurse.

"The doctor said you won't go in for surgery until tomorrow. The baby is too big and it won't come out easily. Be patient and get through the night, everything will be better tomorrow." Miss Rinbu gently rubbed Umeko's belly while pulling up on the iron weight that was hanging at the opening of her womb.

"Ouch! My! I can't take it anymore! Miss Rinbu, please leave the weight there. I am dying of pain!" But Umeko's anguished screams could not move Miss Rinbu's iron-cold heart.

"Why can't I have the operation sooner! I can't make it until tomorrow. Miss Rinbu, do me a favor and ask the doctor to come. Otherwise, give me a knife and I will . . ." Her wailing grew ever sharper and more heartrending.

"Why are you howling like this at midnight? It has been two days, but the baby is in the same position. Without this, how can we get him out? Why did you commit such a sin and get yourself in trouble like this in the first place?"

Sin and get herself in trouble—how could she say such a thing? Umeko was about to tell Miss Rinbu about who had forced her father to join the army and get killed in China, who had driven her mother to her death, blinded her grandmother, and seduced her when she was still an innocent virgin, leaving her in this condition. But Miss Rinbu had already gone, leaving her in the cold, desolate room with the heavy weight.

The pain in her abdomen intensified. At first it had come in spasms, sometimes at intervals of two or three minutes. But now she felt as if a tiger were tearing its way out of her womb. With her feet tied up, she could not move at all. She wanted to pull herself up, untie the iron weight, and knock it against her head to finish off their two lives at once. But with her slightest movement, the baby inside her would squirm violently, like thousands of snakes gnawing at her flesh. On quite a few occasions, she lost consciousness and came to again not knowing whether she was still alive or not.

The next afternoon, Umeko was wheeled on a gurney into the operating room, which was about twelve tatami in size.[2] Inside, she felt it was as dark and dreary as an execution ground. And her whole body shuddered as she heard the clanking of surgical instruments. She did not understand what the doctor was saying to the three nurses; she only felt her heart race as they covered her eyes with a white cloth, tied her feet to the operating table, and even held her hands tightly.

Heavens, was this torture?

At this point she hadn't the least bit of pity for the little creature that had sucked the blood of her body for four and a half months, and knew that in five minutes they would cut it out of her as easily as removing the liver from a slaughtered pig. She really did not care, feeling only that she had suffered too much for it, and that it didn't belong in her body. She wanted to severely punish it and get rid of it.

"Miss Rinbu, please ask the doctor to give me some poison and let me die. I can't take it anymore. I have suffered too much and don't want to go on living.

---

[2]In Japan, rooms are measured by tatami mats. One tatami is about eighteen square feet.

Please be kind and tell the doctor to poison me and get it over with," Umeko, trembling, said in a terrified and tormented voice.

"Quiet down, please. We'll give you an anesthetic soon. It won't be long. In just a moment, it won't hurt." Miss Rinbu gripped Umeko's hands.

They put a chloroform mask over her mouth and she immediately fell asleep.

As she was coming to, she felt a knife scraping her womb like a spoon scooping out a watermelon. But that thousand-pound flesh-gnawing tiger had disappeared.

"The baby was removed intact. The doctor says it will be made into a specimen," said Miss Rinbu with a smile. But Umeko could feel her barbed words, and in her heart she felt deeply offended.

On the third day, she went home. The father of the aborted baby came to see her. She told him about her experience in the hospital, and begged him in a low voice: "Fujima-san, I have suffered all this because of you. If you ever desert me, I will kill myself. When I was in the hospital, I contemplated suicide several times, but I endured for my dear Fujima." She held him tightly and cried like a child who throws herself into her mother's bosom after being bullied.

"Cheer up, my dear Umeko. I won't let you down. You gave up your virginity to me as well as a precious, probably the greatest, little life for me. How could I be so cruel as to leave you? I will marry you as soon as I tell my family and get my parents' approval."

Umeko's broken heart seemed to be mended! Now there was hope for the future. The past was just like a nightmare. *As long as Fujima carries out his promise, won't I soon be living the happy life of a little family?* But beautiful girls are born under unlucky stars. Just as her dream was about to come true, her blind grandmother suddenly fell ill with relapsing fever and died, and Fujima was drafted and sent to fight in Shanghai. Her sole purpose in coming to the front with the Comfort Corps was to find her husband, just like Meng Jiangnü of ancient China, who walked thousands of miles in search of her husband.[3] But who knew that her fate was like a rose in bloom suddenly destroyed by a storm? Her sweet, beautiful dream was smashed by a merciless bomb!

Arriving in Hankou, she received the terrible news that Fujima had died

---

[3]In this famous legend, Meng Jiangnü goes in search of her husband after he is conscripted by the first Emperor of China, Qin Shihuang, to help build the Great Wall of China. When she arrives at the wall, she learns that he has died, and her weeping topples the wall.

on the battlefield. She had now lost the courage to keep on living. But what Fujima's friend, Okamura Sanro, said was perfectly true: she should never sacrifice herself so easily, and she should avenge her husband, Fujima, and her father.

"Umeko, you mustn't be so passive, but live on with courage! Have you ever asked yourself who killed your father and grandmother, who killed your lover?" Those words, like shells fired from a cannon, erupted in her heart.

III

UMEKO STAYED IN Hankou for half a year and could not remember clearly how many drunken Imperial Army soldiers had ravaged her body. From their own mouths, she learned how they had brutally raped women in their seventies and eighties, and ten-year-old girls. She experienced a dramatic change in her point of view during that half year, having seen with her own eyes the Imperial troops raping Chinese women, burying alive young men, massacring old folk and young children, torching people's houses, and looting their belongings. No matter how reactionary a person was, if they were human, they would never forgive the Imperial Army for such cruelty, violating all divine justice and human nature.

Umeko hated it all! Why was there such a nation as Japan? And why had Japan produced such beastly warlords? Why did she have to be born in such a country at the very moment when they were slaughtering the Chinese people?

Being a Japanese subject under this military dictatorship was shameful! They never ceased mouthing high-sounding phrases like "good will" and "assistance," but every cell in their bones was full of poison, bombs to destroy human civilization, flames to wipe out all justice.

One day, she asked Matsumoto, a private first class who kept himself in a perpetual state of drunkenness, "Do you think it is right that the Imperial Army kills, rapes, plunders, and burns like this?"

He replied, "Who says it's right? But what can I do? They order you to do it, dare you say no?" His long sigh revealed that he too had his worries.

"What if the Chinese troops burned your house, looted your belongings, raped your wife and mother, transfused your son's blood into their soldiers? Wouldn't it break your heart?" Umeko's voice grew more and more angry.

Matsumoto, however, kept laughing like a madman. "It's precisely because we know they would never march to Japan that we dare to do all these crazy things!"

"The Chinese would never march to Japan—is that what you think? Why would you think that? Although they are oppressed by the Japanese army, they will stand up one day. How long can they take having their country suffer such disgrace? Marching to Japan, that is absolutely possible. It is just a matter of time."

"Ha ha, Miss Umeko, what a rebel you are! But don't let Commander Matsuoka hear you, or you will get yourself executed!"

Fortunately, as Matsumoto was fond of her and, moreover, was drunk, he did not take what she said very seriously, and was just making fun of her.

"Who cares? What is the point of living like this? I gave up on my life long ago, but I don't want to commit suicide. I want to see how long you guys can lord around."

"Ha ha, you are crazy, out of your mind! What is the use of saying all this? Come here, my sweetheart, and let's drink a few more cups. 'If you find me drunk on the battlefield, don't laugh; from ancient times, how many make it back from war alive?' Do you understand the meaning of this Tang poem?"

The two caroused all night long, and Umeko eventually discovered his secret heart. It turned out Matsumoto had been a college student with an independent mind; though he had detested war for a long time, he had no way to express his true feelings. Therefore he hid his real opinion and disguised himself as a drunkard, spending his time chasing women. He had not expected that Umeko would have such noble ideas about the war and become his comrade. When he introduced his best friend, Okamura Sanro, to her, she said, giggling, "Do you know that he is also my good friend?"

"Really? I can introduce to you my other good friend. Unfortunately he is not in Shashi, but may come here very soon. He is a pilot, a very handsome young fellow. But I wouldn't be very happy if you fell in love with him."

"Are you kidding, Mr. Matsumoto! Who has the time or desire to talk about love? At a moment when the front is engulfed in gunsmoke and the Japanese warlords are slaughtering innocent Chinese people, we should be focusing all efforts on our antiwar movement. What do you think, Mr. Matsumoto?"

"Of course, we should do as you have said. But such talk is just between you and me. Because of all the antiwar activists committing suicide, they're watching us ever more closely. I hope you will be more careful when you speak out and not get carried away by your enthusiasm. It would be better if you pretended to be a pragmatist who cares for nothing but enjoyment. That would be better for our movement."

Hearing what Matsumoto said, Umeko was overjoyed. She had found a true friend to whom she could confide her pain and vexation. As for Matsumoto, attracted by her passion, liveliness, courage, and beauty, his feelings for her had already gone beyond those of ordinary friends and he dreamed dimly of her one day becoming Mrs. Matsumoto.

IV

"UMEKO-SAN, YOU HAVE a guest. Hurry and get up!" Kieko flew in like a little sparrow.

"Who is it?" Umeko asked.

Kieko pulled Umeko up and draped a coat around her shoulders. The guest, probably tired of waiting, had already come in. "Hi, everyone. I am Nakajyo Chigi. Oh, Umeko-san, you really are pretty! Hurry and get up!"

He continued, "My apologies, Umeko-san. I did not wait for you to get up because I have to rush back to headquarters on some business." Nakajyo politely took off his cap and bowed. He wasn't as rude and fearful as the other soldiers.

"That's all right. I should apologize for being ill and unable to get up sooner to greet my guest." Feeling guilty, Umeko slid out of bed to return the courtesy.

Kieko had prepared him a cup of tea and stood aside, waiting on them. "Mr. Nakajyo, please sit down and have some tea."

"Thanks."

As Kieko offered him the tea, she made a point of smiling flirtatiously, feeling sure Nakajyo would like her. However, his attention was completely focused on Umeko instead. Umeko's face, covered by her disheveled hair, looked just like the ancient Chinese beauty Xishi after an illness, and therefore appeared all the more lovable. Her bright eyes exuded profound tenderness; her dainty mouth revealed two rows of straight white teeth; and most beautiful of all were her hands which, just like those of a child, were slightly rounded like small steamed buns and had very slender fingers, definitely hands of a superbly clever girl.

"Umeko-san, do you know Matsumoto-san? He is a good friend of mine. I did not know that you were here until I received his letter today. I searched for you in several places and have found you at last!" Nakajyo's face displayed uncontrollable joy, making Kieko, who was sitting to one side, exceedingly uncomfortable.

"Yes, Matsumoto-san is very good to me. But I let him down this time when I followed orders and left Hankou for Shashi on the night of the 14th before I had a chance to say good-bye. I got sick as soon as I arrived and have not written to him yet."

"That is all right. I will say hello for you when I write back to him."

"Many thanks!" Umeko suddenly felt her face grew warm, and her heart beat fast and her left eyelid twitched. She did not know whether it was because something was wrong with her eye or because Nakajyo's eyes were different from other people's, but she felt that the bright light from his eyes pierced her heart like two sharp arrows. She did not dare to look at him for long but at the same time hoped that he would look at her a little more. She wished Nakajyo would leave the room, but another part of her wished he would never leave her.

"How are you doing here, Umeko-san?" Despite having nothing more to say, Nakajyo was loath to leave just yet.

"Nothing special. Just passing time."

Hearing this, Nakajyo now felt a little disappointed. Hadn't Matsumoto told him that Umeko was a woman with a mind of her own? Then why had she given up on herself? "See you tomorrow. I have business to attend to."

After they saw Nakajyo off downstairs, Kieko turned to Umeko in sour jealousy and said, "Congratulations, Umeko-san! You've found yourself such a handsome lover. And he's an air force pilot! Love at first sight. Ha, ha, ha!"

"Don't be jealous, Kieko-san. If he comes back tomorrow, I will leave the room and let you have the entire time to make sweet talk."

"Come on. I am not that lucky, as you know. Better let me help you complete your good fortune."

As if in a debate, they talked back and forth for quite a while. Umeko pretended to be angry but felt joyful in her heart. Kieko was right: love at first sight. That was exactly how she felt about Nakajyo. She had met many men, but she had never come upon one who attracted her as powerfully as he. She was now twenty years old but had never fallen in love just like that. Wasn't that something miraculous?

She forgot Matsumoto's warning and sowed the seeds of her first love in the field of her heart.

V

TIME FLASHED BY like lightning. Two months disappeared like that, and the love between them grew more passionate with each passing day. At first, they could not stand being separated for one day; later, they could not even be apart for a single minute. Nakajyo was stationed in Jingzhou, about four miles from Shashi, and rode his motorcycle to see her every day. Summer was the best season for love. Men wore short-sleeved silk shirts, shorts, socks, and black or white leather shoes, and strutted about like gallant ancient knights. Women liked to sport summer sandals on their bare feet and wear short sleeves to show off their beautiful fair, soft arms. As she wore only a single layer of clothing, Umeko's charming curves were visible as she walked. Her slim figure drew even more admiring stares every time she strolled down the street. Many officers were crazy about her. But she fooled them by pretending to have a severe case of syphilis, and warned them to stay away. Sometimes, in order to avoid all their pestering and humiliations, she would paint spots on her body with red Mercurochrome to scare them off. But this method only worked with the newcomers, and couldn't fool old acquaintances. She grew increasingly weary of her life as an army prostitute and craved permanent love to heal the deep wounds in her heart. She loved Nakajyo and was willing to give her body and soul entirely to him, for him alone to possess. Similarly, she also needed his whole body and soul. Actually this was not so difficult, because the two of them had won complete victory in their love.

It was already 9 p.m. and Nakajyo still had not shown up. Umeko was on the verge of tears worrying.

He wouldn't break his promise. Something must be preventing him from coming on time, Umeko thought, sitting alone under a tree by the lake in Zhongshan Park. She did not dare to leave to wait at the park entrance, because this was the spot that they had agreed upon the night before. If she were to leave and he showed up, wouldn't they miss their chance to meet?

All of a sudden, two strong hands clasped her waist, and she let out a scream.

"Dear Umeko, have you been waiting long?"

"Oh, it is you. You scared me. Why are you so late?"

A full Chinese moon broke out of the clouds and shone on the lakeside where a tall and a short figure merged into one. Nakajyo and Umeko were deeply intoxicated in their long, sweet kiss.

"What are we going to do, Umeko? The fighting at the front is getting worse. The Chinese have sent fifty thousand troops to attack Shashi. We will send eighty sorties to bomb Chongqing the day after tomorrow. I will risk my life again." Nakajyo told her this important news once he had calmed down a bit.

"What? Attack Chongqing again? With eighty planes! My god, how murderous that would be! Do you have any idea of the bloody aftermath of the bombings? Some families are completely buried beneath the debris. Wives can't find the bodies of their husbands whom they had been together with just moments earlier. Although I have never experienced a bombing, I have seen plenty of the ruin left by our Imperial Army's bombs. How many happy families have been devastated, and how much property saved over a lifetime has gone up in flames? I am begging you, Nakajyo, don't go. I can't see my lover becoming a slaughterer of human beings! Nakajyo, can't you pretend to be sick? We've got to find a safe way out of here. What are you thinking now? Why don't you say something?"

Raising his head, Nakajyo looked at her with a slight smile. "You are a girl and don't understand what men think. I am four years older than you are and, though I may have suffered less, I think about things more than you realize. I have been a murderer for almost a year, but I dare say that I have not killed a single person. . . ."

"Humph! Nonsense! When you attacked Chongqing, Chengdu, Kunming, Guiyang, and other places in southwest China dropping your bombs, you didn't kill anyone? Do you mean you dropped your bombs in lakes and rivers?" Umeko cut him off before he had finished.

"Be careful. We would be in trouble if anyone heard us. Actually, that was exactly what I did. Every time I went on an air attack on Chongqing, I dropped my bombs in the Jialing River or else in the fields. I often flew very fast and quickly left my squad. Otherwise, I would not have been able to do this. If some running dog loyal to the Imperial Army reported on me, would I be alive today?"

"Let me ask you something. Tell me frankly, do you often feel depressed about such a life?" asked Umeko, holding his head with her hands as a child does.

Nakajyo kissed her little mouth lightly and answered, "That is why I said you are still a child and don't understand me. When I first learned to fly, it was purely out of interest and because I wished to be like a bird, flying in the sky day and night, going wherever I pleased. I also admired professional pilots traveling everywhere and hoped that someday I too could fly around the world. After graduation, the air force sent me to China as a fighter pilot. Later I became a machine gunner on a bomber. But my machine gun has never hurt anybody, only strafed the clouds in the sky."

"Hmm, only strafed some clouds in the sky, what nice words! You mean to say you didn't wound any Chinese?" the troublemaker Umeko challenged Nakajyo again.

"Yes, I gunned down some clouds in the sky. Since I flew at such a high altitude and shot upward, there's no way I ever harmed anybody."

"If you were shot down by a Chinese plane, would you be happy?"

"If they didn't hurt me, of course I would be happy. But since we always execute Chinese prisoners, they'd do the same to me if I were taken prisoner."

"No, they wouldn't. The Chinese are a peace-loving nation, unlike we who are so bloodthirsty and murderous. Since the start of the war, they have captured many of our soldiers and have never hurt any one of them. On the contrary, they treat their prisoners very well."

"Yes, I have also heard many soldiers say that those who opposed the war voluntarily surrendered to the Chinese, taking their weapons along with them. However—" Nakajyo paused abruptly. His eyes turned to the bright and clear moon as though there were some unspeakable bitterness in his heart; then he looked down at their two reflections on the lake.

"However what? Darling Nakajyo, don't you think the right thing to do is to surrender?"

"It's not that it is not the right thing, but it would be humiliating. And besides, the Chinese soldiers bitterly despise us, and I'd be a fool to get myself shot to death."

"Nakajyo, don't keep thinking about death. In fact, they would never shoot you. I wish you would launch an antiwar movement and persuade other fellow air force officers to drop their bombs on top of the Japanese warlords, especially on those important military positions and important military and political headquarters."

"It's not as easy as you think. It would be very hard to persuade air force officers to surrender. For one thing, they enjoy political favors and comfortable lives, and they would not risk their lives to surrender. For another, they have their families to consider . . ."

"And? Why don't you continue?" Umeko thought it strange that Nakajyo had suddenly stopped talking. A dark shadow disappeared from the grove to the left.

"It is late, Umeko. Let me see you home. We can talk tomorrow." Nakajyo signaled to her with his eyes. Knowing that someone was approaching, she quickly stood up, smoothing her light blue silk dress that had gotten crumpled from sitting, and felt an unknown melancholy.

"Did someone overhear our conversation?" she asked as they went out of the park gate.

"I think so. Just now I saw someone's shadow in the grove, the shadow of a woman."

"A woman? That doesn't matter; she might have been on a date and would not have taken notice of what we were saying." Nakajyo saw Umeko back to the Fu'an Inn. When she opened the door, she did not see Kieko. As her bed curtain had been put down, she assumed Kieko had gone to the restroom, and poured a cup of water for Nakajyo before seeing him off downstairs.

Then Kieko came back with an irritated look on her face.

"Hi, Kieko-san, back so late? Where have you been?" Umeko asked, sitting on her bed.

"Don't you know? I went to Zhongshan Park on a date with my lover!" As she shot Umeko a meaningful glance, her words were full of jealousy and envy.

"That's great! Congratulations!"

"What for? I'm in love with Nakajyo, but he loves another girl."

"Who would that be? Who?"

"That is what I was going to ask you. Only you would know."

Umeko giggled. To calm Kieko down, she pulled her over to sit next to her on the bed and said, "Kieko-san, I should tell you that the love of a man is nothing to depend on. They just chase whoever is young and pretty. What is there to be jealous about?"

Kieko, just like a mute who, having swallowed bitter medicine, cannot speak of it, forced a smile, then threw herself on Umeko's bed and fell asleep.

VI

THE POWER OF love! Sometimes a mere word from a lover can be more effective than an emperor's edict. As expected, Nakajyo excused himself on the pretext of sickness from the bombing raid on Chongqing. This, however, aroused Captain Inukai's suspicions. On top of that, Kieko had overheard their conversation the other night. She had gone to the park out of jealousy, but ended up hearing their most important secret, which she then reported to Captain Inukai. The captain assigned her the task of spying on Umeko, who, thinking that it was just that they both loved the same man, never suspected that their lives were now in Kieko's hands.

Nakajyo rushed upstairs in a panic two nights later and, seeing that Umeko was alone, whispered to her, "It's not good, Umeko. Someone overheard our conversation the other night, and they've assigned people to follow us. It looks like we cannot stay here safely any longer; they will come for us anytime. We'd better get ready quickly and defect to the other side when the Chinese troops launch their attack!"

"How will we rendezvous?"

"We won't necessarily go together. According to the intelligence, three thousand Chinese guerrillas will come by boat from Changhu to attack Shashi tonight at midnight. Once we hear the gunshots, we will disguise ourselves as refugees and sneak to the front. There I can join the marines . . . thus to join the Chinese army, by voluntarily getting captured." Nakajyo whispered the few words in the middle very softly, cupping his hands at Umeko's ear.

After she heard this, Umeko was so elated that she almost burst into tears. "In the Chinese army, we can live a peaceful and humane life and take part in resistance." But just then her words were cut short by Kieko and a man, who laughed as they entered the room.

The man was Yokozo, who had been ordered by Captain Inukai to tail Nakajyo.

Yokozo said, "What a lucky fellow you are, Nakajyo-san, catching the beautiful Umeko. When do we get to attend your wedding banquet?" The muscles of his ferocious face twitched with his smile.

"Well, we can treat you to wine tonight." Nakajyo purposefully walked up to Kieko and said to her, "Can we also have the honor of your company, Kieko-san?"

"My pleasure! How could I pass up good wine!" Kieko faked a flirtatious manner and shamelessly nestled in Yokozo's arms.

Umeko also joked, "Kieko-san, when can we attend *your* wedding banquet?"

"Well, tonight, too!"

The four of them, in different moods, entered the just-opened New Asia Restaurant. Strangely, it was not as noisy and busy as usual, with only a dozen soldiers drinking in silence, and there had been very few pedestrians on the streets as well. It was as though something terrible was about to befall the city.

Nakajyo was quick to realize why Yokozo had suddenly turned up at such a moment. He had figured it all out and nudged Umeko with his knee, reminding her of their plan that night.

Among the four of them, besides the happy couple Nakajyo and Umeko, Yokozo was in love with Umeko, and Kieko was in love with Nakajyo. They took advantage of the situation to get Yokozo and Kieko drunk.

Like a thunderbolt on a clear day, gunshots suddenly rang out outside the town and came closer and closer. Zhongshan Road was immediately thrown into turmoil, with cars, motorcycles, and panicking crowds stampeding . . . all filling the street. Nakajyo and Umeko took advantage of the situation and rushed out of town to join the fighting troops.

The news that the guerrillas had attacked the city in the night and taken two prisoners spread throughout the Imperial Army in the area surrounding Wuhan, Yichang, and Shashi. They all wondered how Nakajyo and the famous beauty Umeko could have suddenly disappeared. How could Nakajyo, an air force pilot, end up in the marines? What was even more unimaginable, someone saw him firing his pistol at his own officer. He fell down later, wounded, of course.

One day, Yokozo accidentally leaked the secret: "Nakajyo and Umeko were antiwar activists and they deliberately surrendered to the Chinese." Within twenty-four hours, he was put to death by a bullet from Captain Inukai's pistol. Kieko, also a suspect, was sent to jail.

VII

NAKAJYO HAD LONG been nursed back to health by the Chinese army. Umeko looked after him the whole time, giving him great comfort and pleasure.

He said, "Thank you for giving me the courage, Umeko. For a year I had dreamed of surrendering in order to work alongside the Chinese army, but the dream was always defeated by the thought of death. It is only now that I realize that the Chinese are a great and peace-loving people. Someday, Umeko, let's get married in China!"

"That would be wonderful! Now I have no relatives back home except my uncle and aunt. Let's never return to Japan!" With tears of happiness, she clasped his hands tightly.

Three months later. . . .

They had both been sent to Laohekou. Because he had served in the Japanese air force and she was a valiant antiwar activist, the Chinese field commander personally interviewed them and expressed his deep admiration for their understanding of justice and for their struggle for true freedom and peace between China and Japan in East Asia. The commander also instructed Major Lee of the Korean Volunteers Brigade to enroll them to work there. And ever since, there have been two more brave fighters in our anti-Japanese force.

6
Yang Jiang
(B. 1911)

An exceptional comic voice in modern Chinese literature, Yang Jiang was born in Beijing in 1911. She was an avid reader in school and even taught herself Spanish in college; later she went on to do graduate work in European literature at Qinghua University. In the summer of 1935, she married the acclaimed novelist Qian Zhongshu (1910–1998), then a fellow graduate student, and shortly thereafter the couple went abroad to pursue advanced literary study, first at Oxford University and later at the Sorbonne in Paris. Apprehensive about the prospect of war breaking out in Europe and about the welfare of their families back home, Yang Jiang and Qian Zhongshu set sail on a French ocean liner bound for China in November 1938. Qian disembarked in Hong Kong and headed west to Kunming to take up a teaching position in the foreign languages program of United Southwest University, a coalition of universities from the Beijing–Tianjin area that merged during the war. Yang Jiang continued on to Shanghai to care for her elderly father, who had taken refuge in the French Concession. Yang accepted a post as school principal of the new campus of her *alma mater,* the Zhenhua High School for Girls, but the school was forced to shut down when the Japanese annexed the International Settlement at the beginning of the Pacific War in 1941. It was around this time that noted playwright and critic Li Jianwu, who remained active in the flourishing Shanghai theater world after the Japanese invasion, encouraged her to try her hand at drama. The result was four well-crafted plays written between 1942 and 1946, beginning with two European-style comedies of manners, *As You Desire* and *Forging the Truth.* Li was reportedly so impressed by the quality of Yang's maiden play that he personally arranged for director Huang Zuolin to stage its production at the Shanghai Golden Capital Theater, and even signed on to play the role of Xu Langzhai himself. But he was even more enthusiastic about *Forging the Truth,* the five-act play Yang Jiang completed the following year, writing in a review at the time that it marked a milestone in modern Chinese literature, second only to the comedies of Ding Xilin (1893–1974). Indeed, despite the fact that she was a virtual novice as a playwright, Yang Jiang's *As You Desire* and *Forging the Truth* were both box-office hits when they debuted in 1943 and 1944, respectively, and were soon available in print form both in a single volume and in the multivolume compendium of Shanghai drama put together by Kong Lingjing.

Forging the Truth, translated here, pokes fun at modern romance, subtly subverting the classic May Fourth associations among free love, truth, and freedom. An apparently eminently eligible bachelor woos the spoiled daughter of a rich Shanghai businessman, only to be tricked into marriage by her clever cousin Yanhua; in the end, though, it is the clever cousin who is deceived. The fast-moving repartee, the cast of comic characters, and the relentless reminders of the power of money within capitalist culture make for a representation of modern gender relations that is at once entertaining and incisive.

After 1949, Yang Jiang and Qian Zhongshu reportedly declined offers from the University of Hong Kong and Oxford to teach abroad, electing instead to return to Beijing to join the faculty of Qinghua University. Eventually they would become research fellows at the Chinese Academy of Social Sciences, where today Yang Jiang remains a fellow at the Institute of Foreign Literature. During the early post–'49 period, Yang Jiang devoted much of her scholarly attention to translation projects, though her comic predilections remained in evidence. Her most famous translations include *La Vida de Lazarillo de Tormes,* which was published in 1951, and Cervantes' masterpiece, *Don Quixote de la Mancha.* She had completed much of the work on the latter by the mid-fifties, though not until some twenty years later did her eight-volume translation of the novel make its way into print (1978). Unfortunately, despite Yang Jiang's own self-censorship and her cautious measures to steer clear of politically sensitive intellectual and literary projects, she was not immune from political persecution. In 1958, she was forced to undergo a brief re-education program on the outskirts of Beijing, and she was again a target during the Cultural Revolution. Her punishment for being a "bourgeois scholar" was to be assigned the task of cleaning the toilets at the institute where she had previously worked as a researcher. Between 1970 and 1972, she was relocated to a so-called "cadre school" and forced to undertake manual labor on a state farm in the Henan countryside. It was not until the post–Mao era that she resumed her creative writing. Among her most important works from this period are her 1981 memoir of her personal experience during the Cultural Revolution, *Six Chapters from My Life Down Under,* which employs wry humor to capture the tragic banality of that misguided chapter in modern Chinese history, and a satirical novel, *Taking a Bath* (1988), which depicts the travails of intellectuals coping with the successive political campaigns of the immediate postliberation era. Most recently, she has published a best-selling autobiography that focuses on her family life entitled *We Three* (2003).

Forging the Truth

(1944)

Cast of Main Characters

ZHOU DAZHANG—a young man courting Miss Zhang Wanru but in love with her cousin Miss Zhang Yanhua

ZHANG WANRU—the spoiled daughter of a wealthy Shanghai capitalist

ZHANG YANHUA—Wanru's cousin, who lives with the Zhangs

ZHANG XIANGFU—a wealthy capitalist; Wanru's protective father

ZHANG YUANFU—Yanhua's father; older brother of Zhang Xiangfu

LADY ZHANG—the wife of Zhang Xiangfu and Wanru's mother

FENG GUANGZU—Lady Zhang's nephew, a pedantic scholar in love with Yanhua

MOTHER—Zhou Dazhang's mother, an elderly widow

SISTER—Zhou Dazhang's sister

ZHOU SHIKUI—Zhou Dazhang's (paternal) uncle

AUNT—the mother-in-law of Zhou Dazhang's sister; also their maternal aunt

AHMA YANG—a servant at the Zhang residence

LIU SHUN—a servant at the Zhang residence

Act I

Setting: Zhang Xiangfu's parlor, which is sumptuously furnished. ZHANG WANRU *is overcome with boredom as she sits on the sofa flipping through a pictorial magazine. The phone rings.*

ZHANG WANRU (*picking up the phone*): *Wei,* the Zhang residence. You wish to speak to Mr. Zhang Xiangfu? Oh! It's you! (*laughing*) Dad's not home! Calm down! Mr. Zhang Xiangfu is not at home! He's not here! I'm waiting for you! Hurry, hurry, hurry! Fly like a bird! I'll give you three minutes. No way, more than five minutes and I'll really be mad! Hurry, hurry, hurry! I'm waiting for you! (*Hanging up the phone, she laughs and takes out the love letter folded in her book. She reads it over and over again, then heaves a long sigh as she tosses it aside, and walks over to the window. Pulling open the curtains, she looks out*) (ZHANG XIANGFU *is hiding outside the door spying on* WANRU. WANRU *again sighs and goes back to sit on the sofa. She folds the letter back into her book, then stands in front of the oval mirror hanging on the wall and adjusts her hair. She turns around to admire herself, smiles in the mirror, and poses. Suddenly she turns around and sees her father*)

WANRU (*surprised*): Daddy!

ZHANG XIANGFU (*entering the room*): Wanru, whom were you expecting?

WANRU: Whom was I expecting? I'm not expecting anyone!

XIANGFU: When I speak to you, Wanru, don't play dumb! I am not joking with you.

WANRU: I know that!

XIANGFU: Do you? Just now someone here was fixing her hair, gazing in the mirror, turning her head, and giggling. What was all that for, then?

WANRU (*pouting*): Daddy, you're horrible! You're horrible! Why, I was just looking in the mirror—everyone looks at themselves in the mirror. . . .

XIANGFU: Oh, then why did you look in the mirror, then look out the window and sigh?

WANRU: No reason. I was reading.

XIANGFU: That's right, I saw you reading something. Take it out and show me, what were you reading?

WANRU (*quickly putting the book under her arm*): It's homework.

XIANGFU: Not bad, so your love letter has transformed itself into legitimate homework! Take it out and show me.

WANRU: I haven't got it.

XIANGFU: You haven't what? What?

WANRU: I don't have what you just said.

XIANGFU: Wanru, I said take it out!

WANRU (*hugging the book*): I haven't got it.

XIANGFU: Do you hear me? Take it out! (*grabbing the book*)

WANRU: I *don't* have it.

XIANGFU: Wanru! (*tugs at the book, causing Wanru to fall down and cry*) Silly girl, what's the matter now?

WANRU (*crying*): That hurt.

XIANGFU (*consoling her*): I was trying to talk to you, but you wouldn't listen.

WANRU (*whimpering*): I don't have it . . .

XIANGFU: If you don't, then so be it. But I'm warning you, if you say you're not waiting for anyone, you'd better not be waiting for anyone! Starting now, I'm going to sit right here—I won't move an inch—and wait for whomever it is you're waiting for!

WANRU (*pouting*): Go ahead and wait! (*wiping away her tears, she picks up the book and dashes out of the room*)

XIANGFU (*laughing, he sits down. Loudly*): Yanhua! My slippers! (*takes off coat and shoes.* ZHANG YANHUA, *who is fashionably dressed, enters with his slippers*)

YANHUA: Third Uncle. (*bending down to put on his slippers, she takes his leather shoes and is about to exit*)

XIANGFU: Where's your third aunt?

YANHUA: Dunno. (*exiting, she collides with* LADY ZHANG)

LADY ZHANG: Yanhua, I told you to fetch his slippers . . .

YANHUA: I did. (*exits*)

LADY ZHANG: You're back? Why don't you go upstairs and get changed?

XIANGFU: I am not going to move an inch if I have to sit here for half the day.

LADY ZHANG: Are you tired? Why don't you go lie down for a while?

XIANGFU: I am not in the least bit tired. Have Ahma Yang make me some dim sum.

LADY ZHANG (*toward the door*): Ahma Yang, when the dim sum are warmed, serve them out here, the master has returned. (*to* XIANGFU) Didn't you say you wouldn't be back until this evening?

XIANGFU: Who says I can't come back a little earlier?

LADY ZHANG (*laughing*): What? Did the deal on Herder Road go through?

XIANGFU: All 1,800,000 *yuan* worth. I came back to relax. This evening I'm going out to celebrate.

LADY ZHANG: 1,800,000! For such a tiny bit of land!

XIANGFU: It's a building site! It's not for anything else! It's a sure bet! The location couldn't be better, and it's certain to appreciate in value.

LADY ZHANG: What about that house on Jing'an Temple Road?

XIANGFU: The Honghe corporation is willing to put up 3,000,000; Old Wang has agreed to 3,500,000. We'll see . . . (AHMA YANG *enters with the dim sum*) What's this?

AHMA YANG: The tree ears aren't soft enough yet, so this is the leftover bean soup with seeds of Job's tears that the young masters didn't finish. (*exits*)

LADY ZHANG: We weren't expecting you home at this hour.

XIANGFU: Obviously.

LADY ZHANG: What?

XIANGFU: Am I blind? You were all expecting someone else! I'm telling you: if Zhou Dazhang shows up, tell him I'm not home, tell him no one's home, and don't let him in the house.

LADY ZHANG: Did you see him at the door?

XIANGFU: I saw Wanru waiting for him.

LADY ZHANG: How do you know that she was waiting for him?

XIANGFU: How could I not know? (*stands up*) Look! (*imitating* WANRU *looking in the mirror*) This is our Wanru! Why else would she be doing this? If she wasn't waiting for Zhou Dazhang, then who was she waiting for?

LADY ZHANG (*smiling*): Good gracious! Fine father you are, the longer you live the more old-fashioned and inflexible you become! In this day and age, how can things be the way they used to be back then?

XIANGFU: Inflexible! I am the most flexible kind of man there is! These days, how could things possibly be the way they used to be?

LADY ZHANG: Indeed. Back then, so many of my cousins had just started clamoring for women's equality and free love.

XIANGFU: Back then, it was advantageous for women to be free and equal. But these days, freedom and equality don't pay off for them.

LADY ZHANG: That's news to me.

XIANGFU: If we waited around for you to get wind of things, it would be too late for anything. In all matters, time is of the essence. How could I wait for you to hear about anything? If I waited for you to find out which property had appreciated and which had depreciated before I sold or bought anything, would I ever make any money?

LADY ZHANG: Who said anything about business?

XIANGFU: It's the same principle as in business. Nobody engages in things that aren't profitable!

LADY ZHANG: We're letting Wanru make a new friend, not run off with someone. What loss will you possibly incur?

XIANGFU: If she runs away, what loss will *I* incur? I am assessing the situation on behalf of our daughter. These days, insisting on all that female equality stuff doesn't pay off even for girls themselves. Before, it was just rhetoric: "emancipated" and "equal" women like you in fact did nothing more than sit in your parlors being housewives, while the ones out earning a living were still us men. But nowadays people are taking it seriously. Girls are expected to be just like men and go out and earn a living too. But how can men and women be equal when women still bear the responsibility of pregnancy and child rearing?

LADY ZHANG: Oh! So you're saying all this for our benefit, are you?

XIANGFU: Am I wrong? If I were a woman, I would be happy to be one of those old-fashioned young ladies who doesn't have to worry about dating and finding a husband but instead simply lets her parents marry her off. If I weren't satisfied with the match, I could then blame it on my parents and lament my bitter fate. But a new-style girl doesn't even have these small advantages. If your husband turns out bad, who can you blame for having fallen blindly in love? If he breaks your tooth, you might as well swallow it! As for freedom—I'm more concerned about financial security. If I were someone's daughter, I would allow my parents to select my husband and negotiate the terms for me, because then I couldn't lose.

LADY ZHANG: Oh? So in your opinion women these days would be better off submitting to the Three Obediences and the Four Virtues![1]

XIANGFU: Only obedient and virtuous women wind up with good husbands! Who would want to be a "newfangled parlor *taitai*" like you, who thinks all men are worthless and has ten things to say for every one thing he says?

LADY ZHANG: Well, well, well, listen to you, aren't you the one making the speech here? I haven't said more than half a sentence!

XIANGFU: If I were a woman, I would be perfectly happy to follow the Three Obediences and Four Virtues! Let the man go out to make all the money and do all the thinking, I'd be happy to be the servile little wife.

LADY ZHANG: You just wait until I die. Then you can go find yourself an obedient and virtuous wife.

XIANGFU: My word, women can't be reasoned with! Here I am trying to discuss the most significant event of our daughter's life, and she insists on bringing herself into it.

LADY ZHANG: Oh! And you call yourself a reasonable man! Weren't you insinuating that *I* don't obey you?

XIANGFU: You *don't* obey me! I'm telling you: if Zhou Dazhang comes over, tell him no one is at home, and don't let him come in.

LADY ZHANG: What's the point of offending him?

XIANGFU: If you offend him, it's easier to tell him not to call on us.

LADY ZHANG: Why tell him not to call on us?

---

[1] The Three Obediences refers to the Confucian precept whereby a woman should obey her father before marriage, her husband during marriage, and her son in old age. The Four Virtues refers to the "feminine" virtues of morality, proper speech, proper conduct, and diligent work.

XIANGFU: Why do you want him to call on us?

LADY ZHANG: He is the scion of an old scholarly family and the young master of a rich household. He studied abroad, he earned a doctorate, he's young, he's handsome, yet you still don't approve of him?

XIANGFU: You listen to me. We don't know whether he's from a good family or not, or whether he is rich or not, or whether he's well-educated or not. I have been asking around, and nobody knows much about him. He's basically an unknown product with a new brand name, and such business is not reliable.

LADY ZHANG: Now who said anything about business?

XIANGFU: The same logic applies. If you stock your shop with brand-new products that you got on discount, it's plausible that you'll make a profit, but the risk involved is too great. There's no shortage of boys in our family, so in the future they can choose their own wives; but Wanru is our one and only daughter, and thus when I select a son-in-law, it has got to be a reliable transaction, not some act of wild speculation.

LADY ZHANG: Who's asking you to speculate? Zhou Dazhang doesn't have a single friend who isn't famous; and as for his relatives, we've heard of them too. Why don't you just take the time to make some inquiries?

XIANGFU: My dear wife, we are not acquainted with the people he knows. And those relatives of his, we have only heard their names and thus couldn't possibly go around to their houses asking for details. He's just a casual acquaintance of Yanhua's, but you have taken such a fancy to him! We have just one daughter. Can you afford to make her bear the responsibility of taking such a risk?

LADY ZHANG: I'm not telling you to rush out and marry her off to him; take your time to ask around. . . .

XIANGFU: Take my time! Take my time! These days, how can we take time over anything? Take that piece of property over in the Bund, it now costs 5,000,000, but a just day ago it was only 3,000,000! And what about those two dozen towels you bought? If you had bought them a month ago, wouldn't they have been half as cheap? Foreigners say "time is money." Can you afford to throw money away?

LADY ZHANG: You certainly are obsessed with business! In your mind, even marrying off our daughter and choosing a son-in-law is a business deal.

XIANGFU: What's the difference? When you take a fancy to some product that's a sure money maker, before you can bat an eyelid you've got to snatch it up. In today's market, how many girls are there waiting to get married? But how few quality sons-in-law there are! They all have 3 or 4 *yuan* in capital and think they can make a fortune of 300,000 or 400,000. Our Wanru is already 21 years old; do we have time to take things slowly and ask around?

LADY ZHANG: Didn't you just say we shouldn't take any risks? But now you can't wait long enough to make any inquiries! Why don't you just go ahead and throw our daughter away?

XIANGFU: Listen carefully: it's when something's a sure bet that you can't take your time and miss the opportunity altogether.

LADY ZHANG: And do you have a sure bet?

XIANGFU: Not me, you.

LADY ZHANG: Who?

XIANGFU: Indeed! It's just like when you ladies go out shopping—you see all those colorful and pretty things and you completely forget about what you actually came to buy. Whether your eyes are open or shut, all you see is one Zhou Dazhang, Zhou Dazhang, and you've clean forgotten about your very own nephew, who lives in our very own home and whom you see every single day!

LADY ZHANG: You mean Feng Guangzu? Him?

XIANGFU: Him! What about him? Isn't he the young master of a scholarly family? Don't I know enough about your family? You want a scholarly family, isn't that a scholarly family through and through!

LADY ZHANG: Well, of course, he's a fine fellow, but . . .

XIANGFU: But he's a little poor? Is that it? Not rich—well, he may not be rich, because you know his roots, but he comes from a good family.

LADY ZHANG: Wanru marrying a poor teacher . . .

XIANGFU: Is our Wanru afraid of not having money?

LADY ZHANG: But . . .

XIANGFU: But what? Guangzu has been abroad, and I was the one who put him on the ship and the one who met him when he returned, so isn't he an authentic foreign student? Furthermore, since we have watched him grow up, how can we not feel assured of his character?

LADY ZHANG: It's kind of you to praise my nephew, but Guangzu has taken a fancy to Yanhua, not Wanru.

XIANGFU: If he fancies Yanhua, how can he not fancy Wanru? Does a man who smokes Beauty brand cigarettes complain that Three Forts lack flavor? Is this a problem?

LADY ZHANG: Feng Guangzu (*shaking head*) . . . Surely our Wanru ought to be able to marry someone more handsome. . . .

XIANGFU (*slapping the table*): I am telling you, were it not for my motto of "reliability and speed," who knows where this family asset might have ended up!

In Shanghai there are men of all varieties! If all you care about is his looks, and randomly pick one, it's just like spending 10 or 20 *yuan* on a lottery ticket. The grand prize is 5,000,000 and tomorrow you'll hit the jackpot! But seriously, I have calculated this and it is an absolutely wise investment. I have taken a liking to Guangzu, so you go talk it over with him.

LADY ZHANG: And what shall I say? "Here, take our Wanru"?

XIANGFU: Who's telling you to say that? Completely ignoring your daughter's dignity! Just say that I have great respect for him and that he ought to get married. Then bring up him and Wanru together—you understand these sorts of tactics better than I do. (AHMA YANG *enters with a needle in one hand and three or four western-style shirts in the other*)

AHMA YANG: Madame, there's not a single button left on any of Young Master Feng's shirts. Tomorrow he's going to Suzhou for a wedding banquet, but how can he wear any of these?

LADY ZHANG: You sew some back on for him.

AHMA YANG: There's not a single button left, so what's there to sew back on? (*shouting out the door*) Master Feng, did you save the buttons that came off your shirts? (FENG GUANGZU *enters*)

FENG GUANGZU: Buttons? I didn't even notice. Uncle, you're back?

XIANGFU: Um. Guangzu, how does someone as skinny as you manage to pop off all their buttons?

AHMA YANG: I sewed them on tightly!

GUANGZU: Ahma Yang, as I have told you before, you must first research why these buttons keep falling off, for only when you discern the cause can you prevent such an outcome. Sewing them on tightly is no use. There are three reasons why buttons fall off: first, when you iron the shirt you destroy the thread; second, your stitches are too tight, so you ought to make the "neck" of the button longer; and third . . .

AHMA YANG: I have never seen a button with a long neck.

GUANGZU: Give me the needle and thread. I'll do it myself.

AHMA YANG: I don't have a single button. (*handing them over to* FENG)

LADY ZHANG (*loudly*): Yanhua! Yanhua! Bring me that plate of little mother-of-pearl buttons that's in the square paper box in my drawer!

GUANGZU: Ahma Yang, you may go now. Give me the shirts. (AHMA YANG *hands them to him and exits*)

LADY ZHANG (*impatiently*): Yanhua! Yanhua! (YANHUA *enters, hands over the plate of buttons without saying a word, and exits*)

LADY ZHANG: It's as if she's afraid someone's going to catch her and force her to do hard labor. Yanhua!

GUANGZU (*hurries to the door*): It's nothing, Yanhua, we didn't call you. (*to* LADY ZHANG) I can do it better myself. (*takes the shirts, sits by the window, and sews in the light*)

XIANGFU (*shaking head*): Guangzu, this is too pathetic, I can't stand to watch you. Ask Wanru to sew them on for you.

LADY ZHANG (*laughing*): Wanru is even less competent than he is. Give it here, let me see.

GUANGZU: None of you knows how. You have to make the "neck" longer, yet not too long. (*bends overs and sews*)

XIANGFU: Guangzu, as I was saying . . . (LIU SHUN *enters*)

LIU SHUN (*loudly*): Miss, Miss, Mr. Zhou Dazhang is here! (ZHOU DAZHANG *follows him in, sees* ZHANG XIANGFU, *and stops in surprise*)

ZHOU DAZHANG: Uncle, Aunt . . .[2]

XIANGFU (*coldly*): Mr. Zhou.

LADY ZHANG: Young Master Zhou! Won't you please sit down.

DAZHANG: It is unusual for Uncle to be home!

XIANGFU: I am not usually home, am I?

DAZHANG (*seeing* FENG): Oh, Mr. Feng.

GUANGZU (*stands up halfway*): Mr. Zhou.

DAZHANG: Pardon me for interrupting. Uncle, you've been busy recently!

XIANGFU: I've been busy recently, have I?

DAZHANG: Wherever I go, I hear people talking about you.

XIANGFU: About me?

DAZHANG: That's right.

LADY ZHANG: Master Zhou, please sit down. (DAZHANG *sits;* LIU SHUN *pours tea and exits*)

DAZHANG: Yesterday, an old friend invited me out—actually, he's not exactly a friend; his ancestors served as our accountants for generations—they lived well, they got rich; the son purchased an office, so now the grandson is suddenly a wealthy young gentleman too. I myself have never been inclined to accept social invitations. If you attend one banquet, then it often turns into a dozen—but if I don't attend, then people take offense and say that I look down upon them. What am I to do? I have to go. However, I didn't expect that yesterday I would run into quite a few close acquaintances—Ma Zhenbin, the manager of the Huimin factory—does Uncle know him?

XIANGFU: I have heard of him.

---

[2] These are polite forms of address. Dazhang is not related to Mr. and Mrs. Zhang.

DAZHANG: Chen Zihe, one of the top-ranking industrialists today . . .

GUANGZU: I met that fellow once when I was abroad.

DAZHANG: Is Mr. Feng well acquainted with him?

GUANGZU: I don't know him, I just met him once.

DAZHANG: What a formidable man he is! Minister Qian used to say that in the world of industry there are only two truly promising talents: one is Chen Zihe—who thinks rather highly of himself, and he doesn't easily praise others; but he is kind to me, and is always asking when I can help him—he also has tremendous respect for Uncle. . . .

XIANGFU: He knows who I am?

DAZHANG: Well, he doesn't often think highly of other people, but he doesn't let anyone slip by him either. As for someone as talented as Uncle, of course he takes notice.

XIANGFU: What did he say about me?

DAZHANG: Everyone was talking about you. There was also Yu Fei, the manager of Zhen Xing, and Chairman Lin of the Chamber of Commerce—do you know him, Uncle?

XIANGFU: Never heard of him.

DAZHANG: A truly slick fellow who can get around any situation—except once even he got into a jam. For all his slickness, he's a bit of a coward, and hates offending people. Once he came up against a dead end and I was the one who helped him out. . . .

LADY ZHANG: What happened?

DAZHANG: It's a long story about all the jockeying for power that goes on, which would surely bore Aunt. Oh, Uncle, how about this fellow? Ye Jiazhen of the Silver Star Factory . . .

XIANGFU: Never heard of . . . (WANRU *pokes her head up in the window and calls to* DAZHANG, *who doesn't hear her*)

DAZHANG: He's the one who brought you up first.

XIANGFU: Ye who?

DAZHANG: Uncle, let them go ahead and know who we are, but why should we have to get to know every single one of them?

XIANGFU: What did they say about me?

DAZHANG: They were discussing an important matter and saying if only Zhang Xiangfu would join, for he alone would do.

XIANGFU (*nodding head*): Hm, what sort of venture is it?

DAZHANG: They want to pool their capital and open some bank.

GUANGZU (*stops sewing and raises his head*): Such a peculiar phenomenon these days, everyone's opening banks.

XIANGFU: I never pool my capital.

DAZHANG: I heard them say that capital wasn't the issue. It's that there is no one else with the vision, technique, courage, or innate luck of Uncle.

XIANGFU: Ha, ha, ha. It's true, perfectly true! But I have made up my mind never to pool my capital with others.

DAZHANG: And your decision couldn't be more correct. Didn't I once hear that Uncle wanted to build a pharmaceutical factory? It had only one owner and generated gobs of money. But then because that manager suddenly died . . .

XIANGFU: For me, my first motto is reliability and the second is speed. I don't get involved in things I know nothing about.

DAZHANG: Uncle, you are too modest! Why, you could do anything! Just the other day—I was over at the Liu residence, the Liu who has long been the governor of Zhejiang and Jiangsu provinces, an old friend of the family. That day I was at his house, several Shanghai big shots were discussing plans to establish a university, and they said that they wanted to invite you to serve as chairman of the board. . . .

XIANGFU: Ask me! Ha, ha, I would never fall for that! They just want to trick me into bankrolling it.

DAZHANG: Yes, that's why I didn't say anything when I heard it. Uncle, I'm afraid that when a man becomes famous, then everyone comes looking for him!

XIANGFU: Ha, ha, ha, but if he had the ability to get famous in the first place, then he should have the ability not to fall for such traps. (DAZHANG *sees* WAN-RU, *who is outside the window gesticulating that she has waited for a long time. Points at* ZHANG XIANGFU *as if to say, "Daddy's in there, so I don't dare come in" and "and I'm getting impatient."* DAZHANG *makes furtive response*)

LADY ZHANG: What's the name of their university? Have they already hired the faculty? What are the salaries like? Does Young Master Zhou know?

DAZHANG (*quickly*): Whom did Aunt have in mind for a position? No problem, just get me a copy of his resume.

XIANGFU (*patting* GUANGZU *on the shoulder*): Splendid, wait until I'm chairman of the board, Guangzu, and you won't even need to copy your resume, I'll ask you to be the president of the school. Ha, ha, ha, I'll ask you to be the school president!

GUANGZU: President . . . only someone as talented as Mr. Zhou would be qualified for that.

DAZHANG: To tell you the truth, Uncle, I have never been interested in fame. Take the insurance company I now run. It started out with me helping a friend, helping him delegate assignments, doing his writing, more or less being his secretary. Then he decided he was only interested in the stock market, and so he turned everything over to me. I told him I wasn't too keen on being the manager, but he said I had already been the manager for some time. I said that if he forced me, I would resign. . . .

LADY ZHANG: Being a manager isn't so bad.

DAZHANG: Aunt, don't laugh at me. This is precisely my ambition! Whatever kind of work I do, Uncle, I am absolutely unwilling to do it half-heartedly. I put my entire heart and soul into it—so now I have become the manager of a company with my heart and soul! (*shakes his head with mock disdain.* WANRU *is outside the window imitating him, laughing,* DAZHANG *secretly gestures to her.* ZHANG XIANGFU *suddenly appears to have noticed, and* WANRU *swiftly hides*)

LADY ZHANG (*laughing*): The young Master Zhou ought to become an official.

DAZHANG: Aunt can't be serious. If I had wanted a career for purely selfish gain, I could have become an official and made a fortune. Even before I returned from overseas, my friends in Nanjing sent me a letter urging me to come back home.[3] Had I wanted to be an official, would I still be waiting around today?

LADY ZHANG: The young Master Zhou's disposition is too noble for politics and material considerations.

DAZHANG: To be perfectly honest with you, Aunt, young men tend to be rather idealistic—wasn't Uncle once this way himself? (XIANGFU *is glaring out the window*) If a person's ideals are too lofty and he sees how far apart this unfair world is from the ideal world of his dreams, how can he possibly bear it and get along with other people! (*shakes head and sighs*) I ought to be able to transform my environment, for I am the master of my environment. Mr. Feng, isn't that so? (WANRU, *outside the window, sticks out her tongue and pats her chest as if to say "That scared me to death! He nearly saw me."*)

GUANGZU: But one must first research the causes of social injustice, and one ought to research this from several points of view. First . . .

DAZHANG: Indeed. (*motions silently toward the window*) If a man wants to pursue something worthwhile, he ought to study it from every possible angle. I'd rather be an insignificant peon than some official! Once you're an official, you become divorced from reality and the masses, and lose touch with the people.

---

[3]The Nationalist government established Nanjing as the capital of China in 1928.

LADY ZHANG: But really, Young Master Zhou, your ancestors have been officials for generations. . . .

DAZHANG: What! Aunt, who said so? A real man, a true man, conquers the world on his own. If he has to carry around a placard announcing his ancestral legacy in order to accomplish anything, then he's got no hope. As for myself, I am not interested in the fact that my ancestors were officials of some sort, and I have certainly never advertised my ancestral heritage. (WANRU *again pokes her head up.* ZHANG XIANGFU *is standing angrily at the window*) Of course, being filial to one's parents is quite another matter.

LADY ZHANG: As for Young Master Zhou's family, are your father and mother still living?

DAZHANG: My father passed away a long time ago, and ever since I was little my uncle brought me up in the strictest manner: everything I said or did had to conform to the words of the Classics. For instance, because of the rule "When one's parents are living, do not travel afar," they did not approve of me going abroad, and because of the custom "There are three unfilial acts, and not leaving descendants is the foremost," they forced me to marry a young lady of equal social and economic status.

LADY ZHANG: Young Master Zhou is already married?

DAZHANG (*laughing*): Heavens no! I would have to agree to that myself. Had I left it up to them to manipulate my life, seventeen or eighteen ladies would already have been escorted in through the door!

LADY ZHANG (*laughs*): So now they don't interfere anymore.

DAZHANG: Hm, I couldn't allow them to be my masters! Of course, that means I haven't any ready-made fortune either, so I have to depend on myself. (WANRU *pokes up her head and mouths "Be careful!"* ZHANG XIANGFU *notices* DAZHANG *and sees* WANRU *outside the window. He is furious*)

LADY ZHANG: Your mother doesn't worry about you?

DAZHANG: My mother is an extraordinary lady. She is both talented and knowledgeable. It was she who supported my decision to go abroad to study—my maternal grandfather, just like Uncle Xiangfu, always had a good reputation in the business world—in many respects, her character is a lot like yours, Aunt.

LADY ZHANG: How could I ever compare to her?

GUANGZU (*stands up, shaking the shirts*): Preposterous!

LADY ZHANG: What's wrong?

GUANGZU: All my efforts are completely wasted! I sewed the button on the wrong side of my shirt!

XIANGFU: Guangzu, go ask Wanru to do it for you.

GUANGZU: Wanru?

XIANGFU: Tell her to sew them for you, and tell her I said so.

DAZHANG: Mr. Feng has been sewing!

XIANGFU: This is Wanru's work. (*pushes* FENG *out, who takes the needle and thread and the shirts with him; exits*)

DAZHANG (*smiling*): Your daughter is quite accomplished.

XIANGFU: Hm. (*to wife*) Hey, have my shoes been polished yet? I still have to go out.

LADY ZHANG (*shouting out the door*): Ahma Yang!

XIANGFU: Go ask Yanhua, she took them. (LADY ZHANG *exits*)

DAZHANG: Do you have business to attend to, Uncle?

XIANGFU: Ah, I still have to go out! For dinner . . . but I should get there a little early, because there's something I need to discuss. (*looking at watch*) Not to worry, it's not late. Yanhua! My shoes! Hurry up!

DAZHANG (*standing up*): Shall I accompany you out, Uncle?

XIANGFU: Fine! We'll go together—Yanhua!

DAZHANG (*smiling*): Uncle, when you say you'll do something, you really do it. (YANHUA *brings the shoes in and, without acknowledging* DAZHANG, *changes* ZHANG XIANGFU's *shoes for him*)

XIANGFU (*looking at watch*): Let's go.

DAZHANG: Let's go—shouldn't we say good-bye to Aunt?

XIANGFU: You needn't be so polite, let's go. (*to* YANHUA) We're off! (DAZHANG *and* ZHANG XIANGFU *exit.* YANHUA *looks out the window, laughs coldly at* DAZHANG's *back, exits.* ZHANG XIANGFU *reenters*)

XIANGFU: Ha, ha, ha, ha! (LADY ZHANG *enters*)

LADY ZHANG: Where's Zhou Dazhang?

XIANGFU: I saw him off!

LADY ZHANG: How did you see him off?

XIANGFU: He walked out the door with me—what could be better than that? As we were getting on the bus, I said I had forgotten something and told him to go on ahead. Ha, ha, I'm going upstairs to rest for a while!

LADY ZHANG: Have you no shame?

XIANGFU: What is there to be ashamed of? I even saw him off!

LADY ZHANG: And he didn't see through this?

XIANGFU: I wish! (*loudly*) Liu Shun! (LIU SHUN *enters*)

XIANGFU: If Zhou Dazhang comes back, tell him I'm not home, that nobody's home.

LIU SHUN: Yes, sir! (*exits*)

LADY ZHANG: I don't understand your point—even if you don't want him for your son-in-law, must you be so rude?

XIANGFU (*indignantly*): Shall we allow him to come and make eyes with our Wanru through the window . . .

LADY ZHANG: What? You're being paranoid again. Wanru is upstairs.

XIANGFU: I saw her with my very own eyes.

LADY ZHANG: Well, even if it were true, so what? In my opinion, this man has a tremendous future ahead of him. He really will become the minister of finance!

XIANGFU: What minister of finance?

LADY ZHANG: A fortune-teller predicted that he'll become the minister of finance, and that all the money in the country will flow through his fingers.

XIANGFU: Tut tut, Zhou Dazhang said so himself?

LADY ZHANG: A fortune-teller said so—once Mr. Zhou brought up the subject of fortune-telling and said that he didn't believe in such things, but if the fortune-teller's words were on the mark, then someday he would become the minister of finance.

XIANGFU: Would he really do it?

LADY ZHANG: He really would, and he would even recognize you! So don't set your sights too close to home!

XIANGFU: You listen to me: if you make the advertisement too large, you might have to sell your merchandise at a discount. And if you want a loan, you first have to secure credit with hard goods. . . .

LADY ZHANG (*angry*): Business! Commodities! My daughter is not some object for sale! (LIU SHUN *enters*)

LIU SHUN: Sir, Mr. Zhou Dazhang . . .

XIANGFU: I just told you: I am not home.

LIU SHUN: Mr. Zhou Dazhang is waiting at the door to escort you to the bus.

LADY ZHANG: You see, he is such a sincere and earnest fellow.

XIANGFU: Tell him I have already left!

LADY ZHANG: Nonsense, you clearly came back inside and haven't left again, so why make him waste half the day waiting for you?

XIANGFU: Who wants him to escort me to the bus!

LADY ZHANG: Weren't you just saying that . . .

XIANGFU: Damn it, it's getting late. All right, I'm going, I'm going! (*gets his hat and exits.* LIU SHUN *exits*)

LADY ZHANG (*loudly*): Guangzu! Guangzu! (*no one answers; she exits*) (YANHUA *sneaks in, stands at the window where* WANRU *had been, looks out*)

YANHUA: Wanru! Wanru! Oh, Wanru! (WANRU *enters*)

WANRU: Were you calling me?

YANHUA (*laughing*): Come in here and wait, he'll be back shortly.

WANRU: Who are you talking about?

YANHUA: The person for whom you are waiting!

WANRU: Who is waiting for whom? Guangzu is waiting for you upstairs!

YANHUA: Don't bring me into this. Then why was a certain somebody crying?

WANRU: I don't know.

YANHUA: I also wonder why she started crying as soon as she saw a certain person leaving.

WANRU (*pouting*): You're awful. I'll hit you!

YANHUA: Heh! Aren't you the spoiled one! You'll break my bones hitting me like this.

WANRU: Yanhua, you're awful!

YANHUA: *I'm* awful? I rushed in here to tell you to stop crying and that he would be here any minute!

WANRU: Says who?

YANHUA: Says me.

WANRU: How would you know?

YANHUA: Of course I know! So you think he should not have told me, or that what he wants to say he wouldn't tell me?

WANRU: Yanhua, don't tease me.

YANHUA: Calm down, I'll stop teasing you. Of course, whether you believe me or not is up to you.

WANRU: Do you mean he's really coming back?

YANHUA: Of course! Does anyone go to the temple to burn incense for the sake of feeding the fire and the monks rather than praying to Buddha?

WANRU: What do you mean?

YANHUA: Look, he may fool other people, but he doesn't fool me. He tricked Uncle into leaving, but he'll be right back. (WANRU *laughs*) My dear girl, this has all been so amusing!

WANRU: That's enough. We're the same age. You are barely a few days older than me, so don't pretend that you're so much more mature.

YANHUA: One human year equals one divine day; you age according to divine days, so though I'm twenty-one, you're not even a month old yet!

WANRU (*hugging* YANHUA, *she laughs*): My dear big sister.

YANHUA (*struggling to get free, she says coldly*): Control yourself. Just wait here like a good girl.

WANRU: I still think you're teasing me, so I won't wait.

YANHUA: Fine, go upstairs, wash your face, and comb your hair. Anyway, your nose is all shiny from crying. . . .

WANRU (*quickly looking in mirror*): Oh, I look dreadful!

YANHUA: No, the more pitiful you look, the more people adore you.

WANRU (*hitting* YANHUA *like a spoiled child*): I really feel like hitting you! Silly!

YANHUA (*dodging her*): Why hit me? There are other people who would enjoy receiving such treatment from you! (ZHOU DAZHANG *enters;* WANRU *utters a delicate sound of surprise and hurries off*)

YANHUA (*sneering*): Please have a seat, Mr. Zhou. She is just going upstairs to freshen up and will be right back. I was just here consoling her on your behalf, assuring her not to be sad, and that you, sir, would be back soon.

DAZHANG: Yanhua, how did you know?

YANHUA: Pardon me, Mr. Zhou, to you she may be Wanru, but that doesn't make me Yanhua. (*pointing to herself*) Miss Zhang or Madame Zhang, however you prefer to address me.

DAZHANG: Yanhua, since you have not yet become Mrs. Feng, I'd better call you Yanhua while I still can!

YANHUA (*angrily*): Dazhang, Mrs. Feng or not, it's none of your business! You are free to court whomever you choose, but don't impose the name Mrs. Feng on me.

DAZHANG: Yanhua, is it my fault? Is it my decision to impose the name Mrs. Feng on you? Can I stop this from happening? I could, but I wouldn't dare!

YANHUA (*sneering*): Poor Mr. Zhou! What a considerate gentleman you are!

DAZHANG: Yanhua, no matter how bad I may be, at least I have self-knowledge. I know that I'm not as good as other people, and that I can't compete with them. When a man willingly yields, it is a matter of great shame to him! But for the sake of my beloved, for her happiness, I would rather be a coward and a weakling.

YANHUA (*with a cold laugh*): For me! For me! You don't even have the guts to admit your snobbery! Snob!

DAZHANG: Yanhua, you do me great injustice.

YANHUA: As if I had time for that! However, please stop interfering in my business! (*exiting*) And I don't want you to call me Yanhua.

DAZHANG: As you wish, Miss Zhang.

YANHUA: Right, Mr. Zhou. (*exits and again turns head*) And I'll tell you one more thing: Feng Guangzu is a hundred times better than you, a thousand times, ten thousand times!

DAZHANG (*bowing*): My congratulations, Miss Zhang.

YANHUA: Right, congratulate me! In a few days I'll tell you to come and see how I've become Mrs. Feng. (*exits*)

DAZHANG (*lowers his head and gasps in admiration*): Can a man ever get what he desires? (*paces backs and forth*) Oh Yanhua, I mustn't entrust you to the wrong parents. What can I do? (WANRU *hurries in, throws herself into* DA-ZHANG'*s arms*)

WANRU: Dazhang, Dazhang. . . .

DAZHANG: My dear little Wan!

WANRU: I thought I wouldn't get to see you today! My father just had to come home. . . .

DAZHANG: Would I be willing to leave without seeing you?

WANRU: Ever since you left yesterday, I have been speaking with you in my heart, did you hear?

DAZHANG: Of course I heard you.

WANRU: I was calling you, calling you to come back.

DAZHANG: I felt you calling me.

WANRU: Really? Dazhang? As soon as you left, my heart was stretched out this long, this tight—is your heart magnetic? It pulled mine away when you left, but my heart can't be pulled up by the roots, otherwise wouldn't it just be like a piece of taffy that gets longer and longer the more you pull it? When you pull off a strand it drifts about, never touching, never landing . . .

DAZHANG: Now I'm here.

WANRU: It's circling around you, unwilling to come back to me.

DAZHANG: Fine, I've brought it back to return to you.

WANRU (*hiding her hands*): You don't want it, so you're giving it back to me just like that?

DAZHANG: Little Wan, don't pout. Then how shall I return it to you? You tell me.

WANRU: Who wants you to return it?

DAZHANG: Are you upset? Did I say something wrong?

WANRU: Nothing at all.

DAZHANG: Then what's the matter?

WANRU: Get out!

DAZHANG: Where would I go, aren't I entangled in your heart?

WANRU: You've already returned it to me.

DAZHANG: Little Wan, what I gave back to you was *my* heart.

WANRU: Who wants to listen to such old clichés? I'm being honest and telling him what's in my heart—but a certain someone doesn't understand a thing, and merely answers with clichés!

DAZHANG: Little Wan, you gave me your heart and I gave you mine, isn't that correct?

WANRU: Absolutely correct! How could you possibly get a formula like that wrong!

DAZHANG: You want me to say something original?

WANRU: If there is nothing in your heart, then don't say anything at all.

DAZHANG: How could there be nothing—my heart is overflowing with words, and it's too bad that I'm not a clever young lady who can be as tactful and eloquent as you.

WANRU: Who wants you to talk like a young lady? After all, I'm not a man!

DAZHANG: Then I'll talk like a man—but you should know that I am a crude man who has nothing to say, because as soon as I see you my only desire is to devour you.

WANRU (*laughing*): Devour away!

DAZHANG (*laughing*): I'm afraid I'd devour you entirely! It's better to let me worship you like a flower, and let me kowtow and worship you.

WANRU (*laughing*): Worship away.

DAZHANG (*bending down on one knee, he kisses her hand; she laughs loudly*): You're not mad at me anymore? Oh, little Wan, you nearly scared all the words right out of me.

WANRU: What words? Anyway, nothing serious.

DAZHANG: I want to discuss a very serious matter with you.

WANRU (*covering her ears*): I don't want to hear.

DAZHANG: I have to go soon.

WANRU: You're not allowed to go!

DAZHANG: Little Wan, listen to what I have to say.

WANRU: I don't want to.

DAZHANG: Stop this nonsense, little Wan, I'm serious!

WANRU (*pouting, she turns her back*): I have been waiting for him since yesterday. He finally comes, but we can't talk together; I try to send him signals, but not only doesn't he receive them, my father notices, and the next thing I know I have to listen to his lecture! And now you want to discuss something serious!

DAZHANG: Listen, little Wan, it is *our* serious matter.

WANRU (*turning around*): Then what is there to discuss?

DAZHANG: Really? There's no problem?

WANRU: Would there still be a problem?

DAZHANG: Your father doesn't disapprove?

WANRU: Let him go ahead and disapprove!

DAZHANG: If he disapproves, then I won't be able to call on you.

WANRU: Mom has already instructed the gatekeepers to let you in, so there's no one who won't let you in!

DAZHANG: When I came this time again I couldn't see you, and we had to play hide and seek.

WANRU: At least it was fun!

DAZHANG (*staring*): It sounds as though you enjoy the fact that your father disapproves of me. If we get married, will we have to hide from your father and do it secretly?

WANRU (*laughing*): Why not? It'll be just like in the movies, we can secretly slip away and elope!

DAZHANG: And before you know it, your father will disown you and won't give you a dime. Then what will you do?

WANRU: What is there to be scared of? You have money, I have money.

DAZHANG: Your entire inheritance is in your father's hands, and he could refuse to give it to you.

WANRU: He gave it to me a long time ago when he put all the documents in my name.

DAZHANG: What about cash?

WANRU: There's always your cash.

DAZHANG: Mine? No matter how much I have, it wouldn't make any difference since it's all in my mother's hands. Is what I myself have enough for us both to use?

WANRU: I'll just have to withdraw some in advance.

DAZHANG: Little Wan, you think of everything! But this is not a long-term solution, and if your father disowns you as his daughter . . .

WANRU: That would never happen. How could my father disown me? But even if he did, don't worry, because he could never confiscate your property.

DAZHANG: I am poor, you know.

WANRU: Poor is fine. It's not as though I'm marrying you for your money!

DAZHANG: We have to get by.

WANRU: If your mother is waiting for you to get married, then she's bound to give you your inheritance.

DAZHANG: My mother is someone to be reckoned with.

WANRU: I'm not intimidated. Anyway, as I said long ago, I won't live in your house as a daughter-in-law. There are important people in your family, and lots of elders, and customs; I won't live there.

DAZHANG: Of course, we'll have to make our own little household.

WANRU (*laughs*): But will your mother want to move in with us?

DAZHANG: Oh no—she lives with her own family—that is, with my younger sister. My sister's husband is my mother's brother's son, and so my sister was married into my mother's family, do you understand?

WANRU: I don't care. Anyway, I ought to live with my mother and father.

DAZHANG: Weren't we going to elope?

WANRU: We haven't eloped yet! What's the hurry? My father adores me. And as long as I obey him, he'll agree to anything I say.

DAZHANG: But, little Wan, you don't know how awkward it is for me at times. Since my friends don't understand our situation, they're always introducing me to other girls—well actually, it's not that I am introduced to them, but rather they are being introduced to me. Today this family invites me over, tomorrow that family, and if I don't call on them, I offend them, and if I call on them I still offend them, because afterward they ask me if the young lady was to my liking and I never know what to say—since it's little Wan whom I love, how could I have eyes for anyone else?

WANRU: Can't you say that you're already engaged to be married? Didn't you give me this ring? (*showing her finger*)

DAZHANG: I'm afraid your father won't give his consent. . . .

WANRU: Oh, Dazhang, what's there to fear? Enough of this nonsense!—If Daddy doesn't approve, then we'll simply elope! All right? Let's not stay inside any longer, let's go out and walk on the lawn. (*they exit, walking arm in arm*)

YANHUA (*comes out from the back, stares out the window*): Fine, Fine! (*shakes head*) Fine!

Act II

Setting: Zhou Dazhang's home, a flat above his maternal uncle's small grocery store, in which the bedroom doubles as a kitchen. There's a canopy around the bed, next to which is a canvas cot. Against the wall is a miscellaneous assortment of washbowls, a coal stove, a wooden trunk, bowls, small plates, a knife, a pot, and other sundry items. Zhou Dazhang's MOTHER is crouched down on a small stool in front of the coal stove fanning the fire.

VOICE FROM DOWNSTAIRS: Is anyone home at the Zhous' upstairs?

ANOTHER PERSON: Who are you looking for? For Zhou Dazhang? Zhou Dazhang's never home!

MOTHER (*toward the downstairs*): You're looking for Zhou Dazhang? He's too busy to stay home all day!

SISTER (*from offstage*): Ma, the fruit shop across the street wants to settle the bill. . . .

MOTHER: What bill? You go ahead and pay it for your brother.

AUNT (*the mother-in-law of Dazhang's SISTER. She shouts from downstairs*): Zhou Dazhang! Zhou Dazhang! What a fine and competent son he's turned out to be! A fine and competent son! But what a waste to have given birth to such a competent son when you live off your daughter!

MOTHER (*jumps up and grabs the cattail fan and goes to the doorway; shouts downstairs*): Live off my daughter! Since when has a daughter ever gotten to support her mother? Daughters are born to be given away as filial daughters-in-law!

SISTER (*offstage*) Bad girl! (*smacks her daughter*) Shoo! (*daughter cries*) You deserve a big spanking, naughty girl! Go ahead and cry! Cry! I'll smack you again! Why did I have to give birth to a daughter? So I can give you away to someone else to be their maid? To be their wet nurse? To be their housekeeper? Die young, so you don't ever have to be in such an awkward position when you grow up. What's the use of having a daughter? What's the use?

AUNT: Elder Sister, show a little mercy. If you hurt your precious daughter, you'll be sorry. If she follows the good example of her grandmother, who lives with her daughter in her own family's house, then your grandson will be blessed with having four generations living under one roof!

MOTHER (*toward offstage in loud voice*): I do live in my own family's house! Unlike some people who could never go back to their own families!

AUNT (*offstage*): My surname is Wu and so I live with the Wu family. You wouldn't catch me propping up the door of my family in the east by leaning against the walls of my family in the west![4]

MOTHER: Whether you live off your own family or your mother-in-law's family, in any case it's still living off other people! Relying on one's own family is a natural blessing! Tut, tut, tut, whose dowry was it that made the Wus rich in the first place?[5]

SISTER (*leaves her daughter, crying, downstairs and enters*): Ma, can't you hold your tongue?

AUNT (*offstage*): That's right! It's convenient to rely on one's parents. What's the use of having a son? Our good-for-nothing son is worse than Zhou Dazhang. Not only doesn't he support me yet, he treats me like a servant, and I am even at the beck and call of my daughter-in-law.

MOTHER (*to her daughter*): You're telling me to hold my tongue! What shouldn't I have said?

AUNT (*outside*): You're better off depending on your daughter than your son, since daughters tend to stay close to their parents while sons tend to keep their distance! I've got the worst situation of all, since I have to depend

---

[4] She wouldn't depend on her maternal family to support her in-laws' family or vice versa.

[5] In other words, Aunt also supported her in-laws by means of the dowry provided by her natal family.

on my son's wife! Little Mao, don't cry—(*daughter stops crying*) come with Granny and go look at the motorcars go toot toot. But later on, be a good girl and don't have a son or bring home a daughter-in-law, but just live off your daughter. That is your fortune!

MOTHER (*toward offstage*): I have the good fortune to live with *my* family, but I don't depend on my son-in-law! (*to her daughter*) Would she ever be able to go home and live with her family for even a day? She secretly subsidizes her own family, and yet she finds fault with her own daughter-in-law. Whenever our Zhou Dazhang borrows a little money from his uncle, he pays it back; if not, it's because his uncle wants to help him out. Why does she have to keep nagging about it so much?

SISTER: Oh, Brother's been such a disappointment, and he puts me in a very awkward position.

MOTHER: My dear daughter, now you blame your brother too! How has he been a failure? Are you suggesting that after I married you to my nephew, I should not have put you in an awkward position by coming to live here? But when did I ever embarrass you by spending my son-in-law's money?

SISTER: Ma, please, no one's trying to settle accounts with you, so what are you carrying on about?

MOTHER: Your father-in-law invited me to live here because I, his little sister, am dear to his heart, and I don't care what anyone else has to say!

SISTER: Why are you telling me all this? You don't even know what happened.

MOTHER: Does Dazhang owe you for some bill? Did he borrow money from you?

SISTER: How would you know? Brother borrowed my gold ring—that clasping Buddha-hand ring—and it just so happened that the old lady wanted to wear it when she went to the temple to pray. I didn't dare say I had lent it to Brother, so I just said that I pawned it to buy something. She then accused me of pawning it to support my own family.

MOTHER: What did Dazhang want your ring for? You are a fool, and if he loses it, it's not my problem.

SISTER: He said he needed to borrow it for something . . . (*downstairs the daughter cries, and* AUNT *scolds her*) I've got to go—or else she'll start nagging that I don't mind my own child, that I expect her to cook for me, that I never lift a finger . . .

MOTHER: Tell her that it is her good fortune to be able to rely on her son's wife. It's good luck to rely on your son's wife: the whole family prospers and has enough gold and silver to stuff under the bed.

SISTER: Ma, really! I don't see any silver and gold.

MOTHER: Daughter, our family has always done all right! Unfortunately, daughters never get a fair share of the wealth! Your father's family was poor, and my father was only willing to put as much up for my dowry as he would get back from the bride price. Any more, and he feared he'd undermine the wealth of the family.

SISTER: I heard that he lost quite a bit on your dowry.

MOTHER: Rubbish! The truth of the matter is daughters always belong to someone else's family, so no one's ever willing to spend much on the dowry. The family inheritance goes entirely to the sons. They'd rather give it to the wives of their sons and the wives of their grandsons who have joined the family than to their own daughters. What's a daughter? Someone with a different surname!

SISTER: Isn't that the truth! All of your jewelry went to Brother—did you ever give me any of it?

MOTHER: Oh no! My dear daughter! Now you're blaming me? When have I ever failed you? Do I have any other jewelry? Didn't I cash it all in for your brother's studies?

SISTER: I never got to study!

MOTHER: But he's my son! The Zhou family may be poor, but we are still a family of scholars!

SISTER: Oh please! Whose family hasn't read a few books? And that makes us a scholarly family? Some ancestor or another started out as some rich man's accountant and used the boss to help his son become a *yamen* clerk; his family then produced a few sons who held insignificant posts, and now it's as though there have been important officials in the family for generations! Hm! What's it to me!

MOTHER: What's it to you! Since when did you get so high and mighty? It was me who had the wisdom to marry you into my own family so that you'd have plenty to eat and plenty to wear—so you'd always be well fed and warmly clothed—and so some people would have the chance to study! Your aunt looks down on my family because they were in business, but in the final analysis, it is businessmen who are rich.

SISTER: That's why the old lady says who cares about scholars! They're not only pedantic, they're poor! Yet they're all so full of themselves!

MOTHER (*angry*): Let me tell you something, poor as they may be, scholarly families can't be compared to these skirt-wearing abacus counters! Ai! Our Dazhang's fortune has yet to be made, so here we are biding hard times, waiting for the day his luck changes. I'm not bragging, but when that happens your entire family will rely heavily on him in many ways! Now you are such a snob, talking of being pedantic and poor.

SISTER: Ai, Ma, whose side are you on? Whenever I agree with you, you turn around and snap at me.

MOTHER: I am being sincere! Now that you're married, you'll always defend another family in your heart, and you won't listen to anything I say.

SISTER: But you were defending your in-laws too!

MOTHER: Aren't my in-laws your own family?

SISTER: Then aren't my in-laws your own family?—Oh, little Mao is crying. I have to go. (*exits*)

MOTHER (*sighs*): Daughters, they always complain that their own families mistreat them. But as far as families are concerned, daughters are like spilled water, a waste of money.

AUNT (*in a loud voice offstage*): Who said raising children is preparation for one's old age? I'm still the maid! I sweep, cook, wash, and now I even have to look after my daughter-in-law's children! (*sounds of* SISTER *swearing and spanking the child, who cries. In the midst of the crying and squabbling,* ZHOU DAZHANG *enters, carrying a greasy bag*)

DAZHANG: Ma, delicious pastries coming right up! Pork buns.

MOTHER: Still snacking at this hour?

DAZHANG: As I was passing by, they were fresh out of the steamer. When you take a bite, the juices come squirting out. Eat them before they get cold.

MOTHER (*in a loud voice directed offstage*): Little Mao, little Mao!

DAZHANG: It's my treat to you! Why must you always give some to little Mao first?

MOTHER: I'm afraid I won't be able to finish them all, since we are about to have dinner.

DAZHANG: What can't you finish! (*giving* MOTHER *the paper bag*)

MOTHER (*taking out one single small bun, and looking attentively in the bag*): There's only one?

DAZHANG: Oh, didn't I leave you a few? I guess I didn't notice how many I ate—tastes good, doesn't it?

MOTHER: What are you doing buying such fancy ones? My, Dazhang, you do love to spend money. . . . (*watching* DAZHANG *take off his western suit and change into old clothes*) Dazhang, what did you take Sister's ring for?

DAZHANG: Don't ask. I'll tell you about it in a couple of days.

MOTHER: Your aunt has been grumbling about it.

DAZHANG: What is there to grumble about? I'll go talk to her . . .

MOTHER: Don't go shooting your mouth off any further! Sister didn't say you were the one who borrowed it.

DAZHANG: I'll just tell her it was me who borrowed it, I'm not scared!

MOTHER: Ai, Dazhang, your sister has to make a good showing for her own family in front of her in-laws.

DAZHANG: And she has to parade the wealth of her in-laws in front of her own family.

MOTHER: This is what is called "one woman must make a good showing for two families!" And if *you* don't make a good showing for me, they'll laugh at me for sponging off my own family, while you Zhous will joke that my own family can't support me.

DAZHANG: Ma, there you go again, don't say such depressing things—you have me! You're my mother, so why worry about whom you can depend on?

MOTHER: When are you going to pay back the money you borrowed from your maternal uncle to go abroad? I have to listen to your aunt complain about it day and night.

DAZHANG: That paltry sum! Just wait till I, Zhou Dazhang, have made it big, and I'll pay him back, plus three times the interest!

MOTHER: When you make it big . . . (*sighs*) your salary is barely enough to get by on. We don't even have any rice left, so I fixed some fish-shaped flour noodles. (*opens the pot, ladles his bowl full, and places some chopsticks on the table*)

DAZHANG: Great! (*sits down*) Fish noodles are also fish!

MOTHER (*picks up the chopsticks*): And the flour went sour.

DAZHANG: Then I won't have to bother adding any vinegar.

MOTHER: I'm afraid you won't be full.

DAZHANG: I'm not very hungry yet—today I dined at the Zhangs' place—just a simple meal of six dishes: fried shrimp, braised chicken, crispy duck, glazed fish, sauteed "three winters," buttered cabbage, shrimp, and sea cucumbers. . . .

MOTHER: That's seven!

DAZHANG: Seven? Then there must have been seven.

MOTHER: The Zhangs invited you for another meal?

DAZHANG: They even wanted me to stay for supper, but I was afraid you would be lonely here all by yourself.

MOTHER: These days, if there's good food to eat you should take advantage and eat up!

DAZHANG: I wanted to keep you company. Anyway, I had other engagements. A friend invited me to the Meilongzhen to eat, and another asked me out for western food at D.D.'s.

MOTHER: The one who wants to open the factory? Did your new job come through?

DAZHANG: I'll be an assistant manager, at least.

MOTHER: What about the money? Will you make a couple thousand?

DAZHANG: A couple thousand? More than ten thousand!

MOTHER (*temporarily stunned*): What! And you still say you have to wait till you've made it big! Isn't this already a windfall? More than ten thousand *kuai!*

DAZHANG: Indeed! But what's the big deal? If it works out, so be it; if not, so be it. I really don't care!

MOTHER: After you've been working there for a while—for a year or two—our family will finally be back on its feet again.

DAZHANG: What's so great about being an assistant manager? Before this, a bank asked me to be the manager and I wouldn't accept.

MOTHER: Why not?

DAZHANG: It was a brand new bank—one's got to maintain a little dignity!

MOTHER: How much money would you have made?

DAZHANG: It wouldn't have mattered how much, I still wouldn't have accepted the position! That chairman of the board took a liking to me, and was trying to force his daughter on me.

MOTHER: Oh, you mean the Miss Dong you used to talk about? Is she richer than the young miss of the Zhang family?

DAZHANG: She was plenty rich, all right. But she also had a terrible temper and a rather common appearance, so I didn't fancy her.

MOTHER: There's still that Miss Jin, right?

DAZHANG (*shakes head*): Girls like her are a dime a dozen.

MOTHER: Then you fancy Miss Zhang?

DAZHANG: Not yet, but when I do, I'll marry her.

MOTHER: Is the Zhang family willing?

DAZHANG: More than willing; in fact, they're afraid I won't have her.

MOTHER: If they pick a poor son-in-law, they'll save money on the dowry.

DAZHANG: They won't save on the dowry. A western house with a garden, a dozen lane houses, gold, jewelry—the diamond alone is worth several million!

MOTHER: They're willing to lose that much on her! Thousands upon thousands of dollars!

DAZHANG: Yes! That's why a few thousand *yuan* means nothing! Wait until I have thousands upon thousands, then when I go out to make money it'll come rolling in by the millions—not like the hard work I do now, for which I earn next to nothing. I wear myself out completely, yet I only make a few hundred.

MOTHER: Oh Dazhang, then you'll be rich!

DAZHANG: Yes, I'll be rich. You can eat whatever you want and wear whatever you want. We'll have a magnificent garden, a huge foreign mansion, a big motorcar, a chauffeur with a brand new uniform who will address you as "Lao Taitai" and help you in and out of the car, maids and servants to wait on you. . . . (*the two finish eating;* MOTHER ZHOU *washes the dishes,* DAZHANG *dries them*)

MOTHER: And when I'm tired after a long day's work, I'll just call your sister to come and massage my legs.

DAZHANG: Why would you be tired from working? You'll be tired from lounging around! You'll make the maid massage your legs, and have the amah make you some ginseng soup.

MOTHER: Dazhang, this certainly is a windfall. (ZHOU SHIKUI *opens the door and pokes in his head*) Even though I have had to endure a lot of misery and abuse, now my son has become rich and has millions at his fingertips. (ZHOU SHIKUI *enters, holding a pipe*)

SHIKUI: Dazhang has gotten rich?

MOTHER: Uncle, have you eaten yet?[6]

DAZHANG: Uncle, please sit down. Have you had supper?

SHIKUI: Ai, you rich folks may have supper, but we eat old pumpkin and boiled noodles just to fill our bellies as best we can, and still worry that there will be days of hunger ahead.

DAZHANG: We didn't have much to eat either. I am so tired of eating fish and meat they no longer have any flavor.

SHIKUI: So, Dazhang, have you found a new "rice bowl"?

MOTHER: Not yet, he's still working at the same place.

SHIKUI: I have heard—heard you shouldn't count on working at that insurance company much longer.

DAZHANG: Says who?

SHIKUI: Our eldest daughter—she's a governess in your manager's nephew's house—she heard that the manager complains you're not a conscientious worker, that you show up to work late and leave early, and that all you do is chase women.

DAZHANG: Ha, ha, Uncle, what a joke! I want to quit, but they're reluctant to let me go. I have other things to do, and at the moment I can't do any of them.

SHIKUI: Ah ha—I knew you had found a good "rice bowl"! What new venture have you undertaken now?

---

[6]Zhou Shikui is Dazhang's paternal uncle. His mother addresses him as "Uncle."

MOTHER: He has a number of ventures. But our Dazhang has high standards. Though if you ask me, several thousand a month is quite good.

SHIKUI: That's not good enough? Me, I'm just a dead-end scholar doing accounts in a shop. The boss makes all the money, but as for me, all I can hope for is enough for half a meal. With seven or eight mouths to feed in the family, there's never enough fuel, rice, oil, or salt. (*sighs*) I don't know how we are going to get by!

MOTHER: It's like eating an unwashed carrot with the dirt still on it—you eat a bite when you have wiped off a chunk.

DAZHANG: Hasn't Uncle ever considered switching jobs?

SHIKUI: Yes! And as long as we're having a heart-to-heart talk, Dazhang, I was thinking . . .

DAZHANG: Thinking about what?

SHIKUI: Thinking about going into business. I heard that "rice bowl" of yours broke, that's why I've come to form a partnership with you. (ZHOU DAZHANG *smiles slightly*) Of course, you have other good "rice bowls," but I don't care, our partnership can be a sideline. Everyone in the store is doing . . .

DAZHANG: Doing what?

SHIKUI: Doesn't matter what, as long as we have capital, it doesn't matter what we invest in; we'll just stockpile it under the bed and under the table, let it sit there for a few days, then go out and sell it—it's a sure way to make money. The two of us can form a partnership and invest in some merchandise.

DAZHANG: Great, but what about the capital? I don't have any cash!

SHIKUI: Dazhang, don't worry, we're certain to make money on this! I'm telling you, I know about some discounted goods that are three times cheaper than market price. If we purchase them now, in a few days we'll double our capital.

DAZHANG: That's excellent.

SHIKUI: Right, so let's go order them. It comes to 76,000, and we have to pay half up front.

DAZHANG: But, Uncle, as I said to begin with, I have no cash on hand.

SHIKUI: Ai, Dazhang, you are overly cautious. I guarantee you that this is a sure money maker!

DAZHANG: Then Uncle, why don't you first pay your half, and when we've sold the stuff you can keep my half from the profits.

SHIKUI: Ha, ha, Dazhang, what a knack for figures! You're already rich, but you still want to rip off your poor uncle. If I had my half of the capital, would I still come to you?

DAZHANG: But Uncle never would have thought of doing business unless he had some capital!

SHIKUI: Dazhang, stop kidding. I know how generous you are; that's why I came to see you.

DAZHANG: To be perfectly honest, Uncle, I am so poor I don't even have a single cent—

SHIKUI: Dazhang, these are truly the words of a rich man! The richer one is, the poorer one pretends to be! Let's do it this way: you put up half of the 76,000, and when you have earned your money back, we'll split it 40/60—you can take the additional share of the profit. It's no skin off your neck! Anyway, flesh and blood ought to help each other out. When you were young and fatherless, didn't I take care of you?

MOTHER (*straightening things next to the stove. Loudly*): Hey! I want to say something. Dazhang has never depended on his uncle! Ever since he started school, it was my family who supported him. Although he never got a diploma or anything, he was brave enough to ask my brother to lend him the money to go take a dip in foreign gold and return gilded! I'm the one who gave birth to this competent son, and I'm the one who raised him; he never benefited from the Zhou family.

SHIKUI: Sister-in-law, your son's competence and your moral integrity are both the products of the accumulated virtue of the Zhou family ancestors. We are all one family!

DAZHANG: One family! Whenever I need to borrow money, do the Zhous ever treat me as one of the family?

SHIKUI: Oh dear, as they say, "Don't brag about your successes in front of someone who is frustrated about his failures." I have never been lucky, and I have never been able to take good care of others. But it's not as though I were a millionaire who ignored you while you went hungry and cold.

DAZHANG: And if I were a millionaire, what difference would 30,000 or 40,000 *kuai* make to me? You wouldn't have to borrow it, I would give it to you.

SHIKUI: I am not asking for a loan, I am simply asking you to form a partnership. Even if it were a loan, I would return it to you with interest.

DAZHANG: Uncle, you think I don't want to make money? It's simply that I don't have a penny to my name!

MOTHER (*loudly*): I couldn't even afford to buy tofu or vegetables, so have some salty noodle soup.

SHIKUI: A testimony to my sister-in-law's good housekeeping—Dazhang, does a rich man ever carry his cash around with him? He only carries enough to get by.

DAZHANG: If I had enough to get by, would I be living in this dump? I am mired

in debt, and everywhere I go I am insulted. If that insurance company fires
me, we'll starve. Where would I have capital for a little business venture?

MOTHER (*confused*): But Dazhang, what about being the assistant manager of
that factory?

SHIKUI: Which factory?

DAZHANG: Which factory! It's just like our "partnership"—nothing's finalized.

SHIKUI: Dazhang (*shaking head in disbelief*), so you're an assistant manager! I
knew you would be lucky! Such a trivial amount, yet you're still giving me
such a hard time.

DAZHANG: Nonsense. Uncle, they don't even know where the factory is going to
be located yet, so what kind of assistant manager could I be?

SHIKUI: Ha ha, Aunt, did you hear that, he's already the assistant manager, but
there isn't even a factory yet. Who's he fooling?

MOTHER: Of course there's a factory. Just wait till Dazhang pays off his debts,
then of course he'll help you out.

DAZHANG: Uncle, don't listen to Ma, she's confused.

MOTHER: Confused about what? Didn't you just say so yourself? You're an assistant manager, and you'll be earning more than 10,000 a month. . . .

ZHOU: I said nothing has been settled yet. We haven't been able to attract any
investors—so it's too early to brag about any of it yet. (*to his mother*) Didn't
I tell you it didn't matter to me whether any of this works out or not?

MOTHER: Couldn't you still be manager of that bank?

SHIKUI: A bank manager!

DAZHANG: Ma, stop this nonsense. What's all this about being a bank manager?
I never said that either.

MOTHER: Didn't that chairman of the board who wanted you to be his son-in-
law ask you to be the manager?

DAZHANG: And didn't I say I didn't want the girl so I didn't take the job?

SHIKUI: Oh, Dazhang! (*nodding with admiration*) A man must indeed go
abroad. Once he returns he can become an assistant manager, no problem,
a bank manager, no problem, and there's even a chairman of the board who
wants you to be his son-in-law. . . .

MOTHER: There's also the young lady of the Zhang family! She has a lovely disposition, she's pretty, and her dowry consists of property, gold, silver, pearls,
jade, and who knows how much. . . .

DAZHANG: Oh, Mother. . . .

MOTHER: I didn't get any of this wrong!

SHIKUI: Dazhang, why be so secretive about all of this! If you're going to come
into such easy wealth, you've got to let the people around you share a bit . . .

spread the wealth around. Your ancestors' accumulated virtue made you what you are, and so you can't go and forget all about your own family. No, our ancestors certainly would not approve of that.

DAZHANG: Ancestors! Ancestors! What ancestral wealth was ever handed down to me! Some people are born into the high life, but I have had to climb my way up one step at a time and I am still not there! I know perfectly well that they look down on me, that they despise me and mistrust me, but I just grin and bear it and keep on climbing. Ready-made wealth! Some people's ancestors were important officials, but what were ours? All we ever produced was a government clerk! Others have huge estates, but our family? We haven't one tile over our heads, and not an inch of earth beneath our feet—you call that good fortune? From the time I was young, what sort of good fortune have I ever enjoyed? I have just kept my head up as I crawled my way up from the bottom. Let them spit at me and curse me, let them step all over me, and if I make it I'll watch them steam in anger, and if I fail I'll watch them laugh.

SHIKUI: What are you complaining for now? This is the sweetness after the sorrow—you've freed yourself from misery.

DAZHANG: Freed! As if it were so easy! Other people get handed the opportunity to attend high school and college, to get master's degrees and doctorates. I had to borrow money for a ticket to Europe and simply scraped by in the cheapest place I could find for a year and a half. And forget about an M.A. or a Ph.D., I didn't even manage to get a high school diploma out of it. Whose ready-made wealth have I ever depended on? All I ever got were ready-made ridicule and curses!

SHIKUI: Oh! Oh! Dazhang is too modest. They laugh at you and curse you, and yet they still offer their daughters to you! Isn't that right, Sister-in-Law?

MOTHER: That's right. Everyone's after him since they all know that down the road he'll accomplish great things. Everyone is fighting over this son-in-law.

SHIKUI: Then, Aunt, will your family soon be celebrating a wedding?

MOTHER: Absolutely—now that you mention it, I have important things to do. And I still have to fix up this house! But again, I have no money. I'm telling you, Dazhang really doesn't have any money—though eventually he will—and when he does, he certainly won't forget his uncle.

SHIKUI: You're right. I understand that it's not a good time, what with the house repairs. Have someone over to do the work, you can repay me for it slowly. But when the new bride crosses the threshold, just don't forget about your poor uncle.

MOTHER: That goes without saying. Uncle will always be Uncle!

DAZHANG (*indignantly*): Uncle, there's no need to rush, because the new bride isn't going to be crossing my threshold, and I don't have the money to fix up the house.

SHIKUI: The bride won't be crossing the threshold?

DAZHANG: She's really spoiled and would never leave her parents.

SHIKUI: So you won't be bringing her dowry over either?

DAZHANG: How can they send over a house and property?

SHIKUI: If she doesn't move in here, what do you plan on doing? Are you going to live at the girl's house?

DAZHANG: What do you care?

SHIKUI: What about your mother? Will you take her over there as well?

MOTHER (*loudly*): Over my dead body! Daughters-in-law move into their mothers-in-law's homes. I have never heard of a mother-in-law going to her daughter-in-law's!

DAZHANG: What are you getting so worked up about, Ma? I didn't ask you to go!

SHIKUI: Your mother will stay here then?

DAZHANG: Of course she'll stay here.

MOTHER: And you?

SHIKUI: If he doesn't go there, then the groom will be in the east and the bride in the west. How will they ever consummate the marriage?

DAZHANG: This is all a long way off in the future anyway, so what's the rush?

MOTHER: Oh Dazhang, we have to make certain everything is clear. As for going to my daughter-in-law's house to be the mother-in-law, I won't go.

DAZHANG: Don't worry, I promise not to make you go.

SHIKUI: Sister-in-Law, did you hear that? He's making you stay here and live off your daughter. Your son has been given away to another family to be their son-in-law, is that it?

MOTHER: Over my dead body, I would never agree to that! Even though I have been a widow all these years, I struggled to raise you to manhood. But now you're simply going to fly from the old nest and leave me behind without a second thought.

DAZHANG: Ma, what are you talking about? This is all a long way off.

MOTHER: A long way off! When I do things, I like to do them in a timely fashion. I'm going straight to the Zhangs' to sort this out now. (*straightens her clothes, combs her hair, and pats her face. Moving toward the door, she says loudly*) Elder Sister! Elder Sister! Come here!

DAZHANG: Ma, what are you doing?

MOTHER: I am going to the Zhang residence.

DAZHANG (*laughing*): And where would the Zhang residence be?

MOTHER: You think I don't know? Your sister saw you leaving their house, and didn't she ask you the address too? (*toward offstage*) Eldest Sister!

DAZHANG: Ma, you're crazy! What are you going to the Zhangs' for?

MOTHER: The sooner we sort this out, the better. I'm not going to stand by and let them lure my son away with a few lunches and dinners and let some little missy hook my son like some fish! They'll get no such bargain! I gave birth to this competent son! And I will enjoy the good fortune he achieves. (SISTER *enters*)

SISTER: Ma, were you calling me? Oh, Uncle's here.

DAZHANG: Sister, Uncle has driven Ma crazy! Even if I don't have any money to lend him, he shouldn't stir up trouble between a son and his mother!

SHIKUI: Hey! Dazhang, what are you talking about? You two were the ones fighting, don't drag me into it!

Mother (*loudly*): Elder Sister, listen to your mother. Dazhang wants to abandon me and go become someone else's son-in-law.

DAZHANG: That's what Uncle said.

SISTER: Aiya, Brother, you took my ring to give to someone else?

MOTHER: Right! According to the new custom, giving someone a ring amounts to becoming husband and wife! Fine! Go ahead, have a good life and just leave me here with your sister.

SISTER: Brother, this won't do. It's not that I am unwilling to take care of Ma. But she has been here with me for so many years, and I have had a hard time putting up with my mother-in-law's constant nagging about it.

MOTHER (*crying*): I have no reason to go on living. My daughter complains about me and my son has no need for me! I'm going to go and ask that Miss Zhang for a rope to hang myself with!

SISTER: I have never complained!

DAZHANG: What is everyone talking about?

SHIKUI: Sister-in-Law, it wouldn't be convenient to call on the Zhangs at this hour. Let's talk it over tomorrow or the next day. No one's going to treat you poorly. Elder Sister, come here, I have something to discuss with you. . . .

MOTHER: Elder Sister, don't go. Now that I'm thinking about it, I can't stop worrying. Come with me to . . .

SISTER: To where?

MOTHER: To the Zhang residence.

SISTER: You want to call on the Zhangs at this hour? You don't even know them! Uncle, let's go sit downstairs. (*leaving with* UNCLE)

DAZHANG: Ma, why let Uncle stir things up? Would I ever abandon you?

MOTHER: But the more I think about it, the more sense it makes. Why would a young lady from a well-to-do family be willing to come live here? Naturally they would want you to go live there.

DAZHANG: Stop worrying, I just won't marry her. Didn't I just say that I hadn't even taken a fancy to her yet?

MOTHER: A young lady who wears pretty clothes, who flirts with you day and night, sooner or later you'll take a fancy to her.

DAZHANG: Then I just won't go to her house.

MOTHER: Who told you not to go! It's not that I don't approve of her. I merely want to go clarify things.

DAZHANG: Ma, calm down. If you have something to say, I'll tell them for you.

MOTHER (*shakes head*): None of you can say what I have to say. I myself must go—and you don't fool me, all that nonsense about not liking her, who believes you?

DAZHANG: Ma, then let me check the almanac and pick a propitious day.

MOTHER: That won't be necessary; I know tomorrow is an auspicious day!

DAZHANG: Ma, then wait until I buy you a new pair of shoes. . . .

MOTHER (*looking down at her old shoes, sighing*): These shoes really aren't fit to be seen by your in-laws! But don't forget to buy me a pair tomorrow! Oh, I must ask Elder Sister for that address . . . (*exits*)

DAZHANG: Ma! Oh! (*slapping the table*) She'll ruin my plans! (*pacing*) I'll have to act fast!

Act III

Setting: The same as act I, Zhang Xiangfu's parlor. WANRU *is standing beside the telephone; she picks up the receiver, then puts it back down again.*

WANRU (*angrily*): Dazhang! I told you to give me your telephone number, but you keep forgetting! If I have something to say to you, how am I supposed to get hold of you? Even if I shout myself hoarse, he still won't hear me! (*slamming down the receiver, she looks out the window, then glances down at her watch*) (FENG GUANGZU *enters*)

WANRU: Guangzu, you're back?

GUANGZU: It's early and you're already here waiting for someone?

WANRU: Yes! I despise him! I have something to tell him, but I have no way of getting in touch with him.

GUANGZU: What's so important that you're in such a panic? Can't you just wait till he comes and tell him in person?

WANRU: I have to warn him *not* to come! Dad is making trouble again! He's guarding the house, and refused to go out today.

GUANGZU: Isn't that because of all the pantomime you did at the window?

WANRU (*laughing*): Dear Guangzu, you saw me too?

GUANGZU: Who *didn't* see you?

WANRU: Just now a call came that I'm sure was Dazhang, but Dad picked it up.

GUANGZU: At worst you won't see him today!

WANRU: But I have something to tell him.

GUANGZU: You have so much to say!

WANRU: There always seems to be something I forget and don't say.

GUANGZU: The two of you are so fond of each other!

WANRU: So only you are allowed to be fond of someone!

GUANGZU (*embarrassed*): What! We're not like you two—Oh, Wanru, since you admit that you're fond of him, I have something to ask you, and you have to answer me honestly.

WANRU: Fine, I'll answer you honestly. Ask me.

GUANGZU (*sitting down*) I wanted to know, you—you and Dazhang, just how fond of him are you?

WANRU (*laughing*): What do you think?

GUANGZU: Then you—you—have you decided on him?

WANRU (*laughing loudly, she shows him her finger*): Take a look! What is this?

GUANGZU: It's a ring on a finger! Did he give that to you? Does that mean you're engaged?

WANRU: Think what you like, he gave it to me for fun.

GUANGZU: Then when he gave it to you, he didn't say what he meant?

WANRU: Say what he meant?

GUANGZU: Say that he—he—he loves you.

WANRU (*laughing loudly*): I don't understand any of that. What would he say?

GUANGZU: Don't play dumb. I'm asking you, does that mean he asked you to marry him? Is that what he meant? (WANRU *laughs*) Wanru, this is an important matter.

WANRU: Is it?

GUANGZU: Does your mother know about this?

WANRU: Of course she knows.

GUANGZU: I'm saying, Wanru, at this level, one must carefully consider . . . that is to say, whether Zhou Dazhang sincerely loves you or not.

WANRU (*angrily*): He's not sincere, isn't he?

GUANGZU: No, I'm not saying he's not sincere—what I mean is—does he love anybody else?

WANRU: Everyone can be a little wishy-washy!

GUANGZU: Of course, if you're sure, that's great. Because, because I—ah . . .

WANRU: Because you what?

GUANGZU: I have always thought that—it seems to me that Dazhang is in love with Yanhua.

WANRU: You're really something! You'd turn a million somersaults in jealousy! He, in love with Yanhua! But naturally, your beloved is the best in the world, and everyone is in love with her!

GUANGZU: I was just asking.

WANRU: You can stop worrying! Your Yanhua! I beg your pardon, but she is certainly not the one he loves.

GUANGZU: Then, Wanru, tell me truthfully . . .

WANRU: Half a day of questions, and all because you fear that he's in love with your precious Yanhua! What else do you want to honestly know?

GUANGZU: Do you think—Wanru, tell me honestly, is Yanhua a wee bit in love with Dazhang?

WANRU: Yanhua is not foolish, she's perfectly aware that the one Dazhang loves is not her.

GUANGZU: Ah. . . .

WANRU: You can relax about this!

GUANGZU: Who cares if I relax or not? Although she has no one else in heart, I am not in her heart either. . . .

WANRU: You mustn't give up.

GUANGZU: Wanru, do you think I have a shred of hope?

WANRU: Why wouldn't you? Behind your back she's always saying how kind you are.

GUANGZU (*happily*): Really? (LADY ZHANG *enters*)

LADY ZHANG: It's you two! What are you discussing?

WANRU: Dear Guangzu is researching a question.

GUANGZU: I'm not, I'm not, I was merely asking whether . . .

WANRU: He's been beating around the bush trying to ask me whether Yanhua loves him or not.

GUANGZU (*embarrassed*): No, no. . . .

LADY ZHANG (*laughing*): Silly! Why don't you just go and ask her yourself? Wanru, you're also confused. There's no point in you acting as a representative, so go get Yanhua and let him ask her himself.

WANRU: Yanhua isn't back from the office yet.

LADY ZHANG: She has a headache, so she came home early.

WANRU (*standing up*): I'll go trick her into coming down. My dear Guangzu, don't worry, I promise to go far away and not eavesdrop on the two of you.

GUANGZU: Wanru, don't tease me, I—I—I don't have anything prepared . . .

WANRU: You've already memorized what you want to say in your heart! (*laughs, exits*)

LADY ZHANG: Prepare what? It's not as though you're giving a speech or teaching a class—I'm not scolding you, but Guangzu, you're a grown man, and if you can't utter a word whenever you see a woman, if you're going to be so aloof, who's ever going to fall in love with you? What's so great about Yanhua? In what way don't you match her? (*laughs*) Look how embarrassed you are! I'm leaving. . . . (*turning back*) Be brave and ask her. Why would she turn you down?

GUANGZU: Ai, I—I . . .

LADY ZHANG (*laughing, she imitates* FENG): "I. . . . I . . ." I have something to do. (*exits*) (FENG *paces back and forth, rubs his hands, straightens his clothes, pulls on his tie, sits down restlessly.* YANHUA *comes in, rubbing her temples and frowning*)

YANHUA: Where's Third Aunt?

GUANGZU: Yanhua, do you have a headache?

YANHUA: I'm all right. Wanru said that Third Aunt wanted me . . .

GUANGZU: She wanted you to come sit down for a while in here so you wouldn't be all alone in your room.

YANHUA: Oh! I thought she had something for me to do. (*sits*)

GUANGZU: She knew that you weren't very comfortable—you don't have a fever? (YANHUA *shakes her head.* FENG *pours her some tea*) Do you want a sip? (YANHUA *takes a sip*) Another cup? (YANHUA *shakes her head.* FENG *puts the teacup on the table next to the sofa and sits down next to* YANHUA. YANHUA *rests her head against the back of the sofa, closes her eyes, and doesn't say anything*) Is that better?

YANHUA: Thank you, that's a little better.

GUANGZU: Yanhua!

YANHUA (*opening her eyes*): Yes?

GUANGZU: A. . . . um. . . . ha . . . are you feeling better?

YANHUA: A bit.

GUANGZU: Ah, Yanhua . . .

YANHUA: Hmmm?

GUANGZU: Ah . . . ah . . .

YANHUA: What is it?

GUANGZU: I . . . I . . . (*starts pacing*) You . . . you . . . are you better?

YANHUA (*smiling*): Yes, I am yet again a little better.

GUANGZU (*suddenly sits down next to* YANHUA): Yanhua, I have something to discuss with you.

YANHUA (*softly*): What about? So serious!

GUANGZU: You can't call it a serious matter—from the overall perspective of society, it's a very insignificant matter. But to the one or two people involved, however, it is a matter that concerns lifelong happiness, so one can't not see it as a very important matter, and one can't not discuss it very thoroughly.

YANHUA (*moving farther away from* FENG): Please tell me.

GUANGZU: Does your head still ache?

YANHUA: Not anymore.

GUANGZU: That's good, then I'll lay the whole matter out very clearly for you. There are five points. The first point is, that is to say, the basic issue is whether or not this is worth discussing at all. In the past, when young ladies brought up the issue of marriage they would get embarrassed, and as for their own important event, they would get so flustered that they would let other people go and take care of it.

YANHUA: So, of course, it is worth talking about.

GUANGZU: But what we also have to carefully examine is—that is to say, the second point, that is, the problem itself—in other words, what we have to analyze now is, what is the issue?

YANHUA: What?

GUANGZU: Nowadays, some people oppose marriage. What we have to discuss is: should a person get married or not? Some people say that the family is the root of all greed and a great many social ills—and that extortion and so forth starts with marriage. So, is marriage a good thing or not?

YANHUA: What?

GUANGZU: Of course it is obvious, so I might as well be frank. All men and women, no matter who they may be, need to get married. . . .

YANHUA: Enough! *I* don't need to get married. If I ever fall in love with a man, I'll just run away with him.

GUANGZU (*nervously*): Yanhua, we are merely discussing the issue—and I'm not finished—what I just said was the second point—let me first finish giving you the overall outline and then we can discuss the individual points one at a time. The third point is, why haven't I gotten married yet? There are several reasons for this, and I'll tell you them gradually. The fourth point is, can I get married right now? And there are two subpoints here: one is your perspective on this, the other is my perspective on this. The fifth point is the union of these two points, that is to say . . .

YANHUA: That is to say, I ought to marry you!

GUANGZU: Oh, Yanhua, I have never dared to utter that sentence. I always thought that—this—this—this thing called love is quite a marvelous thing that has to be painstakingly fostered. It can't be forced. That's why I have patiently waited for you, one year, two years, three years, even as much as five or six years so that it could grow naturally. This brings us back to my third point . . .

YANHUA (*standing up*): That won't be necessary. Why you haven't gotten married, that's your business. Can you get married now? That's also your own business. Can I get married now? That's none of your business. And the conclusion is: in seventy years, eighty years, or a hundred years, that marvelous "thing" of yours will never grow in my heart and tell me to marry you! (*angrily exits*)

GUANGZU: Yanhua! . . . Ah, how did I offend her this time? Ah! Women! Women! A mysterious work of . . .

YANHUA (*reenters*): If I did marry you, it would only be because I admire university students and have never had the good fortune of attending classes and hearing lectures, and that way I could have private lessons with you! (*exits*)

GUANGZU (*surprised*): This . . . this . . . simply . . . it's not funny, yet it's not upsetting! She . . . she . . . If I can't figure her out then I am not a man! (*sits down on the sofa and angrily wipes off the sweat.* YANHUA *enters again*) You have more to say?

YANHUA (*takes a step, then stops, modestly apologetic*): My dear Guangzu, please pardon me.

GUANGZU (*impatiently*): What?

YANHUA: I have come for an apology.

GUANGZU: An apology? I don't understand how I offended you.

YANHUA: I am apologizing to you. I don't know what came over me just now to make me behave so rudely. (FENG *is silent*) I shouldn't have behaved that way.

GUANGZU (*sighs*): I deserved it.

YANHUA: At first, I . . . when I came in, I was thoroughly prepared to give you my consent.

GUANGZU (*confused*): Consent?

YANHUA: I knew what your intentions were, and I was prepared to give my consent.

GUANGZU (*stands up happily*): Yanhua, you made me suffer at first on purpose, only to now make me happy.

YANHUA (*retreating one step*): That's *not* what I . . . I have come to sincerely apologize to you.

GUANGZU (*grabbing her*): You don't have to apologize! Yanhua, as long as you consent, even if you hit me or called me names, I would still be perfectly willing.

YANHUA: But I'm not keen on hitting people or calling them names. Dear Guangzu, I know you are devoted to me, but I simply can't say yes.

GUANGZU: Why? Yanhua? Oh, Yanhua, you weren't even willing to finish listening to my third point. . . .

YANHUA (*impatiently*): The third point! The fourth point! This is Professor Feng's Marriage Proposal Method!

GUANGZU: You are this mad all because of those five points?

YANHUA: I am not mad. But (*sneering*) what kind of proposal was that?

GUANGZU: You require a specific method? Oh Yanhua, you have seen far too many movies, so now you think that a marriage proposal must be romantic, with all that nauseating talk, but in fact, a sincere person . . .

YANHUA: You needn't say any more.

GUANGZU: Why not?

YANHUA: I have tried with all my might to make myself love you, but I can't. No matter what, I just can't.

GUANGZU: This is curious. Since you can't love me, why are you trying to force yourself?

YANHUA: You still don't get it! I ought to love you. All these years, besides you, who else ever looked after me? When my dad got remarried, he forgot all about me. Third Uncle and Aunt don't really pay much attention to me. You were the only one who was ever concerned about me, who helped me, who took care of me. Is it that I don't know how to be grateful?

GUANGZU: But Yanhua, gratitude isn't the same thing as love. I certainly don't approve of a woman sacrificing herself out of gratitude.

YANHUA: Now that I think about it, in order to express my gratitude and repay you, I actually ought to promise *not* to marry you. You know my disposition: whoever marries me will have plenty to put up with.

GUANGZU: Oh, Yanhua, you do have a short temper.

YANHUA: Exactly, I'm like a huge explosive. There is gunpowder stored in my heart, wrapped in several layers of thick paper, bored to frustration, just waiting to be ignited. *Pao! Pao!* I'd explode an instant, and fly up, my whole body burned to cinders. Only then would I be relaxed and carefree!

GUANGZU: How sorry I feel for you. . . .

YANHUA: But you wouldn't be able to put up with me. I guarantee I would abuse you, trample all over you, bully you; the kinder you were, the more I would torment you. I wouldn't make a good wife—I originally thought I could try hard to become a good wife. But I couldn't—I couldn't love you.

GUANGZU: Because you love someone else. (YANHUA *is silent*) Yanhua, I know I don't measure up to Zhou Dazhang. But Yanhua, you should know—Wanru told me, the two of them are engaged to be married.

YANHUA: I already know.

GUANGZU: If you know, then you ought to hold back your feelings, don't be like the floodwaters that breach the dike.

YANHUA: I have always been that way, unable to control myself. If only I could love you, but I can't. I don't want to love him, but again I can't not love him. Now that we've had this talk, I see myself all the more clearly. Zhou Dazhang is mine, and I must marry him no matter what.

GUANGZU: I truly understand you, and I sympathize with you as well. However—and this is leaving myself aside—after all, they're engaged, and you can't just go and break apart their marriage.

YANHUA (*sneers*): And why can't I? Why can't I?

GUANGZU: You shouldn't.

YANHUA: Why shouldn't I? Should Wanru get to be the pampered little lady? Should I be the wretched slave? Should Wanru get to enjoy all the wealth, while I have absolutely nothing? They exalt her, they fawn on her! In what way do I not measure up to her? In what way?

GUANGZU: Yanhua, you are more clever than her and more beautiful.

YANHUA: What good is that?! This world belongs to her, she has a mother and father who dote on her, while I only have people who dislike me. She gets whatever she wants, I get nothing I want. She needn't care about whether she has money or not, yet I have to sell myself, piece by piece, in order to earn a few lousy *yuan*. Isn't that so?—I won't live for long, since there are only 365 days in a year and each day I sell a little of myself to the office. In the blink of an eye, I'll be old, and what will I have achieved? What's the good of being clever? What's the good of being beautiful? She doesn't have to be clever, and people say she's clever. She doesn't need to be beautiful, since as long as a young woman isn't too ugly, she can dress well and she'll look beautiful. Not only is she clever and beautiful but her disposition is also all right, and her heart's not bad, plus she's generous . . . not like me, who's petty and jealous! Should! Should! Should! All the fire in hell is burning in my heart!

GUANGZU: Oh, Yanhua, if you spend too much time thinking about how unfair life can be, you can't help being resentful. That's why the world has philosophy and religion, and therefore . . .

YANHUA: Who asked you anything about "therefore"? I only asked why. Why? (*stamps*)

GUANGZU (*frowning*): This . . . this . . . Yanhua, how can you ask me? What should I say?

YANHUA: I will ask you! You too are one of God's favored ones. You just muddle along, happily passing the days!

GUANGZU: Oh, Yanhua, you're exaggerating, how would you know whether I feel happy or sad? Not everyone can be like you, like a bomb that might explode with one nudge.

YANHUA: What an accomplishment!

GUANGZU: It's no use getting so angry! I would advise you not to think so much about yourself. Then you won't be so jealous.

YANHUA: I am not such an idiot! Since heaven bullies me, I have to look after myself all the more! Since heaven doesn't love me, should I not love myself? Why should Wanru be the only one who gets a good husband, a rich husband? Why should only her husband be able and handsome? (FENG *sighs, stands up, and paces*) Dear Guangzu, I beg you to forgive me, it's not that I look down on you. . . .

GUANGZU: It's not important.

YANHUA: However, I . . . I . . .

GUANGZU: You love his wealth, and his ability, his looks . . .

YANHUA: Well, of course. Whatever it is they call unconditional love, I don't believe in it.

GUANGZU (*sighing*): Then there's no hope for me.

YANHUA: Why must you say such ridiculous things? I said earlier that I could never be a good wife, but there are plenty of women in the world, and you still say there's no hope for you!

GUANGZU (*sighing*): Yanhua, I didn't think this was the way you felt. (*sighs*) But I don't understand. How do you plan to marry Dazhang?

YANHUA: I don't know. But when I set my mind to do something, I do it— sooner or later. (FENG, *shaking head, sighs*) It won't be that difficult either! As for Dazhang, he loves me. I know he loves me.

GUANGZU: I can only hope that you succeed.

YANHUA: Hoping won't do me any good. You can help.

GUANGZU: How?

YANHUA: Aren't you going to Suzhou to attend your cousin's wedding reception?

GUANGZU: I'm going tomorrow or the day after.

YANHUA: Go today.

GUANGZU (*nodding*): You want me farther away?—Of course I can.

YANHUA: Take Wanru with you.

GUANGZU: I can't take care of that—she said she wasn't going.

YANHUA: Let me tell you some news: she wants to elope with Zhou Dazhang, elope! She said so herself.

GUANGZU: Nonsense, I'll tell Uncle.

YANHUA: You needn't tell him, just take her away with you today.

GUANGZU: She's not a child. Will she let me?

YANHUA: Tell her that Uncle has ordered her to go. In fact, Uncle doesn't want her to have any contact with Dazhang—oh, Uncle, you're back. (ZHANG XIANGFU *enters, wearing slippers*)

XIANGFU (*standing at the entrance*): Wanru!

YANHUA: It's me, Uncle.

GUANGZU: Uncle.

XIANGFU: Ha, ha, I thought Zhou Dazhang had come! (*about to exit*)

YANHUA: Uncle, Guangzu just wanted to ask you about something. Today he is going to Suzhou, and he doesn't know whether Wanru was going there to amuse herself.

XIANGFU: You're leaving today?

GUANGZU: Grandmother wants to have her over for a few days. Third Aunt doesn't have time, so she can come with me.

XIANGFU (*slapping the table*): That's excellent! Tell her to go with you right now! I'll tell her to go!—Wanru! Wanru? Wanru! (*exits*)

YANHUA: See? I was right!

GUANGZU: I'm sure Wanru won't want to go.

YANHUA: She won't dare not go; and Third Aunt will certainly approve of the idea.

GUANGZU (*shaking his head, he sighs*): In any case, whoever wants to go to Suzhou with me can come. I won't force anyone, but I won't pay anyone's way. Yanhua, I have to go and pack my bags. (*exits*) (YANHUA *looks at her watch, looks out the window. Upstairs,* ZHANG XIANGFU *and* LADY ZHANG *can be heard faintly: "Go and take a look at the new bride"—"Bring some Suzhou candies back"—"Hurry up"*) (WANRU *rushes in*)

WANRU: What shall I do? Dear Yanhua! Dad is making me go to Suzhou right now.

YANHUA: The weather's splendid, so you'll be able to go to lots of different scenic spots. Suzhou's a great place.

WANRU: Ah, but . . .

YANHUA: But there is one person who can't go! Tell him to go with you, wouldn't that be great?

WANRU: Yes! Dear Yanhua, this is a disaster! Dazhang is coming to see me in just a while, he may even be here momentarily. But Dad wants me to take the next train with Guangzu, and it departs right away, and Dad is seeing us off himself! Dear Yanhua, what do you think I should do?

YANHUA: Leave him a letter telling him to go to Suzhou.

WANRU: Do you think he'd be willing? (*looks for paper and pen, writes a letter, then tears it up and writes another one*) What should I say?

XIANGFU (*from offstage*): Wanru! Wanru!

WANRU (*loudly*): I'm coming! I'm coming! (*to* YANHUA) What's the big rush! (*tears up the letter, writes another*)

YANHUA (*laughing*): Then don't write him a love letter, just write something simple.

XIANGFU (*offstage*): Wanru!

LADY ZHANG (*offstage*): Wanru, do you still have those two new pairs of silk stockings?

WANRU (*toward offstage*): I'm coming! I'm coming! (*tears up letters*) My dear Yanhua, you write it for me, okay?

YANHUA (*laughing*): Don't be ridiculous, how could I write your love letter? I can only help you pass it on.

WANRU: Who's still writing a letter? (*writing, then tears the letter up*) My dear Yanhua, will you pass on a message for me?

YANHUA: What's the message?

WANRU: Tell him to come to Suzhou—tell him that I went with Guangzu to Suzhou, and that he's to come as well.

YANHUA: If I pass on a message for you, there ought to be a keepsake.

WANRU: Why must there be a keepsake?

YANHUA: To prove that it's a message from you.

WANRU: What keepsake?

XIANGFU (*offstage*): Wanru! Wanru!

WANRU: I'm coming, Dad!—Dear Yanhua, what do you think?

YANHUA: That ring of yours (*pointing to her finger*)—you can ask your two hands to drag him to Suzhou!

WANRU (*smiling*): You would think of that, you naughty girl! (*giving her the ring*) Give it to him, and say—you say something on my behalf. (ZHANG XIANGFU *enters*)

XIANGFU: Wanru, go and change your clothes.

WANRU: I'm not changing.

XIANGFU: Then let's go! Your mother already packed your things. (*loudly*) Guangzu! (FENG GUANGZU *carries in a small case and bag.* LADY ZHANG *enters, carrying a small trunk*)

LADY ZHANG: Wanru, don't forget, when you go by the old store, buy a few things to take with you. I have already told your father.

XIANGFU: I know! I know! How many more times are you going to say it?

LADY ZHANG: Guangzu, send our regards, and congratulate your Sixth Aunt— tell them to come to Shanghai for a visit.

XIANGFU (*stamping his foot*): Arrgh! I simply don't understand why, whenever you ladies go out the door, you have to settle accounts at the very last minute—"Come visit," "Send our regards," even if you've said it all before it doesn't count, you have to say it all again at the last minute. Let's go, let's go, let's go!

WANRU (*nudging* YANHUA): Don't forget.

YANHUA: I couldn't forget. (*they all leave in a clamor;* LADY ZHANG *and* YANHUA *reenter*)

LADY ZHANG: Yanhua, now that it's just the two of us, let's invite some people over to play mahjong.

YANHUA: Oh dear, Aunt, I forgot, just now I believe Wanru said that—that Lady Wang invited you over to play mahjong, or maybe it was Lady Chen— wanted you to go over there right away, I'll ring her up and ask.

LADY ZHANG: Don't, it had to have been Lady Wang! She is the old tiger of the mountain, and she detests going out—but if I go out, then you'll be here all alone.

YANHUA: I'll watch the house.

LADY ZHANG: Then I'm off. (*exits*)

YANHUA (*listening to* LADY ZHANG *leave, she looks at watch*): They're all gone. . . . (*loudly*) Liu Shun, when Mr. Zhou Dazhang comes, tell him to sit in here. (*exits.* ZHOU DAZHANG *enters*)

DAZHANG (*sitting, he talks to himself*): They're all out. (*flips through a pictorial.* YANHUA *enters wearing a splendid dress, pretends as though she's going out*)

YANHUA: Oh my! Mr. Zhou Dazhang!

DAZHANG: Yanhua . . .

YANHUA: What terrible timing, everyone has gone out.

DAZHANG: Yanhua, you look so lovely, where are you going?

YANHUA: Pardon me, Mr Zhou! I have some errands to do, I can't keep you company.

DAZHANG: Will they be back soon?

YANHUA: Be back? They wouldn't be back very soon, now would they?

DAZHANG: Where did they go?

YANHUA: Third Uncle and Third Aunt saw Wanru and Guangzu off to Suzhou.

DAZHANG: They went to Suzhou? Wanru and Guangzu? Whatever for?

YANHUA (*with a mysterious smile*): I don't know.

DAZHANG: Mr. and Lady Zhang went too?

YANHUA: They went, but they'll be back.

DAZHANG: Ah! (*pauses*)

YANHUA: Oh, I nearly forgot something important! (*searching in her bag, she pulls out a paper bag*) This, Wanru told me to return this to you. (*handing him the paper bag*) She also invited you to a wedding in Suzhou.

DAZHANG (*looking in the bag, he sees the ring; surprised*): She didn't say anything else?

YANHUA: She invited you to Suzhou.

DAZHANG: Why didn't you go?

YANHUA: She didn't invite me.

DAZHANG: Why not?

YANHUA: Why would she invite me? (DAZHANG *is silent, plays with the ring*)

YANHUA: Is that an engagement ring? Is she returning it to you?

DAZHANG (*forced laugh*): This an engagement ring? This ugly thing?

YANHUA (*smiles*): Seeing you so disappointed, it would appear that someone has stolen your fiancée.

DAZHANG: Me disappointed? Someone stole your fiancé! Would I still be disappointed?

YANHUA: I don't have a fiancé.

DAZHANG: And I don't have a fiancée.

YANHUA: Just because you have a fiancée, must you assign a fiancé to me?

DAZHANG: I know you don't have a fiancé, and fortunately I don't have a fiancée!

YANHUA (*sneers*): Fortunately! Dr. Zhou has nothing! Everyone hurry and come grab him!

DAZHANG: Yanhua, you're the one who has nothing, so I'll come and snatch you up. (*grabs her hand*)

YANHUA (*pulls away her hand and sneers*): Pardon me, Mr. Zhou, but I have an appointment, excuse me.

DAZHANG: Yanhua, I won't let you leave. (*grabs her*) Tell me what appointment you have, or else I won't let you go.

YANHUA (*laughs*): I'm off to see my lawyer! I'm off see my broker! I'm off to get some things from my safe deposit box at the bank!

DAZHANG: Yanhua, who are you going to see?

YANHUA: I told you.

DAZHANG: That was nonsense.

YANHUA: Of course! That was merely nonsense! Were it true, would Dazhang pair me up with Feng Guangzu?

DAZHANG: Yanhua, you despise me. Is my love so cheap? You know perfectly well that you're the only one I love! The reason I stepped aside was for your own happiness! But I couldn't bear it, so I kept coming back here, and if I couldn't see you, then at least I could occasionally hear about you, and I was always thinking about you. It's so contradictory and so pathetic. I have my pride, and I hate it when others laugh at me, so I invented a pretext—namely, coming to see Wanru. Wanru! Such a brainless little creature! Even if she were made of gold, would she compare to Yanhua? Would I be bought by her? Yanhua, it was merely for your own good that I was willing to step aside—I, Zhou Dazhang, have never submitted to my environment! I submit only to you—unless you don't support me.

YANHUA: Dazhang needs someone to support him?

DAZHANG: Sometimes I am so exhausted that I can't get up. In my dreams, I long for a warm bosom where I can bury my face, and where I can cry my heart out or laugh—I feel as though I've become a hard, empty shell. Even though the outside is hard, the inside is hollow, I am hungry and want something soft to fill me up. Let me be pathetic and helpless in front of you. If I could just pour a little bit of your sympathy into this empty shell, all my fatigue and fragility would immediately be solidified into something as hard as steel! Yanhua, you are mine! (*about to kiss her*)

YANHUA (*half pushes him away, with soft voice*): Dazhang.

DAZHANG: You are mine forever and ever (*puts the ring on her finger*)—since you said this was an engagement ring, it is yours! (*kisses her hand*)

YANHUA (*leans her head on his shoulder*): But Dazhang . . . (*twists the ring around, sighs*) My dad will probably arrive in Shanghai tomorrow and force me to leave with him—leave. . . . You know I don't want to.

DAZHANG: Then let's get married and go on a honeymoon!

YANHUA: You want to get married too? You don't think I'm some silly girl you can toy with?

DAZHANG: Yanhua, feel my heart! Am I toying with you?

YANHUA: But is this all so easy that we can just get married tomorrow?

DAZHANG: Only unless you're a coward and you don't dare.

YANHUA: What do I have to fear? When I make a decision, I follow through on it!

DAZHANG: Then, Yanhua, let's take the early train to Hangzhou tomorrow.

YANHUA: To Hangzhou?

DAZHANG: We'll go see West Lake!

YANHUA: Oh!

DAZHANG: We'll leave first thing tomorrow morning.

YANHUA: Really? Just like that? Are you ready?

DAZHANG: I've got everything with me. Bring your things to the train station.

YANHUA: The earliest train?

DAZHANG: Yes, first thing in the morning. Bring as much cash as you've got.

YANHUA: Of course!

DAZHANG: I'll leave now! I'll get everything ready—Yanhua, listen to how fast my heart is beating!

YANHUA: I'm going to go right now to pack everything.

DAZHANG: Right.

YANHUA: See you tomorrow morning. Shall I ask for leave at the office?

DAZHANG: We'll discuss it at the train station. See you tomorrow. (*exits*)

YANHUA (*looks at him as he leaves*): Is this real? Oh, thank God! Where there's a will there *is* a way!

Act IV

Setting: Same as act I. LADY ZHANG *is sitting on the settee knitting a sweater,* WANRU *is lying on the long sofa eating candy from Suzhou. On the table there is a candy canister, and nutshells.*

LADY ZHANG: You ought to have brought a couple more packs of Caizhi House pine nut candy.

WANRU: We just couldn't carry any more. (*eats the candy*) Ma, I think dear Yanhua definitely ran off with Dazhang. Guangzu says he would bet on it.

LADY ZHANG: Forget them!

WANRU: I'm not mad! He didn't fool me!

LADY ZHANG: What's the point of being mad? He's not worth it!

WANRU: I couldn't care less! Come to think of it, he most certainly had wicked intentions and planned to trick me. (*eats the candy*) It's like pouring water over a rock: the water flows away and the rock dries up again! Neither one gives a damn about the other!

LADY ZHANG: You've broken up with him, so what's there to think about? It's not worth it! There's only your dad who keeps running around placing ads in the newspaper, writing letters—her father should have received the letter by now, but look, he hasn't even gotten a reply!

(*Offstage there are sounds of an argument. In spite of* LIU SHUN's *barricade, Zhou Dazhang's* MOTHER *shouts, "I must go in!" She forces her way in, and* LIU SHUN *follows her*)

MOTHER: You are not the little ghost guarding the gate for the devil! You can't block me! This is the Zhangs' residence, and I need to ask the people named Zhang for my son!

LADY ZHANG: With whom do you wish to speak?

MOTHER: I am looking for someone named Zhang!

LADY ZHANG: Liu Shun, let her come in. If you have something to say, say it.

LIU SHUN: She is looking for Zhou Dazhang, but I told her Mr. Zhou hasn't come, and that we are named Zhang.

LADY ZHANG: What do you want?

MOTHER: I want somebody! You're getting a bargain. You already have a young lady, but you want to seize my son? You think we're going to let you take our posterity, the fruit of eighteen generations of cultivation, for free?

WANRU: What is your relation to Dazhang?

MOTHER: Hm! What is my relation to Dazhang? You even call him Dazhang! Well, don't think you can deny it! If Dazhang's not hiding here somewhere, then I'll be dammed! (*grabs* WANRU) If you don't give my Dazhang back, I will fight with you until I die!

WANRU (*struggles with her*): What are you doing? This old woman is crazy! (LIU SHUN *pulls at* MOTHER. LADY ZHANG *tugs* WANRU)

MOTHER (*to* LIU SHUN): How dare you! How dare you! Do you know who I am? I am a virtuous widow! How dare you touch me!

LIU SHUN: Am I scared of you?

LADY ZHANG: Liu Shun, you may leave. (LIU SHUN *stands outside of the door and pokes his head in*) Mrs. Zhou—your name's Zhou, am I right?—please have a seat, and if you have something to say, go ahead and say it. Wanru, tell Ahma Yang to come and pour some tea! (WANRU *exits*)

MOTHER: Well, at last Madame In-Law—is your name Zhang? Finally, an educated lady with some sense.

LADY ZHANG: Mrs. Zhou, I believe you are mistaken, we don't have any in-laws named Zhou.

MOTHER: Oh, Madame In-Law, we can't take this too rigidly. According to custom, would new relatives have the face to come here before drinking wedding wine? But doesn't it stand to reason, since I am after all the groom's family, and men are superior to women, and the *yang* more valuable than the *ying,* how can we allow you to wipe out our family, when even the imperial family never had such a custom? (AHMA YANG *enters, pours the tea, stands to one side, and stares.* WANRU *also stands at a distance watching*)

LADY ZHANG: But, Mrs. Zhou, I only have one daughter, who is still in school, and hasn't gotten married.

MOTHER: This young lady here? She's not bad looking! She looks and sounds likes an imperial concubine, and she's very suitable for my Dazhang. But just because your daughter hasn't been married off yet, that doesn't mean my son should be married off![7] I have been agonizing over this matter for several nights, and I have been meaning to come over and talk to you about it—is it not true, Madame In-Law, that things are worse today than they used to be, when everyone would meet and talk before the daughter-in-law crossed the threshold . . . our skin is old, what do we have to be ashamed of! (*laughs*) But because these shoes on my feet are worn out on top, I thought my in-laws would laugh at me, so I said to myself, wait a while, wait until Dazhang buys me a new pair—who would have known that he—oh, I really get mad talking about this! A man's heart also faces out. He thought I would stop him, so without saying a word, he moved over here himself.

LADY ZHANG: Nothing of the sort ever happened.

MOTHER: You can't hide it from me. My gold clip, my gold *ruyi*,[8] and even that fine golden bracelet, which my brother had to go redeem for me, he took them all and wrote me a note saying he was going to get married.

LADY ZHANG: Your son, is he Zhou Dazhang?

MOTHER: Oh! My son won't recognize his own mother, is that it? However competent your son-in-law may be, he still came out of this belly of mine!

LADY ZHANG: Oh, Zhou Dazhang's mom!

MOTHER: Call me Madame In-Law, and let's be a little more civil. I've been addressing you as Madame In-Law all this time.

LADY ZHANG: But Zhou Dazhang is no relation of mine!

MOTHER: He wrote a very clear note saying he was going to get married. I can't read, and his sister can't read either. We waited for two days and he didn't come back, so I was worried sick. Finally, his uncle came and read the note, and only then did we know that he was here.

LADY ZHANG: Mrs. Zhou, why your son took your belongings I have no idea, because he didn't come here.

MOTHER: Oh, Madame In-Law, I've saved those few pieces of jewelry all this time to give to my daughter-in-law. I'm a widow who has suffered tremendously, I raised my son to maturity, and I was merely looking forward to him getting a wife soon, having grandchildren soon, so that I didn't live this life for nothing. I have maintained my widowhood until this day. I didn't get to wear colorful clothes; I only awaited the good times when he would be mar-

---

[7] In traditional China, there were different terms meaning "to marry" for a woman (*chujia*) and for a man (*ququn*). Here Mrs. Zhou objects to the notion that her son is being married out (*chujia*).

[8] An S-shaped ornament.

ried, so that I could wear colorful skirts and be the mother-in-law, and have them pay their respects to me. Madame In-Law, think about it. . . .

LADY ZHANG: Old woman, I have already told you: your son is not here. If you don't believe me, ask the gatekeepers.

MOTHER (*angrily*): Madame In-Law, let's be reasonable. Even if you insist on denying it, how can I believe you? Your house is huge, and my son is not a sesame seed—even if he were, even if he were a speck of ash, I would recognize him! (*toward offstage in loud voice*) Dazhang! You might as well come out now, don't think you can hide from your mom! (*crosses to the door*)

LADY ZHANG: Where does the old lady think she's going?

MOTHER: To look for the bridal chamber!

LADY ZHANG: Ahma Yang, stop her.

AHMA YANG (*blocks her*): What bridal chamber are you looking for? We haven't any bridal chamber!

MOTHER (*pushes* YANG): Maid, quiet, wait until I tell Master In-Law, he'll tell you to beat it!

LADY ZHANG: This old woman is crazy, tell Liu Shun to drag her out!

AHMA YANG: Call the police to come and arrest her!

MOTHER: Don't bully people because you think you're powerful! If the police come, you'll still have to be reasonable! Just because my son told you to hide him and you have lots of people here, you think you can bully me? (LIU SHUN *enters, and together with* AHMA YANG *they take* MOTHER *and force her out of the room.* MOTHER *sits down and starts wailing*) I'll fight with you till the end! What's the use of living? The son whom I bore is trading me in for a new family. This world makes no sense, I will crack open my head and die and file a lawsuit with the King of Hell. (ZHANG XIANGFU *enters*)

XIANGFU: What is going on here?

LADY ZHANG: Zhou Dazhang's mom . . .

AHMA YANG: . . . has come to look for the bridal chamber . . .

LIU SHUN: And I told her that her Zhou Dazhang isn't here . . .

XIANGFU: Nonsense. (*to* MOTHER) For whom are you looking?

MOTHER (*quickly stands up*): Are you Master Zhang?

XIANGFU: Who are you looking for?

LADY ZHANG: This is Zhou Dazhang's mom, she came looking for Zhou Dazhang.

MOTHER: Madame In-Law, don't get ahead of me, let me speak my case. Oh, Relative, I have come to find my son. If you're going to take in my son as your in-residence son-in-law, you can't just break off our affection for each other and not let us see each other! For how many days now, I have been worrying myself sick . . .

XIANGFU: So Zhou Dazhang did run off! How long has he been gone?

MOTHER: Oh, very funny, these past four or five days, hasn't he been hiding out here? And you're asking me! When my Dazhang wanted to marry your young lady I was 100 percent for it; however, he can't be like those daughter-in-laws in the imperial household, who once they enter the palace are never allowed to leave again!

XIANGFU: There's no point saying all this, the one Dazhang abducted was Yan-hua! (*to* MOTHER) Hey! Your son abducted our niece, and I have hired a private detective to look for him! In a while your in-laws will be arriving in Shanghai, and you'll have to settle things with them. (*turns toward* AHMA YANG *and* LIU SHUN). You two—out! What are you staring at? (AHMA YANG *and* LIU SHUN *retreat and stand at the door*)

MOTHER: Huh? What did you say?

XIANGFU: Our niece was abducted by your son! I'm just asking you for my niece!

MOTHER: Oh my, oh my! How would I know anything about that?

XIANGFU: Liu Shun, don't let her run off! (*to* MOTHER) In your opinion, where do you think Zhou Dazhang is hiding?

MOTHER: Oh, holy Buddha! If I knew that, would I have rushed over here? I thought you all had hidden him here. Otherwise, everyone better discuss it in a more civil manner.

XIANGFU: You have kidnapped one of our family, and now you want to black-mail us! Liu Shun, don't let her sneak off! First Master will be here shortly and he'll want to interrogate her.

MOTHER (*confused, turns around as if to run;* LIU SHUN *stops her; yells*): Dazhang, you have really made me suffer! I raised a son so I could enjoy some comfort. For the sake of my son, I ate bitterness and endured abuse! Why are you ar-resting me, an ill-fated old lady?

LADY ZHANG: Let her go and let's just forget all about it.

XIANGFU: We can't, we have to arrest her. If she doesn't know where Zhou Da-zhang is, at least we can get some clues from her. Yanhua's father will arrive any minute now, and how will I deal with him if she's gone?

LIU SHUN (*points out*): First Master has arrived. (ZHANG YUANFU *enters with a cigar in his mouth*)

ZHANG YUANFU: Hello, Third Brother, Third Sister—oh, Wanru.

WANRU: First Uncle.

XIANGFU: Big Brother, you sure kept us waiting! Did you just get our letter?

YUANFU: The day before yesterday maybe? Or the day before that? I forget.

LADY ZHANG: We expected that you would come today.

YUANFU: At first, I wasn't going to—but it just so happened that I had something to do, Yanhua's mother wanted to find some matching lace for her dress, and said that the best stuff was in Shanghai. . . .

XIANGFU: Yanhua has run off, and we've been asking around everywhere for her.

YUANFU: If she ran off, then she's gone . . .

LADY ZHANG: She ran off with a man.

YUANFU: Of course she went with a man, she wouldn't have run off with a woman.

XIANGFU: She was abducted by an imposter.

YUANFU: If he tricked her into taking a liking to him, that's fine.

XIANGFU: Oh, then you're not going to go after her?

YUANFU: What for? Women aren't meant to be kept. If you keep them locked up in their rooms and seal the door, they will still escape.

XIANGFU: So you're just going to let her go?

YUANFU (*laughs, puffs out smoke rings in the air*): What's the point of not letting her? She's already gone.

LADY ZHANG (*laughs*): Our big brother is so liberal.

XIANGFU: So, I won't concern myself with it either. (*points at* MOTHER) This is that man's mom, and if you have something to say, say it.

YUANFU: What's there to say? (*sitting on the sofa with his feet sticking out, he calmly puffs out smoke rings*)

MOTHER (*frees herself from* LIU SHUN): I have something to say—I will not fall into your trap! You have kidnapped my son, yet you say my son has kidnapped one of yours! Scare me away, and have a nice family reunion. But I won't be fooled! I am not leaving! I will stay right here, because Dazhang can't keep hiding forever!

XIANGFU: Fine, I'll call the police to come take you away, and make you hand over your son.

MOTHER: My dear relatives, my son is hiding here with you, and I am merely asking you for him.

XIANGFU: My niece has disappeared with your son; we're asking you for her.

YUANFU: Oh, what are you all going on about?

XIANGFU: Going on about! Big Brother, it's your fault. Your daughter is unmanageable, she has caused all sorts of trouble, and she has ruined the Zhang women's good reputation! You may not care, but I have an unmarried daughter.

YUANFU: What's it got to do with this? Yanhua is Yanhua, Wanru is Wanru.

XIANGFU: They are both young ladies of the Zhang household, with the same good name.

YUANFU: There may be some connection, but there's nothing we can do!

XIANGFU: Says who? When you write a bad check, you immediately go and send in some money to make up for the difference! The pair of them ran off, so we have to catch them, bring them back, and help them get married!

MOTHER: Oh dear, my Dazhang clearly said he was coming to get married, but with whom did he run off?

XIANGFU: You're pretending not to know! You yourself said that he was coming to get married, so tell us: where did he go to get married?

MOTHER: He didn't get married here? You tricked him with your dinners and desserts, so does he think about his mother anymore? Would he tell his mother where he was getting married? I want to find him to talk with him, but you keep stopping me. And now you're asking me! I'm telling him to come out and tell us himself! (*makes as if to go upstairs;* XIANG *blocks her*)

YUANFU (*calmly*): Let her search. When she's done looking, you can go over to her house to look too. Isn't it that easy!

XIANGFU: Fine, Ahma Yang—what are you all gaping at?—take her all around to look, so she can see for herself whether he's here or not. (MOTHER *looks back, hesitates, and doesn't dare go upstairs*)

XIANGFU: Go! Go ahead and look!

MOTHER: I am here all by myself, and you could easily kill me.

LADY ZHANG: Absurd! You're the one who said that we are hiding your son, and you're the one who wanted to go look for him; now we're inviting you to go take a look but you won't go. Isn't she unreasonable?

MOTHER: You outnumber me; what if you locked me up?

LADY ZHANG (*laughs*): Why would we lock you up?—Liu Shun, Ahma Yang, leave us. (*to* MOTHER) Come with me. . . . (MOTHER *sees the feather broom in the corner, and grabs it*)

AHMA YANG: Madame, don't do this.

MOTHER: I'm going to hold it for courage, I won't hit anyone.

AHMA YANG (*comes back with a broom*): Madame, you go first, I'll follow.

MOTHER: What are you doing?

AHMA YANG: I won't hit anyone either.

LADY ZHANG: Come on! (LADY ZHANG, MOTHER, *and* WANRU *exit*)

LIU SHUN: I have never seen such an inspection team. (*exits*)

XIANGFU: When they're done inspecting, we can all go together to her house.

YUANFU: For what?

XIANGFU: To make a little inspection.

YUANFU (*calmly puts out his cigarette*): Why must you lower yourself to that old lady? Where on earth is there a child who belongs to his or her parents? When they are young they are parasites, and when they're grown up they are on their own; boys, girls, they're all the same!

XIANGFU: So you're saying that none of us should worry about it?

YUANFU (*slowly*): This is what is called the "son and daughter debt"! We're in their debt!

XIANGFU (*sighing*): The poor girl—I always said that Zhou Dazhang was not to be trusted.

YUANFU: What kind of man is he?

XIANGFU: He's an employee in some company, and his family is just him and his mom.

YUANFU: If he managed to trick Yanhua, then he must be clever.

XIANGFU: I'm afraid they have hard times ahead of them. How much do you plan to give her?

YUANFU: For a dowry? Her own talent is her living dowry, and she can earn two or three percent interest a month on it.

XIANGFU: Shouldn't you at least give her something?

YUANFU: Not even a cent. (FENG GUANGZU *enters*)

GUANGZU: Uncle—oh, First Uncle, when did you arrive? I have found Yanhua!

XIANGFU: You found her? Where is she?

GUANGZU: She sent a letter telling me to meet her at 5:00 at the station.

XIANGFU: Where were they?

GUANGZU: She told me to keep it a secret.

YUANFU: Ha, ha, then keep it a secret for them!

XIANGFU: Why did she tell you to go there? (FENG *doesn't answer*) I know, no doubt she wants money! Um, what else did she say?

GUANGZU: Nothing else.

XIANGFU: She didn't mention Dazhang?

GUANGZU: It is him.

XIANGFU: Zhou Dazhang's mother has accused us of hiding her son, and she is upstairs right now searching for him. (LADY ZHANG *enters*, MOTHER *enters, crying*, WANRU *and the others follow behind*)

LADY ZHANG: Don't cry, he must be hiding somewhere else.

MOTHER (*tearfully*): Dazhang! Where is my Dazhang? I want to wear colorful skirts and be a mother-in-law! Now I won't have a son to bury me when I die. I have nothing to depend on to go on living, and when I die I'll just have to steal cold food at the Junction of the Three Roads.

GUANGZU: Is this the lady?

XIANGFU: Wipe your tears and stop crying, this gentleman has brought your son back.

LADY ZHANG: You found him?

MOTHER (*dries her tears*): Where is Dazhang?

XIANGFU: Don't rush me, I first want to ask you, what do you intend to do when your son returns?

MOTHER: I'll make him go home.

XIANGFU: Do you plan to hold a wedding celebration for your son and daughter-in-law?

MOTHER: Yes! I have already prepared the bridal chamber. I don't have anything else, but I bought some big red candles a long time ago, to light to pray to the ancestors. The bedding on the wedding bed was what I used for my own wedding.

XIANGFU: Excellent. Listen to me, Mrs. Zhou, you hurry back home and put on your colorful clothes to get ready to be a mother-in-law. The bride and groom are on their way back.

LADY ZHANG: You really found them?

WANRU (*to* FENG): Did Yanhua write you?

GUANGZU (*nods*): I have news.

MOTHER: You said my Dazhang is coming back?

XIANGFU: Right, he'll be back soon, bringing your daughter-in-law with him.

MOTHER: Really, you're not teasing me?

XIANGFU: You ask this gentleman here, he's about to go to the station to meet them and bring them back to your house.

GUANGZU: But how shall I meet them? They didn't plan to go home.

XIANGFU: Guangzu, you are so useless. First arrange it with a taxi, and just tell them you're inviting them for dinner and trick them into the taxi. Tell the driver to take you to his home—Mrs. Zhou, where do you live? Tell me the exact address, so we can deliver them home easily.

MOTHER: Seven Horses Road, upstairs from the Wanli convenience store. This store was opened by Dazhang's uncle, who got really rich! In one day he does several thousand *kuai* of business. . . .

XIANGFU: Yes, he must be rich—Seven Horses Road, number what?

MOTHER: 7700, next to the pancake vendor, and across from the fruit store.

XIANGFU: Well then, you go back first and wait, the ladies here will want to get dressed up so they can go to your house for the wedding banquet. . . .

MOTHER: Oh dear, how can I afford to host a wedding banquet?

XIANGFU: Don't worry, I'll arrange it all and have it sent over.

MOTHER: Aiya, In-Law, you are so polite!—Well, I myself have to go get cleaned up and dressed. . . .

LADY ZHANG (*laughing*): So hurry back.

MOTHER: What about my Dazhang?

XIANGFU: This gentleman is going to meet them.

MOTHER: I'll go meet them too.

XIANGFU: If you go, then you'll ruin the plan. Your son doesn't plan to go home, so if he sees you, he'll hide. Hurry home, and wait by the door. Guangzu, you be careful and don't let Yanhua run off again. Mrs. Zhou, when your son gets out of the taxi, drag him upstairs.

MOTHER: I will not let him slip away for my life!

GUANGZU: Then I'm off to meet them.

XIANGFU: Don't forget the address. Guangzu, can you handle this little matter? This is Yanhua's big day, so we have to wrap it up nicely for her.

GUANGZU: Relax. (*looking at watch*) I'm leaving. (*exits*)

MOTHER: It is true. I have to go back and tidy up the house! I'm also leaving.

LADY ZHANG: Hurry back.

MOTHER (*laughing*): You'll come soon! We're relatives now, so don't blame me for my shabby house, Master In-Law, Madame In-Law, Miss, and also this Master In-law, please come over! (*the crowd laughs and accompanies* MOTHER *to the door; only* YUANFU *doesn't move, but sits on the sofa smoking*)

LADY ZHANG (*laughing*): How hard it was to see her off! Even my brain is swelling up.

XIANGFU: It's not over yet, hurry up and make a marriage license, and we also need Yanhua's seal—Wanru, what else does one need to be a bride?

WANRU: Flowers, headdress, and a veil.

XIANGFU: Right, let's go get ready.

LADY ZHANG: What for?

XIANGFU: Once we've apprehended them and brought them back, we have to hold a belated wedding ceremony for them.

WANRU: Hey! Yanhua is marrying him! Hooligan! Imposter!

YUANFU (*yawning*): She's already married, she doesn't need your permission!

XIANGFU: You all have to hurry up! And you have to get dressed up.

LADY ZHANG: I'm not going! Who wants to claim kinship with that old lady?

XIANGFU: This is the big event! Who says they're not going?

YUANFU (*lazily*): You go, I'm going to stay here and lie down for a while.

XIANGFU: You are the host of the wedding, I am the witness.

LADY ZHANG: Wanru and I are not going.

WANRU: Mother, let's go watch.

XIANGFU: Let's go, let's go. For Yanhua, this is her once-in-a-lifetime wedding day. As soon as the ceremony's over, we can come back and that's it.

WANRU: Mama, what should we wear? (*drags* LADY ZHANG *off*)

XIANGFU (*making phone call*): Is this the Big Fortune Restaurant? I want to order one banquet table. . . .

Act V

Setting: Same as act II, in Zhou Dazhang's house. The interior has been swept clean, decorations have been hung, and the red candles have been lit. MOTHER *is wearing a red skirt and is sitting upright in the middle of the room.* SISTER *is dressed in splendid attire, with red flowers in her hair, and jewelry. She is helping* MOTHER *put on her makeup.*

MOTHER (*looking in mirror*): Make it a little redder! I have an honest personality, and if it's supposed to be red, let the red show. (*sighing*) From the time I gave birth to you until now, I have never gotten dressed up the way I wanted to. The day that you got married, I did nothing more than put on a little rouge. . . .

SISTER: Is this okay?

MOTHER (*looking in mirror, she sighs*): Oh, look at me, I sure am old! Elder Sister, you should have seen me when I was a bride! I was fresh as a daisy, my cheeks as red and plump as fresh chicken eggs. (*stroking her cheeks*) They all said I looked like a beauty on a cigarette box![9] (*shaking head, she sighs*) I didn't even get dressed up that many times, and I'm already old!

SISTER: Who's old? My mother-in-law still dresses up like she was eighteen years old, and she even wears big red flowers.

MOTHER: Does she? When she was a bride, with that not-quite-black-not-quite-yellow face of hers, she already looked like she was thirty years old. And now she really is that old. Oh, Elder Sister, it's a pity you couldn't have seen me when I attended her wedding! My hair was slicked back in a fashionable high and round style, like a glossy sesame seed cake, and on this side here (*putting her hand next to her ear*) was a big red flower with big green leaves.

AUNT (*from offstage, loudly*): The guests are here! (ZHANG YUANFU, ZHANG XIANG-FU, LADY ZHANG, *and* WANRU *enter.* WANRU *has a small box under her arm, and is carrying flowers.* AUNT *enters*) The guests are here!

MOTHER: Oh my, two Master In-Laws, Madame In-Law, Miss, please sit down! Please sit! It is cramped in here and filthy—Sister-in-Law, you've also been busy helping me!

AUNT: What are you talking about! We haven't even congratulated you yet! Little Mao is outside with her father keeping an eye out for Dazhang; they should be back soon. (*turning around*) Please make yourselves comfortable. Elder Sister, pour them tea. (*picks up the stool*)

LADY ZHANG: Don't stand on ceremony, don't bother . . . (ZHOU SHIKUI *enters*)

---

[9]Images of attractive young women graced cigarette boxes and many other consumer products in the first part of the twentieth century.

ZHOU SHIKUI: Sister-in-Law, congratulations!

MOTHER: Congrats to you too. (*frantically hurrying about*) Everyone please make yourselves comfortable, and don't be offended by the filth. (*taking out a rag, she wipes the table and stools*)

XIANGFU: Madame, don't rush—if you have dressed, go downstairs and wait at the entrance, lest your son run off.

MOTHER: Aiya, how can I not be ashamed standing at the door looking like this? (WANRU *tries not to laugh;* ZHANG YUANFU *has already found the most comfortable chair and sits there smoking*)

XIANGFU: Move a stool down there and sit behind the door. When you hear the car arrive, hurry and go out.

MOTHER: Then I'd better go down. I'm also going to ask my elder brother help me catch Dazhang—oh, Elder Sister, pour some tea! (*points to her*) That's the sister-in-law of your little miss, my daughter. That is, she was married to my nephew—this is my sister-in-law, my daughter's mother-in-law—take a seat, everyone, I cleaned off the stools with soda water. . . .

AUNT: Go on downstairs! I'll stay here.

MOTHER: Brother-in-Law, you help out too. These two are the masters of the Zhang family, this is the mistress, and this is their eldest young miss.

XIANGFU: Mother Zhou, hurry up and go downstairs!

MOTHER: I'm just on my way. (*exits, then turns around*) Don't stand on ceremony. (*exits*)

XIANGFU (*turns around*): What kind of ceremonial hall is this? We'd better decorate it a bit. Wanru, take out the things, and let's prepare. (WANRU *opens the small box*) Move the table here, spread out the red carpet here. (*everyone moves the table and spreads out the carpet*) Does Zhou Dazhang have a seal?

SISTER: Yes, yes. (*opening the drawer, she looks for the seal*)

XIANGFU: How about Mother Zhou?

SISTER: She has a wooden one.

XIANGFU: That'll do, get them all out and put them on the table—when the groom comes he stands here, when the bride comes she stands here. (*points*) Ah, we still don't have a master of ceremonies . . .

AUNT: Uncle is often the master of ceremonies.

SHIKUI: Ah, ah, I . . . is there a script?

XIANGFU: I didn't prepare one.

YUANFU: Then just don't hold the ceremony.

XIANGFU: Can you do it without a script?

SHIKUI: Well, they'll have to follow what I say, okay! (*outside an automobile honks*)

WANRU: They're here!

XIANGFU: They're here! (*the crowd listens quietly.* MOTHER *forces* DAZHANG *up the stairs;* AUNT *follows, carrying a small suitcase*)

MOTHER: Don't even think about running! You're back! My poor heart has been boiling in oil day and night!

DAZHANG (*freeing himself*): Ma, I'm back, I won't run away again. (*confused, greets the crowd of guests*) (FENG *carries a suitcase with one hand and leads in* YANHUA *with the other*)

GUANGZU (*greets the crowd*): We're here!

YANHUA: What are you doing? (*stares at the crowd*)

XIANGFU: Wanru, be the bride!

SHIKUI (*giving order*): Be the bride! (XIANGFU *pushes* DAZHANG *to stand in front of the table, motions to* FENG *to put flowers on* YANHUA)

YANHUA: Wanru! Third Uncle! Third Aunt!—oh, Dad!

AUNT ZHOU (*silences her*): Tell the bride not to open her mouth! It's unlucky for the bride to open her mouth. (*helping* YANHUA *and* DAZHANG *stand together.* SISTER *stands next to* YANHUA, *and helps* WANRU *drape the veil on her.* WANRU *holds* YANHUA's *flowers*)

XIANGFU (*standing exactly in front of the table*): Come, Elder Brother (*inviting* ZHANG YUANFU *to stand to his left*), Mother Zhou. (*inviting her to stand to his right. Clears his throat*) Everyone, please listen up, ah . . .

SHIKUI: Wedding host, please make a speech!

XIANGFU: I am the chief witness, they (*pointing at* MOTHER *and* YUANFU) are the hosts.

SHIKUI: The chief witness is going to make a speech on behalf of the hosts!

XIANGFU: Everyone listen: Zhou Dazhang and Zhang Yanhua have freely expressed that they are mutually willing to be married and become husband and wife, ah—for many things, the rules can be stretched, and it's not too late to conduct a make-up wedding ceremony; and dispensing with formalities is very common these days anyway. And it just so happens that today is a propitious day. We have lit Longfeng candles, we have spread out a red felt carpet. Bride and groom, bow to each other to become a couple. We hope that you will be compatible for a hundred years, remain happily married till old age, and have many children and grandchildren. Long live their fortune and may their long lives last forever. (*makes a signal to* ZHOU SHIKUI)

SHIKUI: Bride and groom face each other!

YANHUA (*pulling off the veil*): What is this?

AUNT (*silences her*): Brides don't open their mouths!

SISTER: When the bride her tongue won't hold, mountain of rice and tons of gold!

SHIKUI (*ordering*): Kneel!

DAZHANG: Huh? (MOTHER *and others push him down to kneel*)

YANHUA: Dazhang!

AUNT (*to* SISTER): Tell the bride not to open her mouth!

SISTER: When the bride starts to talk, endless wealth will to her walk! (YANHUA *is angry, bites her lip;* SISTER *and* AUNT *push her down to kneel*)

SHIKUI (*ordering*): Kneel! One kowtow! Two kowtows! On your feet! The ceremony's complete!

XIANGFU: Stamp the marriage certificate.

SHIKUI (*ordering*): Married couple affix their seals! (GUANGZU *helps* DAZHANG, WANRU *helps* YANHUA) The hosts affix their seal! (YUANFU *stamps, and* XIANGFU *helps* MOTHER) The marriage witness affixes his seal! (XIANGFU *stamps it*) (YANHUA *pulls off the veil*)

SHIKUI (*ordering*): Bride takes off her veil! Bride and groom, pay your respects to your elders!

YUANFU: Good God, just bow and be done with it.

MOTHER (*dragging the chair to the middle, she sits down*): In-Law, what a thing to say! In times like these, it is rare to have a day like today! If you just stand there, bend your body back and forth a few times, is that a ceremony?

SHIKUI: Pay respects to your mother-in-law! (MOTHER *sits up straight*)

SHIKUI: Kneel! One kowtow! Two kowtows! On your feet! (DAZHANG *kneels down himself;* SISTER *and* AUNT *push down* YANHUA)

SHIKUI: Pay respects to your uncle!

XIANGFU: Everyone just make a salute and be done with it.

SHIKUI: With the two families together? There is no such thing as this ritual!

LADY ZHANG: This kind of kowtow can "tow" till tomorrow.

SHIKUI: Okay, okay, okay. Everyone bow to each other. (*the crowd stands in a line, and bows to* DAZHANG *and* YANHUA)

SHIKUI (*ordering*): Pay respects to the ancestral temple!

YUANFU: We're not done paying respects yet? (YANHUA *stands up straight without moving*)

SISTER: The bride is tired, sit a while. Uncle, let's pray to the ancestors this evening.

MOTHER: Don't rush! Don't rush! (*holding* YANHUA*'s hand*) Sit down for a while and rest! Don't tire yourself out!

LADY ZHANG (*to* XIANGFU): We can go home now. (WANRU *packs the veil and other things*)

XIANGFU (*nodding*): Then go back—Yanhua, you are now one of them, we have formally married you to them, so be a virtuous wife and daughter-in-law. Mother Zhou, you can relax now! The wedding banquet will be sent over shortly, we're leaving now.

MOTHER: Oh dear, relatives, you're leaving before the wedding banquet? You've spent so much money, and you're not going to eat anything yourselves?

LADY ZHANG: We'll eat at home. Come on, Wanru—Guangzu—

MOTHER: Won't you stay a while longer? Elder Sister, Uncle, Sister-in-Law—everyone go and see them off. (*the crowd sends them off*)

YANHUA: Dazhang, what just happened?

DAZHANG: I don't know either.

YANHUA: It wasn't a dream?

DAZHANG: It sure seemed like a play.

YANHUA: This—is this your home?

DAZHANG: Our home!

YANHUA (*looking around*): What a cultured family! (*pointing outside*) That was your wise and proper, talented and virtuous mother? And down below is your uncle's magnificent department store? And that happy woman was your sister! (*laughing bitterly*) My, Dazhang, you really did transform your environment! I admire your skill in transforming your environment!

DAZHANG: Oh, Yanhua, you are in charge of your destiny! I admire your skill in controlling fate!

YANHUA: Fine! You are right! I really understand what you mean! You say fate is what I control, right? I can't blame you, am I right?

DAZHANG: Ai, Yanhua, we are just the same. Let's not blame each other.

YANHUA: I can't compare with you!

DAZHANG: Don't be so modest, Yanhua! Besides you, who else would suit me?

YANHUA: And besides you, who else would suit me? Too bad I don't have the nerve you do! This is "our family now"! You tricked me into coming to this family!

DAZHANG: Oh, for heaven's sake, Yanhua, you are an extremely intelligent person, how could you blame me? If I were a god, if I wanted something, would I not have that which pleased you? But this is beyond my control!

YANHUA: It's beyond your control? Hm, everything is controlled by you! But what I want to do, I definitely do!

DAZHANG: Right, you can conquer fate!

YANHUA: Including you! Starting with you! Remember that!

DAZHANG: Me? I can only transform . . .

YANHUA: From now on, I will supervise your transformations! Including you! Starting with you! Remember that!

DAZHANG: Yanhua, how right you are! You're right about everything, everything! If we depend on my ability to transform the environment, and combine it with your knack for controlling fate, we can be successful wherever we go!

YANHUA (*sarcastically*): Coming from your mouth, everything is positive!

DAZHANG: Nothing that comes from the mouth is dependable, so from now on we must watch out, since the world belongs to us! Come, come drink a cup, this world belongs to us! (*pouring tea, he forces* YANHUA *to clink glasses with him*)

YANHUA (*drinking*): This is lukewarm tea!

DAZHANG: Just pretend it's wine! (*the crowd enters, and everyone helps to move the table and set up the feast*)

DAZHANG (*pouring the wine*): Ma, you must be exhausted having prepared all this! Paternal Uncle, Maternal Uncle, Aunt, Brother-in-Law, Sister, you've all worn yourselves out! Today is a day of great festivities! My father-in-law hasn't made any effort for me yet, but my uncle-in-law has already found me a good official position! (YANHUA *looks down and stands to one side*) My bride is of course not as pretty as my mother! But she is so obedient that if you took a lantern and went and searched, you wouldn't find another like her. In this life of mine, what now won't go my way? Today is my wedding feast, and it is really a happy feast!

CROWD (*lifting glasses*): Congratulations! Congratulations!

7
Su Qing
(1914–1982)

Born Feng Yunzhuang in 1914, Su Qing made her literary debut with the publication of her essay "Having a Boy, Having a Girl" in 1935 in *Analects,* the popular humor magazine edited by Lin Yutang. A year earlier she had gotten married and withdrawn from her studies at National Central University in Nanjing to give birth to her first child. The essay, which Su Qing would later describe as an attempt to alleviate the boredom of being cooped up at home, is a droll reflection on the Chinese family's obsessive preoccupation with male descendants. A few months later *Analects* editor Tao Kangde wrote urging her to submit more work to Lin Yutang's newly launched *Cosmic Wind,* and over the next few years Su churned out a steady stream of amusing essays on topics ranging from contemporary female education to divorce to hairdos. Typical of the style of Lin Yutang and the "nonaligned" literature for which he and his protégés were best known, her essay writing assiduously eschews the serious and often overly strident tone characteristic of revolutionary literature of the day and instead muses on contemporary themes with wit and a sense of ironic detachment.

After the outbreak of the Sino-Japanese War, Su Qing continued writing prolifically in this same vein, regularly contributing to several major Shanghai literary journals, including those associated with the Wang Jingwei regime such as *Reminiscences* and *Talks Amid Hardship* as well as the *China Weekly.* In 1943, having separated from her husband and in need of an independent source of income, she launched her own highly successful literary magazine, *Heaven and Earth,* a venture that apparently had the backing of several high-level collaborationist city officials, including Chen Gongbo, the mayor of Shanghai from 1940 to 1944. These connections, plus the fact that she was said to have accepted a cushy sinecure in the Shanghai municipal government, would later be cited as evidence of Su Qing's reactionary crimes in the postrevolutionary era. (In her own defense, Su Qing maintained that the choices she made during the war were motivated by survival and the need to support herself and three young children.) *Heaven and Earth* featured work by Zhang Ailing, at the time one of Shanghai's young new literary sensations, as well as a number of other contemporary female authors, though Su Qing also used the publication to showcase her own creative work: her essays appeared in virtually every issue until the magazine's demise in mid–1945, and she would also use the magazine's press to issue several individual volumes of her work. The collection *Clear Stream* appeared in 1944, followed the next year by *Waves, Eat Drink Man Woman,* and *Flowing Waters.* In 1944, Heaven and Earth Press also published her novel *Ten Years of Marriage,* which had been received with enormous enthusiasm by urban readers during its serialization in *Talks Amid Hardship.* The novel was Su Qing's most successful creative work, going into some thirty consecutive reprintings after its initial publication and making her one of the most widely read contemporary authors in Shanghai in the 1940s. Typical of her literary sensibility, the work reads as a satirical rewriting of the sentimental tradition of May Fourth women's confession, featuring an innovative first-person narrator who laughs at her own follies as a modern woman trapped (at least temporarily) in an absurdly old-fashioned family, as well as the silly sexism that pervades contemporary society. Critics at the time misinterpreted the novel as being about sex, which, albeit not accurate, as Su Qing pointed out, actually helped boost sales! Su Qing's other major works of fiction from this period include *Sequel to Ten Years of Marriage* (1947), which chronicles the protagonist's adventures as a divorcée, and another quasi-autobiographical novel, *A Straying Beauty* (1948).

In the early years of the PRC, Su Qing responded to a recruitment call by the Ministry of Culture to work in the newly reorganized Shanghai theater world. In 1951, she was assigned to the Fanghua drama troupe, which specialized in *yueju* opera; later she would be transferred to the Red Flag drama troupe. Despite never having worked as a dramatist before, she was prolific throughout this period, publishing numerous plays, the majority of which were adaptions of traditional stories. They included *Quyuan, Baoyu and Daiyu* (based on the classical masterpiece *Dream of the Red Chamber*), and *The Story of Liwa,* and were staged regularly in Shanghai and Beijing.

Although Su Qing reportedly joined two of the newly established CCP women's organizations in Shanghai after 1949, her writing from this era does not seem to sustain the feminist critique that distinguished her wartime literary output. She made the mistake of publishing a series of essays in the Hong Kong-based *Shanghai Daily* that, while not directly critical of the ruling Communist Party, seemed to ridicule certain aspects of the "new society." This, together with lingering suspicions about her activities during the Shanghai occupation, led to her arrest in 1955 by the Shanghai Public Security Bureau on counterrevolutionary charges. She was released from jail in June 1957, but her reputation never fully recovered, and with her writing banned, her literary career went into sharp decline. Su Qing died at the age of 69 in relative obscurity in Shanghai in 1982. Her name was officially cleared two years later.

"Waves," the autobiographical essay translated here, was first published in 1945 and captures Su Qing's distinctly post–May Fourth vision of women's emancipation and national salvation. Whereas writers of the previous generation tended to romanticize the rebellious New Woman, here the author presents a satirical self-portrait of her career as a student activist at a girl's school in Ningbo to throw into sharp relief the discrepancies between the rhetoric and the realities of modern politics.

Waves

(1945)

I

LIFE IS LIKE the sea, a vast expanse when calm, aimless, even stymied. Yet when all of a sudden the waves start surging, roaring and unstoppable, the ones in back pushing the ones in front, those in front pushing those in front of them, that's just the way it is, it's not up to you anymore, you've just got to roll with it. And then the wind stops and the waves die down and what's left is that vast expanse once more, all worn out, the crashing waves mere memory.

When I started middle school at the age of twelve, the air was heavy with gathering storms. My school wasn't any ordinary school, it was the county Normal School for Girls. It was the only place in Yin County where girls could get a middle school education; there wasn't any such thing as coeducation back then, not in anyone's wildest dreams.

The school was located in the middle of Moon Lake, and the dormitory occupied a lovely spot called Bamboo Isle. Bamboo Isle certainly had its share of historic sites. As early as 1041, during the Northern Song dynasty, there was a building where the Master of West Lake came to lecture, though the island was called Pine Island back then. By 1174, in the Southern Song, the venerable Shi Zhongding built the Retreat of True Seclusion there, and renamed it Bamboo Isle. Then Master Shen Shuhui and his younger brother Bing took up residence to the right of the Retreat of True Seclusion, where they each set up a thriving academy. From then on, it seemed every era drew prominent figures to the place, such as Lou Xuanxian and his Bright Brocade Hall, Quan Xieshan, who wrote in the House at Double Chive Mountain, and Huang Jingji, who lectured at Distinguishing the Essence of Loyalty Hut. Local history of such distinction was a favorite topic among the Ningbo elite, and few enjoyed it more than our principal, Master Shi.

Master Shi was a Budding Talent degree-holder from the last dynasty, and an old friend of my paternal grandfather. He had a round, red face and a traditional three-part beard, not all that long, but not short either, that grew from his chin. He was always stroking this beard when he talked, but gingerly, lest he lose a single strand, which would be no laughing matter, indeed, a far sadder affair than if his rimless glasses were to break. Apparently, his glasses only ever broke once in his life, and that was during my first six months at the school. The way I heard it, an upperclass student who had joined the KMT had gathered three or four classmates on the playground early one morning to talk about equality of the sexes, abolishing arranged marriage and whatnot, when she was overheard by my fifth aunt on my father's side (who was also our dorm mother). She ran straight to the principal, her little bound feet in leather shoes pattering across the ground like a drum roll. Master Shi, who had just sat down with a cup of tea, was stroking his beard with one hand while removing his glasses to wipe off the steam with the other. My aunt burst in out of breath, delivering her report in fits and starts. Master Shi had only to hear the three syllables K-M-T for his hands to start trembling. His beard remained intact, thank goodness, but his glasses got knocked to the floor, and though my aunt swooped in to retrieve them, it was too late to spare him that sharp pang of loss, for one of the fine lenses had shattered.

As if the lens weren't enough, Master Shi's heart itself broke over time. Because even though the student who joined the KMT had been forced to "voluntarily withdraw" from the school, a new wind seemed to be sweeping through the upperclassmen. All over campus, on the playground and even in the restrooms, students were huddling together discussing matters in hushed and urgent tones, which caused my poor aunt's bound feet in their little leather shoes no small amount of drumming, all that running back and forth. Master Shi could be heard now to sigh as he stroked his beard. When I first arrived at the school and couldn't figure out what was going on, I asked around; people told me what was happening, and it made sense. But even after my enlighten-ment, there were still some things I didn't get. What was the KMT? And why were people who joined it forced to leave school?

When I asked my aunt these things, she panicked. The blood rushed to her face and she grew more and more flustered as she tried to warn me off this sub-ject. "What did you say? How could you . . . how could a child know about the . . . KMT? Who told you about it? Thank goodness . . . thank goodness, it could be worse, he hasn't found out . . . if he knew, if Master Shi knew—you'd better watch out, don't you ever mention such things again!"

Now I was scared too, and didn't dare say another word to anyone. But Master Shi summoned me to his office that same morning, and my aunt was standing right there beside him. Her face was bright red, whereas his now looked rather pasty, as if his usual rosy glow had been transferred in its entirety to my aunt. He looked as if he'd just lost his temper, but his expression was also traced with grief.

I trembled as I made my bow to him.

He nodded slightly, his left hand holding his teacup, his right hand start-ing to stroke his beard. He said many things to me, many wise and learned things, citing many an ancient text. I didn't understand any of it at first, and I was scared. At long last I finally managed to latch onto the phrase "jade and stone burn together," which probably was intended to mean that if I made trouble with those other girls again, I'd end up going down with them. But I hadn't made trouble with them, I'd only asked a question. I didn't know what my aunt had told him, and I wanted to explain, but he'd already dismissed me with a wave of his hand. This was the first chance I'd had to talk with him since I'd started at the school—or rather, I should say, the first chance to listen to him.

The second time he called me into his office it was because I was wearing my hair in two braids. Girls' schools back then had rules about this: in primary school, girls wore braids; in secondary school they did not, regardless of the student's age—all that mattered was what grade she was in. When I started normal school at twelve, I was the youngest kid there; many eighteen-, nine-teen-, even twenty-year-old primary school students were wearing their hair in braids, but I was supposed to put mine up in a bun. There were all kinds of fancy buns: the vertical S, the horizontal S, just to name two, but I couldn't make any of them. I could only manage the look of the most straightforward sort of girl, the simplest and easiest hairstyle, which was to put my hair in a single braid, coil it up somehow, and then tack it down with hairpins. But running and skipping made my hairpins fall out, and the braid would uncoil and wind its way down my back like a stream down a mountain gully. Someone suggested that since I was too young for a bun to look right on me anyway, I was better off combing my hair into two braids and wearing a coil on each side. Remembering how nice this looked on the servant girls of beautiful women in old paintings convinced me to try it.

I had no idea Master Shi would call me back for another reprimand. This time his face looked even pastier, and his right hand was no longer stroking his beard but clenching it. He said, "Why are you breaking the rules like this? Wearing two braids—what's become of you? The ancients put it well: the sky does not have two suns, nor the people two rulers. This is rebellion!"

Aunt Five was standing there, her face so red she looked overheated, except that her limbs were trembling as though she were cold. I was wondering what a hairdo could possibly have to do with rebellion. It was a mystery to me how anyone could find an analogy between two braids and the sun or a king. Just as I was framing these questions, just as my lips initiated the slightest of movements, my aunt screamed, "What are you waiting for? Go fix your hair! Who told you to wear it in two buns? Who's putting you up to this? Go on, go change it right now!" Choking back my tears, I retreated, feeling enormously wronged.

Thus were my braids reunited, joined together as one. Meanwhile, the entire country of China was falling apart as usual—the vast and mighty Nationalist Revolutionary Army was setting off from Guangdong, sweeping toward Zhejiang.

One sunny spring day the following year, the comrades had accomplished at last their glorious task: the new flag was now flying all over town. Everywhere, that is, except the girls' school, our own Master Shi at the helm. Every office, school, organization—even every fashionable home—was rushing to raise this new red flag with a white sun in a square of blue sky in the upper left-hand corner. Everyone hung the flag as high as they possibly could, and it felt to us young people everywhere we went as if the flags were calling out to us in greeting as they flapped in the wind. As we looked up at those flags, thousands and thousands of hearts rose together, and the cries of those hearts rose higher and higher: *Down with imperialism! Down with local tyrants and evil gentry! Freedom for women! Girls, cut your hair!* And the final demand—coeducation, which made Master Shi positively apoplectic.

He refused to hang the national flag, on the grounds that it would usher in all manner of wickedness. When the upper-level students complained, he simply locked down the campus. So day students boarded at the school for a time, and boarders weren't allowed to leave on Sundays or even official holidays. But eventually the outside world caught wind of it, and flyers went up on walls, pillars, and shop windows all around the periphery of the school. They all said more or less the same thing: OUT WITH THE OLD RETROGRADE! SACK THE DIE-HARD! Of course we didn't get to see them right away. We finally laid eyes on them one day when we sent Amah Zhang out to buy us some peanuts; the candy shop was so cheap they used a flyer they'd ripped down to wrap them up. OUT WITH THE OLD RETROGRADE! SACK THE DIE-HARD! Now these slogans trafficked inside the school grounds too.

Our first full-fledged demonstration was a mass haircutting. As I recall, an upperclassman said to me, "Su Qing, don't you get tired of all that braiding? You look like a little old lady, wearing your hair that way at your age. It's hideous! They wouldn't even let you wear it in two braids, and went and made that special rule. Don't you want to fight it? Work for emancipation?" I nodded, and she lopped off my braid with the scissors, thus emancipating my hair.

When my aunt came rat-a-tat-tatting into the dormitory that night for inspection and found the table littered with piles of hair and a pair of scissors, she was scared out of her wits. She stood in the middle of the room, shouting, "You're all asleep? What's the meaning of this? Where did all this hair come from? Who's on duty here?" She kept firing off questions, but nobody answered—everyone was pretending to be asleep. This just made her madder. She marched over to check the duty roster and, wouldn't you know it, there was my name.

She opened my bed curtain and scoffed, "Su Qing, you mean you're still not awake? Don't you know it's your turn to be on duty?"

I had buried my head under the thin cotton quilt, and when I heard her put it this way, all I could do was blurt out through my giggles from underneath the covers, "Day duty, sure, but not night duty!" She was stunned for a moment, and then yanked down my quilt to find that my hair had been cut so short the ends only just brushed my neck and cheeks.

When she went from bed to bed opening the curtains and found every single one of us with messy bobbed hair, she nearly lost her balance running out the door, screaming in a quavering voice, "It's revolt, it is! Revolt! I'm going to tell Old Master Shi! I know why you've cut your hair: free love! You want free love!"[1] She was acting like a crazy old lady, and we all sat up in bed to watch her and laugh.

Afterward, no doubt because her modesty prevented her from showing up at Old Shi's bedroom door in the middle of the night, she ended up staying

---

[1]The term "free love" refers to personal choice in love, as opposed to arranged marriage.

in her own room, pacing in circles, her little feet in their leather shoes tapping furiously across the floor, making a huge racket most of the night before falling silent at last. The next morning, as we were combing our short hair and admiring ourselves in the mirror, one of the servants by the name of Old Wang came in furiously ringing a handbell to announce an emergency assembly.

The auditorium was a madhouse—let us say, less than orderly. Old Master Shi stood on the stage, flanked by seven or eight teachers, and to his immediate right stood Aunt Five, her face ashen, her eyes lifeless. The principal was wearing a mandarin's long upper garment of gray cotton, and black riding breeches. He looked calm. His beard seemed especially well groomed. He stroked it lightly with one hand, rested the other on the lectern, and began. "Quiet down, please. Everyone come to order!"

The entire room went still. I was sitting in the front row, feeling pretty anxious. Old Master Shi ponderously began. "In my fifteen years here, many of our students have come from families with whom I have enjoyed lasting friendship. Su Qing, for example." Here he relinquished his beard to point at me, and I quickly looked down. "Her grandfather and I were classmates, her mother was also a student of mine, and she's been just like a granddaughter to me. . . . But now, I regret to say, even a girl who could be my own granddaughter has betrayed me. No, she hasn't simply betrayed me. She has gone so far as to spurn the very bedrock of civilization and abandon all semblance of morality. From childhood I had the benefit of a classical education, and I have examined myself thoroughly to see where I went wrong. . . ." By this point, all you could hear was the buzz of laughter from the seats beneath the stage. But for some reason, my heart just ached, and I was secretly swallowing my tears.

He continued, "Don't laugh at me. I know I'm an old die-hard. But I'd much rather be an old die-hard than blindly follow these frivolous youngsters, what with their free luh . . . luh . . . No, I simply cannot utter such a vulgarity, it is turning us all into animals! When a girl grows up and is ready to marry, she should follow her parents' wishes. Now that you've cut off all your hair, how are you going to get your pearl flower ornaments to stay fastened on your wedding day?"

"We're not wearing pearl flowers! We're not getting married!" Pandemonium erupted all over again.

Shi replied, his voice leaden, "No. You'll wear them, of course you will. Women want to be beautiful. Even if it's not a pearl flower per se, you'll wear something in your hair, I know you will. You're going to regret this someday, and you'll end up growing out your hair again. . . ."

"No we won't! No way! We don't want to listen to this."

"You don't want to listen? That's fine," Shi said, his voice growing hoarse now. "I'm going to stop now anyway. I came here today to say good-bye. I've already tendered my resignation to the Bureau of Education. They'll be sending someone to replace me this afternoon, and by tomorrow morning no doubt a brand new flag will be flying around here. Actually, I know all they'll be able to do is hang the new flag; that and short hair, that's what everyone's calling "revolution." . . . Su Qing, you're still a child, you're too young to be their pawn. But remember, the jade burns right along with the stone. Go on home with your Aunt Five today after school."

After lunch, without even waiting for my consent, my aunt hired a boat and took me home. I didn't get to see the flag raised at the school, the flag with the white sun against a blue background on a field of red, even though my hair, apparently, had already been emancipated.

II

I WAS SO lonely living at home. Aunt Five was always nattering at my grand-father, about how times had changed, about how bad girls were nowadays, what with these new haircuts that looked like duck butts. But my grandfather disagreed. He said fixing long hair was a lot of bother, that it was actually bet-ter to cut it off. He even approved of equality for women, and women making contributions to society. There was just one thing that mystified him and that he couldn't accept, and that was "free love."

When my older brother came home for summer vacation, he told us that Old Master Shi was long gone, and they were going to turn the girls' normal school into Sun Yat-sen Public School, which would be coeducational. Grand-father said coeducation was fine with him, that way everybody could learn from each other, as long as there wasn't any funny business with boys and girls in the same classroom.

My brother said, "So what if there was? Lots of people approve of free love nowadays!"

This made my grandfather furious. He shouted, "What does that mean? I'll tell you what it means. It's fornication! It's mating like dogs, is what it is!"

Aunt Five tried frantically to get me to leave the room. "Qing, dear, go see your mother. You don't want to listen to this nonsense!"

I did leave the room, scowling, thinking, *You don't want me to hear it, fine.* It didn't matter, because my brother had been slipping me books, introduc-tions to the Three People's Principles and the like, which I would sneak off and read when I had nothing better to do. Stuck inside the books were things like the words and music to the party anthem cut from the newspaper, or a mimeographed copy of Sun Yat-sen's last will and testament.

I liked to sing, and begged my big brother to teach me the party anthem, but he didn't know the tune. So I had to make my way through the music myself, tentatively humming one note to the next until the thing actually started sounding something very much like a melody. And the president's last will and testament? That treatise was the object of my even greater diligence and adoration. Word by word, over and over, I read it and read it, till I quickly knew it by heart.

When summer vacation ended, my brother went to Sun Yat-sen Public School, and I remained under house detention. As my grandfather put it, provided the boys and girls managed to behave themselves with a modicum of decency, he would let me resume my studies the following semester; otherwise, I would stay home and help out my mother around the house.

I didn't like helping around the house nearly as much as Aunt Five did. We'd be helping Grandmother with the cooking, and somebody would want beef curry. But of course you couldn't get curry powder out in the countryside, so I got sent to Shenda Grocery in town. The owner said, "Listen, girly, you'd better lower your sights. Somebody's got to go fish those clam droppings you want from the bottom of the ocean. We don't carry it, because who could afford it?"[2] Thus foiled in her attempt to make the latest main dish recipes, Aunt Five had to settle for the latest in snacks. Her specialty was banana pudding. The eggs and flour were no problem, but she was foiled again for lack of banana extract.

So Aunt Five would sigh, and Grandfather would sigh right along with her. He wasn't lamenting his lost chances to eat beef curry or banana pudding, however. He was sighing over the letters he'd been getting lately from my brother at school, which reported that the teachers really believed in communism, that they were forever trying to divorce their wives with bound feet. And the students? They opened their mouths with Marx and closed them with Borodin. Boys sat shoulder to shoulder with girls in the classroom, extolling comradely love. Even though roll wasn't called at this school, the random absences that seemed to have been provoked by such seating arrangements were not tolerated. Furthermore, since there weren't enough girls to go around, many boys couldn't sit with a girl, resulting in a great deal of vying for seats.

---

[2]The shop owner has misheard the word for curry powder, *galifen,* as the word for clam droppings, *gelifen.*

They endlessly complained about the unfairness of the seating assignments and insisted on doing them all over again by some fairer method, say drawing lots, or weekly rotation.

Grandfather would invariably heave long sighs after reading these letters, and when he was finished sighing, he would remember the magazines that came in the mail. They were usually printed horizontally, not in the traditional vertical arrangement he was used to, and the effort it took to read them annoyed him no end. He was constantly putting on and taking off and putting on again his old pair of bifocals. Respectfully urging him not to overtax himself, Aunt Five would say, "It's all wicked heresy anyway, why bother yourself?"

Grandfather would reply that the theories behind both the Nationalist and Communist parties were actually quite sound; the problems only came with implementation. If the school had let things get so out of hand that boys and girls couldn't even lay eyes on each other, perhaps it was just better all around to hold off on coeducation for a few years, wait until these kids grew up a bit before trying it again.

Though these were Grandfather's views on the matter, he never shared them with the authorities. But lo and behold, the enlightened authorities saw things pretty much the same way, and within three months Sun Yat-sen Public School was closed. The reason for this, it turns out, wasn't entirely to clarify male-female relations as much as it was to clear (i.e., purge) party ranks of those with questionable political backgrounds.

When my brother came home, he talked nonstop about what went on at the school before it was shut down. He said, "You should have seen it! It was amazing! First we went after the local tyrants and evil gentry, and then the statues of the city god and his minions. Squads of us set out from the school, marching smartly in formation. Later, for some reason only soldiers had the right to march smartly in formation. Then troops of army comrades stormed the school and took up guard at the front and back entrances. They fired their guns into the air to show they were serious, and then started rounding up Reds. They arrested girls in red scarves, anyone with the word 'red' in their name, anyone who had drawn the party flag crooked or had exchanged letters with anyone who had drawn the party flag crooked, or had shared the same dorm or signed the autograph book of anyone who had drawn the party flag crooked."

Some of those arrested, provided their father knew somebody who worked in the party or had some in with a party organization, managed to get out on bail. Others braced themselves for harsh punishment, only later to be released to Hangzhou or Nanjing.

Then there was the story about the pretty schoolteacher in a neighboring county and the old party member who wouldn't leave her alone. The old man sent in one of the arresting officers to plant some Red contraband in her mail basket, which made it possible to bring her in to headquarters for interrogation. When she was thrown in jail, the old party member arrived to exercise his charms. He asked her to marry him. He promised to clear her record if she would. But she was just too young, too innocent, simply too incapable of deceit. She said there was no way she could love him. He had no morals. She really told him off. He got mad, and she was executed. She was beautiful even in death. Those who watched the execution couldn't bear to leave when it was over, so taken were they with her fine lily-white arms. The old party member wept too, they said.

When the pretty teacher was persecuted to the grave, my brother said, "China just lost a female revolutionary."

Aunt Five snorted, "Yeah, right. How can a pretty woman be a revolutionary? Free love is what did her in, and nothing but! You can't blame the old party member."

Looking up at the sky, Grandfather said nothing. I followed his gaze and seemed to see there a pure and innocent young woman, frantically waving her fine lily-white arms and screaming, "I was wronged! Oh, I died such a terrible death!"

The following year, the school that began as the Normal School for Girls and was then transformed for a few months into the Sun Yat-sen Public School once again became a middle school for girls. The principal, a Mrs. Zou, was a pretty woman, recently divorced. She'd had only a year of college, and had attended high school at the Normal School for Girls, where she and Aunt Five had enjoyed a student-teacher friendship. Aunt Five was ecstatic when she got the letter offering her the job of school monitor. She promptly forgot all about the principal's free love sins. Word was that back then Principal Zou had been madly in love with a party member by the name of Mr. Shang, who was now the political training instructor at the school.

I begged to go back to school, and Grandfather finally relented, albeit with a mandate for Aunt Five to redouble her vigilance over me. Everything was pretty much the same when I returned, except now the new flag was flying and the dorms had been freshly whitewashed. Apparently, during the Sun Yat-sen Public School era, a fad for graffiti had run rampant. The boys wrote it everywhere, things like SO-AND-SO IS A FILTHY STINKING WHORE, or NO MORE LOVE LETTERS IN CLASS! and HEY LITTLE SISTER, YOU'VE GOT GREAT THIGHS! Few walls were spared, but the restroom doorways proved an especially popular spot.

Even after the whitewashing, you could still make out some of the writing, but nobody really cared. The boys were gone, fortunately, and the younger men who remained, gatekeepers and cooks and the like, were just servants—and how, as they say, would a toad dare crave the swan? Furthermore, precious things like us would never have given them a second look.

The male teachers, however, were another matter entirely. The older generation had fled at the same time as Old Master Shi, and though Principal Zou had tried repeatedly to rehire them, no one was willing to suffer the indignity of working under a young woman. So the teachers she hired were all about the same age as Mr. Shang. There was a Chinese literature teacher named Mr. Huang, who usually wore a long gray mandarin gown and kept his hair combed sleek and shiny. His face, though, was as long as a horse's, and his eyes were tiny. He swayed when he walked, and every other word out of his mouth was "Bing Xin." He was wont to sigh and declaim, "O, Ocean, my mother!" right in the middle of class. When a mischievous student would respond "Over here," his face would turn bright red. When he taught Mo Zi's "Universal Love," even as he explained the text, he shook his head and said, "Ancient works like this are so depressing, there's really no need to study them. Bing Xin's essays are so soothing, so beautiful, so elegant, so full of . . ." he sighed in rapture.

"Sir, would you please explain universal love?" I blurted this out one day as I stared down his long horsy face.

Without missing a beat, he responded, "Universal love means you love me and I love you."

The whole classroom erupted with laughter. He didn't get it, but I did. My classmates took to teasing me, "Here comes your universal lover Mr. Huang!"

He was always praising me, saying I wrote just like Bing Xin. One of my classmates asked him, "So which of them is better? Bing Xin or Su Qing?" Squinting through his little eyes, he said, "Right now Bing Xin, but in the future perhaps Su Qing." My classmates laughed, but I didn't. Looking at his long horsy face, all I could feel was anger.

Falling for male teachers was a fad among schoolgirls in those days. There was an English teacher named Mr. Zheng; we all called him Red Rat. He parted his hair down the middle and wore thick glasses and a light brown western suit. He really wasn't all that good looking. But the classroom was always deserted right before his class. I could never figure out where everyone was. Later I discovered quite by accident that my classmates were all back in the dorm changing their stockings and putting on makeup.

Paltry though it seems, since we had to wear the regulation black leather shoes that were part of the school uniform, we were reduced to finding fashion victory on the stockings front—light gray, pure black or pure white, or brown, but mostly pink. When Mr. Zheng walked into the room, some of the girls would stretch their legs into the aisles, with the result that when they bowed they were much less "at attention" than "at ease." What's more, some of the other girls bent at the waist in decidedly unorthodox fashion, swaying like willows, as if they were dancing.

For Mr. Zheng, the girls at our school went beyond simply shouting "Down with imperialism" at the top of their lungs; for him, they studied imperialist English with a vengeance. They would recite a lesson over and over again, so softly, so sweetly, till the whole classroom seemed to be filled with the twittering of little birds. Elated, Mr. Zheng would exclaim, "Tomorrow I'll teach you an English play, called *Columbus Discovers a New Continent!*" It ended up that when the roles were assigned, the girl chosen to play Columbus didn't want to at all, and the one who played the Queen of Spain was this inordinately self-satisfied prissy girl who couldn't even say her lines.

And what of Mr. Shang? Even though he was young and good looking, no one went after him, because he belonged to Principal Zou. He loved her so much he insisted on going through the mess of divorcing his wife back in the village. When the mediation phase failed, he took it all the way to court. One of his charges was that she was unfilial to his parents, always cursing at everyone in sight. But when the judge asked them about their daughter-in-law, Mr. Shang's father replied, "She's a fine daughter-in-law. It's that Zou woman that's the problem. My son would never tell such outrageous lies if that slut didn't have him under her spell!" Mr. Shang didn't get his divorce, but that didn't stop him and Principal Zou from moving in together.

He taught politics, so he was always asking about current events. One time he asked me a question about international affairs and when I couldn't answer, he said, "Don't you read the paper?" I said I did. He said, "Well, what sections?" I paused a beat, then replied with a smile, "I read the parts about unsuccessful divorce suits." He was furious, but didn't say a word, just drew himself up to full height, which, as he was dressed in a Sun Yat-sen suit, gave him a certain commanding dignity. I envied Principal Zou, and was a little jealous of her too.

We really didn't get much opportunity to see men at school, but our chances of being seen by them were many indeed. We were called upon to sing the party anthem at every single public occasion. Not very many people knew the song back then, so they'd pick a dozen of us girls to go up and lead it. There I was, always in the front row because I was so short, my voice loud and shrill.

After the anthem, the chairman would read the president's last testament. Some of them couldn't read it very well or would repeat lines they'd already read, which made me so anxious for them that I could barely resist taking over and reciting it flawlessly from memory. If we felt like it, sometimes after the meetings there would be a play or a performance of martial arts or chemistry tricks over at the boys' school. As for programs at the girls' school, our dance performances were hands down the most popular.

I remember the plays from back then—invariably *Resurrection of the Rose, Return to the South, Southeast Flies the Peacock, Three Rebellious Women, One Night in a Café,* and *Sorrows of Youth.* The dances were usually things like "Three Butterflies," "Dance of the Water Nymphs," and "Fallen Flowers, Flowing Waters." The girls who could dance pranced around as if they were the most beautiful creatures on earth. They always wore their uniforms too small, so tight they hugged their bodies. They wore the skirts as short as they possibly could, several inches above the knee, so that they only just covered their bottoms. This left Aunt Five in a predicament that drove her crazy. The only thing that prevented her from yielding to her desperation to yank the skirts down to cover those bare knees was her realization that this would result in baring those bottoms.

Then came the Jinan incident in the spring of 1928, and the dancing stopped. We had all been going out to inspect the stores for Japanese goods to mark for boycott. But since it was impossible to tell Chinese and Japanese products apart, we just picked the prettiest things, pasted them with strips barring their sale, and left the shopkeepers screaming like crazy over their losses. These inspection tours of ours were led by the Student Federation, which in turn followed the guidance of the party, and sometimes worked in cooperation with it. Thus we ran into Mr. Shang virtually every day, and it wasn't long before he fell in love with a student named Zhang Jianying. He wrote her a letter that said, in part, "Scholar Zhang, Why haven't you written me back? I am simply dying for your letter. They say pining eyes can bore through anything, but I'm telling you, even my shoulders are pining for you this way." This letter ended up in Aunt Five's clutches, and with trembling fingers she handed it over to Principal Zou, who said nothing about it.

The next day at assembly Principal Zou was furious. She announced, "Since Mr. Shang is so busy with the boycott, Mr. He will teach political training in his place. Please be sure to give him your full attention," etc., etc. But a few days later Principal Zou called another assembly and announced, "Due to my recent poor health, I have tendered my resignation to the Ministry of Education. I will be replaced by Principal Liu," etc., etc. Everybody knew the real reason she resigned was that Mr. Shang dumped her.

III

THE FIRST ACT of Principal Liu's worthy administration was to retain my Aunt Five. He had been one of the original teachers at the Normal School for Girls. He was short and fat, with buck teeth and little white specks all over his face. He was probably in his forties, and quite stern, so you were always on your best behavior around him. Because we were so intimidated by him, someone was always hissing "Specks Liu" behind his back. And because his belly was so big he actually waddled, some of us took to calling him Nine Months Pregnant, though since we were such tender things the mere mention of reproduction rather predictably left us twittering with embarrassment, so this nickname wasn't nearly as popular as the other one.

Principal Liu taught my grade math. Starting in the fall semester of 1928, the textbook we used was volume 5 of *Essentials of Mathematics* by Duan Yuhua, but we never did get much beyond the first ten pages, because the principal was always too busy imparting pearls of wisdom, invariably on such topics as Communist Bandits and how they were out to use us. This is how his classes went: He would waddle through the door, preceded by his stomach, as the bell was still ringing. Throughout our mad scramble for our seats, he would just stand up front, silently surveying the room. He would wait until we were all standing still at our desks and had given him our proper, respectful bow. If anyone wasn't paying attention and missed the bow, he would stare her down without calling her by name, while announcing to the class, "That one didn't count. Bow again." The one who hadn't joined in the first time would have no choice but to stand back up, blushing with shame.

Once he was satisfied with the bowing, he would hold up the textbook and make a great show of flipping to our page, at which point we would start flipping furiously through our books. The girls who didn't know which page we were on would just look at him, and then he would break into a smile, close the book, and say, "Let's take our time with the book, right now I need to give you some advice." And then he would begin. "First of all, girls get married when they're grown, obviously, but if anyone's fiancé calls on her, the rest of you must by all means avoid coming out to get a look at him. One time I saw a certain student's fiancé come to visit her. . . ." As he spoke, he trained his gaze on Lu Yuexiang, who immediately blushed, not simply with modesty but also with no small part of rage. I tried to explain on her behalf, "That wasn't her fiancé, just a friend." Instead of accepting this as I expected, he suddenly hardened his expression and said, "If he wasn't her fiancé, then he has no business here. The purpose of friendship is mutual edification, and there are plenty of girls here to be friends with, not to mention all of your teachers. There is no need whatsoever to draw upon boys from the outside." Lu Yuexiang's face was nearly purple by this point, when he finally started working around to another topic.

"All in all, this is not a good situation, and we must rectify it. . . . Secondly, since the student association is now self-governing, the scope of its activities must naturally be restricted somewhat. Though you should take orders from the Student Federation, on matters of minor importance you can just send a few representatives over to put in an appearance. There's no need for everybody to go, parading through the streets, offering yourselves up to public commentary for no reason."

"So let them comment, so what? Are we supposed to stop eating because we might choke?" One of the girls tentatively offered this objection.

Then I rather smugly added under my breath, "Besides, if they can comment on us, we can certainly comment on them." No sooner were these words out of my mouth than Principal Liu pounded the lectern, his face darkened with fury, as he shouted, "Who said that? Stand up!" We all lowered our heads, our eyes welling up with tears, unable even to look at him.

"If you have something to say, stand up and say it!" He positively howled with rage, spittle flying. Sitting in the front row and sprayed by his saliva, I couldn't help but shudder with revulsion.

"If no one has anything to say"—here he paused, taking a softer tone all of a sudden—"then perhaps I was mistaken. Now remember, your studies are the most important, and it's only right that you not attend so many extracurricular meetings."

But meetings need people to attend them, after all, and Principal Liu couldn't stem the tide entirely. Though he kept a respectful distance from those party organizations and citizen's groups, he couldn't avoid at least keeping up the appearance of participation, and his method of going through the motions was to sacrifice a few representatives. Pity was, since I had won a few prizes for public speaking, I was chosen as one of them, and representatives had to attend every meeting of every group. In the past, missing classes had been no problem, but after Principal Liu took over we had to ask to be excused, which meant that every semester, through no fault of my own, I ended up with scores of absences on my record. Today I regret this, but at the time I was mighty proud of myself and saw nothing wrong with thinking that I was sacrificing my education for the greater social good.

So I stood on speakers' platforms at little playgrounds and big public rallies and screamed at the top of my lungs. What about? I don't really remember—most likely it was just a bunch of emancipate this, emancipate that. But I'll never forget what it felt like as I tremulously took the stage, my heart quaking, my lips trembling. I did everything in my power to appear calm, me, a short, skinny kid making my way around ten or fifteen party officials, union representatives, and comrades in uniform, my hair parted on the side and covering my left eye, but prepared to address a crowd of thousands straight on. I had no time to imagine what their impression of me might be, what fault they might be finding. My only concern was making myself heard; without megaphones or loudspeakers at these huge public squares, I had to be shrill. But it didn't matter, because when I finished screaming and stepped down and could finally catch my breath, I would feel so relieved, and then suddenly so heroic, as if I were the center of the universe. It occurs to me that I got such attention because it was so rare back then for a girl to be doing anything in public; nowadays nobody gives it a second thought.

The unexpected retribution for this: a military man in his forties wrote me three or four times, enclosing with each letter some free verse of his own recent composition. I still remember two lines of the last poem he sent: "the sick lone goose mourns the swan, hoping in your heart to find a bier to lay it on." Principal Liu and Aunt Five were beside themselves. Under great secrecy they called me into the office, dismissed the servants, and shut the door. Principal Liu remained silent for a moment, his expression grave, and then said, "I am not opposed to 'free love.' But it seems this officer may be too old for you; after all, he's in his forties, and you're only fourteen. Besides, he's from Guangdong, and . . ."

By this point, I was already crying, I was so scared, but Aunt Five, her face ashen, just frantically gestured with one hand to shush me while scrambling over to crack the door to see if there was anyone out there listening, which, of course, there wasn't. Relieved of this concern, she now turned to me and hissed, "You're crying? You've got nerve! You want everyone to hear? What do you think will happen if people find out about this? All right, we'll say no more about it. From now on, no more being a representative for you. You go tell them you're sick and you'll have to quit. . . ." She grew more and more agitated as she spoke, her voice rising in pitch. This time, it was Principal Liu who motioned her to stop, thinking such excessive force wouldn't work anyway. Besides, it appeared from the contents of the letter that I really wasn't to blame, since I'd never written him back a single syllable, and if he kept writing me anyway, what could I possibly do about it? Moreover, it wasn't really in the school's interest to offend someone like him, especially as long as the matter could be handled at the gatehouse. If anyone came asking for Miss Su, he would simply be told that no such person had ever been enrolled at the school; any inappropriate letter could simply be returned to sender. And so the whole affair ended there. From then on I was kept safely inside school walls, all the way up until the lantern parade on National Day, October 10.

It was already the afternoon of the seventh by the time our school was notified about the lantern parade, and since it was up to each school to provide its own lanterns, we wouldn't be getting any subsidies from the central planning committee. When we heard this, we were beside ourselves, bombarding our teachers in every class with questions, trying to get them to tell us how we could start getting ready. But no one would tell us anything! All was quiet in the principal's office, which didn't issue a single announcement about preparations. And all was just as quiet in the daily operations office, which didn't send a single person out to buy lanterns. What were we supposed to do? Witness the impassioned students, the day before the holiday:

"How can we not celebrate National Day? Spineless traitors!"

"Whoever doesn't want to be a spineless traitor has to join the celebration!"

"It doesn't matter if we don't have lanterns! We can just light rolled up strips of paper!"

"Let's go ask Principal Liu!"

"Let's go petition Principal Liu!"

And so the chair of the Student Self-Governance Committee called an ad hoc meeting of the Executive Committee, and the Executive Committee resolved in this ad hoc session to call a general meeting of the student body. It was resolved at this general meeting of the student body to designate seven representatives to petition Principal Liu. And wouldn't you know it, I was one of them.

This time, Principal Liu ignored the others completely and addressed his words of wisdom to me alone. "Su Qing, don't you remember what happened last time? A whole group of girls going out with lanterns in the middle of the night! Hmph! Su Qing, why can't you learn from your mistakes?" By this point, he was shaking his head, as if to suggest I knew no shame. But at that moment, I really had been rendered a bit silly by everyone's high spirits, and when I saw that none of the other representatives was going to say anything, I had no choice but to throw shame to the winds. "But, Principal Liu, lots of people will be there!"

"Yes—men!"

"And girls aren't people?" There was my old equality-between-the-sexes routine again.

Principal Liu sighed and said, "When girls go out, they must have chaper-

ones. . . . Don't laugh! You girls don't understand these things. I can't in good
conscience let you go without chaperones."

My eyebrows flew up, and the other girls' faces showed their anger and disappointment. Meanwhile, the crowd of girls outside the office, craning their
heads to catch the latest developments, had somehow discerned that we had
hit a snag and were busily discussing matters among themselves, while a few of
the bolder among them simply started shouting, "We want to go! We want to
go!" When Principal Liu rose slowly to his feet and made his way unsteadily to
the door, all the girls outside scurried off in giggles. Only then did he return,
pause, and say to us solemnly, "If you really must go, then fine. I will enlist
some teachers to be your chaperones. But you must mind them. . . . National
Day should be a happy occasion. I love my country too. But . . . ai!" When he
lapsed into silence, it occurred to us that since our mission was accomplished,
we really didn't have to listen anymore. We withdrew with the spoils to report
to our classmates.

Sure enough, the next morning Mr. Ma, head of daily operations, hurried
out to buy the lanterns personally, and supper was moved up half an hour.
Our company was now ready to embark. When we had finished counting off,
standing at attention, there were 467 of us. With the shorter girls in front
and the taller ones behind, carrying lanterns of all different colors, our parade
wound like a snake through the streets. As the crowds grew, the jeering and
laughter began.

"Look at all those duck butt haircuts! Say, they're not bad!"

"Two or three of those girls'll be plenty for me!"

"Hey, that one's sure pretty! Look at that one, she's hideous!"

"Look! They're smiling!"

"Look! They're touching their own . . . !"

The older girls lowered their heads, while the younger ones cocked theirs
and giggled. Our gym teacher, Miss Wu, was wearing a magenta knee-length
cheongsam and a long black-and-gold-striped scarf around her neck and down
her back. October was a bit early to be wearing a scarf, but at only seventeen,
Miss Wu had always been delicate. She was just back from Shanghai (where
she'd graduated from a certain physical education teachers' training school), so
she dressed especially well. "Who's this?" the men on the streets asked as they
started noticing her, "the principal's daughter?"

"Or concubine!"

Miss Wu spat back, "Go to hell!" Then her high heel slipped and she fell.
Mr. Ma rushed over to help her up, but she was in so much pain she couldn't
walk, so he had to give her his arm. This set off much whispering in our ranks,

about how they were an "old twosome" (Ningponese for married couple), and how they were "stuck on" each other.

We arrived at Sun Yat-sen Park.

The festivities began, with the reading of the last testament, speeches, and the chanting of slogans. Finally it came time for the lantern parade. Lining up first were the party representatives, then government representatives, the marching band from the orphanage, representatives from every citizens' group, and then, finally, thousands and thousands of students. Those from a certain province-level high school came first, followed by the county-level technical school, and then a trade school. Our girls' school was also county level and should have come next, but our marshal Mr. Ma and the other teachers were so self-effacing, so reluctant to move forward, that several missionary schools just plowed their way in front of us. All the other private schools followed, and we ended up in the rear. It really was our lucky day: a number of women's associations who wouldn't mix with men's groups most earnestly sought to march with us, and of course we had to let them go in front of us too.

Thus the mighty lantern parade began, starting out from the main entrance to the park, where the crowds now formed a sea of bobbing heads. The spirits of the marchers were high, with much talking and laughter and high jinks. When the marshals saw how out of hand everything was getting, they announced that everybody had to stay in line, and suggested that we all sing along with the band. So first we sang the party anthem, and then "Down with imperialists! Down with imperialists! Out with warlords! Out with warlords! On with the revolution! On with the revolution!" We sang these songs over and over again as we approached the park gate, when all of a sudden someone in the crowd shouted, "Let's join the coeds!" In the ensuing uproar, we were a little scared, but also somehow proud of ourselves. But things quickly degenerated as all sorts of lowlifes charged into our ranks, pinching a plump girl on the thigh, or just grinning and leering and cackling salaciously. It was so disgusting you wanted to puke, and with no end in sight, we really were starting to panic. "Yuck! Beat it!" "My lantern's caught fire!" "Mr. Ma!"

Mr. Ma was so frantic his whole head was sweating, and he kept screaming at us not to scatter, to just keep going, keep going! Eventually those up ahead must have figured out what was going on, because some dozen-odd policemen appeared, waving their billy clubs in the air, charging after the lowlifes, and shouting threats. By that point those so intent on pressing their luck knew better than to continue, but they made another huge commotion as they fled. The girls, afraid of getting clubbed by mistake in the fray, were crying and squealing at the police, "Watch out! Look where you're going!" The police, now frantically squealing a bit themselves, responded, "Don't worry, young ladies, my club could never touch you, trust me!" Miss Wu's whole face reddened at this. She tugged on Mr. Ma's sleeve and whispered, "Let's make a run for it back to the school! Hurry!" Lacking any sort of counterproposal, all we could do was stray from the parade and make our dejected way back to school, dragging our lanterns—now crushed, burned, bedraggled to the point of one lone bamboo stay intact—as we went. However staunch an advocate Principal Liu was for social change, society was just as intent on obstructing it.

IV

IN THE AFTERMATH of our participation in the lantern parade (an aftermath that tidily bore out Principal Liu's "prophetic vision"), the student body split into two camps. One group believed that anyone of Principal Liu's years naturally possessed the wisdom of experience, but these girls were too embarrassed to voice their admiration for him aloud. The other group, people more or less like me, persistently refused, for some unknown reason, to acknowledge our defeat in this new game, despite the fact that we had formed no profound or more accurate views of our own to bring to it. Just look at him: Principal Liu positively licking his chops with smugness. No, even worse: delighting in the calamities of others. He hypocritically cast himself in the role of compassionate father, making us the little children who just didn't understand the ways of the world. His face a mask of sorrow and regret, he'd say things like, "I'm in favor of equality between the sexes too, but . . ." or "Of course I want our students to be patriotic, but you know. . . ." This left us no room at all for maneuver; we little pupils were like netted fish in a stagnant pond. If anyone made a peep of dissent, she became morally suspect from the day she was born, because she liked nothing better than going out swinging a lantern, looking for savages to feel her up.

Aunt Five would flare her nostrils at me and say, "Qing, dear, I just don't know why you won't put your intelligence to proper use. For instance, just yesterday Principal Liu was telling me. . . . Anyway, the point is, he really does feel sorry for you. You'd better come to your senses!"

Put your energy into your studies! Settle down! Come to your senses! But heaven only knew what was worth studying. Our Chinese teacher, Mr. Cheng, was a disgusting, red-nosed old pedant. Standing up at the lectern, he'd blow his nose with a loud honk, producing a long stream of snot, which, since he didn't have a handkerchief, he'd wipe with a crumpled-up page from the lecture notes he'd just read. And then he'd stuff the filthy paper into the drawer.

Math was covered by Principal Liu, who would skip over all the hard problems on the grounds that girls weren't going to become engineers anyway, so what business did they have with advanced mathematics? The important thing was to benefit from his daily words of wisdom. English was now being taught by a new teacher, Mr. Jiang, whose recitation voice sounded like someone crunching on pebbles, hoarse and harsh, painful to the ears. His specialty was grammar, apparently, rule by rule by rule, as if it were legal code or mathematical formulae. We would always cram before his tests, but once when he changed the date of the test on us, we all heaved a huge sigh of relief and promptly forgot every last one of those grammar rules.

And then there was Mr. Zhao, who taught party doctrine and was even more miscast than the rest. As Principal Liu explained it, because he'd been unable to hire a real party bigwig (and even if he had, he'd never have been able to live it down if we inadvertently offended him), all in all it was better to just drum up some lackey for the job. This teacher was so ignorant he might as well have been hired for the express purpose of standing up there telling us jokes. He had no idea whether the Grand Canal connected north and south or east and west, nor could he name the principal ports of the eastern seaboard. So we told him there was no need to teach us the general plan for national reconstruction, or better yet, "Why don't you tell us, so we can all have a good laugh, because we need to know, esteemed teacher: Did you nod at the son of some footman of Premier Sun to get this job, or did you carry the briefcase for some provincial-level party committee member?" He'd just smile blankly and take the barbs, along with his dollar's pay for the hour. Whenever he was ten minutes late, we'd yell, "Dock him eighteen cents!" He would seem genuinely apologetic and plead with us to lighten up. If we did, he would tell us what was on the quiz. But the last time this happened he came stumbling in drunk, and when he heard us shout, "Dock him eighteen *fen*," he just raised his eyebrows and smiled as if he didn't have a care in the world. He blathered on about the ports of the eastern seaboard and the Grand Canal, and we went on with whatever we were on about, and before long he was replaced. Later, after I was expelled, I ran into him on the street. He was riding proudly in a private rickshaw, its bright white wheels rolling smartly along, the bell up front trilling. He'd struck it rich.

Now I suppose I ought to explain how I got kicked out of school. In the spring of 1929, the school hired this teacher named Mr. Xu. He couldn't have been more than twenty-seven or -eight. His face was haggard, his skin sallow, and he wore gold wire-rimmed glasses. His voice wasn't particularly commanding, but he carried himself with such composure that he immediately inspired respect. He taught history, but he said it was fine if we didn't know a whole lot about ancient events, as long as we had a general sense of premodern society—who the hell cared about the names of the emperors, let alone their pretty concubines? He turned dead serious, though, when it came to the history of the last hundred years. He gave complete and thorough explanations of every idiotic personage, every infuriating event, and every single humiliating treaty. At times he would even burst into tears as he spoke, and we would be beside ourselves with indignation as we listened to him. The bell ending class rang and we ignored it, the bell for the next period must have rung too but no one noticed; he was still lecturing passionately, and we were still hanging on his every word, when Principal Liu walked in, preceded by his belly.

"Ignore him!" I shouted, just glancing at him before swiftly returning my attention to Mr. Xu's face, wanting him to continue, to go on and on.

"Pay him no mind!" My classmates must have noticed him too, but everybody was hoping history class could be extended, and we could just forget math.

Instead, with a cry of alarm, Mr. Xu noticed him too, and could only hastily wrap up his lecture, grab his roster book, and leave. Then Principal Liu took the podium, grinning from ear to ear, and began dispensing his words of wisdom as usual, teaching us to be well-behaved, law-abiding students, well-behaved, law-abiding people, well-behaved, law-abiding eaters and drinkers; telling us how we shouldn't go looking for trouble, because society would never tolerate "extremists."

We knew whom he meant by "extremists," and, feeling defiant on Mr. Xu's behalf, I just had to disagree. When our views betrayed our unstinting admiration for Mr. Xu, Principal Liu's face turned vicious, and the little freckles stood out so clearly you could have counted them one by one. But since he wasn't about to abandon the deportment of the well-bred, he refused to let his anger show; he just bit his lower lip in a way that contorted his whole mouth, as if he were feigning a smile or grinning hideously. "Now let us turn to the irregular polygon. . . ." He grabbed a piece of chalk and started drawing on the blackboard, but he used so much force that the chalk snapped in two. Apparently his anger hadn't quite abated. After that, whenever anything not to his liking happened, he immediately suspected that Mr. Xu was behind it, aiding and abetting the students.

One time we staged a hunger strike. It started with the cook cutting too many corners—the vegetables were getting worse and worse, and fewer and farther between. We would get a yellow croaker too small to go around a table of seven; it looked like some kind of baked gadget, it stunk, and the flesh had the texture of face powder. If the cook couldn't bear to part with the roots when serving spinach or bean sprouts, we could live with that, but apparently the kitchen staff was just as fond of the mud, for our every mouthful tasted like dirt. At times we took matters into our own hands: we'd scrape leftovers from the other dishes onto one serving dish and go find a bug to add to it, preferably a fly, of course. Then all seven of us would bang on the dish with our chopsticks and shout at our server, "Come look! Hurry! There's a fly in the food! That means you have to bring us two more dishes: one for replacement, and one for your penalty." Those at neighboring tables would add their voices to the clamor, and the unfortunate cook would always relent and provide another dish. But after we pulled this trick once too often, the cook refused to pay up any longer. From now on, he said, every dish would be inspected before we started eating it. If a bug was found then, he'd replace the dish, but anything that happened after our first bite, forget it. We weren't satisfied in the least, but since Principal Liu considered this fair, there was nothing we could do but grumble to ourselves.

As luck would have it, one morning when everybody had just about finished off a pot of rice porridge, somebody spooned up a dirty rag from the bottom. The brown gunk from the rag had been stirred through the whole pot, so everyone was retching, trying to puke, but it was too late—the germ-laden swill wouldn't come up. Thus began the dining hall riot. We banged on the dishes with chopsticks, pounded the tables, kicked over stools, and made a real mess of the place, but the unwavering rationale from the kitchen was, "So who told you not to inspect your food before eating it?" We said, "But who could have known you'd be so mean? We knew to look in the serving bowls, but how could we know the problem reached as far as the bottom of the porridge pot?" Truth be told, Principal Liu wanted to get the cook to provide a fresh pot, but we would have none of it. We insisted that the cook be held fully responsible for guaranteeing that we wouldn't contract any stomach disorders, which, we pointed out, would be no laughing matter. But wouldn't you know it, this only reminded Principal Liu of something else on his mind—Mr. Xu had ulcers.

Apparently, when he was in college, his girlfriend was in high school, so he paid all their expenses. But since he came from a poor family that had nothing to spare for the two of them to live on, all he could do was scramble after odd jobs trying to make ends meet, and since he wasn't eating well either, over time he developed ulcers. And then heart disease. Since he didn't hold out much hope for his future, he left college after three years to work, which gave his girlfriend the chance to attend college without worry. Principal Liu had never cared about Mr. Xu's health before; rather, it was the fact that the teacher had never graduated from college that inspired our principal's deepest regret. Who could have known that our little dining hall riot could cause such a misunderstanding? Now apparently even Mr. Xu's stomach trouble was grounds for suspicion: clearly, he was guilty of instigating the riot. And once again my own Aunt Five couldn't resist chiming in, because she just had to show how clever and cutting she could be. With a derisive laugh, she said to us, "I always thought stomach problems were brought on by sacrificing yourself for a woman, not eating porridge." Angrily refusing more porridge, we ran out of the dining hall to the dorm, pretending to be sick. It wasn't long before Aunt Five arrived under orders to lock down the dorm. Banished to the corridors and the courtyard, we stood around in helpless fury. Some of the girls clutched their bellies, screaming and moaning. We lasted through lunchtime with no resolution in sight, but then we started sending servants like Old Wang and Mama Wu on bread runs to the little shop at the school gate. Principal Liu didn't cough up the money to buy us noodles until 3:30 that afternoon. He also told us that the cook would be docked the next day by having to provide an extra meat dish for every table. Mr. Xu, however, was driven straight to his sick bed with exasperation.

Mr. Xu lived alone at the school, and when he took to bed, not a single teacher, from Principal Liu on down, went to see him. Nor was anyone doing anything about his meals. So we organized a dozen-some students to visit him in little groups. But then Aunt Five delivered Principal Liu's mandate: "No girls allowed in male teachers' quarters." So then we pooled our money to buy flowers and things like bread, crackers, and cookies, which we had Old Wang take over to him. Surely there couldn't have been anything wrong with this, but Principal Liu managed to find some pretext for chastising Old Wang, after which he refused to make further deliveries. When Mr. Xu went into the hospital, we didn't even know about it at first; it was something like a week later before we found out. Then everybody started getting themselves excused from classes so they could go visit him. When Aunt Five eventually found out what was behind our absences, she and Principal Liu were furious. He told the office to stop excusing students from classes for any purpose that involved their departure from school grounds. One Sunday, we just got about a hundred of us together and stormed the hospital en masse. Who knew Aunt Five and a number of office staff were posted there waiting for us? They claimed the doctor had told them that since Mr. Xu's heart condition was so serious, he required complete and total rest and quiet. Principal Liu, for his part, stressed that so many girls in such a hurry to see a young male teacher was sure to become big news for people. We crowded through the hospital gate, shouting,

"Who cares if we're news, we just want to see him a minute!" Next thing we knew, they were hashing it over, and after a while Aunt Five came and told us that it really was in the interest of his quick recovery that we not disturb him too much. But each grade could choose two representatives to visit him, she said, and then we'd see where things stood.

When we got back to school, too many students were gone to call an assembly on a Sunday. And when we named our representatives on Monday, the office refused to let them off school grounds, saying we'd have to wait until Sunday, our next day off. Unfortunately, I was a representative again this time, so whenever I ran into Aunt Five, she had plenty of awful things to say. "This Mr. Xu of yours has a girlfriend, you know," she'd announce, her voice laced with derision, "and he's really quite ill this time. Principal Liu has already sent her a telegram telling her to come, so I don't know why you should get yourselves so worked up over him." Or she'd say, "He may seem like the quiet type, but he's really quite the ladies' man, which is the only reason so many of you girls are on his side." These comments of hers just made us madder and madder.

In the end, a notice appeared on the bulletin board one drizzly morning. Written on a little slip of paper, it read, "One of our faculty, Mr. Xu, has died after an illness. All middle school–level history courses from this day forth will be taught by Mr. Cheng." That fine specimen of the nose-blowing old pedant. Now the drawer beneath the lectern would be stuffed with two classes' worth of soiled lecture notes. We had no interest in those stale formulaic tales about the olden days; we wanted to know about our own world, our own country, our own society, what Chinese people of our own day ought to be doing. History is a mirror, and we wanted to see real live people in it, not just skeletons from the distant past.

We had to have a memorial for Mr. Xu! But the school wouldn't allow it. His girlfriend was the one in charge of funeral arrangements. The principal sent a memorial couplet anyway, but it never got hung, since she was in no shape to organize a funeral or anything like it. She just bought a coffin, added the corpse, put it in the guild hall, and that was it. When we called an ad hoc meeting of the student association, though, the principal actually delegated some teachers to suggest that members of the student self-governance committee go pay our respects and also send a memorial couplet written on white cloth. We could ask Mr. Cheng to choose the phrases. But I would have none of it. "No way! Why have the cat mourn the mouse?" The chair of the student association shot me a glance. Then a number of girls stood up and started criticizing the school and the principal. At that point, the chair suggested we table the matter and discuss it again at our next meeting, but I said, "Why bother? Let's just forget it, he's already dead. There was never any need for this meeting to begin with." Then somebody else leaped to her feet to wield her own powers of persuasion, and the discussion was on again. In the end, we came up with two resolutions. One was that every student wear a velvet flower in her hair, and the other that we cancel all history classes for the rest of the semester. But the faculty delegates said the school would never agree to that.

The chair said, "Since our faculty delegates have said our second resolution is unacceptable, I think we should abandon it. As for our decision to wear white flowers in our hair, we should ask the principal for permission before proceeding." I said, "You can't just abandon a resolution! And everybody surely has the freedom to decide whether or not to put a flower in her hair; why should we have to ask the principal's permission?" Many of the others agreed with me, and the chair completely overreacted. She said, "Okay, Madame Su Qing, you get up here and take over. I'm obviously unqualified, and I quit." Tears were running down her face as she spoke. That started everyone clamoring for me to be chair, and somebody took a real dig at her and said that anyone who would be such a crybaby was never qualified to begin with. But of course I refused to take over, and the teacher delegates said that once a chair had been selected you couldn't just pick another one, and the meeting fell apart after that.

The next day, everyone refused to go to class because we wanted to have another meeting. Principal Liu insisted that we go to classes first, the chair pretended she was too sick to call a meeting, and from there things devolved into a student strike. That evening Principal Liu called in those of us who had been chosen as the class representatives to visit Mr. Xu in the hospital. He said that if we observed school rules and returned to class, everyone else would naturally follow suit. We responded, "The whole school's refusing to go to classes, it's not just us. Why should we be the ones to go back first?"

"How is it they picked you as class representatives in the first place, if you weren't the ones out there helping Mr. Xu fan the flames?"

"First of all, Mr. Xu never fanned any flames, and second of all, we were picked to visit the sick, not to lead the way in class attendance."

Principal Liu resorted to veiled threats; we refused to budge; and when we left, neither side was very happy. On our way out of his office, we ran into our student association chair and I asked her, "Are you feeling better now?" She came up, took my hand with a great show of sincerity, and said, "I think we'd better just return to classes for now, or else I'm afraid we'll really have to pay—Liu has asked me for a list of names; he wants to know who's fanning the flames!"

By Sunday morning—the day on which class representatives were to have visited him in the hospital—Mr. Xu was dead, and all that was left was that little announcement flapping on the bulletin board. Curiously, another notice written in a nearly indecipherable hand was stuck right next to it, announcing the expulsion of those same class representatives, on the grounds that we had incited the student strike, albeit, the notice added, with outside instigation. No doubt the instigator was Mr. Xu. What a pity he was no longer a part of this suspicious world!

The flames went right on burning, bigger and higher too. Yet the resolution of the whole thing amounted to nothing more than the removal of both notices from the bulletin board, the appointment of a new history teacher named Wen, and the reclassification of our expulsion to voluntary withdrawal from school. But the price we paid was the same either way: a middle school diploma had been within our grasp, and we'd lost it just like that, for nothing.

The chair of the student association asked Principal Liu to be her godfather not long afterward, and she graduated first in her class the following year.

It seems to me that when waters rise, no one can calm them. And when water is deathly still, it's hard to stir up a wave. Why not just take all our cues from nature? I'm energized by an approaching thunderstorm. When it passes, I'm brought back down to this lonesome earth once more, as uncertain and aimless as ever.

8
Fengzi
(1912–1996)

Born Feng Jiren in the southern province of Guangxi, Fengzi was the youngest child in a large family. When she was little she was tutored in classical Chinese by her father, a rather conservative-minded scholar and poet. Later, she attended Fudan University in Shanghai, where she took part in the progressive student movement while majoring in Chinese literature, developing a special passion for modern spoken drama. As an undergraduate she joined the Fudan Drama Troupe, adopting Fengzi (Phoenix) as her stage name, and after college she became a professional stage actress. Although her family reportedly disapproved of her career choice, she performed throughout the country in leading roles in a number of high-profile plays, including Cao Yu's well-received contemporary dramas *Thunderstorm* and *Sunrise*. Both plays interrogate patriarchal family structures, a topical theme that clearly touched the imagination of contemporary educated audiences. Fengzi's own feminist concerns and her interest in contemporary Chinese women's culture led her to serve briefly as the editor of *Women's Monthly* magazine before it folded in 1936. This magazine was sponsored by the Women's Bookstore, a small and relatively short-lived Shanghai-based publishing house devoted to supporting female artists and writers in the mid-thirties. One of the founders was Yao Mingda, a professor at Fudan University whom Fengzi likely met during her college days. Prominent women intellectuals associated with the Women's Bookstore included Wu Shutian, Chen Baiping, and Zhao Qingge; Zhao and Fengzi would remain close friends.

During the war, Fengzi joined the exodus of intellectuals to the interior, where she remained active in the performing arts in Chongqing and Kunming in addition to working as a special war correspondent for *New People's Herald*. She also edited a column for *Peace Daily*. Her trenchant essays (*sanwen*), including many attacking the rampant corruption of the KMT regime, established her as an important essayist of this period.

After Japan's surrender in 1945, Fengzi returned to Shanghai, where she was invited to serve as the editor of *In the World,* a left-wing magazine with ties to the Communist underground. During this period, she also worked for the openly leftist Shanghai Kunlun Film Company. Having already made her debut on the silver screen in the late thirties, she now landed a part in *Unstoppable Spring* (1947), a film whose star-studded cast included China's premier male actor, Zhao Dan (1915–1980). It was around this time that Fengzi met Sidney Shapiro, a Brooklyn-born lawyer who was later to become a prominent literary translator at the Foreign Language Press, and they were married.

In addition to Fengzi's important contribution to modern Chinese drama, during the forties she also published several major works of fiction, including her full-length novel *The Silent Singing Girl* (1946). Other publications include *Meandering on the Stage* (1945), a collection of essays that reflect on the contemporary drama world, and *Eight Years* (1945), a volume of sketches based on the author's personal experiences and observations of life during the war.

After moving to Beijing on the eve of the Communist victory, Fengzi was eager to contribute to the new society, volunteering to help with the rehabilitation of prostitutes when brothels were officially banned in the early postliberation era and later serving on a land-reform team in Jiangxi province. She decided to retire from the stage after the People's Republic of China was founded in 1949, but she remained active in the cultural realm by working with the Beijing Art Players and publishing film and drama reviews. Eventually she accepted a position as editor-in-chief of *Playscripts,* the official monthly magazine of the Chinese Dramatists Association. During the Cultural Revolution, she and her colleagues from the association were sent to a cadre school in the countryside, where Fengzi remained until 1975. In 1979 she officially joined the CCP, and throughout the post–Mao era she remained active as a critic, with essays on contemporary plays and films frequently appearing in newspapers and the periodical press. Several collections of Fengzi's short stories and essays, including her very last collection, *Mirages* (1998), and a memoir have been published in mainland China in recent years.

"The Portrait" (1947), the short story featured here, employs sophisticated formal techniques to unfold what at first glance appears to be the mysterious tale of a young wife's disappearance. The author's narrative perspective, however, gradually reframes Lu Xun's famous query about the New Woman Nora, asking the reader to ponder what happened to the men Nora left behind when she left home.

The Portrait

(1947)

Chapter 1

"WHY DO YOU always look so despondent? Why can't you just look in my direction? What is it that you're looking for? Wei! Why not share your worries with a friend?"

Zhong Yuguo repeated the same questions to himself as he stared at the three-by-five-foot, half-length portrait on the wall. The young woman was dressed plainly in everyday clothing. A youthful glow rose from her cheeks. Perhaps the artist had held his brush with a less than certain hand—the *qipao* with tiny flowers betrayed an overly slender figure. The eyes that should have sparkled were instead glazed over with a foglike melancholy. She gazed off into the unknown distance. Not once did she look in the direction of the old friend who now sat this evening in lonely contemplation beside her portrait; nor did she pay the least bit of attention to the compliments he paid to the painting or his enthusiastic praise of the subject. It was as if she cared not that others existed, as if she were indifferent to even her own existence. It was as if she lived on in the hearts of several people but simply could not bear the excessive nature of friendship, and so had quietly and without warning disappeared. She wasn't dead, but then where was she? No one knew. Her whereabouts were a riddle that more than a few hoped to solve.

Facing the portrait of this young woman, Zhong Yuguo seemed to forget himself. He seemed to forget that his sideburns had long ago turned to white, that he was now an old man and no longer the young, energetic fellow he had been fifteen years ago. Back then he had just returned from studying abroad and was confident that he'd make a name for himself. Who knew that after too much time spent away he would discover his ideas, beliefs, and methods to be always just a bit out of sync with the rest of the nation? Failure after failure sent him finally into an uncontrollable depression. It was at that very moment that by chance he met her, a teenager named Li Ziwei. She was young and vivacious, with a pair of eyes that looked out on her new world with anticipation. She knew absolutely nothing about life. He taught her what she needed to know. What was the meaning of life? She began to wonder about the same things he wondered about. Each day, he would write her a long letter. Those letters enriched both her spiritual life and her knowledge. Those letters were her education and gradually became proof of his love for her. She knew she ought to love him. She knew she ought to repay this man who seemed to live for her. But what was love, after all? To love meant to enter a shared spiritual world. Love was a conclusion, a result. Love meant that two people from two different walks of life faced a shared frontier.

Love and marriage. How could a girl not yet twenty, a girl who had just begun to live, conclude a period in her life awash with sunlight and so full of vitality? Ziwei was determined to use her own powers of deduction to answer these troubling questions.

Thus began her despondence.

"You're too young. You don't understand me."

"I don't understand you?"

"No, you don't understand the world. You know far too little."

". . . . ."

"If you love me, you shouldn't fear me."

". . . . . ."

"You're afraid of marriage, but everyone has to get married sometime!"

"I—I think I'm too young. If you truly love me, why won't you agree to my proposition and just wait ten years?"

What a child she is, he thought. How could a thirty-something-year-old man possibly consider waiting ten years to marry a teenage girl? He couldn't help but laugh out loud at her proposition. She was just a child. He thought he could convince her. He even thought that perhaps he would come to possess her via his own actions. But then, after a year of unrequited love and daily letters, love letters that took more out of him than preparing his lessons, he was rewarded with more endless waiting. This weather-beaten man had lost all ability to appreciate the heart of a young girl in love for the first time. She loved him, almost blindly. His letters were food for her spirit. If the postman was late, she felt as if she had lost something. She indulged in reveries and daydreams. She thought of him constantly—in class, while sleeping, even when she ate. She was steadfast in her plan, however. She refused frequent meetings and even on holidays she would hide away, taking long walks alone on the outskirts of town. She felt comfortable chatting with the azure sky, the alabaster clouds—for she lacked the courage to tell the world that she was in love, how lucky she felt to be loved. She imagined that perhaps in five years' time, once she had graduated from college and was living on her own, she would ask her parents for the freedom to choose her own husband. Naturally, he would be her choice. She envisioned her life five years from now, brimming with happiness like an overflowing glass of wine. Just the thought of it made her blush. One moment she would be lost in silence, the next she'd be sharing laughter with friends, then she'd disappear without the slightest trace. Classmates who didn't know her well said she had changed. Only those close friends who knew her secret were left to share her burden. A great disparity in age doesn't always provide for the best of loves. She attached such importance to matters of the heart—and how she loved to daydream! But reality could never be as beautiful as she imagined it to be. Who would have the heart, who had the power to cast off her illusions?

A year passed, a year of unrequited love that now, looking back, was even more indistinct, more vaporous than a dreamscape. The woman in the portrait had lost all traces of her youthful charm. Only the eyes that stared off into the unknown betrayed the poetry she once possessed. But even her eyes revealed a furtive sort of torment. The silence of her words descended like a fog and eclipsed all with its hazy shadow.

"Why do you always look so despondent? What are you looking for? Perhaps you blame me. Perhaps you hate me. Perhaps you blame me for not waiting for you; you hate me for not keeping our promise. You're right. I got married. But I got divorced too. I've been alone to this day. When I finally found you ten years ago, you were already someone else's wife. You had a wonderful home. Why would you suddenly leave? Mushi was a good husband. He's still waiting, but there's no word of you. Your old friend, the one you once shared everything with, is waiting as well. But it's as if you've forgotten his existence altogether. No one understands you, yet so many people await your return. So many of us still love you. If only you'd come back. You who won't even look in my direction—who would've guessed that you could become so heartless?"

If talking to oneself could be a diversion from loneliness, then it's no wonder that Yuguo's daily soliloquies took him back to those dreams of yesteryear. He treasured the portrait. He kept it on display. There wasn't a person around who didn't know that he had once had such a lover, that because he couldn't accept her almost preposterous proposal, they both had married other people. As for her, reality opened her eyes again and again. She was no longer that girl who loved to dream. She no longer lost herself in love letters; even the most exquisite missive could not capture her interest. Her youthful love was now an absurd, laughable memory. No, that's not right either—it wasn't a memory. She had no time for memories. She admitted that it was he who had taught her how to love and reality that had taught her how to live. Just as there was a great disparity in age, so too were their philosophies quite different. He couldn't understand her. And her? It was altogether possible that she had already erased him from her memory. Recollections in one's later years are often quite bitter. There was no question that the portrait of the young woman that hung in Zhong Yuguo's study embellished his twilight years, reflected his mood, and was tantamount to a scathing mockery. "Why must people live in the past?"

Memories of the past were Zhong Yuguo's entire life.

Chapter 2

WAR CHANGED EVERYTHING. Bombs destroyed cities and altered the ancient faces of more than a few remote towns and villages. Once people realized that their nation was at stake and that final victory would be achieved only after a long, protracted struggle, everyone—individuals and entire families—abandoned the mentality that trusted in chance and biding one's time and took up the sacred cause of national salvation. Excitement took a back seat and everyone began taking a long-term approach to life. If people couldn't head off, gun in hand, to the front line, then they were going to give their all for their nation and for the war. The population in the southwest soon increased by the tens of thousands.

A humble little ancient town, where donkeys and horses ambled unhurriedly along slate roads both day and night, began unexpectedly to flourish because of the war. The customs of this old town were simple and sincere. The people spoke little, but the breadth of their kindness rivaled the limitlessness of the sky. Visitors soon fell in love with the place, with their amiable hosts, the natural scenery and the mild, warm sun that illuminated a perpetually azure sky.

Spring was never-ending; everywhere flowers were in bloom. The local patois had not one vulgar word. There were more colorful parrots than sparrows, and they'd often land on your window lattice to keep you company as you read. Like a mythical legend, this bewitching place embroidered itself into everyone's memory. It mattered not which road one took into town. The scenic beauty of these highlands thousands of feet above sea level brought heaven to earth. Both the sights and the ways of the townspeople made visitors reluctant to leave.

In the northwest corner of the town, on a tranquil narrow road lined with bamboo, sat a four-sided compound with the traditional red lacquer windows and black doors. In three side rooms that faced east lived a young married couple, Li Ziwei and her husband, You Mushi.

Their home seemed to overflow with youth and happiness. Their life seemed like a glass of good wine or an expressive poem. Mushi was not a poet. He was even more intelligent than a poet; he was a philosopher. He loved this house that provided shelter from the storm, the tiny room that made one want to pick up a good book and read. All that was needed were a few friends and some good wine. There was no need to write about it—life itself was a beautiful poem. Spring filled the room and flowers bloomed in the garden. Life had grown so peaceful that even words seemed superfluous. You didn't have to imagine parrots; their colors surrounded you. Ziwei, although no stranger to silence, sang joyously, and the room was filled with vitality because of her. The living room often rang with witty laughter, and over time their home became a frequent refuge for a number of their single friends. There were poets and artists, scholars and professors. The envy of all his friends, Mushi was more than content. But too much happiness is bound to bring trouble.

Not far off was a school. In order to make sure he had the proper research environment, Mushi got himself a small study at the school and set daily office hours. Home was for eating and sleeping; there was little trace of Mushi otherwise, even on holidays. And what of his colorful parrot? Li Ziwei, once vibrant, had grown mute and uttered not a sound all day. Everyone complimented her on being a virtuous, intelligent wife. She could handle the household, cook and clean. She entertained guests and after meals listened patiently to the brilliant conversations and debates. She was all that a woman was supposed to be. She was well versed in national and world affairs and made an excellent pot of coffee. She had the depth of a philosopher and the breadth of a writer. She tolerated the constant and tedious haranguing of her spirit. She thought she might begin to look at different arguments in order to better answer the questions that nagged her. She walked among the fiery red camellias of March. She visited a summer resort in the Western Hills. She sailed upon Dianchi Lake in autumn. In a winter meant for quiet chats around the fireplace, not a drop of rain could be hoped for, to say nothing of a silvery snowflake or two. Spring all year round made one idle and lazy. In frustration, she couldn't help but lament that the northern winds were so far away. Her expression sank under a fog of despondency.

It was the painter Chen Yiyang who memorialized that expression with his brush. In a month's time, he created a three-by-five-foot, half-length portrait for admiring friends of the couple.

Everyone praised the portrait and mused often about the lady in the painting. Many were aware of Ziwei's past and knew that she had once had a lover,

Zhong Yuguo. Zhong had even once been entertained in their living room. Naturally, people continued to weave stories from Ziwei's romantic past. They thought it strange that she was content to curl up quietly like a cat might at home. Gossip soon became prophecy as people began to predict that a storm would soon descend upon this peaceful haven. And isn't that what happened? Look at that expression. That expression itself is a riddle—one not easily solved. Do-gooders began to pay more attention to Ziwei. Wasn't that the case? Ziwei's expression truly was buried beneath a fog. All day long, she stared off into the distance in deep concentration. Her eyes were like a bottomless lake. Still waters run deep, and the depth of this lake proved the distance that separated Ziwei from others, including her husband, Mushi. Often the person closest is most likely to overlook what's in another's heart. The person closest may not be the one who understands his partner best.

Falling in love means that two people begin a journey toward a shared spiritual life. But falling in love alone cannot bring two people from two different walks of life to live together behind the same fence. This is one of life's most basic contradictions. Someone who's used to searching for answers couldn't help but ponder this one.

Contemplating a question is different from daydreaming. Daydreamers may not be able to bear a shattered reality, but those in search of a spiritual life will be even less satisfied with reality itself—even though it's that same reality that inspires change.

Ziwei grew agitated.

Her old friends were scattered across the country. These young people who had once worked together were now struggling for a greater cause. They had sacrificed their own happiness and were now enduring hardships with great perseverance so that others might experience happiness. Several of them lacked her capacity for hard work, but reality had taught them a maturity she didn't possess. They—men and women—reached out to her, sending enthusiastic summons in her direction. Ziwei was perplexed, but her consciousness remained hazy. She didn't know which way to turn. She was enchanted by the aromas that filled the garden, and the warmth of springtime had made her lazy. She began to contemplate a new spiritual life. She began to think of the icy north and the severity of winter. She longed to hear the sound of gunfire at the front line. This new era was a smelting furnace of sorts, and she yearned to be molded into new form. She didn't hide her thoughts. In her innocence, she asked her husband to leave behind their peaceful little home and forge a new path elsewhere. Her naïveté, her enthusiasm simply became fodder for her husband's after-dinner conversations with friends. "Look here! Our woman warrior!" Her self-respect was battered. This bird could not escape her cage, but oh, how she dreamed of flying!

"It's all these dreams that are destroying you! You ought to find some way to occupy yourself. Let work be your diversion. Or . . . read more. But don't be fooled by those stories. Real life is ordinary. Novels are nothing but fantasies concocted by their authors."

To Mushi, Ziwei was just a girl who liked to daydream. He thought she was just lonely. He failed to recognize the spiritual emptiness that plagued her. He invited friends over and brought more excitement into their home, but this only made it worse. Ziwei grew more and more troubled.

A caged bird won't fly far. The world is just too big. Ziwei pondered this problem all day long. Her thoughts were like a violent wave that couldn't be checked. They roused a great power deep inside of her. She thought: *I don't care if the world is huge. I want to live.*

> I doubt that love and home are all that life is made of. There must be something else. If you don't agree with my methods and you refuse to escape this old life with me, I hope you'll forgive me for going it alone. If you think that in abandoning this home I'm forsaking you, there's nothing more for me to say. Neither love nor home can fill this void. I had no idea that the person I would come to share my life with would be so distant from me in spirit. I can't calm down. There are all sorts of voices calling to me. I can't explain my thinking clearly enough. I can only use my actions to forge the reality I'm in search of. . . .

Early one morning Mushi awoke to discover that his colorful parrot had already escaped from her cage! This was the letter Ziwei left behind. Ziwei had actually left him. Unbelievable. This girl who so loved to daydream was even more senseless than those daydreams suggested. She loathed their life. She didn't love him! Why? Why?

The sun continued to shine with its usual springtime warmth. The blue sky was as clear as ocean waters. But these rooms had lost their poetic charm. Losing Ziwei meant losing everything. Mushi realized that this wasn't a dream. Those happy days were gone, like a dream never to be revisited.

Mushi recalled how they had fallen in love. He thought about their marriage. Two short years—he had been so sure Ziwei was completely caught up in their life. Like a small skiff avoiding life's storms, she should have been anchored in his port for life. Who knew that she would test even rougher waters and, leaving everything behind, sail off for distant places? "You were right—our spiritual lives were so far apart!" For the first time he realized that he didn't know her at all. The painful thing was, he loved her. He couldn't lose her. Even more agonizing was the fact that he couldn't go after her. He resolved to live an ascetic life, relinquishing all to await her return. He trusted that a woman's fate was like that of a caged bird. Regardless of how far she flew, one day she would no longer be able to brave the storm. One day she would need to rest; she would need a home.

Time flows like a river, in one direction, never to return. Mushi quietly bore the pain that tore at his spirit. His perseverance was astonishing. He spent his days buried in books and grew increasingly eccentric in his ways. Everyone felt sorry for him. They felt sorry for Ziwei as well. No news arrived. Mushi avoided friends and recoiled from the pity that came from their kindness. He refused to speak of the past. It was as if he had completely forgotten. The only reminder, the portrait of Ziwei, had been retired from the wall at some point, never to reappear. Where had the portrait gone? Someone mentioned that they had seen it at an exhibit. Someone else speculated that it had been purchased. Those who knew the artist, Yiyang, declared this an insult. Yiyang would never sell the painting. And it certainly couldn't have been Mushi. No one felt comfortable asking Mushi, and Yiyang had no idea how the portrait ended up in an exhibition. He was determined to find out how the painting had disappeared. He resolved to bring the truth to light.

Chapter 3

JUST AS THE portrait of Li Ziwei, as well as the person herself, had begun to fade in people's memories, a fortuitous opportunity arose for Yiyang to travel to another foggy mountain town. Even more astonishingly, he discovered the long-lost portrait hanging in Zhong Yuguo's living room. It was mounted in a luxuriously carved, gilded frame, so he had difficulty recognizing his own work. But those eyes, that utterly despondent expression, brought his memories back to life. It was Ziwei! Yiyang was so pleasantly surprised that he let out a cry. This sudden miracle was no match, though, for the hidden worries that had been brewing all these years. Could it be that the life Ziwei had been searching for was right here? He didn't like Zhong Yuguo. He was nothing but an old man who never practiced what he preached. He had used his experience and social standing to win the trust of young people. But what had he given them in return? He had courted more than a few women, but hadn't truly loved any of them. Even his wife finally divorced him. As for Ziwei, he said he loved her, but he never truly possessed her. They'd managed to stay friends. But many felt that such a friendship was an insult to Ziwei's reputation and honor. Of course Ziwei never concealed her past; nor did she fear others' criticism. But when the married Ziwei spoke of her past with friends, she didn't give a very positive impression. After her disappearance, rumors spread. Since Zhong Yuguo was recently divorced, perhaps he was responsible for this tragedy. Yiyang spared no time in refuting such accusations. He felt he understood Ziwei. A woman so bent on improving herself would never sink to such a level. But could it be true? How else could the portrait have ended up in Zhong Yuguo's possession? The more he thought about it, the less comfortable Yiyang felt. He was struck by the desire to run from the room before his host appeared. He feared that the rumors were in fact reality, and he couldn't bear to watch the portrait come to life before his eyes. He was afraid that Ziwei was the mistress of *this* house. But something held his attention. He stood motionless, staring, gazing at the portrait. He considered how he might vanish with the painting. *This is my work! It's my right.* He repeated this to himself over and over again, as if he were speaking directly to his host. It was as if he were preparing to make a speech, but before he could run through his notes, his host appeared before him.

From early afternoon through dusk, then from dusk deep into the night, over several bottles of wine and a final pot of coffee, the story of the portrait, the story of the woman in the painting, moved both the storyteller and his listener. Their long discussion dispelled many of Yiyang's misgivings. He felt a sense of pity for the difficulties this man with the graying sideburns who now sat before him had experienced. Yuguo could tell a story, and his control of the facts, especially the romantic facts, made this one all the more worth listening to. Once Yiyang understood the relationship that had existed between Yuguo and Ziwei, he couldn't help but give their most sacred friendship his blessing. Finally, he sighed and said:

"Perhaps it's better this way. You can hold on to that time. You're an old friend of hers. Perhaps you'll see her again. I still hope that the portrait returns to its rightful owner, that the painting will once again hang in Mushi's living room. It's really too bad that I could only paint her outer appearance, but I couldn't know her inner being."

"Who really knew her?" Yuguo sighed deeply.

It was true. Not only did Yiyang and Yuguo *not* understand her, but Mushi, her own husband, never figured her out. She seemed to have loved her husband and to have enjoyed her friends, but her spirit inhabited another world. She lived with Mushi and often spent time in the company of friends, eating and talking. The first impression she gave was of a lively, vivacious woman who was easy to be around. Only those who tried to get closer to her realized the silences that separated them from her world. Her foggy expression said a lot about her despondency, but it could not reveal the source of her depression.

"I didn't understand her. She had changed too much. It was just too strange!" Yuguo, half in recollection, continued, "Two years ago in winter, she suddenly showed up here in my living room. My wife and I sat with her and accepted the gift she brought—the portrait."

"Please keep it for me for now. I still have a long way to travel, and it will be inconvenient to take such a thing along."

"Where are you off to? You're by yourself?" I asked her.

She smiled. "Naturally I'm by myself. Otherwise I wouldn't have brought the portrait with me."

"Then . . . what about Mushi?"

"He . . . I did it for him. I was afraid it would just add to his grief. So I decided to 'abscond' with the painting." Again she smiled, but it was a forced, reluctant smile.

"What is going on?"

"There are so many people, so many things that just can't be explained in terms of everyday convention. I'm afraid I have no answer to your question."

"Her thoughts seemed to drift and her tone of voice was quite mysterious, but there's one thing I'm sure of—her expression wasn't the one you've captured in this portrait. Hers was clear and determined. And those weren't her eyes. I'd known her for so many years, since she was a girl, and I knew those eyes." Yuguo couldn't help but flaunt their romantic past a bit, and for a moment grew animated. "But those aren't her eyes. Those look like something from an illustration in some sort of book. They're not the eyes Ziwei should have had. Ai, I can't explain it. Anyway, she changed.

"I never saw her after that. Years passed without a word of news. Life has changed for so many of us. As for me . . ." Yuguo let out a sigh, but didn't go on. There was no need to mention the details of his divorce. Yiyang had heard it all before.

"As for the war, who knows when it will end? I'm not being negative or pessimistic, but the longer things drag on, the more likely it will be that the common people suffer the most. I'm not a soldier, so I suppose I shouldn't be saying such things. If it weren't for this war, my family would still be a family—and Mushi would never have had to let Ziwei go. Don't you think?"

"Are you saying that Mushi let Ziwei go?"

"Why not? The environment determines everything. Naturally, I'm not blaming Mushi. But in their case their personalities determined both their environment and their lives. This is a tragedy of individuals, of society, and of an era.

"Of course, they're both still young. Perhaps they'll love again. But Ziwei is in search of a life, not a lifestyle. She probably won't ever marry again, but she'll never lack emotional stimulation. People go on about her romantic affairs with this man and that, but this man and that are still here in this town. Ziwei, in the meanwhile, is long gone. The concerns of a married man are far greater than those of a woman brave enough to leave her husband. She has an extremely strong personality. She would never ruin her own future for love."

"But isn't she simply ruining herself instead?" Yiyang asked apprehensively.

"Naturally, she's chosen a dangerous path. And those who love her ought to be concerned for her future."

Exactly. Those who love her ought to be concerned about her future. But how should one show concern? How *could* one show concern? Where was she? No one knew, or knew whether or not she was even safe. As he faced the half-length portrait, Yuguo grew silent.

The artist Chen Yiyang finally consented to leaving the portrait with Yuguo. He was, after all, its partial owner. The portrait became Yuguo's companion. He even took it along on his travels and exhibited it wherever he went. He grew used to talking to the painting. This connoisseur of Li Ziwei's portrait had no idea of the stories it had left to tell; nor did he realize that the owner of the portrait, You Mushi, well on his way to middle age, still waited in loneliness, in anticipation that his colorful parrot would fly back home.

Chapter 4

ODDLY, THE PORTRAIT eventually vanished from Yuguo's living room. The thief left a note behind: "Forgive me. I've taken the portrait back without your consent. I haven't found her, but I'm determined to uncover what became of her. I'm about to begin a difficult journey. I'm taking the portrait with me in hopes that it will help me ascertain whether or not she's still alive."

"It was Mushi! Could it be Mushi?" Yuguo grew excited.

After reading the note, he had a hard time believing that a person who had locked himself in his study for years would suddenly pick himself up, grab the portrait, and run off to the ends of the earth in search of Ziwei. "Is this possible?" Yuguo mumbled to himself, as an indescribable feeling of jealousy crawled like an insect through his psyche. Losing the portrait was like losing a god. He couldn't live without the painting; he couldn't live without the memories needed to fill the emptiness inside.

Determined to retrieve the portrait, he immediately went to find Mushi at the address left on the note. In Mushi's home, he found a young man much older than his years. Yuguo's excitement grew uncontrollably, but he stuck to his plan.

"Yiyang agreed. I'm supposed to hold on to this portrait. I must keep my promise."

"What promise?"

"It's a secret."

"Could it be that there are still secrets between you and Ziwei?"

"No, you've misunderstood. The secret is in regard to you."

"Me?"

"Yes, Yiyang asked me to keep the portrait. He believes that one day it will hang again in your living room."

"Are you mocking me?"

Yuguo couldn't help but laugh nervously, then almost immediately continued somberly, "I'm not mocking you. Don't get so excited." Yuguo realized that he would have to think of a way to convince Mushi, so he quickly changed the topic.

"You're just too excitable. You might do something rash and destroy it. Yiyang treasures this portrait because Ziwei adored it. Naturally, it should be in your possession. But more important, you should try to rebuild your family, especially now that you're determined to find Ziwei. I will not break my promise. Once you're a family again, I promise to return the painting to you."

Yuguo was desperate to trick Mushi, but in reality he was lying to himself—all for the portrait. His voice shook as he spoke. He hated Mushi; he despised his heartlessness. Time and again, Mushi had ripped his dreams to pieces. He once possessed Ziwei and now he wanted to lay claim to her memory. What right did he have? What right? *If Ziwei were meant to be yours, why did you let her go? She's gone. You couldn't have her. And now you want to make me suffer? Like a common thief, you took a painting that's rightfully mine.* Common courtesy was not lost on Yuguo as he swallowed a few last curses meant to inflict that final, fatal blow. The tide could not be turned back, though—Mushi's heart was irretrievably lost. He had closed the door. Yuguo didn't stand a chance.

Back home, the living room seemed so empty, so gloomy without the portrait. For the first time, he noted how dark the room actually was. Even at night, an electric lamp wasn't enough. He dreaded being alone there, but he couldn't break the habit of sitting quietly, facing that wall. Now it was nothing but a wall. Facing the spot where the portrait once hung, he couldn't help himself; his private conversations with the lady in the painting continued, even though the painting itself was gone. He aged years in a matter of days. The pain was unbearable—a lost love, divorce—his life was in a shambles. And now the portrait was gone. His spirit, his emotional state could take little else. Seemingly on the verge of insanity, he cursed everyone and everything. He swore that he would figure out some way to destroy the portrait. If he couldn't have it, no one should. But Mushi was gone. How could he possibly locate the portrait?

Several years passed.

Mushi was said to have gone abroad, probably taking the portrait along with him. As old age approached, Yuguo grew less able to bear the pain of having lost it. He couldn't give up. He waited and dreamed that one day the portrait would reappear. Morning and night, he prayed silently before that blank wall. He believed that his sincerity would move Ziwei, that Ziwei would one day fly back to him and spend those final years by his side.

Out of pity for his old friend, who was resigned to living on memories alone, the artist Chen Yiyang decided to find a woman who resembled Ziwei so that he might create another portrait to give Yuguo as a gift.

He asked several friends to find him a model. Days later, he received an anonymous letter. Upon reading it, he couldn't help but cry out in surprise:

"Could it be Ziwei? She's still alive—still here in this world!"

The letter had been hastily written.

I've heard that you'd like to paint a portrait for an old acquaintance and that you need a model with similar features. I'd love to meet with you. Perhaps in my face you might find traces of that same old friend. Don't be surprised, though, that I'm no longer young. Even your brush won't be able to retrieve my lost youth. Perhaps you might be inspired; and if you still consider me a friend, you may even wish the new me well.

It had to be Ziwei. They agreed to meet and when they did, Yiyang hugged her as if she were a long-lost lover. He hadn't realized until that very moment that he too had been in love with her. The Ziwei before him was like the sun in springtime, vivacious and full of energy. She was no longer young—the Ziwei of old was gone—but youth's beauty is no match for the intelligence that comes with experience. Her eyes were still bright and determined. If nothing else, her inner being was more youthful. She was so frank, so warm. As she spoke of life after her departure and how she had come to recognize reality, every sentence drew Yiyang more closely to her. She laughed when she heard why he was planning to paint another portrait.

"Is it worth wasting so much time and energy on a person who lives in the past?"

"How can you be so heartless?"

"I realize that everyone will blame me and call me heartless. But I refuse to make excuses. There are far too many things left undone in this world. It's not hard to catch hold of a young woman's shadow. Because I respect you as an artist, I wish you would create more meaningful works."

"Are you saying that painting your portrait would be meaningless?"

"Don't paint me. I'm just an ordinary person. Mine is but an ordinary life. I no longer swim in that sea of emotions that I knew when I was young. I have my work. Or perhaps I should say, I have my career. I'm willing to do more for others. It's as simple as that. I have nothing to hide. Think about it—what's the point of painting my portrait? Would such a painting change someone's life? Yuguo would sit all day staring at the portrait and talking to himself. His spiritual life would forever be locked in the past. You say you pity him, that I'm cold-hearted. But is it wrong to be cold-hearted toward such a stubborn, selfish person? I don't understand how I could have ever loved him. The mind of a young woman is a strange place. Now as I think back, how laughable a young woman's emotions seem to me."

"But young love is the most precious kind."

"You believe that too?"

"I even envy Yuguo because you loved him first and not me."

"Yiyang!"

Ziwei fell silent. It was obvious that she knew how to deal with such impasses. There was nothing left to discuss. She declined Yiyang's request; she refused to let him paint her portrait again. The portrait and the stories it told finally divulged that she, Ziwei, had been the cause of a series of tragedies. She despised those who lived in the past. She saw that the artist was destined to be another Yuguo, another Mushi. There was nothing to worry about. She had already made up her mind. She felt no regret over their meeting, although she now knew that Yiyang would never be able to wish the new her well.

And so concludes the final episode of the story of the portrait. Yiyang never again saw Ziwei. Both she and the shadow of her younger self disappeared into the crowd without a trace. Those foggy eyes were never to appear again. In Yiyang's recent memory, those eyes were now as bright and determined as the scorching sun. It was that pair of eyes that took Ziwei to a place Yiyang would never know. They left a lasting impression in the artist's memory. At one point he thought to reclaim the precious memory with his paintbrush, but alas, he was unable to bring that final impression back to life.

April 1, 1947
April Fool's Day

9
Lu Xiaoman
(1903–1965)

Remembered in modern Chinese literary history primarily in connection with Xu Zhimo (1895–1931), one of the most celebrated May Fourth poets, Lu Xiaoman had literary aspirations of her own. The well-bred socialite daughter of a distinguished family, Lu was born in Shanghai in 1903 but moved to Beijing when she was about nine years of age. There she attended the western-run Sacred Heart Academy and studied English with a private tutor. She was famous for her beauty. Her much-anticipated marriage was arranged in 1920 to Wang Geng, a Princeton and West Point graduate whose family was native to Wuxi. Several years later, now a married woman, she was introduced to Xu Zhimo, who reportedly fell madly in love with her, and their romantic affair soon erupted into one of the major society scandals of the mid–1920s. Xu fled to Europe, returning only when the dust had settled and Lu's divorce was firmly secured. When the couple eventually wed in Beijing 1926, with Hu Shi and Liang Qichao present as their witnesses, the event attracted coverage in the mainstream media. After the wedding, they moved to Shanghai, where Lu Xiaoman became quite popular for her amateur opera performances in benefit shows at such theaters as the Empire, the Olympic, and the Carlton. She was even featured on the front cover of the popular urban pictorial *Young Companion* in 1927. Their celebrity marriage would be short-lived: Xu Zhimo was killed in a plane crash in 1931, on his regular commute back from Beijing, where he had a teaching position, leaving Lu Xiaoman widowed at the age of twenty-nine.

Although Lu Xiaoman allegedly displayed an artistic flair from a young age, excelling in dance, opera singing, and Chinese painting, her relationship with Xu appears to have inspired a new interest in literary creation. In 1928, she co-wrote a five-act play, *Bian Kungang*, with Xu. According to the writer and literary historian Su Xuelin, Xu formulated the dramatic structure, while the story and the dialogue can be attributed entirely to Lu Xiaoman. The play is a tragedy that revolves around the title character, a kind-hearted widower who remarries only to have his new wife become bitterly jealous of his memories of his late wife, with fatal consequences. The play was published under both of their names in *Crescent Monthly* magazine.

Lu Xiaoman's literary aspirations were also in evidence when, in 1935, amid the flurry of publications of love letters of famous literary couples, she published *Love Letters to Mei*, a fascinating collection of letters and diaries she and Xu Zhimo had written at the peak of their illicit romance. The volume appeared on what would have been Xu's fortieth birthday and seems to have been largely motivated by a desire on Lu Xiaoman's part to make her side of their legendary affair known. Above all, as she claims in the preface, she hoped to put an end to the vicious rumors that, even ten years later, continued to circulate about their controversial affair and subsequent marriage. In three parts, the book powerfully conveys the intensity of their mutual devotion but also the moral quandary Lu found herself in. The juxtaposition of Xu's diaries with her own also highlights quite distinct perspectives on love and literature, no doubt informed by their respective positions as a well-established poet and a young married woman bound by her upper-class, old-fashioned family. In the end, whereas Xu Zhimo comes across as rather selfishly submerged in his private emotional universe, Lu Xiaoman grapples with their relationship in terms of a need to balance desire with moral concerns, medical issues, and the mundane considerations of domestic duty.

After the founding of the People's Republic in 1949, Shanghai mayor and poet Chen Yi helped Lu Xiaoman secure a position at the Shanghai Institute of Culture and History, and later she taught at the Shanghai Academy of Chinese Painting. She died of a respiratory disease in 1965, and was thus spared the upheavals of the Cultural Revolution. Her final request to be buried next to Xu Zhimo was denied.

"The Imperial Hotel," the short story selected here, was commissioned for Zhao Qingge's edited volume *Untitled*, a major postwar collection of contemporary women's writing published in 1947. The story employs an array of modernist narrative techniques, including stream of consciousness and a fragmentary plot structure, to conjure up the decadent urban milieu of wartime Shanghai while depicting the difficult circumstances a young middle-class mother faces. The work thus offers a refreshing stylistic approach to social inequality, opportunism, and wartime hardship without the sermonizing that such themes often elicited.

The Imperial Hotel

(1947)

WANZHEN SAT ON the edge of the bed watching Erbao sleeping feverishly, his small face apple red, eyes shut, breathing labored, the sound of phlegm churning in his throat as though he wanted to cough it up but couldn't. From his condition it was obvious he was in pain even in his sleep. Wanzhen was beside herself, not knowing what to think because there was simply too much to think about.

Wanzhen was a young college graduate who had married her classmate Zhang Lisheng fresh out of school. A year later she had given birth to a daughter, and by the time she was pregnant with Erbao, China was at war with Japan. Lisheng couldn't just abandon them to follow the government to the interior, so he stayed on in Shanghai. But from that point on, life was uncertain. When Erbao was born, Lisheng had suffered the indignity of accepting a menial position with the puppet regime to support the family. Naturally, with five mouths to feed, relying entirely on his income was extraordinarily difficult, so Wanzhen took on the housework herself. She had her hands full all day long minding the two children. But Lisheng's mother helped out with the meals, so for all the hardship, the family actually got by just fine.

Now Erbao was three already, but ever since he had been weaned he had been a sickly child. During the winter he had come down with chills and a fever that lasted several months, and no sooner had he gotten better than he caught pneumonia. For the sake of this child they had sunk into debt, but lately it all seemed so hopeless. Each day as Lisheng watched the boy gasping for breath and sweating as he coughed, it pained him more than being stabbed straight through the heart with a knife. They could see that the child desperately needed an injection, but Lisheng had long since drawn an advance on his salary, western doctors were so terribly expensive, and the medication would not be easy to buy. So Wanzhen made up her mind to get a job herself to help make ends meet. However, nothing had come of friends' efforts to help her find employment. Then, the day before last she had been elated to see an advertisement in the newspaper for a female staff worker at the Imperial Hotel. After the two had talked it over that evening, Lisheng was of the opinion that taking a job like this was beneath her. But Wanzhen insisted on giving it a try. Besides, wasn't it better to rely on oneself than to rely on others? When it came to survival, who cared what their friends and relatives might think? So off she went with the paper to apply.

The Imperial Hotel was a deluxe establishment with a ballroom patronized by foreigners and upper-crust Chinese. The ladies' lounge in the ballroom needed a female attendant fluent in English to oversee the sale of cosmetics and accessories.

Because she was so well educated, the manager had great respect for her, and she had been asked to begin work the very next day. However, yesterday, her first night on the job, she got the feeling she was not cut out for this sort of work after all. Never before had she encountered ladies of this breed, and within the space of just a few short hours it was as though she had been transported into another world. By the time the clock struck midnight and she returned home, she was in a trance, her head so bewildered she couldn't speak. When Lisheng saw her in such a state, he urged her not to go back. Wanzhen also sensed the inconvenience of night life and began having second thoughts. But today, seeing that Erbao's condition had not improved, that there was no way to fill the prescription that the doctor had written the day before, and that the child was running such a high fever that his cheeks were burning up and he had difficulty breathing, she couldn't bear to sit there watching him suffer and do nothing.

She sat at the foot of the bed transfixed. If she went back to work this evening, she could ask the manager for a small advance on her pay; otherwise, what hope would there be? So as she looked over at the child, she quietly made up her mind. Glancing at her watch, she saw it was nearly seven o'clock already; outside it was getting dark. She stood up, and when she felt the child's forehead to check his temperature it was so hot she couldn't keep her hand there. Her heart ached and she felt as though she might cry. Then, frowning and shaking her head, she stood up and walked over to the bureau, picked up a wooden comb and fixed her hair, turned around and reached for a short, rather worn-out coat from the clothes rack and draped it over her shoulders, went to the inner room, and said to her mother-in-law, "Ma, don't wait for me to eat. I've decided to go to work now, and once I get an advance on my wages, then first thing tomorrow morning we can go buy Erbao's medicine! Tell Lisheng later."

Without waiting for a reply, Wanzhen rushed out. As soon as she got out the door she hopped in a rickshaw and, not even bothering to settle on the fare, told the puller to hurry up and take her to the Imperial Hotel. As she sat in the rickshaw she was overwhelmed by sadness, and tears welled up in her eyes. She could barely control her emotions. Unable to fathom the depth of her sorrow, she had put her own concerns aside, seeing only Erbao's small face, burning up as red as an apple, breathing feebly, looking as though he couldn't hold out much longer! For this reason, she was oblivious to everything and ready to do whatever it took to get some money to treat Erbao's illness. As for what she and her husband had discussed the night before, she didn't give it a second thought. Her sole concern now was that if she were late the manager would be angry and not want her to work there anymore, so she hurried the driver on: "Can't you go any faster? I have urgent business."

"We're there, can't you see it's right up ahead? What's the big rush?" The rickshaw puller was a bit surprised but figured that the lady didn't know the area well or else couldn't read, since right there in front of them was a neon sign flashing THE IMPERIAL HOTEL. She jumped down from the rickshaw and dashed inside, only now remembering that just as she was leaving the night before the manager had told her to come in early today, since business was always best on Saturdays and the place would be packed by early evening. As she remembered what he had said, she dreaded his reproach and her heart pounded in anticipation. And indeed, when she came in through the doors she could see the manager already there, scolding employees with animated gestures. When he saw her, he rushed up and said, "Hurry up, Miss Wang! How come you are later today than yesterday? Quite a few guests have arrived, and Little Hong has already asked for you twice, so hurry and get up there!"

Before the manager was done speaking, Wanzhen had already started up the stairs, and the minute she entered the lounge, Little Hong called out to her from across the room, "Miss Wang, here you are at last, the manager is frantic and wants us to get ready! We've been waiting for you to get out the face powder and rouge so we can set up. Why are you so late?"

Wanzhen didn't have time to answer as she rushed over to open the glass display case and take out the necessary items, which she handed over to Little Hong and Little Lan. She instructed them to put a small amount of powder in the powder box on each dressing table while explaining how they were to greet the patrons who came in.

Little Hong and Little Lan were both middle-school graduates who could speak some English. Because of the hardships during the war and because neither had any family, they had no choice but to quit their studies to find work. Even though Wanzhen had only met them the night before, she appreciated their spirit. She was especially taken by Little Hong, who was pretty and clever, and spoke Beijing dialect. Last night, as soon as they were introduced Little Hong had followed her around everywhere, and Wanzhen agreed to look after her like a younger sister. Therefore, today as Wanzhen handed the items over and watched her take them away so cheerfully, she bowed her head and smiled to herself, feeling inexplicably relieved, even momentarily forgetting her own troubles. Only when she had tidied up did Wanzhen finally sit down, letting out a deep sigh. She looked around the room. The mirrors on the dressing tables reflected the pale yellow whitewashed walls, giving off a refined luster, and making the room appear all the more spacious and grand. Except for the merry laughter of Little Hong and Little Lan emanating from the inner rooms, now there was not even the faintest sound. The air felt rather thick, and Wanzhen thus once again began thinking about her sick child. All she hoped now was that the guests would hurry up and start arriving so the long night would pass by quickly and she could ask the manager for an advance to buy some medicine. Nothing else mattered. She supposed that by now Lisheng must have already gotten back home and would be taking care of Erbao. She remembered how excited she had been the previous night sitting on this very chair, and how intrigued she had been by all the brand-new sights and sounds. She had been like Liu Laolao, who was so utterly enthralled when she visited Grand View Garden.[1] She had even started to enjoy her job, and this elegant, spacious room that naturally was so much more comfortable than their cramped, poorly lit quarters at home. But later on, when she hopped in a rickshaw to go home, her mood again shifted and it occurred to her that what she had witnessed was a lot like the novels she occasionally read, with scenes she had assumed could not possibly be true, things she could scarcely imagine.

Thus she returned home with a perplexed and heavy heart, and not until she had told Lisheng all about it and mulled it over carefully did she conclude that to keep working there would be too risky. She made up her mind not to go back the next day.

Who would have thought that here she would be, sitting on this chair again today? Now that she thought about it, she grew uneasy.

Just then peals of laughter rang out outside, followed by four or five ladies pushing open the door, giggling and chatting as they burst in and proceeded into the inner rooms, all except one tall and slender young matron who changed her mind before going in. First, she glanced around the anteroom and peered over at Wanzhen, then sauntered up to a dressing table, where she stood in front of the mirror and gazed at her full, round face and her equally

---

[1] Reference to a memorable rustic relative in *Dream of the Red Chamber* who is overwhelmed by the material grandeur of the Jia family mansion when she visits for the first time.

well-proportioned figure. She flashed a proud smile, stepped forward, then picked up a comb to straighten a few loose strands of hair. She inspected herself from side to side, then looked down to get a lipstick out of her pocketbook, which she reapplied, all the while softly humming a tune from the opera *Jade Hall of Spring,* as though no one else were in the room. Meanwhile, out came another woman in a long crimson gown, who had to be five or six years older than the young woman—clearly a seasoned socialite who could just smile without even saying a word and win a person over. Her charm was such that her white complexion seemed all the more tender and lovely. As soon as she saw the young lady there humming Peking opera, she immediately walked up behind her with a smile, and affectionately wrapped her arms around her shoulders. Looking at her in the mirror, she said, "Good gracious! You're gorgeous enough as it is, what are you doing putting on more make-up? Didn't you see how Jiaoqi couldn't keep his eyes off you at dinner? He didn't even notice when Mr. Zhu poured him more wine. If you get even more made up, he'll be completely entranced! Save the make-up!"

"Oh, nonsense! You never stop. Nothing from your mouth ever sounds nice. You fail to mention that you yourself spend hours doing your face, and who knows how long you spend admiring yourself from side to side when you get dressed?"

"Oh, I've thought of something! Stop fooling around, let's talk about something serious, okay?"

"What have you got to be serious about? You just want to learn some new opera, or design some costumes, or find some limelight." Having said this, the fat lady stood up in front of the dressing mirror and started shaping her eyebrows with an eyebrow pencil.

"Do that later, I have something to discuss with you," said the slender one, taking her hand.

Seeing her looking so anxious, the fat one realized that her friend really did have something important to say, so she put the eyebrow pencil away, sat down, and murmured, "Well, what is it?"

"It's Lin Caixia. Do you get the feeling she's been acting differently lately? The past few times we invited her out, she made all sorts of excuses, whereas she used to be so eager to go out with us. And when she does come she has to leave early, and she's even reluctant to teach us opera now. She's been teaching us that same allegro section of *Jade Hall* for ages now. Apparently she has to force herself, and she's not at all enthusiastic the way she used to be."

The fat woman listened and restrained her smile, keeping silent for several moments before looking up and replying in a low voice, "It's true. If you hadn't said anything I would not have noticed, but now that you mention it, I agree she's changed a lot. Just now at dinner I overheard her saying something about some Mrs. Zhang whom she only met three times who gave her a Hunanese embroidered cushion. Then she brought up a Mr. Li somebody or other who gave her a feathered head ornament. It made me feel bad—it was as though our gifts weren't worth mentioning! It's rather insulting, don't you think?"

"Indeed. Actresses don't understand the first thing about friendship. So I wanted to run this by you now because they'll be back shortly and it won't be convenient for us to talk. From now on, we mustn't be so friendly with her, and if she wants to come out with us, that's up to her. If you get a chance, mention it to Mrs. Li and tell her not to be so doting. We can find something else to amuse ourselves with. Don't just throw your money down the drain. Do you know what I mean?"

Just as they were conversing, their three companions emerged from the inner rooms, one of whom was slightly older than the rest. She looked dignified and quite chic, as if she were an aristocrat, and even though she was well over forty, she was beautifully attired. If it hadn't been for the lines of wrinkles around her eyes, from afar one would never have guessed her age! Another one was dressed like a northerner trying to imitate Shanghai style, and at a glance it was apparent she was either a drum-song singer or an actress. Even the way she walked was like an actress on stage! And then there was one who couldn't have been more than thirty, who looked quite poised. Just watching her walk gave away her whole personality—so serene and haughty. She was still gazing blankly at the western-style landscape painting hanging on the wall when the older woman approached the dressing table.

"Just look at the two of you! The minute you're together you just can't stop nattering away. Wherever do you find so much to talk about? But nothing nice is ever said behind people's backs, so you must be whispering about me again, aren't you?" said the distinguished matron to the fat one, half in jest, as she took the slender one's hand. At that point the two pulled her over and whispered something in her ear.

As soon as Lin Caixia came out, she had spotted the long glass display case in front of Wanzhen. Because of the tiny electric lights inside the case illuminating the golds, silvers, reds, greens, and various other colors on top of the glass, everything seemed especially elegant and dazzling, and immediately caught her fancy. So without even pausing to chat with the ladies, she went over by herself. First she eyed Wanzhen briefly with a look of amazement, for this was the first time she had ever been to such a grand hotel. She had never seen cosmetics and accessories for sale in a ladies' lounge before and she wasn't sure what tone of voice to take with Wanzhen, so she just stared at the merchandise in the case, longing yet not daring to ask about it. Wanzhen smiled slightly and said to her, "If there's anything you'd like to look at, please go ahead."

Hearing this, Lin Caixia was unsure how she was supposed to respond, so she looked around for reinforcements. "Mrs. Li, come over here quick, isn't this purse exquisite! And that gold brooch too!"

As Lin Caixia called out to her, she also beckoned the two other ladies over with her hand. Mrs. Li trotted right over obediently, happily instructing Wanzhen to show Lin the things she wanted to see. Wanzhen thus took them all out and spread them on top of the glass counter, turning on the small electric lamp on the counter as well, so that they glittered all the more brilliantly. Lin Caixia looked mesmerized, as though she would have stuffed them all into her own little handbag were it not for the fact that she knew it was quite beyond her means to buy them all. Thus an indescribably strange expression crept over her face, and she glanced at Mrs. Li, then turned to look at the two others who had just walked up, and, all smiles, asked, "Mrs. Li, Mrs. Wang, which do you think is the prettiest? I've been looking at them for so long that I can't tell. I've never seen such things anywhere else; they must be imported!"

At this point the slender woman went over to Lin Caixia and held the gold brooch up to her chest to see how it looked and, laughing slyly, said, "Why, Ms. Lin, on you it looks even prettier. If you don't buy this, you'll have passed up a good opportunity. I think you should buy them all. You mustn't think twice about it." Having said this, she shot a glance at Mrs. Li and the fat woman.

Mrs. Li looked at her with uncomprehending eyes, while the fat woman smiled and added coldly, "Indeed, it's as though they were made just for you, Ms. Lin, they wouldn't suit anyone else. Stop this nonsense and hurry up and get out some money to pay for them! You can put them on straight away."

Poor Lin Caixia. Clutching her pocketbook in one hand, she was at a complete loss. She certainly hadn't expected these two to act so uncharacteristically, and she was so mortified she was rendered speechless. Ordinarily when they all went out shopping together, she need only express the slightest interest in something and without even saying a word, they would fight to buy it for her. But not tonight. Even Mrs. Li was somewhat mystified. Wanzhen watched the expressions on each of their faces; it was truly more fascinating than a play. She even felt a little sorry for the actress, and thought her quite pitiful.

At this moment, Mrs. Li became somewhat embarrassed and walked over to put her hand on Lin Caixia's shoulder, saying, "Ms. Lin, have whatever you like, my treat. It's getting late, so why don't you go back out and dance? And afterward, weren't you going over to my house to teach us the slow part of *Jade Hall*?"

As she heard this, Lin Caixia's expression immediately changed; she rolled her eyes and, with an indifferent and thoroughly artificial laugh, said, "Oh, I almost forgot, I still have to go to rehearsal!" With that, she spun around to leave, ignoring the merchandise on the countertop and not uttering another word. By now Mrs. Li was extremely concerned and at once caught up with her, asking, "But Ms. Lin, didn't you promise that after we went out dancing you would spend the rest of the evening at my house? How can you have rehearsal in a little while?"

The slender woman glanced at the fat one, and the two smirked knowingly at each other. They then excused themselves from Wanzhen, whispering as they walked out. Observing this scene, Wanzhen felt sad, reflecting on the fact that while they had the means to amuse themselves extravagantly, she could ill afford legitimate expenses, let alone frivolous amusements. They were all human beings, yet what disparities divided them.

She was just mulling this over when through the door barged a woman with a black cape draped over her shoulders. As soon as she came in, she threw it off and handed it to Little Hong, who was standing at the entrance, all the while humming the popular English tune "Merry Widow."[2] As she walked up to the mirror, Wanzhen examined her carefully in the pink hue of the lamp—how lovely. Wanzhen could scarcely believe that there was such a beautiful creature on earth! She was neither too thin nor too fat, not too tall or too short, and she was dressed in a western-style black velvet evening gown with a red back, and had on silver leather shoes. The collar revealed just a bit of snowy white skin. Her complexion was flawless, and her big, radiant eyes exuded intelligence and vitality. Slim and graceful, she stood in front the mirror combing the long hair cascading down her shoulders. How charming! She appeared to be slightly tipsy, and from the way she giggled at the faces she made in the mirror, she seemed quite pleased with herself. But from the expression in her eyes, one could also see that her heart was in turmoil. Just then, the hand that had been applying make-up abruptly froze as she stared vacantly at her wedding ring. An uncomfortable look came over her face and after a moment or so of struggle, she managed to pull the ring off and tossed it into her handbag with a snide smile. Before the bag was shut, another comely young lady came in through

---

[2]Famed comic operetta by Franz Lehar that was adapted for the 1934 film by the same name.

the door who, upon seeing her at the dressing table, at once heaved a great sigh of relief, clapped her hands together, and said, "You rotten girl! You just disappeared on us without saying a word, so we all had to go search for you. I guessed you'd be in here. And sure enough, I was right. What are you doing?"

"Ah, Linna!" the young lady in black turned around and said with affection. "I've had a bit too much to drink and my head is feeling rather dizzy, so I came in here to rest for a moment. I am sorry you had to come looking for me."

"Oh please, stop this nonsense. What's this about drinking too much? I know perfectly well that you're hiding in here plotting something. It's hard to say just what kind of wicked scheme you've come up with this time, but I've known for ages that whenever Xiao Chen's away, nothing is off limits as far as you're concerned. Fine, wait until he gets back, and I'll tell him all about the naughty things you've been up to. I saw that look in your eyes when you were drinking with Mr. Liu. Those looks you were giving him made him speechless—I found it terribly amusing."

"Okay, okay. But you're one to talk—what about you? What's the difference? And you thought I didn't notice. You're even better at it than me; even with Lao Jin at home, you've managed to slip out for some fun, and who'd have guessed how friendly you've become with Xiao Wang lately? Didn't he even give you a new purse last week? I've only met Mr. Liu twice, so how could there be anything between us? So don't talk rubbish."

As the woman in black teased her companion, she tapped lightly on the table with the big comb and looked in the mirror as though she were figuring something out. When the other woman heard this, her color changed immediately and she said, her smile gone, "Don't make such wild accusations. I have no choice. We've been friends for over a decade now, so neither of us needs to try to fool the other. I've always been perfectly candid with you and have never kept secrets, and if anything is the matter I've always been up front about it. You're the one who doesn't tell the whole truth! If you really want to know, Lao Jin's regular salary is abysmal, and the money he brings home each month isn't nearly enough to cover ordinary household expenses, let alone my personal expenses, so I have no choice but to scrounge around for a bit of extra income by coming out to 'amuse' myself. At the moment, practically everything I have on and am using were gifts from friends."

"Who would disagree with that? But here you are scolding me, and my situation is no different. I'm even worse off. You know that my marriage was arranged by my parents when I was too young to know any better. It was not until this past year that I came to fully realize that my husband only earns about as much as Lao Jin. And with such a huge family, it's never my turn to spend any money. So all I can do is try to find out some way to get out. I, for one, am not about to sacrifice my youth. But you must on no account tell him, do you understand?"

"True, you are younger than me and you can indeed figure out some way out. But it's all over for me, what with the children and that old-fashioned family. It's hopeless, so I might as well make do with what I've got. But let's not talk any more about this now, Mr. Liu is waiting impatiently. He's not bad, that fellow; the two of you could be friends." With that, she quickly grabbed the young woman in black and skipped out.

As Wanzhen stared at them as they were leaving, she began to wonder whether she was actually watching a play. Could there be such odd characters in the world?

She was in a daze thinking this over when suddenly the sound of the door opening jolted her back to reality. All she saw was a young lady who looked to be about seventeen or eighteen years old, and certainly not old enough to be out of school yet. Frantic, staggering back and forth as though she were so drunk that she could barely walk, she hurriedly steadied herself against the back of the sofa before collapsing onto it. She covered her face with both hands, her shoulders heaving as though she were sobbing or gasping for breath.

Startled, Wanzhen quickly rose to her feet and went over and, after looking at her for a moment, asked, "Miss, are you feeling ill? Do you need anything?"

At this point, the young lady slowly put her hands down, revealing a face as white as a pear, and with eyes half shut, murmured, "Thank you for your kindness, could I have some water? I'm awfully dizzy!"

Wanzhen immediately went to the entrance to the inner rooms and instructed Little Hong to quickly pour her a glass of water. Then she went back over and perched on the edge of the sofa, and felt the girl's hands, which were ice cold, then her forehead, which was burning up. Little Hong brought over the water and Wanzhen held the cup in one hand while using the other to lift the girl's head. The girl drank a few sips of water, then slumped back with her eyes closed. Her chest rose up and down, as though she were deeply troubled. But before a few minutes had elapsed, she suddenly sat up and said to Little Hong, "Thank you! Could you please go outside and check whether there's a man out there wearing formal evening attire holding a shawl?" When she had finished speaking she leaned back again, closed her eyes, and clenched her fists, as though she were straining to overcome some pain. At this point Little Hong walked back in smiling, and with a look of surprise on her face, said that there was indeed a fellow of that description standing outside the door, pacing back and forth!

When the young woman heard this, she sat up at once, head drooping, and began randomly tugging on her hair, tapping the floor with her toes, not knowing what to do. Seeing this, Wanzhen was concerned, for she had no idea if the young woman were really ill or something else was troubling her.

"Are you feeling better? Can we get you anything else?"

"Thank you. I think I can manage now, just let me rest a moment and I'll be all right."

Wanzhen could only signal Little Hong to go. And she herself returned to her seat. She wondered, *What is wrong? What kind of trouble could the young woman be in? She looks so upset, it's as though she were being tortured, not out having fun! Then why bother going out?* At that, Wanzhen again felt uneasy, and the atmosphere in the room all of a sudden seemed to have changed and she had difficulty breathing. But she couldn't put the young woman out of her mind and kept her eyes fixed on her.

The woman was still sitting on the sofa with her chin cupped in her hands, looking down at the floor, tapping her foot to an irregular beat that betrayed her inner turmoil. Her body would stretch out, then draw back, as though she couldn't make up her mind whether to stand up or not. She was at a complete loss as to what to do with herself. Her poor face turned from red to white in distress, and she looked as though she were ready to burst into tears. Suddenly she glanced at her watch, and with a furrowed brow and clenched teeth, she stood up resolutely, as if she had reached some decision. She strode up to the mirror, picked up a wooden comb to tidy her disheveled hair, then went to open her purse. At this point she clearly felt too dizzy to stand up, so she had to steady herself on the dressing table, pausing there for a moment with her eyes shut. Then she staggered back out toward the door. Wanzhen wanted to catch up to help her, but by the time she was halfway across the room, the young lady had reached the doorway, and just at that moment a group of people came bursting in, the two parties nearly bumping right into each other. As soon as Wanzhen saw the group come in, she immediately spun around in alarm and scurried back to her station, for among them was the fat Mrs. Wang, who had come in the day before and chatted with her at length, as though she wanted to be friends. She had even invited her for dinner at her house this evening. At the time, she had casually accepted Mrs. Wang's invitation, afterward forgetting all about it; she was only reminded now that she saw Mrs. Wang again. She dreaded that Mrs. Wang might inquire. She feared that silver tongue and hoped that tonight she would just leave her alone. If only there were someplace to hide.

Other than the fat and somewhat older Mrs. Wang, the rest of the group that had come in was young and gorgeously decked out, adorned with so much diamond and jade jewelry it was obvious they were all ladies of wealth. There was just one young woman who one could tell at a glance was fresh out of school. The clothes she wore were plain, and even her manner seemed at complete odds with theirs. She trailed behind them nervously, as though she felt totally ill at ease, with a panic-stricken look on her face. Seeing all these rich ladies surrounding her, she wanted to walk right back out, but they wouldn't let go of her hand, making it very awkward for her. As Wanzhen observed them she thought it quite unusual, and wondered what kind of game they were playing.

The fat Mrs. Wang appeared to be the commander-in-chief. As soon as she came in she grabbed the one woman who was slightly older, just a little over thirty, but who still dressed as though she were in her twenties. She was wearing a black velvet outfit with a bead trim, of medium length, not too tight. She had snow-white skin, and a pair of black eyes that didn't seem overly big when she laughed, giving the impression that she was quite agreeable. Mrs. Wang pulled her over to the dressing table, sat down on the chair in the middle herself, and told her to sit on the back of the chair. Smiling broadly as she watched the others go into the inner room, she said smugly to her companion, "Mrs. Zhang, do you think this Miss Li is pretty? One little remark from Minister Chen, and I've been running around all week long, and it was by no means easy. I managed to trick her into coming here with us, but I wonder whether he'll be pleased when they are introduced later? It certainly is difficult to be of service!"

"She's pretty, and as soon as you dress her up a bit she'll be prettier than us all. You, make a mistake? Your social skills are renowned. Everyone knows that you have a hand in everything your husband does! And I heard that he was promoted again! After you've taken care of this, I'm quite sure the minister will be most satisfied, just watch! Next month I expect your husband will be promoted yet again."

As Mrs. Zhang spoke, she stood up and faced the fat Mrs. Wang, leaning against the dressing table with a cigarette in one hand. On her face lurked an icy sarcasm and a strained smile, and she peered out of the corner of her eye at the smoke rings she was blowing, as though she were somewhat disdainful of her companion. The fat Mrs. Wang was a smart woman, and seeing her friend's attitude, she grasped immediately what was going on, so she rolled her eyes and with a smile on her face raised her hand as if to slap her, at the same time exclaiming in a charming voice, "Enough! Someone is trying to have a serious discussion with you, and all you can say is a load of rubbish.

You're one to talk. Look at how obedient Minister Liu has become—if you ordered him to head east he wouldn't dare head west, and the minute you say you want something, he does exactly as he's told. Tonight he even skipped that important meeting so he could come out dancing with you. Is this not your magic charm? And you go on about me! Hmm!"

The fat Mrs. Wang was apparently a little displeased by what her companion had said, so she immediately struck back, her barbed words causing Mrs. Zhang's cheeks to flush red. She was irritated, but there was no way to take it to heart, since they were accustomed to such banter, and anyway, just now, hadn't she been the one who had offended her companion in the first place? So she might as well calm her anger. She beamed and affectionately grabbed the hand that fat Mrs. Wang had extended as if to slap her, saying in a tender voice, "Look, I was just joking, but you are so short-tempered, you don't know how bad I feel! I am sympathetic about all your hard work. Aren't we in the same boat? It is not easy being a wife. We have to take care of household affairs and deal with the outside world, with our husbands trying to take advantage of every opportunity. If we don't handle a situation properly, or not to their liking, they call us stupid. And if you make things worse, who's to say they won't leave you at home and go out looking for someone else, right? Are we not busy from morning till night? And isn't all our running around for their sake? Sometimes when I think about it I get so annoyed!"

Meanwhile, Mrs. Wang sat perfectly still with her head down, listening to her companion, and felt so moved! Her own emotions had been stirred, so she fell silent and didn't say a word; however, time did not permit her to go deeper into thought, for those in the inner room had already filed back out, the first one being a woman dressed in pale blue with an embarrassed look on her face. She cried out, "Mrs. Wang! Hurry and come convince her! Even with all the nice things we have been saying, Miss Li refuses to change her clothes. Come over here! We want to see your skills at work."

The next one to emerge was that plainly dressed girl, accompanied by a relatively young matron. The girl's face hadn't a speck of powder on it, nor any rouge; only her eyebrows has been lightly painted, making her look all the more delicate. Nor had her hair been curled; it was only slightly wavy on top. She had on light gray cotton clothes and her demeanor was poised and gentle, though ever since she had come in she wore a strained smile on her face, one that concealed pain, as though she were deeply troubled. At this point, she walked over to Mrs. Wang and murmured, "Mrs. Wang, please forgive me, you've been ever so kind, but ordinarily I can't bear to wear other people's clothes. I had no idea that we were coming to a ballroom this evening, so I didn't change, and I know that I'm dressed inappropriately for a place like this, so let me go back home! Next time, I'll be more prepared, all right? In any case, I can't dance, and just sitting there will look bad and people will laugh. I wouldn't want you to look bad either."

The young woman was desperate to find some way to extricate herself from the situation, loath to stay any longer, but had no choice but to go along with them. The fat Mrs. Wang was determined not to let her get away, so no matter what she said, she had a quick comeback. Mrs. Wang rushed up to her and clasped her hands affectionately, and said, "Never mind, Miss Li! It doesn't matter if you don't change, in those clothes you look all the more pure and dignified. Of course you can't get all dressed up the way we do. With your education, it is perfectly understandable. At any rate, you don't have to dance. We will wait until you've learned how. However, your hair is a bit of a mess! Come over and let me fix it for you, otherwise the foreigners will laugh at us Chinese for so lacking decorum that we don't even comb our hair! Wouldn't you agree?"

Before she could refuse, Mrs. Wang pulled her over to the dressing table and planted her down firmly in front of the mirror, picked up a comb, and began to do her hair. Miss Li was so anxious that her cheeks flushed; she sat there forlornly, but she couldn't cry. What a pitiful sight to behold.

Wanzhen watched all this with bated breath, resenting the fact that she couldn't go to Miss Li's rescue, for by this time she could see what the group was up to. She secretly rejoiced for not having fallen for their trap the night before, since Mrs. Wang's invitation to dinner at her house no doubt had been made with the same wicked intentions. She loathed them and felt sorry for Miss Li. She wished she had the chance to warn her, but how could she? In the midst of all her frustration, she could hear Miss Li pleading, "Mrs. Wang, you mustn't trouble yourself, my hair is most unruly and can't be fixed just like that. Your efforts are in vain! Anyway, since it looks terrible, I think I'd better just go home! My mother doesn't know that I'm here; she's waiting up for me, and if I'm late she'll worry. When we left, you just said we were going out to dine, and she even told me to make sure to be back by ten o'clock. You'd best let me go! Next time, we can make plans beforehand, and I'll come out with you to have fun, all right?"

"Don't worry, I can explain all of this to your mother. After we go dancing, I promise to take you back home myself and I will apologize in person. I assure you she won't blame you." Mrs. Wang combed the girl's hair as she spoke, meanwhile shooting a glance at Mrs. Zhang to hurry up and buy a hair clip, for with a clip it would be fine. Mrs. Zhang understood immediately what she meant and went up to the counter and had Wanzhen get her one, as well as a lipstick and a gold silk purse, and inquired how much it came to, meanwhile taking out a thick wad of bills from her purse, which she counted out one by one.

Although Wanzhen did just as she was asked, her anger could no longer be contained. How she wished she could get away from this pack of demons right then! She knew they were up to no good. No wonder yesterday Mrs. Wang had been so friendly chatting with her; no doubt she had wanted to invite her over for dinner to set her up with someone too, and yet yesterday she had assumed Mrs. Wang was being sincere and actually wanted to be friends. Now she understood. They probably had some use for her as well. The more she thought about it, the more furious she became, and she didn't hear a single word of what Mrs. Zhang was saying. All she could think about was how to crush the demons. If only she could rescue the innocent young girl, but now all she could hear was Mrs. Zhang standing in front of her, shouting at her for all she was worth, "Miss, what has come over you tonight? Are you not feeling well? I have repeated myself several times, but you haven't heard a single word I've said!" Mrs. Zhang said this with a soft, perplexed laugh, looking as though she expected an immediate, satisfactory reply.

Wanzhen would have liked to have cursed her to her face but was unsure where to start, so all she could do was hold back her anger. Courtesy demanded that she respond politely, because this was what her job called for. Still, it was impossible to go through the motions submissively, and she could barely control the tenor of her voice as she said, slowly and frostily, "Fine, whatever you have decided on, I'll add it up."

Taken aback, Mrs. Zhang had no choice but to quickly hand over the hair clip and other items and settle the bill, and took them without even having them wrapped up. She could sense that something was wrong but, having no idea what was the matter, was tactful enough to know that the less she said, the better. And Wanzhen? At this point, her heart had gone out to the young lady, and she wondered whether or not she would be forced to go with them. When she looked over, all she could see was Mrs. Wang seeming very pleased at having combed the girl's hair. Naturally, it looked much better than before, but the young lady didn't take any notice whatsoever, lost in thought with her head down and a worried look on her face. Beside her, Mrs. Wang was murmuring all sorts of compliments, but she didn't seem to hear a word. After thinking for some time, she suddenly lifted her head and, with an imploring look on her face, said with urgency and regret, "Mrs. Wang! Please don't bother. You see, it's after ten already, nearly eleven, and if I don't get home my mother will surely be furious. I may be all grown up already, but my mother still sometimes punishes me as though I were a child! My upbringing was very strict and old-fashioned: when my father was still in Shanghai he would beat my brother even though he was already in college. Daughters have even less leeway to misbehave at home, and if it weren't for the fact that my father is in the interior and can't send us money for household expenses, my mother never would have permitted me to go out to work. She has told me repeatedly not to socialize in public. If I don't obey her, she will not allow me to work. So you had best let me go home! I appreciate your kindness, and in a few days, once I have spoken with my mother, I can come out again with you."

Hearing this, the fat Mrs. Wang appeared somewhat moved and was quiet for a moment in thought; then suddenly her expression changed, as though she had made up her mind to definitely not let the opportunity slip by. She hastily took the girl's hand, like a loving mother cajoling her child, lowered her voice, and with an imploring look said, "That's enough! My dear girl, don't make this any more difficult for me. At least you should grant me some face, I've been bragging to the others that I could get you to come out even if they couldn't, so aren't you now putting me in an awkward position?" At this point she lowered her voice further and assumed a serious tone. "What's more, the minister himself is coming to dance shortly! If he finds out that you are putting on such big airs, that won't be good, and who's to say he won't get angry and report you for having committed some serious offense, or have you fired, how exasperating would that be! Just sitting with him for a while won't hurt, and once he's pleased he'll give you a raise, even getting a promotion won't be a problem. Think about it, some people would give anything to get close to him but never get the chance, while you've got such a wonderful opportunity but are giving him the runaround. What kind of fool are you?" Hearing this string of palaver, the young lady hung her head without saying a word, wavering.

Meanwhile, Mrs. Zhang had walked over to show them her purchases. Mrs. Wang snatched up the clip and put it in the girl's hair, the one protesting it, the other insisting. Just as this fuss was unfolding, two more women suddenly burst in through the door, the one in front wearing a western-style evening gown, loudly cursing as she strode in, the slightly younger one behind her in a *cheongsam* looking completely mortified, trying to catch up with her. At this moment, the atmosphere in the room suddenly grew tense, with all eyes riveted on the two of them. Wanzhen was already feeling dizzy, and as though she could barely breathe. How she longed to get away from this dreadful room and go someplace quiet to be alone for a moment! But now that these two had come in, she forgot everything and just stared wide-eyed, wondering what kind of antics they were up to. She heard the first one, now sitting at the dressing table near Wanzhen, tapping a wooden comb on the table loudly, fuming to the young woman sitting to her left: "Splendid. Just splendid! So this is the good friend you introduced to me, the one who is so well mannered, the one who values friendship, the one who is so well educated? What a despicable thing she has done! What nerve does she have to face me! Just outrageous, what do you want me to say?" With this, she picked up the comb in rage and vigorously combed her hair, though from the look of it she was completely unaware of what she was doing. She was simply beside herself with anger. When the woman with her heard this, her face grew apprehensive and she was so nervous that she mumbled, "First, calm down, I still don't understand what exactly has made you so angry. We're all old friends, so you should forgive them if you can."

"Don't you sound calm! At any rate, it didn't happen to you; if you were me, you would be furious too."

"What dreadful thing did you find out about?"

"Just listen, and I will tell you! Just now we were all getting ready to go out after dinner at my house, right? We were all smoking and putting on our coats in the drawing room, right? It was me who asked Henry to go upstairs to lock the doors and to tell the maid to put little Peipei to bed early and that we would be home late. Not long after he left, Manli also went upstairs. At the time, I thought nothing of it, assuming she had gone up to the bathroom. But after we had been chatting for quite some time, they still hadn't come back down. You and Little Zhang were engaged in a lively conversation, so you didn't notice, but I already thought it curious, so I tiptoed upstairs without saying a word. On the way up I could already hear the faint sounds of two people laughing, so I tiptoed all the way up to the door, pushed it open lightly—luckily it wasn't locked, though they probably didn't hear me anyway, because when I walked in to take a look, what a fine sight, there they were in each other's arms kissing passionately! Tell me, what am I supposed to do, tell me!"

By this point, having quickly run through her account, she demanded that the woman beside her say something, as though she were the one who had done something wrong, so the woman didn't quite know what to say! Perhaps it was the incident itself that had caught her off guard, for she murmured, "Oh, no wonder you're mad," as though she were talking to herself.

"I was so mad then that I nearly wept, but I just turned around and went back downstairs without saying anything, and they came down right after me. We all waited at the door for the car, and I have been furious ever since."

"Oh my! Now I finally get it. No wonder you were so quiet in the car and ignored us all! I see!"

Although she responded to her friend in a low, calm voice, the color had drained from her face and her eyes peered down at her nose, as though she were reflecting on some terribly complicated situation and didn't like hearing what her friend had said.

"Well, look at you! Why don't you speak up? Tell me what to do. How should I deal with her? Shall I tell everybody? Or should I keep it to myself? I just don't know what to do anymore. Here I am discussing it with you and you're being so vague! Like you weren't even my friend at all!"

"You mustn't get too worked up. We are all people with social standing, and there's no point making a big scene. Figure out some other way to handle this. Anyway, now that Manli knows you know, she'll be too ashamed to stay friends with you, and as long as you warn your husband, I expect he won't carry on anymore either. Making a scene would be embarrassing for everyone, don't you think?"

After she heard her friend's calm speech, the woman's anger receded and she was less hysterical than before. She scanned her friend's silent face for a few moments, then slowly stood up and murmured, "Okay. I hear what you are saying, and you're right. There's no point making a scene. The thing I should remember is what type of person she is. Later on if she comes in you can have a word with her so that she knows. Even if I keep quiet, ask her if she has the nerve to face me. I don't intend to speak to her ever again." With that, she strode out, leaving the other there with her head resting in one hand, staring at the cigarette in the other, looking utterly dejected. By this time, the atmosphere in the room had grown extremely still. Only now did Wanzhen, who had not taken her eyes off the pair from the moment they came in, listening with bated breath, take a deep breath. By the time she looked up, she saw that everyone else was gone except the one sitting there quietly as though she were the only person in the room. Wanzhen did not know what to think.

All of a sudden Little Lan came rushing in as if something terrible had happened.

"Hurry—you have a phone call. It's probably your family looking for you. They said it's urgent and no matter how busy you are, you are to take the call. Hurry up." When she had finished speaking she pulled Wanzhen to go, but Wanzhen was so petrified she couldn't even speak and her body felt numb, as though she had just awoken from a bad dream. She had no idea where she was, but when she had heard the call was from home, she remembered everything, she remembered that her Erbao was sick! A phone call now? *I hope nothing has happened*—she didn't dare think beyond that; she was so afraid she broke out in a cold sweat and her heart beat so rapidly she could barely stand up. Little Lan didn't pay attention to what she said but just grabbed her and ran inside, where she picked up the telephone receiver to say hello, but then couldn't go on. She could only hear Lisheng's voice saying, "Is this Wanzhen? What happened? Did you ask the manager for an advance? Baobao is completely delirious from fever, we must hurry and go buy some medicine to make his fever go down, otherwise it'll be too late. Do you understand? Hello! Why don't you say something?"

As Wanzhen listened to Lisheng's anxious cries, she lost her bearings and her heart ached, and her mind was so jumbled she didn't know what to do. The truth was, ever since she had arrived at work she hadn't had time to worry about any of this, and only now was she reminded of Erbao's little face burning up, apple red. It wasn't that she didn't want to get her hands on some money right away, but she . . . "Hello! Hello! Are you there? When can you come home? Can you come back early with the medicine? Why don't you say something? I'm so worried."

"Okay. I understand, I can be back in half an hour." She managed to force out this single sentence, then, without waiting for him to reply, hung up the receiver. She had started swaying, unable to stand up straight anymore, and looked as though she might collapse. Alarmed, Little Lan went over at once to help her walk back to the outer room. Leaning against her, as though in a dream, Wanzhen kept moving forward, but her heart ached so much she was on the verge of tears. At this moment, she needed some peace and quiet to clear her head, but circumstances would not permit it. Before she had even returned to her seat, she could already hear a woman there arguing vociferously with the one who a moment earlier had been sitting quietly at the mirror; one sentence after another pierced Wanzhen's ears, making it impossible not to listen. Meanwhile, the face of the woman sitting there had turned pale and, staring wide-eyed at the woman standing in front of her, she said harshly, "I'm telling you, stop dreaming! Henry will always belong to me. Even before he married Lily he was my lover, and the only reason he married her was that I couldn't marry him. I won't allow you to have a relationship with him, so hurry and give it up, otherwise I shall never let you get away with it. You'd better watch out!"

When the woman heard this, she threw back her head and burst out laughing, a laugh that was at once natural and perverse. Slowly and coldly she enunciated, "Ridiculous, you say this with no compunction, but Henry is not your husband and you have no authority over him. I am free to like or dislike whomever I choose. It is nobody's business. I can do whatever I please, and I don't need you to interfere."

At this point, Wanzhen's head was spinning and she didn't know what to do, and listening to this meaningless chatter made her feel as though her heart were about to explode, as though she were suffocating, as though she were losing her mind. She glanced around at the dazzling lights and gorgeous colors in the room, a room that naturally was much more comfortable than any in her own home, but she now felt that there was something utterly dreadful about this place, and she could barely sit still. The serene atmosphere could no longer contain the fires raging in her heart. All she could feel was a burst of heat on her face, and her heart raced so fast that she could see stars spinning before her eyes, like a person being hounded to death. The sound of the two ladies there quarreling in front of her, word upon word relentlessly bombarding her ears, she didn't want to listen. . . . She couldn't squeeze one more thing into her brain, but with them sitting there in such close proximity, word after word struck her ears; how she wished she could curse them or shout at them to get out! She simply couldn't bear it any longer, so she rose to her feet and was going to berate them, but at that very moment she didn't know where to begin. She was so anxious her face flushed, and she gasped for breath and felt agitated. She had to get away, otherwise she would go mad. She could no longer control herself, all she could feel was the air in the room growing so heavy that it would crush her, she had to get away, she wanted to get away—she simply couldn't wait for anything else to happen, so she dashed out the door, not giving anything another thought. As she fled past the dance floor she seemed not to even see it, nor did she hear the music swirling around her. She looked straight ahead, as though she were all alone; she just looked ahead and walked quickly, oblivious to where she was headed, apparently having lost all sense of control. When she reached the second door, the manager happened to be there taking care of some guests, and when he saw her in this state he thought something must have happened inside, so he immediately went up and inquired, "Why, Miss Wanzhen, what's the hurry, what has happened?"

Wanzhen paid him no heed, scarcely hearing a word he said, and kept walking without the slightest expression on her face. The manager called out after her, but to no avail.

In a single breath she walked all the way from the front entrance to the grounds outside, which were lit up on all sides with neon lights. Since the open space surrounding the building was quite expansive, it was converted into a dance floor during the summer, and here and there shrubbery, flowers, and trees had been planted. It felt quite peaceful, and in one breath Wanzhen had run to the lawns to the left, where she sat down at random on a stone bench. Only when she had lightly exhaled did she feel her chest relax. The evening breeze blew against her head, waking her up a little. She felt as through she were just waking from a dream, and she began to remember her predicament. She had to decide what to do.

She seemed to hear Lisheng's voice on the telephone, a voice thick with anxiety and resentment, and listening to it made her heart break. She was perfectly aware at this moment how desperately Erbao needed medicine to save his young life and how utterly crucial the money was. Little Erbao with his small apple-red face loomed there before her eyes. How could she not love her young son! With wave upon wave of grief, she wished she could just die on the spot! She stood still, alone beside the bench, then walked forward a few steps, then back a few steps, turning it over and over again in her mind. She should do her maternal duty: under no circumstance could she allow Erbao to die out of neglect. She should put the little one first. Thus she again began to make her way back, one slow step at time, toward to the main entrance, wanting to go in to ask the manager for an advance on her salary so she could ring Lisheng to come pick it up, then hurry to go buy some medicine for the child. But as she approached the entrance, she could already hear the undulating strains of music inside! Meanwhile, Erbao's little face had disappeared, and all she could see were the faces of those ladies from before appearing before her. She recalled everything about that room, and started feeling dazed all over again. She walked up to the entrance, wanting to go in, but her legs wouldn't carry her any farther, and already she felt as though she couldn't breathe as comfortably as she had outside. Again she felt short of breath, and that heavy, almost perfumelike aroma, she couldn't bear it anymore, so she turned around and headed back toward the lawns—thinking—thinking about that evening, about all she had seen and heard in the space of a few short hours, and then replayed it in her head all over again. It truly was too complex and too bizarre. She had never before read about such things in novels, let alone personally observed them. Was this really the true character of contemporary society? She simply did not understand, and if she were to work here every evening, how could she possibly bear it? Was she really meant to associate with such insufferable people?

After she had gotten back home the day before she was restless the whole night, for she had sensed that this was another world from the orderly life of peace and quiet to which she was accustomed, in which everything was simple and easy. But now all of sudden she was expected to become an entirely different kind of person. How could she not be upset? So after she and her husband talked it over she had planned to quit the job, for she'd rather be a little poor and wait for something else to come along. Then this afternoon when she had seen how high Erbao's fever was, and how there was no money at home to buy medicine, her emotions got the better of her and she was prepared to sacrifice herself, to give it another try, at most to work for a month for Erbao's sake, and borrow some money to bring home this evening. But now she made up her mind not to condone this sort of lifestyle, because even if she saved Erbao, at the very least her own spirit would be destroyed, maybe even her entire future. The more she weighed this, the more alarmed she became; she feared that when the time came she would no longer be in control of herself and her very character might be altered. And anyway, weren't life and death a matter of fate? Maybe Erbao's illness wasn't that all that serious, and even if she had the money to buy him medicine there was no guarantee he'd ever get better; even if he died, that was fate too. Besides, in the future she could always have another child. . . . With that thought, it was as though a great weight had been lifted from her heart, and she instantly felt relieved. She let out a sigh and looked up at the dark blue sky covered in golden yellow stars that made the dim light of night seem particularly serene. Around her the air was extremely refreshing. At this moment, there was not a single distracting thought in her mind, she only felt as quiet as the night, and she was happy. She was willing to give up on ever finding a job, because no matter what kind of work she might find, she would need to have several outfits made and to buy several pairs of leather shoes, and if you added all that up, her salary might not even be enough, much less enough to help out with household expenses. Her whole body relaxed considerably, free of worries, free of anxieties. She had it all figured out. She stood up and walked briskly toward the front gate, not turning back even once to look at the neon-lit dance floor. She went straight out the main gate and hailed a rickshaw. As she headed home, calmly facing the evening breeze, her mood was completely different from what it had been on her way here. Now she felt only that she was a rather fortunate person.

10
Zong Pu

(B. 1928)

Niece of the renowned May Fourth "New Woman" writer Feng Yuanjun (1900–1974), Zong Pu (Feng Zhongpu) was born in Beijing but spent much of her youth in Kunming, where her family had evacuated in the wake of the Japanese invasion in 1937. Her father, Feng Youlan, was an eminent neo-Confucian philosopher trained at Beijing University and later under John Dewey in the United States. Schooled from an early age in classical Chinese literature, Zong Pu graduated from the prestigious Qinghua University in 1951, having earned a degree in English literature. It was around this time that she first began writing fiction, occasionally publishing short stories in the local periodical press.

In the years following the establishment of the People's Republic of China, Zong Pu landed a job at the state-funded Chinese Federation of Writers and served on the editorial staff of *Literary Gazette* and *World Literature*. Later, she was appointed as a research fellow at the Foreign Literature Institute of the Academy of Social Sciences, where she worked until her retirement in 1988.

"Red Beans," the story that brought her national literary fame, was first published in the prestigious magazine *People's Literature* in 1957 at the height of the Hundred Flowers Movement, a campaign that called on artists and writers to give voice to the darker and more contradictory facets of contemporary socialist society. Set on the eve of the Communist victory, the story revolves around two college sweethearts whose relationship painfully unravels as the young woman comes to realize how little their visions of the future share in common. While the author's sympathies clearly lie with the progressive female protagonist Jiang Mei, the psychological anguish the character undergoes as she weighs the merits of pursuing a fulfilling personal relationship and contributing to society highlights how individual desires and collective ideals are not always perfectly aligned. Unfortunately, at a moment of highly volatile cultural politics, no sooner was the story published than it was attacked by party critics as inappropriate subject matter for socialist-era literature and labeled a "poisonous weed" for dwelling on the pull of romantic love.

Largely because of this controversial story, Zong Pu was branded a rightist and, like a great many others who had boldly voiced "dissident" views in the mid–1950s, she was obliged to make public self-criticisms. As further punishment, she was eventually "sent down" to Hebei province in the late fifties to undergo reform and reeducation through labor on a state farm, but the experience does not appear to have significantly shaken her commitment to current literary policy. The novel she completed during this period, *Peach Garden Maiden Marries Wogu*, upholds the prevailing precepts of socialist realism in narrativizing the theme of peasant participation in the collectivization campaign. Over the next decade, Zong Pu's literary output also included a series of lyrical essays that fuse her classical training with topical concerns.

The upheavals of the Cultural Revolution marked both a period of intense personal suffering and a long hiatus in Zong Pu's literary career, but she made a strong comeback as an award-winning practitioner of "scar literature" in the early post–Mao period with such soul-searching stories and novellas as "Melody in Dreams" (1978). Subsequent works, such as her Kafkaesque "Who am I?", also interrogate the vicissitudes of recent Chinese history, but are marked by more self-conscious formal innovation and thus exemplify the modernist trend that characterized Chinese fiction in the 1980s.

Red Beans

(1957)

The sky was overcast and snowflakes were swirling around; the cover of snow softened the winter's desolation. Jiang Mei was carrying a small case along a path that wound through the university campus. The artificial hills through which the path led were unchanged, and the wisteria trellis could still just be made out behind them. The maples in the little wood were now all heavy with the white snow. It was, in the words of the poem, "as if suddenly one evening the spring wind came and all the pear trees burst forth in blossom."

The snowflakes flying into her face refreshed and exhilarated Jiang Mei. She remembered the day six years ago when she had left the university to start work: she had walked along the very same path. A smile crept over her thin lips; her pace quickened unconsciously and she soon reached the West Block, the dormitory that had been her home for four years.

On entering the building Jiang Mei put down her case, took off her scarf, and shook the snow from it. Everything was silent. She had heard that the building now only housed unmarried teachers and university employees, very different from the days when it had been a student dormitory. A sign on the door of the room where the old caretaker, Lao Zhao, used to live caught her eye: RECEPTION.

"Is there anyone here?" Jiang Mei called out as she looked around. It was all the same, so familiar: the broad staircase and the dim corridor lit only by a solitary globe. A sign on the notice board announced a Youth League meeting that night, and next to it there was a poster about a union election written on bright red paper. These were the only things that gave some life and color to the drab interior.

"Who is it?" a quavering voice asked from inside the reception room. The door opened and an old man dressed in a neat cadre's suit appeared.

"Zhao," Jiang Mei cried in delight. She ran over and hugged him. "You're still here?"

"Is that Jiang Mei?" Zhao rubbed his eyes in amazement and took a good look at Jiang Mei. "It really is you. A while ago the University Services Center told me that a new cadre had been assigned to the Party Committee, and told me to get a room ready.

"They did say that the new cadre was one of our graduates, but I had no idea it would be you. It's been six years now, but you haven't changed a bit. I don't know why, but young people today just don't seem to age. I'll take you up to your room. What a coincidence! It's the same room you lived in when you were a student here."

The caretaker chatted away as they walked up the stairs. As Jiang Mei listened, the feel of the banister under her hand brought her straight back into contact with her student days again.

Her old room was unchanged, except that one of the beds had been taken out and some other furniture put in its place. From the window you could see the little wood and even the small lake beyond it that was covered in lotuses in summer. When Jiang Mei looked around the room, her eyes fell on a crucifix hanging on the wall. The color of the cross was much darker now. The sight of it hit her hard. She felt dizzy for a moment but then steadied herself to ask Lao Zhao, "Why is that still here?"

"At first they said we should get rid of all superstition, so we started taking them down. Later they said they should be regarded as works of art, so we just left the rest alone."

"Why? Why did you have to leave this one?" She gazed blankly at the cross and then sat down on the unmade bed.

"Another coincidence, that's all." Lao Zhao picked up the cleaning rag that had been left on the desk. "I've got the room ready. You just settle in and take it easy while I go and get some boiled water for your Thermos."

After Lao Zhao had gone, Jiang Mei stood up and stretched out her hand to feel the crucifix, but pulled it back as if scared that she might cause pain by touching the wounds. She just stared at the wall. Then suddenly she grasped the right hand of the figure on the cross and gave a pull. The crucifix swung open like a door to reveal a small hole in the wall. Jiang Mei stood up on tiptoe and looked in. Her face turned a ghostly pale. "It's still here," she muttered to herself. Carefully she lifted a little black velvet box that was sitting on an ivory base out of the niche.

She sat down on the bed and opened the box with a shaking hand. Two red love beans sat in the box on a delicate silver ring like two drops of blood. They were lustrous with a cool, fresh glow. The passing years had left no mark on them.

Jiang Mei knew how much happiness and sorrow was contained in this little box. She picked the two red beans up, and as she did the past seemed to float up in front of her like a cloud; tears blurred her eyes.

It had all started eight years ago. Jiang Mei had just turned twenty and she was in the second year of university. It was the unforgettable year of 1948: that bitter, exciting year of tears and decision. Before 1948 Jiang Mei's life had been just like a calm brook flowing undisturbed along a mountain valley, unruffled by strong currents. Her childhood had been comfortable at first. Her father had been a university professor before working for the government. One day, when Jiang Mei was only five, he had gone off to the office and never returned. She remembered being sent off to live with an aunt for a month and when she came back home, she discovered that her pretty mother had become haggard, with huge, sad eyes; she seemed to have aged at least ten years. They said that her father had died suddenly of acute enteritis.

Her father's death had not interrupted Jiang Mei's education. At high school she had a few very close friends and they would often chatter till the small hours. But when she got to the university, she found that the students only turned up for lectures and disappeared afterward. Unless you were involved in extracurricular activities, you would never even know the names of your fellow students apart from those who lived in the same dormitory.

Jiang Mei had spent her university days in the classroom and playing the piano, and her evenings reading in the library. On Saturdays she would go home, always being greeted by her mother on the steps with their pots of well-tended oleanders on either side. Life for Jiang Mei then had been as remote from the world's troubles as those pink oleanders.

She remembered another snowy day like today, just after the Chinese New Year of 1948. She was just leaving the practice studio, still humming the tune she had been playing on the piano. The snow made her feel buoyant, and she had an urge to shake the heavily laden branches of the pines that lined the path back to the dormitory and make the whole world dance in a whirl of snow. As she stretched out her hand, she felt embarrassed and stopped. Instead, she brushed her hair with her hand and made sure the old-fashioned hair clip that her mother had found in a clothes chest a few days before was in place. The clip was made up of two wires of black and white beads on which two red love beans were attached. Her new roommate, Xiao Su, liked it and made her wear it.

A young man hurried along the path toward the studio. He was tall and thin, dressed in a gray silk scholar's gown with a blue cotton jacket over it. He was looking down, his eyes were fixed a few feet in front of him; he seemed completely oblivious to everything. Perhaps it was the air of excitement and energy about Jiang Mei or her glowing cheeks that broke his concentration and made him look up at her. His face was delicate and ivory-colored, with clear and regular features. His eyes were large and had a mysterious, dreamlike quality about them. Jiang Mei thought that although he had looked up, he had not really seen her. It made her feel sad.

That night Jiang Mei lay sleepless on her bed. Images kept flashing through her head: she thought of her mother, of how they had kept each other going over the years, and of how little joy there had been in her mother's life. It was as though some unknown sorrow had swept over her, leaving her ebony hair gray and lifeless. Her mother despised officials and the rich, and Jiang Mei had inherited this feeling, and the aloofness it brought with it. This aloofness now seemed ridiculous.

She knew that the reason she found it funny had to do with Xiao Su. Xiao Su was Jiang Mei's new roommate, and though they had not been together for very long, they were already good friends. Xiao Su had said that Jiang Mei was like someone from another world. She had used the word "aloof," and said that it was both a good and a bad thing. Jiang Mei did not really understand what she meant. Now, for some reason or other, all of these thoughts were floating around in her head.

The room felt large and empty. Xiao Su still had not come back, and Jiang Mei was anxious to see her roommate's chubby pink face. She was always so comforting, giving Jiang Mei both knowledge and strength. People who studied physics were always clever, Jiang Mei thought, and Xiao Su was a fourth-year physics student now. Yet in Xiao Su's case it was not just that she was a fourth-year physics student. There was something more, something deeper, that Jiang Mei could not quite put her finger on.

Xiao Su opened the door and came in.

"What's this? Still awake, Little Bird?" "Little Bird" was Xiao Su's nickname for Jiang Mei.

"I can't get to sleep. I was hoping you'd come back soon."

"What's wrong?" As she spoke, Xiao Su cut a slice off the large radish that she'd brought back with her and gave it to Jiang Mei.

"I was waiting for the radish, and for you to tell me something." Jiang Mei looked into Xiao Su's open and honest face and thought of how taken her mother had been with Xiao Su when she brought her roommate home with her the week before. Later her mother had told Jiang Mei to do as Xiao Su said, and regard her as an elder sister.

"What do you want me to tell you? Do you want me to be like a kindergarten teacher and tell you a story? Here, I'll give you a little book to read instead."

Jiang Mei took the book that Xiao Su passed to her. It was called *Between Life and Death.*

The two girls sat down together and began reading in silence. Jiang Mei soon found herself in another world. The book described the sufferings of the people of China and their struggle for a new life—a life of material sufficiency and true freedom—the type of life that everyone needed.

"Everyone?" Jiang Mei hugged the book to her chest and thought about what she had just read. For twenty years her life had been like that of one of the pink oleanders on the steps at the front door of her home. Yet, like her mother, Jiang Mei detested the rich and the powerful. Sometimes her mother would comment sadly, "Everyone should be allowed a decent life, no one should be hounded to death." The "everyone" her mother spoke of was the same as the people being spoken about in the book. Yes, life should be for everyone.

"Xiao Su," Jiang Mei broke the silence as she leaned back on her pillow, "even an ordinary person like me wonders about the meaning of life. But I've never come up with any answers. You and now this book have given me something to think about."

"There's much more to learn." Xiao Su looked at her warmly. "You really are a good person. You've helped me forget all about how angry I was when I came in. That fellow Qi Hong in my class really makes me furious."

"Qi Hong? Who's he?"

"He lives in his own dream world, just practicing the piano all the time. He's completely self-centered; no one can make him give a damn about anything."

Xiao Su picked the book up and continued where she had left off. Jiang Mei looked at the book too, but could only see that delicate ivory-colored face as she tried to read.

The snow had stopped falling and the ice had begun to melt—winter was coming to an end. Jiang Mei wore a gray woollen overcoat instead of her black fur one, and with her favorite red scarf on, she looked like a picture of spring. She and Xiao Su were getting busier all the time. Jiang Mei had become involved in the "Everybody Sing" Choral Society, as well as the New Poetry Society. She loved the warm and happy sound of the songs they sang. The roar of the drums at the opening of the "Yellow River Cantata" so excited her that she could barely breathe. In her spare time she read Ai Qing's and Tian Jian's poems, and even wrote some of her own: "Fly, fly, fly to a place of freedom." She became known as "Little Bird" to all of her friends. She felt closer to Xiao Su than ever before, and every morning when she got out of bed she would go over and call out to her "Elder Sister Su" to get up.

Jiang Mei practiced the piano and saw Qi Hong every day, though they had yet to speak to each other. At first they had always passed each other on the pine-lined path. Then it was on the staircase. Later Jiang Mei would walk out after playing to find him leaning on the banister as if he had been there a long time, and always wearing that expression of indifference.

One warm spring day, Jiang Mei walked out of the studio to find Qi Hong standing outside as usual. She had been going through Beethoven's "Moonlight Sonata," but just could not get it right; so she had given up in frustration. Qi Hong was in an unusually amiable mood and he asked her, "Why did you stop?"

"I can't get it right," Jiang Mei replied, somewhat surprised.

"You're probably concentrating too hard on your fingers. Don't think too much about them, just keep your mind on the melody and you'll get it right."

When he sat down at the piano, the icy keys gave forth softness and warmth under his fingers. Anyone else's face would have shown a dreamy absorption in the music, but not Qi Hong's. His spirit seemed to flow in every movement and his eyes were as bright as if he were seeing it all in reality for the very first time.

What type of man is he? Jiang Mei asked herself. *A physicist who plays the piano with such an extraordinary expression.*

After a while Qi Hong stopped, stood up, looked at Jiang Mei, who had been standing by the piano, and gave her a slight smile. "Weren't you listening?"

"Yes, but . . ." She tried to explain. "I was thinking . . ." But just what she had been thinking she would not have said.

"Shall I walk you back?"

"Aren't you going to practice?"

"No, I don't feel like it. It's too nice a day."

That was how they took their first walk together. On their walks they looked at the tender sprigs of jasmine and the lotus leaves floating on the lake. Later they lost themselves in the delicate fragrance of the lotus flowers and the heavy aroma of cassia. Then it was winter again, and the snowflakes danced in the air. The snow and the somber winter days. . . .

They talked about music all the way back. Qi Hong said, "I adore Beethoven. Such a giant. His works are so rich but also so simple. Every note is full of poetry."

Jiang Mei's eyes showed that she understood he meant poetry in the widest sense.

"You like Beethoven too, don't you?" he continued. "They say Chopin couldn't stand Beethoven. He loathed his music."

"Yes, but I like Chopin too."

"So do I. The bittersweet quality of his music. . . . People have so much in common, yet so much separates them." The detached look returned to his face. "Physics and music can transport me to a real world, a scientific and beautiful world, not like the pointless, messy, and foul world we live in."

He saw her to the door of the dormitory, gave a nod, and was gone. He had not even asked her name. For some reason Jiang Mei felt once again the disappointment that she had experienced the first time she saw him.

That evening, when she was on her way back to her room from the library, a soft voice called out from behind her, "Jiang Mei."

"Who is it? Qi Hong?" She turned around and saw his tall, slender form in the shadows.

"How do you know my name?" Qi Hong asked, the moonlight revealing the warm expression on his face.

"How do you know mine?" Jiang Mei replied. She felt as though she had known him for such a long time that she did not need to answer him.

"I've known it all my life," he replied softly.

They stood in silence. The moonlight cast their shadows along the ground.

Whenever Jiang Mei came out of the library alone there would always be that soft, warm call. They grew closer to each other, and their walks from the library to her room took longer and longer. Jiang Mei never asked why; she only wished that they could walk even farther, so that their discussions about Beethoven and Chopin, Su Dongpo and Li Shangyin, Keats and Browning would never end. They both loved the Song dynasty poet Su Dongpo's poem, "The River City":

Ten years have passed,
Who lives on, who has died
None can know.
Though not longing,
I can never forget.
A solitary grave so far away,
How can I speak of my sorrow?

They tried to imagine what they would both be like in ten years' time. They spoke of time, space, and the meaning of life. . . .

Once Qi Hong said, "Man lives for freedom. It's a wonderful word. The freedom to be oneself, to do what you want. . . . What do you think of my definition?"

His tone of voice was bantering, but in fact he was being serious.

"But I read in a book that recognition of necessity is the only real freedom." She had been reading *Philosophy for Everyone*. "A person can't just exist for himself. Could you survive if you were alone?"

"Ha!" he commented. "I'd forgotten that you're sharing a room with Xiao Su."

"Yes, and we're the best of friends."

A plum tree in blossom by the path caught his attention, and he said that the word "exciting" should be used to describe it. Jiang Mei agreed, and their discussion on freedom came to an end.

Jiang Mei half knew that on some questions she and Qi Hong would never agree. But she did not dwell on it; she just enjoyed being with him as often as possible.

One Sunday, instead of going home she went with Qi Hong to the Summer Palace. It was a beautiful spring day. The park was a mass of flowers and full of life. Everyone had shed their bulky winter clothes and looked delightfully unencumbered.

Jiang Mei and Qi Hong went walking beside Kunming Lake toward the south bank, which was almost deserted. The warm spring breeze was their only companion. The shiny new green of the weeping willows beckoned them as they talked about the beauty of the spring and life and they approached the Jade Belt Bridge.

"Look how clear the water is." Jiang Mei happily ran under the large arch of the bridge. She was laughing and was just going to run her hands through the water when Qi Hong caught up and put his arms around her on the bottom step.

"Watch it. One more step and you'd have fallen into the water." He brushed her bangs aside. "Don't you realize that I've just saved your life? Now you're mine, little girl."

"I'm yours." Jiang Mei felt as though nothing else existed in the whole world. She leaned on Qi Hong's chest. Deep down inside she felt a surge of tenderness swelling up that swept over them and dissolved them into one.

Qi Hong lifted her head with his hands.

"Are you crying?"

"Yes. I don't know why, but I feel so moved."

Qi Hong looked at her tenderly. Their reflections floated on the water of the lake.

"The first time I ever saw you was on that snowy winter's day. Do you remember? I knew then that I wanted to be with you forever, just as the two love beans on your hair clip are always together."

"I didn't think you'd even noticed me."

"I couldn't help it. You shine like the sun; who wouldn't notice you?" His tone was so passionate and his face looked full of life.

They walked along the lonely embankment, happy and free because they were alone. Jiang Mei looked into his eyes and said, "Qi Hong, if only we could go and live on a deserted island surrounded by the ocean, just the two of us."

Qi Hong shouted with joy and put his arm around her waist. "That's just what I want to do. I hate the whole human race except you."

Jiang Mei had only said that she wanted to be on a deserted island with him because she loved him so much. She could not understand why he had started talking of hate. She looked at him with astonishment. She could see the warmth he felt for her in his eyes, yet behind it there was something so distant and cold, it made her shudder.

Qi Hong noticed that there was something wrong and changed the subject. "Are you feeling cold, my little girl?"

"I'm just wondering, how can you possibly hate . . ."

"Your sweet love is so precious, I wouldn't even want to swap places with an emperor." Qi Hong started to recite some lines from one of Shakespeare's sonnets. His voice was full of emotion, but Jiang Mei suspected that he cared more for the poetry than he did for her. She simply said that she was feeling cold, and they held each other closer.

Jiang Mei's kindly and frail mother did not take to Qi Hong. Jiang Mei once asked her what was wrong with him, and, with a smile on her troubled face, her mother had said that though he was extremely clever and even quite handsome, there was something lacking in his character. Just what it was, she would not say. Even though Jiang Mei loved him deeply, she could not help feeling that there was something missing, something not quite right. It was not the type of feeling that a girl in love should have, but it was there, and it gnawed at her and haunted her nights. She wanted to see him, to hear him tell her how much he loved her, yet nothing could get rid of that feeling. Her mother's comments only made it worse. And there was Xiao Su.

May was a very busy month. There was something on every night. On the fifth there was a poetry recital. The last item on the program was Ai Qing's poem "The Torch." Jiang Mei was going to take one of the parts in it, that of the girl Tang Ni. She had wanted to avoid reciting poetry altogether, but she was the type of person who came out in goose bumps when she heard a poem being recited. Xiao Su knew she would not need too much persuading. She asked Jiang Mei, "Do you like this poem?"

"Oh, yes."

"Would you like even more people to be able to enjoy it?"

"Of course."

"Very well then, you can help recite it."

So that night she found herself on the stage. She heard her own clear voice carrying over the shadow-engulfed audience and then echoing in their hearts. She felt as though she really were the girl Tang Ni, marching in a demonstration with a torch in her hand. It was a feeling that she had never had before, something completely new and unfamiliar. Xiao Su was just like Li En, the girl's mentor.

Jiang Mei's excitement increased as she spoke, the blood rushing to her face. She felt as though she were one with the hundreds of people in the audience; they all seemed to breathe as one body, feel with one heart.

"The night makes off, wailing on distant plains." The chorus was spoken with such energy that she felt as though she were being carried along by a surging wave.

Back in their room when the reading was over, Jiang Mei said to Xiao Su, "Now I know what it means to be together with others, all sharing the same understanding, the same hopes, the same love and hate."

Xiao Su looked at her intently, and asked, "Do you have the same thoughts and dreams as Qi Hong?"

Jiang Mei was so surprised at Xiao Su bringing up Qi Hong that it broke her train of thought. Her expressions, smiling happily until a moment before, became serious.

"I don't know how to tell you, but I feel deep down that there are some things that Qi Hong and I will never agree on."

"I know, Little Bird. You're a good girl; though your world is limited, you're pure and good. Qi Hong hates everyone; he thinks that people always use each other. The only type of love he knows is a mad possessiveness, and the only person he really loves is himself. I've been a classmate of his for four years, and . . ."

"How can you say such things? I love him, I love him." Jiang Mei forgot all about the differences she had with Qi Hong; in a flaming temper, she slammed the door behind her.

"Come back, come back," Xiao Su shouted. She opened the door and found Jiang Mei weeping in the corridor.

"Are you going home this Sunday? If you're not, there is something I'd like you to do for me."

Jiang Mei always did whatever Xiao Su asked. She sensed that Xiao Su was working for some great and noble cause; her life seemed to be linked to the lives of millions of others; she was so warm she could have given life to a stone. Jiang Mei looked up as Xiao Su came toward her. "What do you want me to do?"

"You're not going home then?"

"I'd been thinking of going back. They say that flour costs three million a bag now. I just got paid for a few of my poems that appeared in *Dagong Bao* a few days ago, and I was thinking of giving the money to my mother." She suddenly felt exhausted and sank into a seat.

Xiao Su was going to make a comment that even someone as isolated from the world as Jiang Mei knew about the problems of inflation, but she checked herself and said, "I have the rough drafts of a few wall posters that have to come out on Sunday, and I'd like you to go through them for me. Edit out whatever you want to and try to make them more readable, then write them out clearly. As I'm going into town tomorrow, I can take the money to your mother if you want."

She gave the manuscripts to Jiang Mei and said thoughtfully, "Let's have a good talk in a few days."

After breakfast on Sunday, Jiang Mei sat down at her desk and started looking through the manuscripts. How was it that such short and carelessly written articles had such force? The call for democracy and freedom from starvation that ran through all of the pieces touched her deeply. The same excitement that she had felt on the evening of the poetry recital stirred her again. The figure of Tang Ni appeared before her.

There was a knock at the door. "Jiang Mei."

It was Qi Hong. She turned toward the door to see him standing there, gazing at her with adoration.

"Oh, it's you."

"I went to your place looking for you last night, but your mother said that you hadn't been back, so I came straight back to school without even going home." He walked over to the desk and took Jiang Mei's hand.

On hearing Qi Hong mention his home, Jiang Mei had a vision of a lavish parlor with Qi Hong's banker father counting his silver dollars. It was so different from the world of the articles she had been reading. Even Qi Hong, warm and cultivated Qi Hong, was from another world than theirs; but she was still happy to see him.

"What are you up to? Wall posters? I've heard you've been reciting poems too. Does all this mean that you've joined the democracy movement? My poetess!"

Jiang Mei did not really appreciate the tone of his voice, and she motioned to him to sit down.

"I came to see if you wanted to go out with me. It's such a beautiful day; it'll be summer before you know it. So I've come to take you to the world of Peter Pan to do some spring cleaning." They both loved the story of Peter Pan; their love was really built on fairy tales, on flowers that would have to fade, on clouds that would be scattered and on a moon bound to wane.

"I can't today, Qi Hong," she said apologetically. She pulled her hand out of his, and tidied the manuscripts on her desk. "Xiao Su has asked me to . . ."

"What, Xiao Su again? How come you're always at her beck and call?" Qi Hong asked impatiently.

"Because what she says is right."

"But you know how much I want to be with you, to go with you to listen to the newborn cicadas chirping and see the lotus leaves growing on the water. Remember, I get what I want." His good-humored tone had vanished, and he seemed to be talking about Jiang Mei as though she were some book or object that he owned.

Jiang Mei stared at him in surprise.

"You might even go on demonstrations next. You're a real idiot. All you think of is Xiao Su." He was angry, and it had made his face dark and menacing. Then he suddenly softened his tone. "Come on, go out with me, little girl."

Jiang Mei bit her lip hard. Just then someone called out, "Jiang Mei, Little Bird. Come and see if these cartoons we've done are okay."

She wanted to go out, but Qi Hong was standing in front of her and would not let her pass. She walked around the desk, but again he moved to block her way. She was beginning to get upset but still could not budge him. It was not long before her hair was in a mess and the hair clip that she always wore was on the floor. Before she had time to pick it up, Qi Hong had trodden on it, scattering black and white beads all over the floor. Jiang Mei felt as though her heart had been crushed underfoot. Her strength deserted her and she sat down, weeping for her humiliation.

Her tears were just what Qi Hong wanted. He picked up the two love beans from the clip and caressed her shoulder.

"Forgive me, please forgive me, it is all my fault. I want to be with you more than I can say. I need you. . . . Don't cry, little girl, don't cry." But she did not stop sobbing, and he started to get worried. "I'll never make you angry again, I promise."

Jiang Mei felt that this was all pointless. She raised her head and wiped away her tears. Although she realized that she would not be able to finish the posters, she was determined not to go out with him. She sat staring out of the window.

"Come on, don't be angry with me. I'll make a box for you to put the beans in. They'll remind me never to upset you again. Where shall we hide them?"

Later on he put the beans in a delicate little box, which was placed behind the crucifix in Jiang Mei's room. Qi Hong had found the niche by chance one day, and after that whenever Jiang Mei lay on her bed she would look up at the figure of Christ and think how tired he looked, burdened with the worries of the world.

It was not the last upset they had. Arguments and tears became part of their relationship. Every time they met they would quarrel, yet they could not pass a day without seeing each other. Their love was like opium, for though it caused them both pain, neither of them could give it up. Jiang Mei became so thin and pallid that her mother could not help crying. Qi Hong's usual look of indifference turned into one of anxiety and depression. His lack of faith in life made him mistrust his love as well. So he was always jealously guarding his love and happiness, and watchful of Jiang Mei.

As Qi Hong withdrew more and more from the life around him, Jiang Mei began to learn about the world. She had come to realize that the exploitation of the many by the few had to be ended. She felt in her goodness that everyone should have a decent life. The soaring inflation had begun directly to affect her own peaceful little world. The bank where her mother had been keeping her savings closed down, forcing them both to depend totally on her uncle. Jiang Mei hated being a burden. She yearned for a new life and a new society. For her, the Communist Party had become a beacon lighting the way to freedom and happiness. Though that beacon was still dim and distant, it was visible.

Jiang Mei's mother was plagued again by her old illness, anemia. The doctor advised emergency medication and daily injections of liver extract. He warned that delay could be fatal. But where would the money come from?

Jiang Mei's uncle could barely meet his own expenses now, so they could not possibly turn to him. One word to Qi Hong would have solved everything, but she could not bear to ask him. The situation made her feel constantly depressed, and she could no longer sleep at night. Xiao Su quickly noticed that there was something wrong, and it did not take her long to find the reason.

"You can't put off the treatment any longer," Xiao Su protested with that look of determination that Jiang Mei saw on her face so often. "I'll let them give her my blood. You can see how fat I am, Little Bird, I can afford to give away quite a lot." Jiang Mei embraced her emotionally.

"It's no use, Xiao Su. Your blood type is the same as mine; we can't help her."

"What can we do to get some money together?"

One evening a few days later, Xiao Su burst into the room excitedly.

"Look, Jiang Mei!" she shouted as she waved a wad of notes in front of Jiang Mei's face.

"Su, where did you get all that money?" Jiang Mei asked.

But before waiting for a reply, she started laughing. She laughed out of happiness and relief. It was the type of laugh that Qi Hong longed to hear, but never did.

"Never you mind. Take it and get your mother treated." Xiao Su gave her a mysterious wink.

"No, you have to tell me where you got it, otherwise I just won't feel right."

"Forget it, I'm going to bed." She stopped laughing, took off her blue jacket, and sat down on the bed. She looked exhausted. Jiang Mei noticed a piece of sticking plaster inside Xiao Su's elbow. She went over and took Xiao Su's hand, looking first at the plaster and then at her face.

"What are you looking at?" Xiao Su asked as she pulled her hand away and snuggled under the quilt.

"You've been giving blood."

"Sure," she replied casually, "I sold some blood. Not just me though, several of us did it."

It often happens that just an expression or a gesture can wound deeply, or even destroy a friendship in an instant. In the same way, even a needle mark can cement an undying friendship. Too moved to speak, Jiang Mei knelt down by the bed and covered her face in her hands.

That Saturday, Jiang Mei wanted Xiao Su to take the money to her mother personally. She agreed, and they went home together. Jiang Mei was made to promise not to tell where the money had come from. They arrived to find Jiang Mei's mother too ill to get up; a relative had been sending meals over. As she stood by the bed looking down at that frail figure, Jiang Mei could not hold back her tears. Xiao Su also began to cry: for her it was not just Jiang Mei's mother who was lying ill in front of them, but one of the millions of suffering mothers of China, their hearts heavy with sorrow, crushed by oppression.

That evening the two of them made some noodles and ate them at Jiang Mei's mother's bedside. Their presence made the older woman feel much better, and she sat up and ate with them. When she had finished, she said, "This illness has really made me into an addle-minded old fool. When your aunt came today she asked me whether I had a stove. I thought she'd asked if I had a dog. So I told her yes, we used to have a dog called Fifi. . . ."

The two girls burst out laughing. As they laughed, Jiang Mei thought of Qi Hong: there was no way he could ever understand this way of life or these emotions; and she knew that there was no way she could ever tell him.

In June the movement to oppose American support for Japan reached its climax. Jiang Mei was far more interested in politics than she had been before. She had a feeling that America was plotting something new. It was self-evident that any attempt by the Americans to prop up Japan, a country that had oppressed China for eight long years, would arouse massive hostility among the Chinese people.

One day she was sitting in front of the window with Xiao Su, reading with growing indignation a statement in the paper made by the American ambassador to China: "If the Japanese become a hungry and unsettled people, then they will continue to be a threat to peace. This is just what the Communists want. If we really want to work for the majority of people, then we must eliminate all possible factors that could give rise to communism." It was obvious what the Americans were up to. When they had read it, Jiang Mei said angrily, "It's our business whether we are going to have communism or not."

Xiao Su smiled. "Do you know what communism is?"

"No, I don't," Jiang Mei replied honestly, "but I'm sure that it means a better life than the one we have now. People will all be . . . well, they'll all be like you."

Xiao Su laughed. "What's wrong with things as they are now? You get good white rice to eat, you wear colorful *cheongsam*s, what's so bad about that?"

Jiang Mei leaned on Xiao Su. She was thoughtful as she spoke.

"This is a dog-eat-dog society, not just materially but spiritually as well." She stopped for a moment and then continued, "Xiao Su, you don't have any idea of just how lonely I am."

Xiao Su patted her shoulder kindly.

"The road of life is never smooth. You always have to struggle with bad people and with yourself."

Later on, whenever things became difficult she would remember these words.

On the ninth of June, Jiang Mei took part in an anti-American demonstration organized by students of Beijing University.

On the morning of the ninth, she got out of bed when it was still dark and put her medical kit together; she was in the first aid team. She looked over at Xiao Su's bed, which had not been slept in. What had she been doing all night? Perhaps, Jiang Mei thought, she would soon be using the bandages and gauze in her kit on Xiao Su. She felt uneasy about her friend and the others in her group. As her hands grasped the medicines in the kit, she felt both excited and disturbed.

"Come on, Little Bird, let's go," someone called to her from outside.

Jiang Mei ran over to the sports field just as the red morning sun was rising over the rooftops of the village to the east. Xiao Su was in the crowd. She looked awake, but the pallor of her face showed that she had not slept all night. When she saw Jiang Mei and the others, she smiled in satisfaction.

"Jiang Mei."

"Xiao Su." Jiang Mei returned the greeting as she slipped a large apple into Xiao Su's hand. Qi Hong had given her the apple the day before. An occasional piece of fruit or sweet was all she ever accepted of the endless stream of gifts that Qi Hong bought or had sent to her room in the West Block.

The long ranks of demonstrators started out. They walked silently along the street in the direction of the city, holding all types of placards. It gradually became lighter as they went. A male student looked over at Jiang Mei and asked, "Is your medical kit heavy? I can carry it for you."

She replied with a smile, "Would a soldier let someone else carry his gun?"

He looked at her from head to foot. She was wearing blue trousers and a white shirt with a red woollen waistcoat over it. He asked, "Do you want to be a soldier for always?"

She opened her eyes wide, and after a moment of thought said earnestly, "Yes, always."

The marchers reached the Xizhimen Gate of the city wall at seven o'clock. It was closed. Someone shouted out, "We won't go back to the university until the gates are opened."

Someone else yelled, "Come on, let's break it down."

The banners bobbed up and down as a feeling of excitement passed through the noisy crowd. Xiao Su was moving through the lines calling out, "Stop shouting, and don't break rank. A delegation has already been sent to get the gates opened."

Jiang Mei wished that she were a fairy with a magic wand who could make the gate open. She realized how ridiculous this was, and knew that she would have to wait for the return of the student representatives; they would be far more effective.

At nine o'clock, the gate finally opened and the demonstrators poured into the city, joining up with the students from the universities in the city who had been waiting for them. Warm welcoming shouts could be heard on all sides. Jiang Mei felt tears well up in her eyes, and she looked down at her feet so that no one could see her face.

The demonstration began. Everyone shouted the slogans, "Down with American involvement in Japan," "Freedom," "Independence," in unison as they marched. The slogans exploded in the air, leaving the military police who were standing on the pavement looking fearful and uneasy. Jiang Mei was so excited that she could barely concentrate on shouting. With each footstep she felt a little bit closer to the light of that distant beacon.

They walked along Xisi and Xidan and then along to Tian'anmen, after which they went through Nanchizi and to the Democracy Square of Beijing University. As they passed by the Tian'anmen Gate, Jiang Mei looked up at the magnificent structure and felt a pang of pity and shame. How many insults, how much defilement had Tian'anmen suffered from its unworthy children. She even felt that the crumbling vermilion wall was waiting and hoping that a new society would soon appear so that the people of China and Tian'anmen could be proud once more.

At Democracy Square they held a rally, at which some teachers addressed the crowd. Whether from fatigue or some other reason, Jiang Mei's earlier exhilaration had passed, and she could not concentrate on the speeches. She was thinking of the university campus, deep in the shadows of the early summer dusk. She thought of the West Block, and of the young man who was waiting below her window. She held the medical chest that hung over her shoulder tightly and felt slightly dizzy.

Xiao Su walked over and asked her in a whisper, "Are you feeling all right?"

"Yes, yes, it's nothing," she replied cheerfully. She cursed herself for thinking of him just then.

By the time they got back to the school, all the lights were on. Jiang Mei dragged herself back to her room, her legs feeling like blocks of stone. There was a knock at the door and she felt a tightness in her stomach, as though something bad was going to happen. She leaned against the bedstead, sipping hot water. The door opened, and in came the caretaker, with a frown on his forehead and a squashed box of sweets in his hands. He put the box on the table and said, "Well I never, Miss Jiang, well I never! Never saw a man in such a temper in all my days. Did they raise your Mr. Qi on rooster's blood or something? When he dies he'll go straight to the Ice Hell to cool off, otherwise he'd burn down the King of Death's palace."

"What do you mean, 'your Mr. Qi'? Don't say that. What happened?"

"He came looking for you this afternoon. When I told him that you had gone in the demonstration, he hurled the sweets that he'd brought you down the steps. The box broke open and the sweets all fell out. I reckoned that he could have bought a sack of flour for the money he spent on them, so I couldn't bear to see that waste. I said to him, 'Mr. Qi, Miss Jiang isn't here. You could just leave what you brought her, why fly off the handle?' That really set him going. His face went white and then red, then he threw a tea mug through the window. Look! There's broken glass everywhere. I think he was off his head. Then he took off without another word. Threw three million on the steps as he went, too. Suppose he did that to pay for the window and the mug. What do you think?"

"Don't say any more." Jiang Mei waved her hand feebly. "Just get the window fixed and buy a new mug."

"I thought it was a real waste, the sweets, I mean. So I picked them all up and put them in the box for you."

"Take them home. I don't want them, they're not mine." Xiao Su had come in a few seconds earlier and had overheard some of the conversation. She washed her face and feet, tidied things up, and sat down at her desk to write. Jiang Mei sat leaning against the bedstead in silence.

After a while Xiao Su stopped writing and looked up. "What's up, Little Bird? If you keep on like this you'll destroy yourself. Don't you realize that? Deep down Qi Hong is just selfish, violent, and cruel. Why make yourself suffer like this? Break it off with him. Come over to us, we all welcome you, love you . . ." She walked over and put her arms around Jiang Mei's shoulders.

"But, Qi Hong . . ." Jiang Mei had not really taken in everything Xiao Su had said.

"Forget him." Xiao Su cried out, almost losing her temper. "You're a good girl, kind-hearted, clever, and capable. The type of love you have for him will only poison you. Forget him. Promise me that you'll forget him, Little Bird."

Jiang Mei had never even thought of breaking off her relationship with Qi Hong. She did not really know how he had marched into her life in the first place, and she could not imagine how she could possibly chase him out of it now. "Forget him?" she said weakly. "Yes, I'll forget him when I die."

This made Xiao Su really angry. "What a thing to say! What are you doing talking about death? I want to go on living, and live a life that means something."

For some reason Xiao Su seemed sad as she said this. Jiang Mei noticed that there was something wrong, something out of the ordinary; it made her forget her own pain. Xiao Su stood gazing out of the window for a moment, deep in thought. Then she turned to Jiang Mei and said, "It's dangerous, Little Bird. After I'm gone you'll still want to come our way, won't you? Whatever you do, don't stay with Qi Hong—he'll destroy you."

"Go away?" Jiang Mei took Xiao Su's hand. "What do you mean? I want you to stay with me."

"I'll be graduating soon, and my family wants me to go back to Hunan to teach." Although she was from Hunan and her father was a teacher there, Jiang Mei had the feeling that there was something not completely true in what Xiao Su said.

"Graduate?"

"Yes, graduate."

Xiao Su did not graduate, nor did she return to Hunan. She went off one day to take the last of her exam papers and did not come back. Jiang Mei was just finishing writing a book report for her English literature course when some students came rushing in to tell her what had happened. The book she had been working on was Emily Brontë's *Wuthering Heights*. She had discussed the book with Qi Hong; he had such profound views on it that Jiang Mei felt he should understand more about life than most people. Yet for some reason he did not.

The news that Xiao Su had been arrested soon jolted Jiang Mei back to reality. She rushed out of her room without a thought for her essay, which had fallen to the floor when she had jumped up. A number of other students ran out of the building with her toward the school gate. But the long, straight road that led to the city was empty. There was only a delicate fragrance from the trees along the road. Jiang Mei leaned against one of them as she muttered to herself, "Where is she? Where's she gone?"

A classmate told her sadly, "They shoved her into a paddy wagon. She'd be at the police headquarters by now."

Everything was whirling around, and the strength had completely drained from her legs. She sank to the ground helplessly. The others gathered around her and someone helped her to her feet. "What's wrong?"

"Pull yourself together, Jiang Mei."

In a second everyone was talking, offering advice and encouragement. Suddenly someone shouted angrily, "Blood, tears, and arrests only make people see things clearer."

It was true, Jiang Mei thought. All they had done by arresting Xiao Su was make more people determined to be like her.

Jiang Mei did not know where everyone went, for the next thing she knew, she was walking along, supported by Qi Hong. He was speaking to her: "When I heard from the radicals in our department that you'd fainted, I guessed that it must have been because of Xiao Su, so I came straight over."

"That's right; weren't you taking the math exam together? They said she was arrested in the classroom." Jiang Mei only felt like talking about Xiao Su.

"Yes, it was during the exam. Just goes to show what trouble being in the democracy movement can land you in. I warned you time and time again, but you insisted on seeing so much of her. . . ."

"What? What are you saying?" Jiang Mei cried out, her eyes flaring angrily. "You're heartless." She pushed his arm away and ran back to the dormitory as quickly as if a devil were chasing her.

She rushed into her room and threw herself on the bed. After a while she felt Qi Hong's hand on her shoulder. He had been shocked and mystified by her sudden fit of temper, and he knelt down beside the bed cautiously.

"Have I upset you again, Mei? It's just that I'm jealous of Xiao Su, you care too much about her. Where do I stand? Sometimes I really hate her. I feel that she's the one who is keeping us apart. . . ."

"No, it's not her. Our paths are different, that's all."

"What? Different? How? Sure, we don't always have the same views on things and we argue a lot, and I've got a bad temper. But none of that matters. I know that I couldn't live without you. Mei, I haven't said anything to you, but with the political situation going from bad to worse, my family has decided to move to America. They want me to go too, to study."

"America?" She sat up.

"Yes, and you too, Mei. I've told my father all about you, and though you've always refused to go home with me, he feels as though he already knows you. I often show my parents your picture and tell them about you."

He took out his leather wallet and showed her the picture that he had stolen when he had gone to her home. It was a photo of Jiang Mei when she was seventeen. Her eyes seemed to be smiling though her dark lips were slightly turned up at the corners, making her look as though she were angry with someone.

"I told them that you are like a beautiful poem, or a lovely melody."

Nobody could say nice things about Jiang Mei as well as Qi Hong.

"That's enough." She stopped him tearfully. "Nothing will keep you here in your own country, then."

"Mei, if you go with me you can continue your studies at a university there, and we'll be together forever. Nothing will ever keep us apart."

"That's enough, don't say any more." She could not say anything further.

Jiang Mei felt crushed and did not know what to do. She could not bear to see Xiao Su's empty bed; the white sheets hurt her eyes. She went home before Saturday. There was a blackout that evening, and she found her mother sewing in the flickering light of a candle. She looked old and frail in the dim light. Jiang Mei felt a pang of sadness and wanted to call to her; tears sprang to her eyes.

"Mei!" Her mother looked up and put down her work.

"Mom, they've taken Xiao Su away."

"Arrested?" She knew her daughter's friend well and felt a deep affection for her. But she seemed half indifferent to the news and sat silently in the shadows as if she had not heard.

"Mom, Xiao Su's been taken away." Jiang Mei sobbed again.

"As I expected," Jiang Mei's mother murmured.

Jiang Mei threw her bag on the table and ran over to kneel and put her arms around her mother's legs.

"You knew?"

"No, but I had a feeling that it would come to this." She sighed and put her thin and bony hands over her face. She paused a moment before continuing. "It is time that I told you: your father disappeared just like that fifteen years ago. He was never sick; they said that there was something wrong with his thoughts. He was a stubborn man who wouldn't play their games. He had some other ideas too, but I never understood quite what they were. He never did anything violent, never hurt anyone. But he just disappeared mysteriously." With these last words, she started sobbing.

So he had not died from a disease. No wonder Mother always kept saying that people should not be unjustly killed, as he had. Jiang Mei wanted to shout it out loud. As she sobbed, her mother stroked her hair, wetting it with tears.

Jiang Mei had seen her mother weep before, but never so passionately. How much pain and hate she must have felt over the years. Her mother's tears falling on her hair gradually calmed her down. She wanted no more of this murderous society. The pain of hesitation and inner struggle disappeared, as if some powerful force had helped her choose her future path. She pressed her mother's rough hands against her tear-soaked cheek and sobbed, "Father . . . my father."

Behind them, the door opened softly. The candlelight threw Qi Hong's tall, thin shadow against the wall. Her mother gave him a startled look, but Jiang Mei did not raise her head although she recognized him. He addressed Jiang Mei's mother with conventional courtesy and then said to Jiang Mei, "Why did you come home today? I've been looking for you everywhere."

Jiang Mei continued to ignore him as she raised her head and said to her mother, "He's going to America."

"Yes, aunt, and I want to take Jiang Mei with me," Qi Hong hurried to add. "Might you go?" The trembling hand brushed Jiang Mei's head.

"I'll do whatever you tell me to do, Mom." She clasped her mother's knees and looked up at her tearfully.

"You decide, Mei."

"Then you agree to let her go?" Qi Hong asked, confident that, as always, things were turning out as he expected.

"No, my mother knows that I'll make the right decision. She knows that I'd never go." Jiang Mei stood up and faced Qi Hong. He was soaked in sweat, but was aware only that Jiang Mei was crying.

"Let's not have another upset, Mei," he said, wiping her eyes. "Why should we always quarrel?"

"You two talk it over," Jiang Mei's mother said, picking up her needlework. "But Mei, don't forget your father."

Qi Hong's gaze was fixed on Jiang Mei and he did not notice the old woman leave the room. Jiang Mei returned his stare blankly, letting him wipe away her tears with his handkerchief.

"It looks as though we'll have to part," she said. "The love between us just isn't strong enough to make us throw away our lives."

"But we'll be able to be happy and comfortable together. . . . We won't be throwing away anything. There's no need to part." He took her hand and started passionately kissing her fingers.

"If you want to be with me, stay in China." She was still looking at him without emotion.

"Stay here? Come on, little girl. Do you want me to run around sticking up posters and going in demonstrations with you, is that it? We're different from the rest of them. You can't really want me to give up my physics, my music, my whole way of life. You want me to abandon wisdom so that I can wallow in the mud with the herd? Silly girl. You don't understand what life's really about. Wait until you are a little older, then you won't be so naïve."

"Silly, am I? Better to be silly."

"No, you must come away with me."

"If I go with you then I'll be throwing everything away—my country, my mother, and even my own father." Her voice was so low that even she could just barely hear what she was saying until she startled herself with the vehemence with which she spoke of her father.

"But Mei, you've got me," Qi Hong cried like a spoiled child. Yet, seeing the strange look in Jiang Mei's eyes, he unconsciously let go of her hand. Then with uncontrollable yearning and anger he grabbed her by the shoulders and spoke in a low, deliberate voice: "I wish I could kill you and take you with me in a coffin."

"I'd rather be told that you were dead than know you were living in such a cowardly way."

The wind was howling outside and it was raining hard. Suddenly in the storm came the sound of something breaking. Qi Hong held Jiang Mei to him, and in the flash of the lightning she could see the pot of oleanders lying shattered on the steps. She felt a pang in her chest, as though her heart had been broken like the plant pot.

Although everything had seemed so final that night, Qi Hong and Jiang Mei were still inseparable. Their long walks by the lotus pond and in the woods continued, yet there was no end to the arguments and tears.

In October, the situation in the northeast became very tense. The People's Liberation Army was sweeping down toward Beijing, liberating many cities as it advanced. In response, Chiang Kai-shek formulated a new policy: "Maintain the status quo in the northeast, protect north China, and clean up central China." Although this was supposed to ensure stability in the north, all the well-to-do people there began streaming south. Qi Hong's family had flown to Nanjing at the beginning of autumn, from where they went to Shanghai and then America. Qi Hong was left in Beijing by himself. He had told his family that he had to finish his thesis before he could get his degree, but he was staying on in the hope that Jiang Mei would have a change of heart. He could not believe that she would not go with him, and wished he could abduct her. He became paler and touchier as time went on; his eyes took on a malevolent look.

Qi Hong's strained features and broody expressions haunted Jiang Mei's dreams. They were no longer the simple and untroubled dreams of a young girl. The tense political situation, Xiao Su's arrest, Qi Hong's love for her, and her own confused feelings had made her understand many things. At a demonstration against the Guomindang's slaughter of students in the northeast, Jiang Mei did not take her first aid kit but walked proudly in the front ranks holding a large banner that read, END THE SLAUGHTER, GIVE US LIFE, LET US PROTEST! She led the others in calling out the slogans as they marched. She felt that she was protesting on behalf of her dead father as well as her mother and Xiao Su. She wanted to fight for the liberation of humanity, for a completely new life.

After liberation, when Xiao Su was released from jail and became a radio announcer for Radio Beijing, Jiang Mei learned that the underground had wanted her to join the Democratic Youth Union, but because of her relationship with Qi Hong they felt they could not be sure of her true position, so they let the matter drop. When she heard this, Jiang Mei let out a sigh but did not say anything.

The winter of 1948–49 was the eve of liberation for Beijing. Throughout the city people were saying, "The lanterns hung in every house are to welcome Mao Zedong." All the high officials and rich people made their escape. Qi Hong was getting daily telegrams urging him to leave from his family, who had booked him a flight. Jiang Mei spent most of her time discussing with her fellow students how to protect the school and prepare for the liberation of the city. She was in a state of constant excitement. It was as though she was waiting to receive a generous gift, and she dreamed about what life would be like after liberation. Yet at the same time her decision not to go with Qi Hong was gnawing at her. She felt both exhilarated and depressed at the same time.

One evening, Jiang Mei was sitting in the library trying to read. Qi Hong had gone into the city earlier that day and still had not returned. She could not concentrate and looked up expectantly at everyone who came in. He still had not reappeared when the library closed. Only then did it occur to her that he might actually have left Beijing. If so, then she would never see him again. But she had to see him one more time, just this last time. She felt like calling out his name, hoping that somehow it would bring him to her. But she bit her lip to stop herself and walked out of the library quickly.

Outside, the first snow of the year had fallen. It had not yet frozen over, and the light from the lamps along the path made the ground sparkle. Jiang Mei walked straight over to the male students' dormitory. She wanted to see if the light in his window was on; although she had never been in his room, she knew the window very well. There was a poplar tree outside the window, and Qi Hong had told her how the rustling of its leaves had kept him company through many sleepless nights. Peering through the swirling snowflakes, she found first the poplar and then the window behind it. It was dark. Her heart sank as she stood there, her legs too weak to move.

Perhaps he was so tired after getting back from the city that he had gone straight to sleep. Maybe he still had not returned. She walked into the building and went up to Qi Hong's room. She knocked at the door, but it was locked. He was not there.

Will I really never see him again? The question tormented her as she left the building. She did not notice a friend who was in the New Poetry Society when he walked past, nor did she hear his greeting, "Hello, Little Bird."

She was barely able to get back to the West Block. She was so drained of strength that she decided to lean against the wall for a rest before negotiating the stairs up to her room. Then she noticed that her light was on. The room had been empty and cold since Xiao Su had left. Now whenever she came back it was always dark. But tonight the light was on; it made her feel warm all over. She rushed upstairs, calling Qi Hong's name as she went.

He was inside waiting for her. The worried expression on his face made him look much older. He rushed to take her hand. Weary and a little relieved, he said, "Thank goodness you're back. I thought I'd never see you again." Jiang Mei was silent. She knew that if she spoke he would realize how worried she had been and how much she needed him. But he was going to leave her forever.

"I'm catching an early flight tomorrow morning, so I have to go to the airport tonight." He continued anxiously, "Well, is everything decided? Do we really have to separate?"

"Separate . . . ? I'll never see you again?" She was looking at the crucifix on the wall, and thought she could see the two red beans in the little box behind it.

"We don't ever have to part, Mei. Just say you'll go with me. Just one word, my little girl."

"No, I can't."

"You can't? You can't make this small sacrifice for me? You said that all you wanted in the whole world was to be with me."

"What about you?" she asked, her eyes accusing.

"Me? What I'm doing is the right thing. I couldn't bear to see the woman I love become one of the 'masses.' You have to come with me, you know that. I've never begged for anything as I'm begging you to go with me now. Mei, please, do as I say."

"No, I can't."

"Is that really true? You could watch a person dying in front of your very eyes and do nothing to save him? Once dead and gone, he'll never come back. Once I go, I'll never come back. You'll be sorry. Oh Mei, my Mei." He was shaking her hard by the shoulders.

"No, I won't regret it."

He looked into her eyes, still illuminated by that strange flame, and sighed. "Very well then, at least come downstairs and see me off."

She helped him put on his scarf and straighten the collar of his overcoat. They walked down the stairs in silence.

The snowflakes were floating in the vast night sky. It was very still. As they came out the door, a small car drove up and a hefty chauffeur jumped out. Qi Hong motioned for him to wait, and he walked over to a lamp with Jiang Mei. He looked at her and shook his head. "Do you know that I was going to force you to go with me? See, I've got a car and two plane tickets. But I realize that if I made you come, you'd hate me for the rest of your life, wouldn't you?"

He took an airplane ticket out of his pocket and hesitated for a moment, perhaps in the hope that Jiang Mei would suddenly change her mind. Then he tore it up, letting the pieces disappear among the snowflakes. "Good-bye Mei, my poetess, my revolutionary."

Qi Hong spat the words out bitterly. She looked at him. His face was twisted with pain, his eyes were red, and a drop of blood was swelling on his lower lip. Somehow his disturbed expression made her think of the indifference in his face the first time she had met him.

She wanted desperately to say something but could not. It was as though her throat were full of knives. She cried inside, *I must endure this minute, just this last minute.* She felt Qi Hong's icy lips touch her forehead, and then heard the sound of the car starting up.

In a moment all that was left was the whiteness, a swirling whiteness that filled the sky and buried the whole world.

The last words she had said to Qi Hong were, "I won't regret it."

Jiang Mei did not regret it. Qi Hong was being sarcastic when he called her a revolutionary, but later she actually became a worker for the Communist Party. Her mother, whose health improved greatly after liberation, declared proudly, "Jiang Mei's father did not die in vain."

It was snowing. The red love beans in Jiang Mei's hand were wet with tears.

"Jiang Mei, Little Bird," the caretaker was calling to her from outside the door. "You've got lots of visitors. Party Secretary Shi, Lao Ma, Mr. Zheng, Comrade Wang, and Little Rat. . . ."

He was cut short by the sound of laughter. Jiang Mei's eyes were full now not of tears but of laughter. She put the beans and the little box down and stood up.

11
Ru Zhijuan

(B. 1925)

*B*orn in Shanghai in 1925, Ru Zhijuan was raised by her grandmother in relative poverty after her mother died and her father
abandoned her and her four siblings. Circumstances did not
permit her to start primary school until she was ten, and she had only
enjoyed a few years of formal education when her grandmother passed
away and Ru was temporarily placed in an orphanage in Shanghai. According to her own account, she was largely self-taught and read whatever
she could lay her hands on, citing in particular the influence of *Dream of
the Red Chamber;* the fiction of Lu Yin, who was then one of the more
popular "New Women" writers; and the works of Lu Xun. In 1943, she
followed in the footsteps of an older brother and enlisted in a theatrical
troupe attached to the New Fourth Army of the Communist Party. Later
she was assigned to a propaganda team and spent the next several years
working on a variety of literary and cultural projects to mobilize audiences for the cause of national resistance. She was formally accepted into
the CCP in 1947.

After the founding of the People's Republic, Ru was transferred back
to Shanghai and appointed editor of *Literature and Arts Monthly* in 1955.
Her short story "Lilies" brought her literary acclaim in 1958, winning
high praise from veteran writer and critic Mao Dun. Above all, he was
impressed by the story's rhythmic pace and well-crafted narrative structure. Set during China's civil war in the late 1940s, "Lilies" is told from
the perspective of the I-narrator, a female propagandist assigned to a first
aid post, who observes the developing rapport between a courier in the
People's Liberation Army and a newly married peasant woman. Typical
of Ru's work, the story's interest lies in the author's subtle characterization
and psychological insight into her subjects rather than the development
of an intricate plot. This story and much of her early fiction appeared in
leading journals such as *Harvest, Shanghai Literature,* and *People's Literature* as well as in her collected volumes *Tall Aspens* (1959) and *The Quiet*

Maternity Ward (1962). The former proved popular and went into multiple reprintings after its initial publication.

In the story translated here, written in the 1950s amid a public debate about the role of socialist housewives, the author traces a middle-aged woman's determination to put the spark back into a lackluster marriage in the heady context of socialist reconstruction. Ru composed quite a few works that optimistically depict the ways state policy dramatically reshaped women's domestic identities and familial roles in the postliberation era; this story offers an especially fascinating examination of the shifting dynamics of love and labor (and the love of labor) in socialist culture and the unique challenges this posed to women. The story first appeared in *People's Literature* magazine in 1959.

In her early post–Mao writing, Ru Zhijuan's narrative themes moved in a new direction as she began crafting critical realist fiction that sharply condemned the Communist Party's recent social and economic policies. In her award-winning "A Badly Edited Story" (1979), for example, Ru lays bare the strain placed on the much exalted relationship between the peasantry and party authorities when cadres co-opt "revolution" for the sake of personal gain and ambition. Ru has also emerged as powerful figure on the contemporary literary scene, serving on the editorial board of the influential *Shanghai Literature*. In recognition of her important contribution to modern Chinese literature, Ru was invited to the United States to take part in the prestigious International Writers Workshop at the University of Iowa. She was accompanied by her daughter Wang Anyi (b. 1954), who has since risen to become one of China most well-respected contemporary authors.

The Warmth of Spring

(1959)

THE SKY WASN'T yet light and the first streetcar to set out from the yard had already passed, emitting a rumble grumble sound. As if pushed by someone, Jinglan sat straight up out of her sleepy dreams. Only when she saw how early it was did she relax and carefully crawl out of bed. Fearing she'd wake up her husband beside her, she didn't turn on the light but groped in the dark to cover up Dabao and Erbao with the quilt they'd kicked off in their sleep. And in the same movement she hung up the coat that her husband Mingfa had thrown down on a chair. Then she contentedly picked up the vegetable basket. This was Jinglan's routine: every Sunday or, more precisely, on any day that Mingfa would be eating at home, Jinglan would wake up at the crack of dawn and go to the market to buy him some tasty meat, fish, or vegetables.

"Jinglan!" The sound of the door creaking woke up Mingfa after all. "Where are you off to so early?"

"To buy groceries." Seeing her husband awake, Jinglan was quite pleased, keenly interested that he might tell her what he felt like eating. So she asked, "Mingfa, what would you like to eat?"

"Whatever." Mingfa rolled over and went back to sleep.

"Whatever" echoed in Jinglan's heart. It was always the same. What would you like to eat? "Whatever." To wear? "Whatever." What should we buy for our home? Also "whatever." Yet when he spoke with an old master worker or even with his apprentices at the factory, he was completely earnest, and would never say "whatever." This saddened Jinglan. She was busy from dawn to dusk, buying the groceries, cooking the meals, washing clothes. When the sky was light she'd do needlework; when night fell and she could no longer see what she was doing, she'd wind knitting wool. In the summer she wouldn't use a fan. When mosquitoes bit her, she'd just rub her feet together a little. To make her family happy and comfortable, her hands were never idle for a single minute. Yet her husband would always say "whatever," "whatever," as if everything to do with the family were irrelevant to him.

Jinglan gently sighed as she went out the door. The street was deserted, and seemed much wider than during the day. The streetlights were still lit and the roadsides were engulfed by shadows from the trees. The street was extremely quiet, just an occasional milk cart speeding by, the milk bottles jangling as they knocked against one another. A moment later the sound receded, and everything was silent again. All she could hear were her own footsteps lightly pattering on the cement sidewalk.

Over the last two years, Jinglan vaguely sensed that a wall had arisen between herself and Mingfa. All said, Mingfa hadn't ever lost his temper with her. Nor had he wronged her in any way. Each month as soon as his salary reached his hands, he turned it over to her in full. Sometimes he even took her out to see a movie. Yet in his eyes Jinglan could no longer find the former glimmer of tenderness and delight. Why? She wasn't sure. . . .

All at once, the streetlights went out. The sky was already light. In the deep azure sky lingered a few morning stars not yet hidden from view. On the street the traffic and people gradually picked up.

We have what we need at home, and I have money for meat and vegetables in my pocket. With a life like this, am I still not satisfied? Jinglan silently scolded herself, wishing she could throw off her depressed mood.

The food market was already bustling. People were crowded around several stalls with seasonal foods. Some vendors without business called out to solicit customers. Jinglan bought a basketful of meat and vegetable dishes. She was about to head back home when she caught sight of a wooden tub at a fishmonger's stall piled high with freshwater shrimp as big as her fingers. Each translucent blue shrimp wriggled around, squirming vigorously.

"Shrimp, such giant shrimp!" Jinglan's heart brightened up, and without hesitation she spent nearly a *kuai* to buy a half kilogram. Jinglan was a frugal person. Normally she would think hard about spending even a couple of *jiao*. And shrimp weren't even one of Mingfa's favorite foods. She felt that the important thing wasn't eating the shrimp, but rather the fond memories of her, Mingfa, and their whole family that they would evoke. . . .

* * * * *

"SHRIMP, SUCH BIG shrimp!"

The third year after liberation, Mingfa had a job again, and their lives were resuscitated like a sick person who's been cured. Jinglan and the children moved back from the countryside to live with Mingfa, and they settled down. They no longer had to worry about basic necessities. On one occasion, another Sunday, Jinglan had brought back a half kilogram of big live shrimp from the market. "Come quick. Such big shrimp!" Jinglan put the shrimp in a washbasin, where they wriggled about. Mingfa and the two children crowded around the basin to look, picking up straw sticks to poke the shrimp and laughing for joy.

"Remember, Mingfa?"

"I remember, Jinglan. How could I not?" Mingfa looked up tenderly at his wife, and hugged his two sons to his chest. Husband and wife were absorbed in the same fond memory.

One summer day two years before liberation, Jinglan took the two children to live in the country. Mingfa came back from the city after losing his job. Having no land in the countryside, how was the family of four to live? But people have to live somehow. So each evening the husband and wife took turns going down to the riverside to catch little fish and shrimp. Fishing all night, they'd have a half kilogram of fish and shrimp for Mingfa to take in to town. Once he'd sold them, he'd use the money to buy some six-grain flour to ease their hunger. One evening Jinglan walked to a far-off bend in the river downstream to fish for the night. The next day at the crack of dawn she rushed home with the bamboo basket, wild with joy:

"Shrimp! Such big shrimp!"

Mingfa took a look and, sure enough, in the basket were giant translucent blue shrimp, each jumping wildly.

"Great. They must weigh more than a half kilogram." Mingfa looked at his wife's exhausted and yet excited face, and his heart grew heavy, as if weighted down by iron. Yet he nonetheless uttered an expression of happiness.

The children were still young and didn't understand the grown-ups' misery. They just knew that their stomachs were hungry. So seeing the big shrimp made them eager for something to eat. After they watched their dad pour the shrimp into the bamboo basket to take to town to sell, they trailed behind him, crying. Mingfa's heart suddenly felt as if it had been pierced by ten million fishhooks. He looked at the children, then at his own big, sturdy hands. What couldn't this pair of hands do? They could turn out various precision parts using a lathe. They could handle the hardest steel and iron. Yet now these hands were carrying a small bamboo basket, and once in town he would have to place this bamboo basket at his feet and cry out to peddle its contents. His nose tingled in rage. How he hated everything about this society! In irritation, he left behind the children following him and strode off with tears in his eyes.

To remember such past hardships in the midst of happiness always brought sweetness. That was how Mingfa and Jinglan had been, one tightly hugging the children, the other gazing over with boundless happiness. The two said nothing, but their hearts thought the same thing and felt the same emotion. They felt that their present life was glorious and happy. Especially Jinglan: as far as being a wife was concerned, there was nothing more satisfying than this.

Jinglan bought the shrimp and slowly walked back home. Again and again her heart carefully mulled over all these recollections. Yet what she thought about most wasn't selling shrimp before liberation, but that time they bought shrimp after liberation. From beginning to end, her memory of this event was crystal clear, Mingfa's every word and smile, each expression, each little motion. She mulled it all over again like a text that she could recite by heart after reviewing it just once. From beginning to end, she remembered how she had brought shrimp home, simmered them to a bright pink, and brought them to the table, and how Mingfa had gazed at her with such tenderness, as if to say, "Jinglan, we've shared sweetness and bitterness, we've finally endured through it all. . . ." Every time Jinglan remembered this scene, she'd laugh to herself. Now, looking at her basket, she again smiled faintly.

"Daydreaming, Jinglan?" There was someone pulling at her sleeve.

Jinglan was startled and raised her head. It was her neighbor, Sister Zhu, whose fat body blocked the road as she called out to her in a loud voice. Sister Zhu was the chair of the neighborhood women's association. A month earlier the neighborhood had organized a production and social welfare co-op, and she thus served as the head of the production team Jinglan had joined, the team making microphones. She had once spent two years as a worker in a cotton mill, and she was a forthright person. As soon as she caught hold of Jinglan, she said, her face completely serious, "Our group is going to have a production meeting tonight. We have a mission."

"Oh!" responded Jinglan.

"So will you come or not?" Suspecting that Jinglan's attitude wasn't sufficiently unequivocal, Sister Zhu became anxious.

"I'll be there." Jinglan almost always showed up for their meetings. However, she would always knit as she listened, and she never spoke up herself. She felt as if she attended the meetings simply to hear about the decisions the others had made. She went along with whatever everyone else decided. Sister Zhu knew of this shortcoming, so she pressed her, "Jinglan, you must also make a great leap forward. Be ready to speak up."

Jinglan lowered her head smiling, and muttered "I . . ." then fell silent. Sister Zhu couldn't resist shaking her finger at Jinglan before hurrying off.

Jinglan reached the door of her home and, looking at the shrimp in the basket, couldn't stop her heart from leaping. What would Mingfa say? He would walk over and smile. Dabao and his brother would crowd around . . . the happy scene of the family looking at shrimp a few years ago seemed to appear before Jinglan's eyes. She suppressed her excitement, pushed the door open, and walked in. As soon as she entered, she discovered that the room was completely solemn and silent. The children were awake, but were reading books on their beds. Mingfa had thrown on a shirt, and his hair was sticking up where he'd been scratching his head. He was leaning over the table, drawing something on paper, and didn't bother looking up. The washbasin with water for them to brush their teeth that she'd set out stood untouched, just as she'd left it. The air in the room seemed completely subdued. Jinglan had to swallow the words on the tip of her tongue as she placed the shrimp in a bowl in silence, and then put it in the most noticeable spot on the chest of drawers. Thereupon she directed the children to wash up for breakfast. But even when the children had finished breakfast and gone out to play, Mingfa's head was still buried in his drawing. Jinglan could no longer maintain her calm. "Mingfa, I bought shrimp today."

"Oh!"

"Look, such big shrimp!" Jinglan summoned the strength to calm her words, but her voice didn't sound very natural.

"Oh!" Mingfa still didn't raise his head.

"Mingfa, look . . ."

At this point Mingfa turned his head around and saw Jinglan standing there holding a bowl of big shrimp, looking agitated. Only now did he seem to understand what she'd said. "You got shrimp. Good. Good." He smiled to express his delight, and immediately turned back to his drawing. That smile reminded her of how, as he left for work, he would humor the children when they made faces to show that they didn't want him to go. Now it seemed that he not only had forgotten their bittersweet memory but also had no desire to talk with her.

Jinglan took the bowl of shrimp and quietly walked into the kitchen. Tears welled up in her eyes.

Spring had just arrived, but her heart felt icy. She now felt ever more clearly that a wall separated her and Mingfa. Yet she didn't sense that Mingfa's world was broader than hers, or that his concerns were any greater than hers, or that the things he loved were loftier than those she loved. She just felt wronged, and her tears poured out.

As waves of emotion flooded Jinglan's heart, she felt confused, yet her hands quietly peeled the shells off the shrimp. One by one, she carefully cut them. In this mood she prepared Sunday lunch. She did not forget to warm 200 grams of high-grade Shaoxing wine for Mingfa. Nor did she forget to attend the meeting when evening fell. As soon as the time arrived she found two socks in need of mending, took her needle and thread, and went to the production committee meeting.

A month earlier, Jinglan had gotten involved as soon as the neighborhood launched the production and social welfare co-op. She felt that since everyone was participating, she should too. The first few days, she felt rather unaccustomed to being there. Each afternoon during the break, she'd hurry home to check that her children had come home from school, whether they'd gotten into any trouble, whether the boiled water had been used up. Only later did she get used to things. During production, she'd do whatever she was told. And once her shift began, she wouldn't raise her head but worked every minute for a full eight hours. The women in the group praised her for her diligent and steady work. Besides feeling happy, she was taken by surprise. She felt that, as with the housework, she really didn't have to expend too much energy. But there were also those who criticized her for not taking enough initiative at work. She felt they were correct, yet, not knowing how to take initiative, she also felt a little at a loss.

At this evening's meeting, Sister Zhu rallied everyone to buckle down to fulfill 10,000 urgent orders within seven days. When Sister Zhu was finished speaking, the representative from the factory spoke. Pulling a creased piece of paper from his pocket, he read out a slew of figures. It was like when Jinglan calculated her shopping expenses each evening, but the numbers he recited were much bigger. At first Jinglan couldn't take it all in. Nor did she understand the account he was calculating, but she noticed his earnest manner and the rapt attention with which he spoke. She was reminded of Mingfa. What was he hunched over his desk every morning drawing? It was also creased paper like this, and it was also with this rapt attention. Probably, just like this representative, he wanted to mobilize everyone to step up production. What part of this work could so captivate a person? Today she began to wish to understand, and she continued to listen attentively.

The meeting entered the discussion phase. As usual, Jinglan sat on the side listening. Although she did not speak up once, she felt that some of what others said perfectly captured what she was thinking, whereas in the past she neither spoke nor imagined doing so. At the end of the meeting she discovered that she had broken her usual rule and had left some of her sewing unfinished. Of the two pairs of socks she had brought, she had only mended one and a half.

When Jinglan returned home, it was already past ten. Mingfa and the children were all sleeping quietly. She didn't feel like going to bed. Nor did she feel like working, so she sat down at the table. She felt as if her head were spinning with a jumble of thoughts. But when she sat down to try to disentangle them, her mind suddenly went blank.

The creased papers on which Mingfa drew his plans were spread out on the table. Several squares and circles had been meticulously sketched on them. She couldn't figure out why in the end Mingfa had crudely crossed them all out. The first sheet was like this, and the second sheet, for all together twenty-four sheets.

He's so earnest. In no way is he a "whatever" person! Jinglan repeatedly smoothed the edges of the sheets. For a short while, her heart again felt in a jumble.

Next door in number 16, someone knocked on the door. Sister Zhu had returned. She always came home at this late hour, and she always called out to be let in with such a loud voice. As soon as she called at the door, the whole deeply sleeping alley would stir. She would knock and yell loudly. Her husband was an old master electrician, also the kind of person who would forget all about eating when immersed in his work. As soon as Sister Zhu yelled outside the door, he already replied that he was coming. But Sister Zhu would still loudly scold him. At night her voice sounded especially loud.

"Some people work themselves to death. Aren't you the lucky one, turning in so early."

There was a creaking sound, and her husband opened the door, saying, "Oy, serious, doing a shitload of work and coming home every night as if you've won first place in the imperial examination."

"What? You look down on my work?" Sister Zhu would fire back, but her voice conveyed an inexpressible sense of triumph.

"I wouldn't dare. Wouldn't dare. Don't I feel absolutely honored to be able to open the door for you every night?"

There was a chuckling sound as Sister Zhu laughed and pushed shut the creaking door.

Jinglan stood up, opened the window, and let out a deep breath. She felt utterly dismal. She didn't rise any later than Sister Zhu. Nor did she go to bed any earlier. Sister Zhu toiled busily, but Jinglan didn't rest either. Nor was Mingfa inferior in any way to Sister Zhu's husband. So why were they so harmonious when she was like this? . . . The alley was pitch black. There were no people or noise, just the rectangular bars of light shining on the wall opposite her and Sister Zhu's adjacent front apartments. The wall was still covered with big-character slogans sending off those going to assist with construction in other parts of the country. The writing was still fresh: CONTRIBUTE OUR YOUTH TO THE FATHERLAND! The black characters on the white wall looked all the more solemn, straight, and forceful.

✳ ✳ ✳ ✳ ✳

JINGLAN TURNED HER head and looked at Mingfa. Mingfa lay on his side, obviously already sound asleep. How she pitied him and how he'd toiled all day. Yet when she thought of how he no longer held her in his heart as he had in the past, she couldn't help but feel a pang of sorrow. She quickly turned off the light and lay down on the bed. She felt that all this—Sister Zhu's laughter, the giant shrimp, the pages Mingfa had crossed out, the numerous figures the workers' representative spoke of, and then CONTRIBUTE OUR YOUTH TO THE FATHERLAND . . . these various sounds and images all at once converged and indicated something to her. Her heart was very unsettled, and she mulled it over for some time. Finally a figure firmly gripped her attention: 7–10,000. That was what everyone kept repeating at today's meeting: in 7 days they needed to fulfill 10,000 orders. The hands of the clock pointed to

12. A streetcar sped by, still emitting that rumble grumble sound. An ordinary Sunday had ended.

The next day at work, Jinglan toiled as usual without lifting her head. Usually when she worked, however, it was as if she were thinking about nothing one moment and everything the next, whereas today one thing persistently came to her mind: 7 days, 10,000 items, 7 days, 10,000 items. The more she thought, the more she suspected that she herself was working too slowly. Her speed didn't pick up as a result, but she did work herself into a sweat. She glanced over at Sister Zhu, who wasn't working in the workshop but was all alone squatting down in the courtyard, manipulating an old electric fan with great care.

Isn't she anxious? Jinglan thought it strange. She waited until the end of the shift, then walked over to ask Sister Zhu what she was doing. Sister Zhu was the kind of person who loved to talk and loved to laugh, a real chatterbox. But now her whole face was grave and she said quietly:

"I'm making a machine. Using a machine would speed up the process of filing off strips of rubber for rubber cords. The last time I toured an industrial exhibition I saw a machine like this."

"A machine?" Jinglan immediately thought of Mingfa's numerous sheets of paper with the giant crosses on them. "Would we be able to make one?"

"Sure. Why not?" Sister Zhu knit her brow and said, "The machine needs a disk about so big. A wood one would do. Any ideas?"

"Me?" Jinglan shook her head and then wracked her brains, looked at Sister Zhu, and said timidly, "There's a round stump in the kindling pile at my place. Could we take that and see if we can whittle a disk ourselves?"

"Absolutely. Why not?" Sister Zhu's voice got louder.

"Then I'll go get it and give it a try." Jinglan rushed home, rummaged around in the kindling pile for that round piece of wood, set it aside, ran to the cafeteria to buy food for dinner, then swiftly wiped off the table, took out bowls and chopsticks, and called Dabao, his brother, and their dad to come eat. After completing all this, only then did she pick up the round piece of wood and head back to the workshop.

She and Sister Zhu whittled the wood with a knife and sanded it down. Blisters erupted on their hands. A wood disk finally emerged. Jinglan returned home much later than usual, and she was exhausted, but there was an uncommon happiness in her heart.

When she returned home, the children told her that they had eaten dinner with their dad, and that he had already gone back to the factory to work an extra night shift. She sat at the table and discovered that Mingfa had left her quite a bit of food. The children watched their mom eat and told her that Dad had saved all the best morsels for her.

"Oh!" Jinglan answered happily, but an inexplicable spasm of distress made her nose tingle. The joy she'd felt just a minute ago at having made the wood disk nearly evaporated.

It wasn't until the start of her shift the next day that Jinglan remembered that wood disk. In the end, had it been usable? She rushed into the workshop and saw that a new big-character poster had been pasted up in the "Democracy stand" facing the wall, and many of the women had gathered around to read it. As usual, Jinglan didn't much concern herself with this sort of thing. She couldn't spot Sister Zhu in the crowd, and as she was turning to leave, by chance she looked up and jumped in fright. It turned out that her own name was written on the red paper. *Why have they written about me? What did I do?* Jinglan hastened quietly to push her way through the crowd of people and began to read carefully. The big-character poster praised her and Sister Zhu for daring to think and daring to venture technological innovation. It specifically mentioned Jinglan's initiative in seeking the kindling. At the same time, everyone hoped that they would succeed soon and all the more guarantee that they would fulfill 10,000 orders. As Jinglan read, her face grew hot and her heart throbbed. Never did she think that whittling a piece of kindling would suddenly bring her so much praise. At this moment, the girls noticed her and gathered around, all chattering at her at once. She couldn't make out who was saying what, but she understood that everyone was saying the same thing: demanding that they hurry up with their machine. For it could replace manual labor and improve their efficiency so that they could earnestly, definitely complete the 10,000 items and prove that housewives were not only industrious but ingenious. It would enable their tiny production group to make a great leap forward like a factory. Looking at each woman's fervent face, Jinglan could only nod constantly, unable to get out a single word.

In all her life, she had split no small number of kindling wood pieces. Whether she split them well or badly, when had anyone ever asked a half smidgen about it? Firewood won't burn when damp, so a meal can't be cooked, but at worst a family eats a little later. But today . . . Jinglan suddenly realized that what she was whittling last night was no longer a piece of kindling, but rather a disk for a machine. It was a small brick tile in socialist construction.

"Are you daydreaming again?" Sister Zhu grabbed her from behind. "I was calling you at the top of my lungs and you still didn't hear me. Let's get going. The wood disk didn't work."

"It didn't work?" Jinglan's mind thundered and at once swept away her various thoughts. Now she knew what great bearing the success or failure of this device would have. So she followed Sister Zhu to the workshop and concentrated her full attention on studying the problem.

The wood disk was fairly hard. Pressing down sliced even the steel wire inside the rubber cord. Sister Zhu suggested mounting a thick strip of flexible rubber onto the wooden disk, and Jinglan agreed. So the two went in search of a worn-out bicycle tire. But when they wrapped it around, they saw that the tire was patterned with uneven bumps and crevices. When the disk was turned, certain spots couldn't bear the strain. The tire was unusable.

"I'll go rummage around at the junk stall and see if there might be some smooth thick rubber." Once she had a concrete measure for seeking resolution, Jinglan knew where to direct her efforts. So she and Sister Zhu divided the work. Sister Zhu repaired spare parts at home, while Jinglan went in search of rubber.

The sun shifted from the east to the center of the sky, and then from the center it slanted toward the west. The cafeteria served lunch and then dinner. When six o'clock struck, the dinner menu was written on the cafeteria blackboard, and they began serving. As if on fire, Jinglan's two children, Dabao and Erbao, searched for their mom in the alley. Sister Zhu followed behind them, raising her voice to ask each person she saw whether they had seen Jinglan. Jinglan hadn't come back for lunch, but at one point that afternoon someone had seen her return full of enthusiasm. She'd bought some thick smooth rubber, but when she wrapped it around the wood disk, it still wouldn't go on evenly. Then she disappeared.

At this point Jinglan was squatting in front of a leather worker's stall, watching the master leather worker cover the disk with the rubber, tear it off, and rewrap it. The rubber was as thick as two silver dollars, and no matter how good his craftsmanship, he couldn't cover it smoothly.

At dusk, the sky grew overcast and hazy, and the cold draft in the wind grew chillier. Pedestrians quickened their steps. Jinglan and the leather worker were both dripping with sweat. As he worked, he grew ever more impatient and progressively lost confidence, so Jinglan felt increasing turmoil in her heart. In the past if she couldn't finish a task, at most Dabao and Erbao wouldn't have new shoes to wear, or Mingfa wouldn't have a sweater to wear for a new season. But this would affect the whole production group. It would affect the production mission of the factory. Jinglan had never shouldered such a heavy burden. Nor had she ever experienced this kind of anxiety. She continuously praised the leather worker to pump up his morale. But he looked up at the sky, threw his small hammer into the toolbox, and pushed the wood disk and the rubber back in front of Jinglan. "It won't work. The rubber is too thick. I need to close shop."

Jinglan looked up, and sure enough the sky had darkened. Only at this point did she suddenly remember dinner and the fact that she had the rice and meal tickets with her. She gathered everything up and hurried home. In over a dozen years, Jinglan had never neglected her duties in this way. She knew full well that it was nothing alarming. Mingfa wouldn't be too hard on her, and the children wouldn't suffer too great a wrong. But she couldn't suppress the panic in her heart.

Once she got home she saw that Mingfa was working the swing shift and hadn't returned. The children were eating a steaming hot dinner. Dabao explained that Mrs. Zhu from next door had gone to a meeting and said that if it ended early enough she would come to see Jinglan. He also told her that it was Mrs. Zhu who had bought them their dinner.

"Oh!" Upon seeing that Mingfa wasn't home, Jinglan's heart settled down a little. Yet another kind of worry raided her heart again. *What will we do if the rubber doesn't work?* Her stomach growled, but she held her bowl and stared blankly.

Beneath the window some girls from the production group were questioning Dabao:

"Has your mom come back yet?" "Is the wood disk ready yet?"

The more Jinglan listened, the tighter her heart grew. She hastily set down her bowl of food, told Dabao to put his little brother to sleep nicely, and ran over to the workshop with the rubber and the wood disk.

Jinglan sat alone under the electric light and used a razor blade to whittle meticulously at the rubber. Again she whittled down the rubber, and again she wrapped it on the disk. But now the thickness was uneven, with one section higher, another lower. This wouldn't do at all. Since it didn't work, she tried again. She whittled one piece, then another. When she had to scrap the third piece, she stopped working. She seemed to see each woman's hopeful, fervent face and that brilliant red big-character poster, the creased paper held by the factory representative, the voice full of trust, and Sister Zhu's worried expression.

Tomorrow is day three. What will we do if we can't complete the job? Jinglan's eyes filled with tears and she sat as wooden as a carved dummy. Some family's clock struck twelve with a ding-dong sound. *Mingfa should be home. Have the children kicked off their quilt?* Her habitual concerns, cultivated over the years, swept over her at this point. But they flashed once and were immediately chased away by the pile of rubber in her hand.

What to do? *Somehow I must think of a way.* Jinglan wiped away her tears, but they immediately welled up again in her eyes. As she looked at it, the piece of rubber seemed to be getting thicker and more cumbersome.

"Jinglan!" In the stillness of the spring night, this call sounded like a thunderbolt. Jinglan was startled and turned her head to see Mingfa standing in the doorway.

"Mingfa!" Jinglan couldn't say why, but again she couldn't suppress her tears. Once let loose, they came streaming down.

"Jinglan, what's wrong?" Mingfa walked over to her.

Although Jinglan said that she was anxious about not being able to make the wood disk, she was still extremely delighted to see her husband arrive. She wiped away her tears and explained how they were trying to engineer a disk. Mingfa listened, relaxed his knit brow, and, without speaking, stretched out his hand to pick up the rubber and the wood disk. He examined them, compared them, and then said, "Wouldn't it work fine if we just made a roller using this thick rubber?"

"Exactly! Exactly, exactly!" Jinglan's eyes lit up, and then on second thought she said, "But how can we get it perfectly round?"

Mingfa said, "It'll work once we smooth it out on our factory's lathe."

Having suffered enough with the pile of rubber, Jinglan was still doubtful and had some questions, but Mingfa was already pulling her out the door.

The street was quiet; the streetlights were swaying in the wind. There were no more trolleys, so the two walked shoulder to shoulder in the middle of the road.

"We need this first thing in the morning. Do you think it'll be ready in time?" Jinglan asked softly, but in the quiet night her voice sounded especially resonant.

"It'll be ready in time. It'll be ready in time," Mingfa answered with complete assurance. Jinglan didn't make a sound. As long as it wasn't finished, she still felt nervous.

A night eatery by the side of the road had not yet closed, and a fluorescent light shone in the dining area, though the seats no longer held any customers. She didn't know if Mingfa was truly hungry or just wanted to show his confidence that "It'll be ready in time." Nor did he care whether or not Jinglan agreed. He just pushed her into the restaurant, sat down, and ordered two bowls of noodles.

Time was so tight, yet he wanted to eat a night snack. Jinglan felt some displeasure, but she also feared that her husband might truly be beside himself with hunger. She sat uneasily, frequently looking over at the eatery's electric clock, reticent with the concern that weighed down her heart. Facing her sat Mingfa, scrutinizing his wife up and down. He felt that he had never before loved his wife as he did now. Nor had he ever sensed life's beauty, fullness, and happiness as he did now. In order to accelerate the cause of socialist construction, he had raised his targets, and his wife was now also exerting great efforts toward this goal. They said nothing, but they were both thinking the same thing, just as if remembering the time before liberation when they eked out a living by fishing, and their thoughts evoked the same emotion.

At last the mixed noodles were served. Out of habit Jinglan used her chopsticks to put her toppings in her husband's bowl, then buried her head and ate. She didn't notice how the noodles tasted. All that loomed in her mind was the rubber disk. For a moment the round disk turned into an ellipse. The next moment edges and corners reemerged. In the twinkling of an eye, it returned to its original shape.

"Our woman general has suffered hardships. You should eat up."

Suddenly Jinglan saw a pair of outstretched chopsticks, and between them was a giant, bright red shrimp. . . .

A shiver ran through her whole body. She raised her head to see her husband gently looking at her with boundless fondness.

Ah! How well Jinglan knew this gaze! And yet she found it utterly strange, for it seemed even kinder and more beautiful than the one she knew. Jinglan felt a little bashful, but tears welled up in her eyes. That wall that she could neither touch nor see had completely disappeared.

Suddenly all these thoughts surged in at once upon Jinglan. They excited and shocked her, and she couldn't move her chopsticks for a long time. But like an ocean wave, all this rushed in at her and then swiftly receded. Before she could fully understand why this had suddenly come about, she heard the sonorous ring of the Huangpu River Customs' big clock—the depth of night—it was 1:00 a.m. Suddenly Jinglan woke up and realized that the truly important problem had yet to be resolved. How much depended on whether or not the machine would revolve by daybreak today! She looked at Mingfa, and Mingfa looked right back at her. This time no tears were in Jinglan's eyes, and she didn't feel sheepish. With her gaze she hurried him along, and she hastened to peel off the shell of that big red shrimp, remembering as she shelled it how she had bought shrimp on Sunday, unaware that her face blushed slightly.

Walking out of the restaurant, Jinglan hugged the wood disk and the rubber as she and Mingfa walked shoulder to shoulder in the middle of the road. The whole city was asleep; only the shadows of the trees swayed along the roadside.

"Mingfa, can you be sure you can smooth it into shape?" Jinglan still couldn't set her heart to rest.

"Silly pumpkin, what do I do for a living? In my hands steel becomes round if you want it round, long if you want long. How could I fail to tackle a little piece of rubber like this?"

"Are you sure?"

"Of course I'm sure."

The two walked closely together without speaking, but felt that their hearts were tightly bonded. For a common goal, they were walking the same road.

The night grew deeper, and the wind blew harder. Suddenly a bolt of thunder rumbled, followed by a light sprinkle of rain. Mingfa took off his jacket and covered his wife's shoulders. The two swiftly advanced with long strides.

The first sound of spring thunder had rumbled. Although a hint of cold still lingered in the wind, Jinglan felt extremely warm.

12
Chen Ruoxi

(B. 1939)

B orn into a working-class Taiwanese family, Chen Ruoxi (Chen
Jo-hsi) graduated from National Taiwan University, where she
and several fellow aspiring writers (including Bai Xianyong,
Ou Yangzi, and Wang Wenxing) founded the experimental bimonthly
journal *Modern Literature*. Some of her earliest short stories were translated into English and published under the auspices of a contemporary
literature project sponsored by the U.S. Information Agency. In the early
sixties she went overseas to pursue graduate work in the United States,
receiving an M.A. in English literature from Johns Hopkins University
in 1965. Rather than return to Taiwan, political conviction prompted
her and her husband to repatriate to the People's Republic of China.
They landed in Beijing in 1966, on the eve of Mao Zedong's Great Proletarian Cultural Revolution. They had to wait two years for their work
assignments (during which time Chen gave birth to their first child)
but eventually were assigned jobs at the Hydraulic Engineering College
in Nanjing. They finally decided to leave the PRC in late 1973, but the
harrowing seven years spent there provided Chen with inspiration for a
series of influential short stories about the Cultural Revolution. Noted
for their journalistic style, these stories first appeared in the periodical press in Hong Kong between 1974 and 1976 and gained the author
a loyal following among readers in Hong Kong, Taiwan, and abroad.
The acclaimed volume *Mayor Yin* (1976), a collection of this work, was
soon made available in a number of foreign-language editions, earning
Chen considerable international recognition as well. These stories, plus
her semiautobiographical 1978 novel *Repatriation,* provide a gripping
account of the cruel absurdities of life and the disillusionment of the
Chinese intelligentsia during one of the most turbulent and tragic eras
in the history of the People's Republic. Considering the dearth of fiction
published within China during these years, Chen's testimony represents
a unique contribution to modern Chinese literature whose value cannot
be overstated.

After leaving mainland China in 1974, Chen and her family were on the move for several years before finally settling in the United States in 1979. Chen accepted a teaching position at the Center for Chinese Studies at Berkeley, while continuing to produce a steady stream of essays, articles, short stories, and novels in both Chinese and English. Much of her fiction from this period, including her novels *Breaking Out* (1983) and *Foresight* (1984), explores the diverse experiences of diasporic ethnic Chinese living in North America. Some of Chen's work has now been published in mainland China.

Residency Check

(1976)

I DIDN'T KNOW Peng Yulian very well. Although we were close neighbors—my bedroom window faced hers and the front door of her apartment—we had no opportunity to chat because we worked in different units. On those occasions when we did meet on the way to and from work, she always smiled warmly, exposing her white, even teeth and looking at me with moist, glistening eyes. I could not help meeting her glance and answering her smile with one of my own. The old women who lived in the university dormitory called her a siren behind her back, most likely because they were jealous of her captivating eyes.

As far as we women were concerned, Yulian was by no means a beauty, and was, in fact, very short. But since she took such good care of herself and was very particular about what she wore, her figure always appeared well proportioned. Her breasts, large and curvaceous, attracted immediate attention. She always had her hair cut and blown dry at the large hairdresser's near the Drum Tower, and although she wore it in the same bobbed fashion as everyone else, hers was always nicely fluffed, in what the girls called the "Shanghai style." Her skin was dark, her nose was a little flat, and she had a large round face that didn't seem to suit her small stature. But her eyes were big and bright and so expressive that when she looked at you, they held all manner of allurements. Men were captivated by her, so naturally many of the women looked upon her with envy and malice.

The first time I actually talked with her was on a winter morning soon after I moved into the compound. We were pushing our bicycles out our front doors at the same time that day, and we had shopping baskets hanging from the handlebars. She called out good morning to me, I returned her greeting, and we rode together to the market. The weather was terribly cold, and I was bundled up in a padded jacket, padded trousers, padded shoes, a fur-lined coat, and a snow cap. I was wearing so many layers of clothing that it was a real effort just to get on my bicycle. But Peng Yulian was wearing only a pair of Shanghai-made maroon woolen slip-on shoes with flaps over the insteps; navy blue woolen trousers, a gaily patterned silk padded jacket, closely fitted so as to show off her figure; a maroon woolen cap; and black gloves. With the snow covered ground as a setting, she looked particularly lovely and enticing. It takes a lot of nerve to wear such bright colors, I thought.

Our breath was turning to mist, and I commented, "I never thought that Nanjing winters would be so cold!"

"I never did like Nanjing," she said frankly. "It's freezing cold in the winter and stiflingly hot in the summer. Now Shanghai has a nice climate. If you have a strong constitution you can get through the winter nicely with only a heavy sweater."

I surmised from these exaggerated words of praise that she was from Shanghai. People from Shanghai always seem to have a superiority complex, and to this day the Communist Party has been unable to transform it.

"What a mean bunch they are!" she suddenly blurted out, as she stomped down heavily on the pedal. "They *would* choose a snowy night to come around and make their residency check! Did they check you out last night too?"

"Yes."

I shivered, just thinking about the night before, when I had crawled out of a warm bed to be interrogated, and then got back into a cold bed with icy hands and feet.

"They come to my place every time they have one of their residency checks; their mothers'—!"

That was the first time I'd ever heard a woman utter this classic curse. I lowered my head and dared not look at her.

I too was fed up with residency checks. There was little anyone could say if they checked every household, but on those occasions when a random check was held, only a few families in each building were picked out. People claimed that anyone who is a problem case is checked every single time. My apartment was one of those that was always checked, but no matter how much I resented it, I didn't dare complain.

"I wonder why they had another random residency check last night," I said.

"What else, except they found themselves with nothing to do after dinner?" she said with a sneer. "According to the people who work in the clock factory,

Nixon is on his way to Beijing, and public safety measures are being taken everywhere. It would seem that those public safety measures have reached all the way down to us."

By then we had arrived at the marketplace, and since there was such a crowd of people there, neither of us felt like talking anymore. We parted company and lined up to buy food.

Following that first meeting, I took special notice of Peng Yulian because of her husband, Leng Zixuan. They seemed to be an unlikely couple. First of all, there was a marked disparity in their ages. Although Yulian was approaching her middle years, in general appearance and in the way she made herself up, she was holding on to her youth. Her husband gave quite the opposite impression, and seemed to be on the decline. It was said that Leng was not yet fifty, but his face was already deeply furrowed and half his hair had turned gray. He was bald around the temples, and his receding hairline left a broad expanse of forehead. Although he wore glasses, he was so terribly nearsighted he'd hunch his back and thrust his head out whenever he wanted to see something. In sharp contrast to his wife, he hardly ever smiled, and he was so reticent that he shied away from greeting any of his neighbors. The blank, faraway expression on his face always gave me the impression that he had some knotty problem on his mind.

One summer day just before evening fell, I caught a glimpse of him through the window. He was standing outside, leaning against his front door, and looking blankly up into the sky. His mouth was open and he was absolutely motionless, like some kind of fossil. Only when his daughter, who had come out to call him to dinner, tugged at his jacket, did he snap out of it. He lowered his eyes, adjusted his glasses with one hand, and stared at his daughter with a puzzled look.

He was an old man, no question about it, and I felt a little sorry for Yulian. But during the first year that I lived in the dormitory I saw Leng Zixuan only a few times, since he spent most of the time away performing manual labor.

The very day that I moved in, the secretary of the Party committee in my department came over especially to acquaint me with the political status of my neighbors. She mentioned Leng Zixuan again and again, calling him an "old-time rightist." Later I occasionally overheard my fellow teachers refer to him as an "old political target," for he had been attacked in several political campaigns. He had been in detention for over a year in conjunction with the Cleansing of the Class Ranks and had also been found wanting during the recent One Attack, Three Antis campaign. This latest misfortune had come about in a most peculiar manner: One of the teachers—no one knows who—

had written "Chinese Communist Party" on a piece of scratch paper, and Leng had added the word "dogs." Someone had retrieved the crumpled piece of paper from the wastebasket and forwarded it on up, and as a result one more account had to be settled on top of all the others. Reeducation through labor was ordered, and so an associate professor became a standing member of the May Seventh Cadre School labor force, which kept him away from home from then on.

But the incident that really aroused my interest in Peng Yulian occurred in the summer of 1972. One evening Zhou Min, who worked in my department, called on me and asked me to go with her to a meeting of the neighborhood committee. Besides being colleagues, we lived in the same building. I spent quite a bit of time with Zhou Min because I liked her kind, gentle ways.

"What kind of meeting is it this time, Xiao Zhou? If it's another planned parenthood meeting, I'm not going. I've already been to several of those, and I've filled out all the required forms."

"No, that's not it," she said with a giggle. "This time it's about the Pan Jinlian affair."[1]

"Pan Jinlian?"

"I'm talking about your *honorable* neighbor, Peng Yulian."

She pointed through my bedroom window, then hurried me along. "Come on, let's go. You'll find out what it's all about when we get to the neighborhood committee meeting."

The meeting was being held in another building, in the apartment of a carpenter named Chang. Since Mrs. Chang didn't work she regularly served as the committee chairwoman, and every time there was a meeting she kicked her husband out of the apartment.

By the time we arrived the room was already filled with women, and as I looked around I saw that all of the Lengs' neighbors were there; every block representative was in attendance, even tottering old Guo Nainai and Shi Nainai. The room was buzzing with their chatter. Zhou Min and I found seats on the corner of the bed. I finally realized that they suspected Peng Yulian of having an extramarital affair and were discussing ways of keeping her under surveillance.

"Do they have any proof?" I turned to ask Zhou Min.

---

[1] The notorious heroine of the sixteenth-century novel *Jin Ping Mei,* who was something of a nymphomaniac.

"Proof?" Shi Nainai, who was sitting in front of me, turned around. "We have all kinds of proof! There have been several eyewitnesses. With my own eyes I once saw a man slipping away from her place early in the morning. Ptui! What a piece of trash! Another time someone was seen sneaking into her place in the middle of the night. You just know he had to be up to no good. That shameless hussy doesn't even give a thought to the fact that she has a ten-year-old daughter!"

It came as no surprise that Shi Nainai should speak so harshly of Peng Yulian, for she had been widowed as a young woman and had raised two sons by herself. One of them had joined the army and the other was a Party member, so among all the people in our dormitory compound she was the most highly respected. It was only natural that she could not tolerate the slightest moral lapse.

"She is shameless, all right!" seventy-year-old Guo Nainai railed. "While her man is out performing manual labor, she is blatantly carrying on with other men. How will she ever be able to raise a daughter like that? Every time I see her all made up like some kind of demon I just want to throw up!"

"You said it!" Zhou Min added critically. "Her outlandish clothing has already been criticized several times, but she'll never learn her lesson and change her ways!"

"Change her ways? Why, she's out there flaunting herself in front of us!" Shi Nainai added with considerable spirit. "Do you all remember last summer when she wore that transparent pink silk blouse? She was wearing her brassiere so high that her breasts swayed and jiggled as she swaggered back and forth in the compound. Yan Nainai was making some comment about it to her when she cut her short and mumbled that big breasts are for men to suck on. Just imagine saying a thing like that! Poor Yan Nainai was so embarrassed she blushed all over and was almost in tears as she walked away."

"Didn't Chairwoman Chang also criticize her clothing once?" A woman who lived next door to Peng Yulian seized the moment to denounce her. "She didn't dare talk back to her face, but the moment the chairwoman stepped out the door, she started to bellow, 'You expect me to start dressing up like a widow before my old man is even dead!'"

Chairwoman Chang's temper flared up. "If we don't straighten her out," she said, "the moral atmosphere of the whole dormitory will be destroyed. And if the young girls follow her lead!" She clapped her hands to get everyone's attention and called the meeting to order.

"Mei Laoshi"—I never dreamed that I'd be the first person called on—"your place is directly opposite hers. Have you noticed any indiscretions?"

"Indiscretions?" I was caught completely by surprise, and since the place was filled with people, I began to stammer. "I'm . . . not aware of any."

"The reason we asked you here today was to discuss ways of catching her just once," the chairwoman stated. "Your window is opposite hers, which means you can see and hear anything that goes on inside. So we're going to rely on you to keep this area covered."

I couldn't do that, but I didn't dare refuse. While I was pondering my dilemma, Zhou Min poked me in the back, so finally I grudgingly acquiesced to their request.

"That's fine," the chairwoman said in a louder tone of voice, as she looked over the crowd of people with satisfaction. "That takes care of her front door, and we have Shi Nainai and the others to keep an eye out in the rear. Now we have to come up with the specific steps to be taken."

"This is what I would do," said Guo Nainai, who was always very verbal during meetings despite her advanced age. "The moment we see a man entering her house, we go to the university security section and have them make a search. Then once we've caught her we can hold a big group session and soundly criticize her!"

This met with unanimous approval. Suddenly Zhou Min asked, "What if she refuses to open her door?"

"That's right," the chairwoman said, her resolve beginning to waver. "We must have an excuse for going into her house."

"How about a residency check!" someone shouted out.

"Good idea!" several people agreed, applauding.

"Who would dare refuse to open her door for a residency check?"

The plan of action was thus decided: Anyone who saw a man entering Peng Yulian's place was to make an immediate report to the neighborhood committee, which would post sentries at the front and rear. Then they would place a call to the university security section and ask them to send someone to catch the adulteress.

At this point the meeting should have come to an end, but since Peng Yulian was such a notorious figure, once we began talking about her we couldn't stop. We all seemed to have forgotten our fatigue after a hard day's work, and we were concerned only that we not miss a single tidbit of news. We craned our necks and cocked our heads as we listened intently. I had never been very clear on the Peng Yulian matter to begin with, and now here I was with the assignment of keeping watch over her. Naturally, in order to gain a true understanding of the person under my surveillance, I sat there from start to finish, taking in every comment, no matter how casual.

I discovered that this wasn't the first time she'd gotten into trouble. Back in 1963, during the Four Cleansings campaign,[2] Leng Zixuan had gone with his labor group to Sheyang county to participate in the Three Togethers movement—eat together, live together, and labor together with members of a commune. Before long, the Party secretary of his department, Ma Sui, began hanging around Peng Yulian on the pretext that it was his duty to look after the welfare of the members of his department. This Ma Sui was good-looking, fair, and had a real gift of gab, so Peng Yulian soon fell under his spell and into his grasp.

At the time, all her neighbors could see what was going on, but since Ma Sui was, after all, a Party secretary, no one dared breathe a word about it. At first he would just come over for a secret rendezvous and leave after they'd had their fun. But as time went on he grew more brazen and would actually spend the night at the Lengs' house when Mrs. Ma was out of town on an assignment. The affair became common knowledge throughout the dormitory district, and even Mrs. Ma got wind of it, though she never let on. The neighbors were incensed by the whole sordid affair, to say the least, but no one had the heart to tell Leng Zixuan.

After finishing with Peng Yulian, Ma Sui took up with the wife of the boilerman at the school. But they did not handle themselves very discreetly, and they were discovered by the woman's husband. A public uproar followed and Ma Sui was forced to make a formal written statement of self-criticism. The Party secretary of the school did everything within his power to hush up the scandal, but as luck would have it, his efforts were thwarted by the ushering in of the Great Cultural Revolution. The boilerman joined the ranks of the rebels, and his wife came forward to denounce Ma Sui. He was ordered to make a clean breast of things, and when he submitted his confession, there was a resounding outcry. It turned out that he had been involved with a total of five women at the school, mostly teachers, including Peng Yulian; the methods he'd used and the details of the affairs shocked and disgusted the people.

During the outcry the streets were covered with wall posters denouncing Ma Sui, all the way from the school gate to the cafeteria, and they were pored over by a continuous stream of people. This was the first that Leng knew of the scandal involving his wife, and talk had it that within just a few days half his hair turned white and his walk became a shuffling gait, as though he had

---

[2]*Siqing yundong*. A campaign in which the people and the lower-level cadres were called upon to give a clean account of their political and ideological stand, family background, and financial situation.

aged ten years or more. For the longest time he spoke to no one, and he acted like a mental incompetent. Some people were even afraid that he would try to take his own life.

"Didn't the two of them have a big fight or anything once the scandal was exposed?" I asked Zhou Min.

She smiled and said, "That's the strange part about it all. Shi Nainai has lived opposite the back door of their place for more than ten years, and she says she's never once heard them have an argument!"

"Really?" This puzzled me too. "But since the whole street was buzzing with the affair, I imagine Peng Yulian had to write a confession, didn't she?"

"A confession?" Shi Nainai turned around to break in on our conversation. "Don't even mention that 'confession' of hers! We had one talk after another with her, until our tongues nearly fell out, but all we were able to squeeze out of her was one page. Now I don't know how to read, so I didn't see it, but those who did weren't satisfied with it. You want to know why? Because she wasn't being truthful, that's why! She stubbornly protested that she was being wrongly accused, and that the only reason she'd had any dealings with Ma Sui had something to do with removing her husband's rightist label. According to her, falling into his hands had been unavoidable, and she said something about how it would have been harmful to her husband if she'd breathed a word to anyone about it. I think she was under the illusion that we would all go out and erect a memorial arch for her or something!"

Carpenter Chang walked in the door as she was saying her piece. We all looked at the clock. It was already past ten, so we quickly brought the discussion to an end and left.

One evening as I was walking home with my son, after picking him up at the day care center after work, I saw Peng Yulian riding her bicycle toward us. She had a large speckled hen in the nylon mesh bag on her handlebars. When she saw us she stopped and jumped to the ground.

"Why didn't you ride your bike today, Mei Laoshi?" she asked good-naturedly.

"One of my colleagues borrowed it," I answered with a smile. She had a joyous look on her face, and she was composed, as usual. Her black, shiny eyes, even her dark skin, which was accentuated by her snowy white teeth, were attractive. She was wearing a pair of blue cotton slacks and a white Dacron blouse under a lightweight gold sweater. She didn't look all puffy like everyone else, but rather delicate and lively, and everything fit her just perfectly. Not only were the colors of her outfit well chosen, but even the way she wore her clothes was different. In Nanjing the women wore sweaters underneath their coats—no one wore them as outer garments. The talk had it that only factory girls from Shanghai dared to do that, and even in Shanghai they attracted a good deal of attention as they walked along the street. Peng Yulian showed a great deal of nerve in dressing so conspicuously and parading around in the dormitory district of a prestigious university. It was easy to understand why she was looked upon as an immoral person.

The moment my son spotted the chicken his eyes widened and were riveted on it. With a flurry of gestures, he began to shout, "Mommy, a chicken! A chicken!"

Feeling a little embarrassed, I was glad to take a cue from his words. "Where did you get such a big hen?" I asked.

"Someone from the Swallow Hill Commune brought some over to sell near our factory." She smiled again as she spoke. "Three-fifty apiece. I know that's pretty expensive, but it's a fine chicken and well worth it. My philosophy is to eat whenever the food's available. It's better insurance to store things in your stomach than to deposit the money in the bank, as some people do." She laughed, evidently pleased with her witticism. Then, seeing that the child's eyes were still on the chicken, she bent over and asked him, "Your name is Jingjing, isn't it? Do you like to eat chicken?"

He tugged at my sleeve. "Mommy, I want to eat chicken!"

Before I could say a word, Yulian turned to me and asked seriously, "Would you like one? You can have this one! It's no trouble for me to get them."

"No," I quickly demurred, "no."

"If not now, then perhaps I can get one for you the next time they come around."

I could see by her face that she wasn't making the offer just to be polite. Nonetheless, I momentarily lost my composure. Shaking my head and making signs with my hands, I said, "No! No! I . . . I don't like chicken."

"Really?"

She stared at me incredulously. The smile slowly disappeared, and her face darkened. I avoided her eyes, as I felt my cheeks flush.

"Then let's just forget the whole thing," she said in an obviously forced tone. "So long, then. I'd better be going."

As I watched her ride off, I breathed a sigh of relief.

"Xiao Mei!"

I turned to see Zhou Min, who'd come up behind me during all of this.

"What's going on between you and Peng Yulian?"

I told her we'd met on the road and that she'd offered to give me the chicken. "She's quite a forthright and ingenuous girl, that one," I concluded aloud.

Zhou Min nodded. Then, in a low voice she said abruptly, "You wouldn't know, but she was once a model worker."

"A model worker?" I could scarcely believe my ears.

"That's the truth!" Zhou Min could not keep from smiling. After a moment she took my son's hand, and the three of us walked slowly to the dormitory. On the way she confided to me, "Outside of her fondness for prettying herself up and her extramarital affairs, there's nothing really wrong with Yulian. As for her family background, her father was a vegetable farmer in Minhang village near Shanghai, which makes him a member of the prestigious Five Red Elements. She joined the Communist Youth League as a young girl, and was on the point of being admitted into the Party when she was dismissed from the League because of her affair with Ma Sui."

"That's pretty severe punishment," I said.

"The Nanjing Clock Factory, where she works, took that action only after constant pressure by the rebel faction here at our school. At first they argued that since she'd been seduced, the blame should rest with the man, not with the woman."

"Do they know who the man is this time?"

Zhou Min shook her head. "According to Shi Nainai it's not someone from this area, so most likely he's from the clock factory."

"If they catch him, the people at the clock factory won't have any excuses this time around."

Zhou Min raised her eyebrows and said with a smile, "That's hard to say. The Nanjing Clock Factory can't fill the demand for their wristwatches, and since they can't meet production quotas as it is, why would they concern themselves with matters like this? Besides, the problem of relations between the sexes in factories is nothing new, unlike political questions, which can always be expanded and magnified. At most, it's nothing more than a decadent lifestyle, and the worst that can happen is that they have to write out a confession. But that Ma Sui affair was a moral outrage, and the people were incensed over it. They demanded that he be dealt with severely, and the university had no recourse but to report to the provincial authorities and request that he be demoted and take a cut in salary. Their request was denied by the provincial authorities."

"Why was it denied?"

"They said that even though the situation was bad, it couldn't be considered rape, since all the teachers and workers had gotten involved with him of their own free will. They considered it a matter of lifestyle, which could be dealt with through education. Naturally, the university was put in the bad position of being unable to face up to its own people, so after much negotiating the provincial authorities finally transferred him to another university."

"Really, there doesn't seem to be . . ." I was going to say there was no such thing as right or wrong anymore, but I held back and said indifferently, "No wonder Yulian has done the same thing over and over."

"Xiao Zhou," I said, talk of Peng Yulian reminding me of her husband and how the two of them seemed so different, "don't you get the feeling that Peng and Leng aren't well suited to each other? She's still so full of life, and he looks like he's on his last legs."

"He has aged a great deal these last few years," Zhou Min said by way of agreement, though there was a sympathetic ring to her words. "You may not believe it, but in the past it was she who chased after him."

"Really!"

Zhou Min laughed when she saw how startled I was. But she quickly assumed a more serious air as she continued, "You couldn't know, but the Leng of the pre-antirightist campaign and the Leng of today might just as well be two different people! He was promoted to associate professor in 1967—I remember it distinctly, since that was the year I was sent here to teach. At the time his wife had been dead a year, and he had no plans to remarry. He met Yulian quite by chance at the home of one of his colleagues. She fell for him the moment she laid eyes on him, and she took the lead in getting him to go rowing with her at People's Park. In no time at all he was hooked, and the two of them were constantly together. Three months later they were married."

"Incredible!"

"Hai! Naturally, he was a totally different man in those days. He was quite spirited then. Just think, an associate professor in his early thirties! Why, he walked with such style, with his chest out. People even copied his way of walking. He'd been a star pupil at Nanjing University—it was called Jinling University then—and a young man of real brilliance. He excelled in everything, including poetry. But he had too high an opinion of himself, and he was awfully naive. During the Hundred Flowers Campaign he took the slogans seriously and really blossomed out with attacks on the cultural and educational policies of the Communist Party and the government. As a result he was the first person in the school to be labeled a rightist element."

"Quite a . . ." I was about to say "typical bookworm," but I couldn't be so unfeeling, and so I just heaved a long sigh.

"There was a time when the people in his department entertained the idea of removing that label from him. But then his department head discovered that he'd written a poem that he called 'Snow,' a title that Chairman Mao had used, and had set it in the form of 'Spring in Qinyuan,' just as Mao had done. But the mood of Leng's poem was dismal and chilling, quite the opposite of Mao's. As far as everyone was concerned, Leng was purposely throwing out a challenge, intending it as a satirical attack on Mao Zedong. So not only did he not lose the label, but he was lucky he didn't find himself wearing it to the crematorium!"

"Did you see the poem?" My curiosity was aroused.

Zhou Min shook her head. "That Leng Zixuan isn't one to back down. Even though he wrote several confessions, he insisted that he'd only written what he saw and felt, and he steadfastly denied that any satire had been intended. Some people demanded that the whole poem be made public, but the department authorities weren't willing to have this unhealthy influence spread any further, so they kept it classified, together with his written confession. The entire department hotly criticized and discussed the affair for a while, even though hardly anyone knew the actual contents of the poisonous weed."

By this time we'd passed through the main gate of the compound, and, probably because we were within range of the eyes and ears of others, Zhou Min said nothing more on the subject. We said good-bye and each of us headed home.

One night soon after that my dreams were suddenly shattered by the sound of someone knocking on a door. I awoke and pricked up my ears. Sure enough, someone was knocking on the Lengs' door. That Yulian is sure a sound sleeper, I thought; the noise woke me but there wasn't a peep from her. Then I heard a man shout impatiently, "Open up in there! Residency check!"

Another residency check! Just hearing the words disgusted me, as I knew there would be no more sleep for me the rest of the night. Being nervous and a poor sleeper by nature, I found it next to impossible to close my eyes again if I awoke during the night. Since the residency check was sure to include my place, I figured I might just as well get up and wait for them so I wouldn't be flustered at the last minute, and also to prevent my son from waking.

I turned on the light, got dressed, dug out my residence documents, and sat in front of my desk by the window to wait. Just then the clock on the wall began chiming the hour—it was midnight, a typical hour for a residency check. I lifted a corner of the curtain to look outside. It was pitch black except for a light coming from the Leng apartment. Their front door was ajar, and I could see someone moving behind the window, but since a curtain separated us, I couldn't see clearly. I let my curtain fall back into place, and began to flip through a book.

As expected, in about the time it would take to drink a cup of tea, someone came knocking at my door. I walked over leisurely, opened the door, and with the same motion handed over my residence documents.

"Oh, pardon us, we're not here for a residency check." At this I grew uneasy. The first person through the door turned out to be Mrs. Chang, the chairwoman of the neighborhood committee. There was an unwonted look of apology on her face. She was followed by two men who belonged to the school security section and a woman whose face seemed familiar to me—most likely she was a member of one of the school workers' families.

"Here's why we've come," Chairwoman Chang was saying. "We suspect that Peng Yulian is up to something. Earlier this evening someone saw a man sneak into her place and did not see him come out. Just a while ago we entered her place on the pretext of a residency check but we didn't find a man inside. Yulian was red in the face, like a thief who's been caught in the act, but since she hadn't violated any law, we couldn't very well make her open up her trunks and cabinets so we could look through them. We think she hid him somewhere, so we've come to ask you to keep an eye on her and to be sure to report anything suspicious to the neighborhood committee."

There was nothing I could do but assent, and after a few more admonitions by the chairwoman, the four of them departed.

As if I had nothing better to do than meddle in things like this! Anger filled my heart as I undressed, turned off the light, and got back into bed. But just as I had feared, after this ordeal, any chance of going back to sleep had vanished. I tossed and turned in bed, and like someone who has drunk a lot of strong tea, I grew more and more wakeful. That damned Peng Yulian! After all that tossing about in bed I couldn't keep from cursing her. Everyone in the neighborhood had to lie awake nights because she got herself into trouble! But then I thought of how she had been in imminent danger of being disgraced in front of everyone, and I ended up by being glad for her. But just who was the man? Here I was, living opposite her, and I'd never noticed an unfamiliar man entering or leaving her house. In a big dormitory like this, I thought to myself, with all these people living close together, there naturally were many tongues to wag. Who knows? Some gossip may have raised a false alarm, which started the people talking and gave rise to a groundless disturbance.

After giving rein to my thoughts for a while—I had no idea what time it was—I noticed the faint light of day coming in through the window, and then the shape of the window itself gradually became visible. Since sleep was out of the question, I decided to get up and get dressed, make myself some tea, and then amuse myself by writing in my diary.

I happened to pull back a corner of the curtain and glance out the window. Imagine my shock when I saw the Lengs' front door open slightly and without a sound. Then a head peeked out through the opening and looked left and right. It was followed stealthily by the rest of the body. With lowered head and hat pulled low, the figure tiptoed toward the rear gate of the compound. In my agitation I didn't get a good look at the person's face, but there could be no doubt that it was a man—I wasn't mistaken about that. The Lengs' door was already closed when I looked back; there were no lights in the house and the curtain was pulled down all the way. Suddenly one corner of the curtain was raised, and someone's face was pressed against the glass. The instant our eyes met we both withdrew and lowered the curtains as quickly as possible.

I remained standing beside the window for a long time, my legs rubbery, my hands clasped tightly together and pressed against my breast, as I tried to stop my heart from beating so wildly. If I live a hundred years, I'll never forget Peng Yulian's wide staring eyes. Was her look one of terror, mortification, or defiance? I shall never know.

Before the day was out, news of the Peng Yulian affair had spread throughout the school and the dormitory. By sheer coincidence, Zhou Min had risen early that morning and noticed a man with his hat pulled down over his eyes. She saw him walk very nervously toward the rear gate, open it with a key, and leave. When Chairwoman Chang came over in the morning for information, Xiao Zhou reported what she had seen. Actually, she hadn't seen which place he'd come out of, but everyone eagerly jumped to the conclusion that he was none other than Peng Yulian's lover. People said that the chairwoman recalled seeing a key lying on a table while the neighborhood committee members were making their residency check the night before. She surmised that Peng Yulian had hidden the man in the wardrobe, but in the excitement she hadn't had time to hide the key. Once Chairwoman Chang figured this out she stamped her foot and yelled, "What a shame!" But there was nothing to be gained by regret, and since they hadn't caught the culprit, naturally they had no case against Peng Yulian. She continued to ride her bicycle around the dormitory area in complete freedom, like someone without a care in the world.

The news inevitably reached the May Seventh farm in northern Jiangsu. The farm closed down for a few days before New Year's, and on the eve of Leng's departure for Nanjing, his section leader called him in and told him about the affair. He advised him that if he wanted a divorce, the school authorities would be willing to consider his request since Peng Yulian had repeated her offense time and again.

But to everyone's surprise, Leng stated without any show of emotion, "If Yulian wants a divorce, I'll consent to it anytime, but under no circumstances will I bring up the subject myself."

This bit of news became *the* topic of conversation. Some expressed wonderment and admiration for his "magnanimity," while others called him a spineless weakling who would not let go of a "worn-out shoe." Then there were those who gleefully predicted that it would be strange indeed if he didn't beat her within an inch of her life the moment the two of them were together!

But as it turned out, on the day that Leng arrived home, Yulian, her face beaming with joy, brought home an old hen, and as she plucked its feathers she was even humming to herself. Her neighbors kept their ears pricked up all night, waiting for the sounds of an argument that never came. At this point the school notified Leng that he was to teach a language course, so he no longer had to take part in manual labor. From then on I saw him often; sometimes he would be walking all alone in the schoolyard, while at other times he would be sitting next to the window in his quarters, lost in thought and looking up into the sky for hours on end. On my way to and from work I also ran into Yulian quite often, and she greeted me with a smile as always, but she never again stopped to chat.

Glossary

"A Badly Edited Story"	剪輯錯了的故事
A Bomb and an Expeditionary Bird	炸彈與征鳥
"A Certain Stop on Beining Road"	北寧路某站
"A Piece of Flesh"	一團肉
A Straying Beauty	歧途佳人
A Woman Soldier's Own Story	女兵自傳
Ai Siqi	艾思奇
All-China Women's Federation (Fulian)	全國婦女聯合會
An Unofficial Biography of Huan Xiu	桓秀外傳
Analects	論語
Ancient Melodies	古歌集
"Another Man's Wife"	生人妻
Antirightist Campaign	反右派運動
As You Desire	稱心如意
Autobiography of Lu Yin	盧隱自傳
Bai Lang	白朗
Bai Wei	白薇
Bai Xianyong	白先勇
baogao wenxue	報告文學
Baoyu and Daiyu	寶玉與黛玉
Beidahuang	北大荒
Bian Kungang	卞昆岡
Big Dipper	北斗
Breaking Out	突圍
Cao Yu	曹禺
Chen Baibing	陳白冰
Chen Boer	陳波兒
Chen Gongbo	陳公博
Chen Ruoxi	陳若曦
Chen Xuezhao	陳學昭
Chen Yi	陳毅
China Weekly	中華週刊
Clear Stream	浣錦集
Cosmic Wind	宇宙風
Crescent Monthly	新月月刊

"Crossing the Tong-Pu Railroad"	過同蒲路
Daughter	挑戰
"Diary of a Concubine"	姨太太日記
Ding Ling	丁玲
Divorce	離婚
Du Junhui	杜君慧
Eat Drink Man Woman	飲食男女
Eight Years	八年
"Essentials and Ambience of Life"	衣食住行與生活的氛圍
Feng Jiren	封季壬
Feng Keng	馮鏗
Feng Youlan	馮友蘭
Feng Yuanjun	馮沅君
Feng Yunzhuang	馮允庄
Fengzi	鳳子
The Field of Life and Death	生死場
Fighting out of the Dark Pagoda of Spirits	打出幽靈塔
Flowing Waters	逝水集
Foresight	遠見
Forging the Truth	弄真成假
The Fourteen of Us	我們十四個
"Fragment from a Lost Diary"	肉刑
"The Girl Umeko"	梅子姑娘
Goddess of Freedom	自由神
gongnongbing	工農兵
Gongsun Yang: A Statesman	公孫鞅
Guan Lu	關露
Guizhou Daily	貴州日報
Harvest	收穫
He Xiangning	何香凝
Heaven and Earth magazine	天地
Hu Lanqi	胡蘭畦
Huang Zhang	黃彰
huayu kongxi	話語空隙
Hunan Women's War Zone Service Corps	湖南婦女戰地服務團
Hundred Flowers Campaign	百花運動
"The Imperial Hotel"	皇家飯店
In a German Women's Prison	在德國女勞中
In a Japanese Prison	在日本獄中
In the World	人世間
Interviews at Yan'an	延安訪問記
Ji Hong	季洪
jiefang	解放
The Land	土地

Lao She	老舍
Last Night	昨夜
League of Left-Wing Writers	中國左翼作家聯盟
Les Contemporains	現代
Li Jianwu	李健吾
Liao Chengzhi	廖承志
Liberation Daily	解放日報
Life Bookstore	生活書店
"Lilies"	百合花
L'Impartial	大公報
Lin Yutang	林語堂
Ling Shuhua	凌淑華
Literary Gazette	文藝報
Literary Monthly	文學月報
Literature and Arts Monthly	文藝月刊
Liu-Wang Liming	劉王立明
Love Letters to Mei	愛眉小札
Lu Jingqing	陸晶清
Lu Xiaoman	陸小曼
Lu Yin	盧隱
Luo Qiong	羅瓊
Luo Shu	羅淑
Mao Dun	茅盾
Market Street	商市街
May Seventh cadre school	五七幹校
Mayor Yin	尹縣長
Meandering on the Stage	舞台漫步
Mei Niang	梅娘
"Melody in Dreams"	弦上的夢
Mirages	人間海市
Miss Linli	琳麗
Modern Literature	現代文學
Mother	母親
My Tragic Life	悲劇生涯
National Dispatch	國訊
New Life Campaign	新生活運動
New People's Herald	新民報
New War Diary	新從軍日記
Notes from America	美國札記
On the Songhu Battle Line	在淞滬火線上
Ou Yangzi	歐陽子
Peace Daily	和平日報
Peach Garden Maiden Marries Wogu	桃園女兒嫁窩谷
Peng Zigang	彭子岡

People's Daily	人民日報
People's Literature	人民文學
Playscripts	劇本
"The Portrait"	畫像
Qian Zhongshu	錢鐘書
Qiu Jin	秋瑾
The Quiet Maternity Ward	靜靜的產院
Quyuan	屈原
Radiant Spring	關不住的春光
Raging Dreams	沸騰的夢
Rainbow	虹
"Red Beans"	紅豆
The Red Detachment of Women	紅色娘子軍
Reminiscences	古今
Remote Love	遙遠的愛
Repatriation	歸
"Residency Check"	查户口
Ru Zhijuan	茹志鵑
Shanghai Literature	上海文學
Shen Zijiu	沈茲九
Shi Jimei	施濟美
The Silent Singing Girl	無聲的歌女
Six Chapters from My Life "Down Under"	幹校六記
Song of Youth	青春之歌
Song Qingling	宋慶齡
"Sophie"	蘇斐
Southeast Travels	東南行
Spring Camellias	春茶
The Story of Liwa	李娃傳
Su Qing	蘇青
Su Xuelin	蘇雪林
"Suffering Women"	受難的女性們
Sunrise	日出
Surviving the Storm	浮沉雜憶
Taking a Bath	洗澡
Talks Amid Hardship	風雨談
Tall Aspens	高高的白楊樹
Tao Kangde	陶亢德
Ten Years of Marriage	結婚十年
texie	特寫
"The American South"	美國的南方
"Third-Class Hospital Ward"	三等病房
This Human World	人間世

"Thoughts on March Eighth"	三八節有感
Thunderstorm	雷雨
Tian Han	田漢
tie guniang	鐵姑娘
To Be Working Is Beautiful	工作者是美麗的
Torrents	奔流
Untitled	無題集
Wandering Through the Liberated Zones	漫走解放區
Wang Anyi	王安憶
Wang Wenxing	王文興
Wang Ying	王瑩
War Diary	從軍日記
"The Warmth of Spring"	春暖時節
"Waves"	濤
We Three	我們仨
The White-Haired Girl	白毛女
"Who am I?"	我是誰
Women of New China	新中國婦女
Women's Bookstore	女子書店
Women's Cries	女性的吶喊
Women's Echoes	婦女共鳴
Women's Light	婦女之光
Women's National Resistance and Salvation Alliance	中國婦女反日救國大同盟
Women's Life magazine	婦女生活
World Literature	世界文學
Wu Guifang	武桂芳
Wu Shutian	吳曙天
Xia Yan	夏衍
xiafang	下放
Xiao Hong	蕭紅
xiaopin wen	小品文
Xie Bingying	謝冰瑩
Xu Guangping	許廣平
Xu Zhimo	徐志摩
"Yan'an Forum on Literature and Art"	延安文藝座談會
Yang Gang	楊剛
Yang Jiang	楊絳
Yang Mo	楊沫
Yao Mingda	姚名達
Yellow River	黃河文藝月刊
Young Companion	良友
Yu Ru	郁茹

Yuan Changying	袁昌英
yueju	越劇
Zhang Ailing	張愛玲
Zhao Qingge	趙清閣
Zhao Yiman	趙一曼
Zong Pu	宗璞

Supplemental Readings

I. Critical and Historical Research

Andors, Phyllis. *The Unfinished Liberation of Chinese Women, 1949–1980*. Bloomington: Indiana University Press, 1983.

Bai Shurong and He You. *Bai Wei pingzhuan* 白薇評傳 (A critical biography of Bai Wei). Changsha: Hunan renmin chubanshe, 1982.

Barlow, Tani, ed. *Gender Politics in Modern China: Writing and Feminism*. Durham: Duke University Press, 1993.

Brownell, Susan and Jeffrey N. Wassestrom. *Chinese Femininities, Chinese Masculinities: A Reader*. Berkeley: University of California Press, 2002.

Chen Jingshi. *Xiandai wenxue zaoqi de nüzuojia* 現代文學早期的女作家 (Early modern women writers). Taipei: Chengwen chubanshe, 1980.

Chen Mingshu, ed. *Ershi shiji Zhongguo wenxue dadian: 1930–1965* 二十世紀中國文學大典 (Compendium of twentieth-century Chinese literature, 1930–1965). Shanghai: Shanghai jiaoyu chubanshe, 1996.

Chen Qingsheng. *Kangzhan shiqi de Shanghai wenxue* 抗戰時期的上海文學 (Shanghai literature during the war of resistance). Shanghai: Shanghai renmin chubanshe, 1995.

Chen Xuezhao. *Surviving the Storm: A Memoir*. Trans. Hua Ti and Caroline Green. Ed. Jeffrey Kinkley. Armonk, NY: M. E. Sharpe, 1990.

Chow, Rey. *Woman and Chinese Modernity: The Politics of Reading Between West and East*. Minneapolis: University of Minnesota Press, 1991.

Croll, Elisabeth. *Feminism and Socialism in China*. New York: Schocken, 1978.

——. *Changing Identities of Chinese Women: Rhetoric, Experience, and Self-Perception in Twentieth-Century China*. London: Zed Press, 1995.

——. *The Women's Movement in China: A Selection of Readings*. London: Anglo-Chinese Educational Institute, 1974.

Cui, Shuqin. *Gender and Nation in a Century of Chinese Cinema*. Honolulu: University of Hawaii Press, 2003.

Ding Maoyuan, ed. *Chen Xuezhao yanjiu zhuanji* 陳學昭研究專集 (A collection of research on Chen Xuezhao). Hangzhou: Zhejiang wenyi chubanshe, 1983.

Dong Bian, ed. *Nüjie wenhua zhanshi Shen Zijiu* 女界文化戰士沈茲久 (Women's cultural warrior Shen Zijiu). Beijing: Zhongguo funü chubanshe, 1991.

Dooling, Amy D. *Women's Literary Feminism in Twentieth-Century China*. New York: Palgrave Macmillan Press, 2005.

——. "Desire and Disease: Bai Wei and the Thirties Literary Left." In Charles Laughlin, ed., *Contested Modernities in Chinese Literature.* New York: Palgrave Macmillan Press, 2005.

——. "In Search of Laughter: Yang Jiang's Feminist Comedy." *Modern Chinese Literature* 8 (1/2) (1994): 41–68.

——. "Reconsidering the Origins of Modern Chinese Women's Writing." In Joshua Mostow, ed., *The Columbia Companion to Modern East Asian Literature*, 371–377. New York: Columbia University Press, 2003.

Duke, Michael S. "Personae: Individual and Society in Three Novels by Chen Ruoxi." In Michael S. Duke, ed., *Modern Chinese Women Writers: Critical Appraisals*, 53–77. Armonk, NY: M. E. Sharpe, 1989.

Evans, Harriet. *Women and Sexuality in China: Female Sexuality and Gender Since 1949.* New York: Continuum, 1997.

Ferry, Megan. *Chinese Women Writers of the 1930s and Their Critical Reception.* Ph.D. diss., Washington University, St. Louis, 1998.

Feuerwerker, Yi-tsi Mei. "Women as Writers in the 1920's and 1930's." In Margery Wolf and Roxanne Witke, eds., *Women in Chinese Society*, 143–68. Stanford: Stanford University Press, 1975.

——. *Ding Ling's Fiction: Ideology and Narrative in Modern Chinese Literature.* Cambridge: Harvard East Asian Series, 1982.

Findeisen, Raoul David. "From Literature to Love: Glory and Decline of the Love Letter Genre." In Michel Hockx, ed., *The Literary Field of Twentieth-Century China*, 79–112. Honolulu: University of Hawaii Press, 1999.

Gerstlacher, Anna, et al., eds. *Women and Literature in China.* Bochum: Brockmeyer, 1985.

Gilmartin, Christina Kelley. *Engendering the Chinese Revolution: Radical Women, Communist Politics, and Mass Movements in the 1920s.* Berkeley: University of California Press, 1995.

Goldblatt, Howard. "The Cultural Revolution and Beyond: Yang Jiang's 'Six Chapters from My Life Down Under'." *Modern Chinese Literature Newsletter* 6 (2) (1980): 1–11.

Goldman, Merle. *Literary Dissent in Communist China.* Cambridge: Harvard University Press, 1967.

Gunn, Edward. *Unwelcome Muse: Chinese Literature in Shanghai and Peking, 1937–1945.* New York: Columbia University Press, 1980.

He Yubo. *Zhongguo xiandai nüzuojia* 中國現代女作家 (Chinese modern women writers). Shanghai: Fuxing shuju, 1936.

Hegel, Robert E. "Political Integration in Ru Zhijuan's 'Lilies'." In Theodore Huters, ed., *Reading the Modern Chinese Short Story*, 92–104. Armonk, NY: M. E. Sharpe, 1990.

Hu Lanqi. *Hu Lanqi huiyilu 1901–1936* 胡蘭畦回憶錄 (Memoirs of Hu Lanqi). Chengdu: Sichuan renmin chubanshe, 1985.

Huang, Nicole. *Written in the Ruins: War and Domesticity in Shanghai Literature of the 1940s.* Ph.D. diss., UCLA, 1998.

Kao, Hsin-sheng C. *Nativism Overseas: Contemporary Chinese Women Writers*. Albany: SUNY Press, 1993.

Kao, George, ed. *Two Writers and the Cultural Revolution: Lao She and Chen Jo-hsi*. Hong Kong: Chinese University Press, 1980.

Kong Qingmao. *Yang Jiang pingzhuan* 楊絳評傳 (A critical biography of Yang Jiang). Beijing: Huaxia chubanshe, 1998.

Lan Hua R. and Vanessa L. Feng, eds. *Women in Republican China: A Sourcebook*. Armonk, NY: M. E. Sharpe, 1999.

Larson, Wendy. *Women and Writing in Modern China*. Stanford: Stanford University Press, 1998.

——. "The End of 'Funü wenxue': Women's Literature from 1925 to 1935." *Modern Chinese Literature* 4 (1/2) (1988): 39–54.

Laughlin, Charles. *Chinese Reportage: The Aesthetics of Historical Experience*. Durham: Duke University Press, 2003.

Lee, Leo Ou-fan. *Shanghai Modern: The Flowering of a New Urban Culture in China: 1930–1945*. Cambridge: Harvard University Press, 1999.

——. "Dissent Literature from the Cultural Revolution." *CLEAR* 1 (1) (1979): 59–79.

Lee, Lily Xiao Hong, ed. *Biographical Dictionary of Chinese Women: The Twentieth Century 1912–2000*. Armonk, NY: M. E. Sharpe, 2003.

Li Yu-ning, ed. *Chinese Women Through Chinese Eyes*. Armonk, NY: M. E. Sharpe, 1992.

Li Youning and Zhang Yufa, eds. *Zhongguo funüshi lunwenji* 中國婦女史論文集 (Collected essays on Chinese women's history). Taipei: Taiwan Shangwu yinshuguan, 1981.

Lieberman, Sally. *The Mother and Narrative Politics in Modern China*. Charlottesville: University Press of Virginia, 1998.

Lin Wei. *Ershi shiji nüxing sanwen baijia* 二十世紀女性散文百家 (Twentieth-century women essayists). Fujian: Jiaoyu chubanshe, 1993.

Liu Jianmei. *Revolution Plus Love: Literary History, Women's Bodies, and Thematic Repetition in Twentieth-Century Chinese Fiction*. Honolulu: University of Hawaii Press, 2003.

——. "Feminizing Politics: Reading Bai Wei and Lu Yin." *Journal of Modern Literature in Chinese* 5 (2) (2002): 55–80.

Lu Tonglin, ed. *Gender and Sexuality in Twentieth-Century Chinese Literature and Society*. Albany: SUNY Press, 1993.

Mao Dun. "Tan zuijin duanpian xiaoshuo" 談最近短篇小説 (A discussion of recent short stories). Originally published in *Renmin wenxue* 6 (1958). Reprinted in Hong Zicheng, ed., *Ershi shiji Zhongguo xiaoshuo lilun ziliao*, vol. 5, 1949–1976, 275–286. Beijing: Beijing daxue chubanshe, 1997.

Meng Du. "Guanyu Yang Jiang de hua" 關於楊絳的話 (On Yang Jiang). *Zazhi* (May 1945):110–12.

Meng Yue and Dai Jinhua. *Fuchu lishi dibiao*. 浮出歷史地表 (Emerging from the horizon of history) (1989). Taibei: Shibao wenhua chubanshe, 1993.

Meng Yue. "Female Images and National Myth." In Tani Barlow, ed., *Gender Politics in Modern China: Writing and Feminism*, 118–136. Durham: Duke University Press, 1993.

Ng, Janet. *The Experience of Modernity: Chinese Autobiography of the Early Twentieth Century*. Ann Arbor: University of Michigan Press, 2002.

Nüzuojia jutuanhui 女作家聚團會 (Colloquium of women writers). *Zazhi* (April 1944).

Ouyang Wenbin. "Shilun Ru Zhijuan de yishu fengge" 試論茹志鵑的藝術風格 (A discussion of Ru Zjijuan's artistic style). Originally published in *Shanghai wenxue* 10 (1959). Reprinted in Hong Zicheng, ed., *Ershi shiji Zhongguo xiaoshuo lilun ziliao*, vol. 5, 1949–1976, 333–343. Beijing: Beijing daxue chubanshe, 1997.

Palandri, Angela, ed. *Women Writers of Twentieth-Century China*. Eugene: Asian Studies Publications, University of Oregon, 1982.

Pang, Laikwan. *Building a New China in Cinema: The Chinese Left-Wing Cinema Movement, 1932–1937*. Oxford: Rowman and Littlefield, 2002.

Qiao Yigang. *Zhongguo nüxing de wenxue shijie* 中國女性的文學世界 (The literary world of Chinese women). Wuhan: Hubei jiaoyu chubanshe, 1993.

Qing He. *Yang Sao zhuan* 楊騷傳 (Biography of Yang Sao). Shanghai: Haixia wenyi chubanshe, 1998.

Sang, Tze-lan Deborah. *The Emerging Lesbian: Female Same-Sex Desire in Modern Chinese Literature and Culture*. Chicago: University of Chicago Press, 2002.

Shanghai shehuiyuan wenxue yanjiusuo, ed. *Shanghai gudao wenxue huiyilu.* 上海孤島文學回憶錄 (Memoirs on the Shanghai *gudao* literature). Shanghai: Shanghai shehui kexue chubanshe, 1985.

Shanghai shehuikexue yuan wenxue yanjiusuo, ed. *Sanshiniandai zai Shanghai de zuolian zuojia.* 三十年代在上海的左聯作家 (Leftist writers in 1930s Shanghai). Shanghai: Shanghai shehui kexueyuan chubanshe, 1988.

Sheng Ying. *Zhongguo nüxing wenxue xintan* 中國女性文學新探 (A new exploration of Chinese women's literature). Beijing: Zhongguo wenlian chubanshe, 1999.

Shih, Shu-mei. *The Lure of the Modern: Writing Modernism in Semicolonial China, 1917–1937*. Berkeley: University of California Press, 2001.

Stacey, Judith. *Patriarchy and Socialist Revolution in China*. Berkeley: University of California Press, 1983.

Su Xuelin. *Ersan shishi niandai de zuojia yu zuopin* 二三十年代的作家與作品 (Writers of the twenties and thirties and their works). Taibei: Guangdong chubanshe, 1979.

Tan Sheying. *Zhongguo funü yundong tongshi* 中國婦女運動通史 (A comprehensive history of the Chinese women's movement). Shanghai: Funü gongmingshe, 1936.

Tan Zhengbi. *Dangdai nüzuojia xiaoshuoxuan* (Contemporary women's fiction). Shanghai: Taiping shuju, 1944.

Thakur, Ravni. *Rewriting Gender: Reading Contemporary Chinese Women*. London: Zed Books, 1997.

Wang Jialun. *Zhongguo xiandai nüzuojia lungao* 中國現代女作家論稿 (A discussion of modern Chinese women writers). Beijing: Zhongguo funü chubanshe, 1992.

Wang Jing M. *Jumping Through Hoops: Autobiographical Stories by Modern Chinese Women Writers*. Hong Kong: Hong Kong University Press, 2003.

Wang Lingzhen. *Modern and Contemporary Chinese Women's Autobiographical Writing*. Ph.D. diss., Cornell University, 1998.

Wang Yixin. *Su Qing zhuan* 蘇青傳 (Biography of Su Qing). Shanghai: Xuelin chubanshe, 1999.

Wang Zheng. *Women and the Chinese Enlightenment: Oral and Textual Histories*. Berkeley: University of California Press, 1999.

Yang, Mayfair. "From Gender Erasure to Gender Difference: State Feminism, Consumer Sexuality and Women's Public Sphere in China." In Mayfair Yang, ed., *Spaces of Their Own: Women's Public Sphere in Transnational China*, 35–67. Minneapolis: University of Minnesota Press, 1999.

Zhang Jingyuan. "Breaking Open: Chinese Women's Writing in the Late 1980s and 1990s." In Pang-yuan Chi and David Der-wei Wang, eds., *Chinese Literature in the Second Half of a Modern Century: A Critical Survey*, 161–179. Bloomington: Indiana University Press, 2002.

Zhang Naihua. *The All-China Women's Federation: Chinese Women and the Women's Movement: 1949–1993*. Ph.D. diss., Michigan State University, 1996.

Zhang Yingjin. *The City in Modern Chinese Literature and Film: Configurations of Space, Time and Gender*. Stanford: Stanford University Press, 1996.

Zhao Qingge. *Wutiji* 無題集 (Untitled). Shanghai: n.p, 1947.

——. *Changxiang yi*. 長相憶 (Forever recalling each other). Shanghai: Xuelin chubanshe, 1999.

Zhu Hongzhao, ed. *Yan'an fangwen ji* 延安訪問記 (Interviews at Yan'an). Guangzhou: Guangdong renmin chuban, 2001.

Zhu Lianbao, ed. *Jinxiandai Shanghai chubanshe yinxiangji* 近現代上海出版社業印象記 (A modern history of the Shanghai publishing industry). Shanghai: Xuelin chubanshe, 1993.

Zhuang Haoran. "Lun Yang Jiang xiju de wailai yingxiang he minzu fengge" 論楊絳戲劇的外來影響和民族風格 (On the foreign influences and national characteristics of Yang Jiang's dramas). In *Huaju wenxue yanjiu*, 111–128. Beijing: Zhongguo xiju chubanshe, 1987.

Zhongguo funü yundong lishi ziliao 中國婦女運動歷史資料 (Materials on the history of the Chinese women's movement). Vol. 1: 1840–1918; Vol. 2: 1918–1937; Vol. 3: 1937–1945. Beijing: Zhongguo funü chubanshe, 1991.

II. Additional Translations and Primary Souces for Individual Writers

Bai Wei

Bai Wei zuopinxuan 白薇作品選 (Selected works of Bai Wei). Changsha: Hunan renmin chubanshe, 1985.

Beiju Shengya 悲劇生涯 (My tragic life). Shanghai: Wenxue chubanshe, 1936.

"Jumping Through Hoops." Tr. Jing M. Wang. In Jing Wang, ed., *Jumping Through*

Hoops: Autobiographical Stories by Modern Chinese Women Writers, 43–74. Hong Kong: Chinese University Press, 2003.

Linli 琳麗 (Miss Linli). Shanghai: Shanghai shangwu shuju, 1926.

"Wo toudao wenxue quanli de chuzhong" 我投到文學圈裏的初衷 (My original intentions for joining the literary world) (1934). In *Bai Wei zuopinxuan*, 28–38. Changsha: Hunan renmin chubanshe, 1985.

"Wo xie ta de dongji" 我寫它的動機 (My motives for writing it). *Funü Shenghuo* 1 (1935).

Zhadan yu zhengniao 炸彈與征鳥 (A bomb and an expeditionary bird). Shanghai: Beixin shuju, 1929.

Zuoye 昨夜 (Last night). 1933; reprint, Shijiazhuang: Hebei jiaoyu chubanshe, 1994.

Chen Ruoxi

The Execution of Mayor Yin and Other Stories from the Great Proletarian Cultural Revolution. Trans. Nancy Ing and Howard Goldblatt. Bloomington: Indiana University Press, 1978.

"The Fish." Tr. Nancy Ing. *The Chinese PEN* (Winter 1977):1–15.

"'I Love Chairman Mao'." Excerpts from the novel *The Repatriates*. Tr. Howard Goldblatt. In George Kao, ed., *Two Writers and the Cultural Revolution*, 159–70. Hong Kong: Chinese University Press, 1980.

"In and Outside the Wall." In Hsin-sheng C. Kao, ed., *Nativism Overseas: Contemporary Chinese Women Writers*, 25–51. Albany: SUNY Press, 1993.

"The Last Performance." Tr. Timothy Ross and Joseph Lau. In Joseph S.M. Lau, ed., *Chinese Stories from Taiwan: 1960–1970*, 3–12. New York: Columbia University Press, 1976.

"A Morning for Chao-ti." Tr. Lucy Chen. In Lucy Chen, ed., *Spirit Calling: Five Stories of Taiwan*, 3–10. Taipei: Heritage Press, 1962.

"On the Miseries of Writers in American Exile: Sanitized Versions for Taiwan, Hong Kong and the People's Republic." Tr. Kim Besio. In Helmut Martin, ed., *Modern Chinese Writers: Self-Portrayals*, 187–92. Armonk, NY: M. E. Sharpe, 1992.

The Old Man and Other Stories. Hong Kong: Chinese University of Hong Kong, 1986.

"Reunion in Nanking." Excerpts from the novel *The Repatriates*. Tr. Howard Goldblatt. In George Kao, ed., *Two Writers and the Cultural Revolution*, 159–70. Hong Kong: Chinese University Press, 1980.

The Short Stories of Ruoxi Chen, Translated from the Original Chinese: A Writer at the Crossroads. Tr. Hsin-sheng C. Kao. Lewiston, NY: Edwin Mellen, 1992.

Chen Xuezhao

Surviving the Storm: A Memoir. Tr. Hua Ti and Caroline Green. Ed. Jeffrey Kinkley. Armonk, NY: M. E. Sharpe, 1990.

Chuncha 春茶 (Spring camellias). Beijing: Zuojia chubanshe, 1957.

"Gei nanxing" 給男性 (To men). *Xin Nüxing* (December 1926).

Gongzuozhe shi meili de 工作者是美麗的 (To be working is beautiful) (1949). Hangzhou: Zhejiang renmin chuban she, 1979.

Nanfeng de meng 南風的夢 (Dream of southern winds). Shanghai: Zhenmeishan shudian, 1929.

Tudi 土地 (The land). Beijing: Renmin wenxue chubanshe, 1953.

"Xiandai nüxing de kumen wenti" 現代女性的苦悶問題 (Woes of the modern woman). *Xin nüxing* (January 1927). Tr. Amy Dooling. Reprinted in Amy C. Dooling and Kristina M. Torgeson, eds. *Writing Women in Modern China: An Anthology of Women's Literature from the Early Twentieth Century,* 169–173. New York: Columbia University Press, 1998.

Xingfu 幸福 (Happiness). Shanghai: Shenghuo shudian, 1933.

Yi Bali 憶巴黎 (Remembering Paris). Shanghai: Beixin shuju, 1929.

Yan'an fangwenji 延安訪問記 (Interviews at Yan'an). Hong Kong: Beiji, 1940.

Yanxia banlu 煙霞伴侶 (Travel companion in the twilight mist). Beijing: Beijing guangbo xueyuan chubanshe, 1993.

"A Young Nurse in Manchuria" (1946). In Li Yu-ning, ed., *Chinese Women Through Chinese Eyes,* 247–251. Armonk, NY: M. E. Sharpe, 1992.

"Zuihou de xin" 最後的信 (The last letter), 115. *Zhenmeishan: Nüzuojia hao* (1928).

Fengzi

Banian 八年 (Eight years). Shanghai: Wanye chubanshe, 1945.

Huaxiang: Fengzi sanwen xiaoshuo xuanji 畫像–鳳子散文小說選集 (The portrait: A collection of Fengzi's essays and fiction). Beijing: Beijing chubanshe, 1982.

Renjian haishi 人間海市 (Mirages). Shanghai: Shanghai wenyi chubanshe, 1998.

Shapiro, Sidney. *I Chose China.* New York: Hippocrene Books, 2000.

Taishang taixia 台上·台下 (On and off the stage). Zhongguo xiju chubanshe, 1985.

Wusheng de genü 無聲的歌女 (The silent singing girl). Shanghai: Zhenggong chubanshe, 1946.

Wutai manbu 舞台漫步 (Meandering on the stage). Shanghai: Dalu tushu zazhi chubanshe, 1945.

Hu Lanqi

Hu Lanqi huiyilu 1901–1936. 胡蘭畦回憶錄 (Memoirs of Hu Lanqi). Chengdu: Sichuan renmin chubanshe, 1985.

Dongxian de chetui 東線的撤退 (Retreat from the eastern front). Hankou: Shenghuo shudian, 1938.

Songhu houxianshang 在淞滬火線上 (On the Songhu battle line). Hankou: Shenghuo shudian, 1938.

Zhandi ernian 戰地二年 (Two years on the battleground). Hu Lanqi, ed. Laodong: Funü zhandi fuwutuan, 1939.

Zai Deguo nülaozhong 在德國女牢中 (In a German women's prison) (1937). Chengdu: Sichuan renmin chubanshe, 1981.

Lu Xiaoman

Aimei xiaozha. 愛眉小札 (Love letters to Mei) (1936). Beijing: Dongfang chubanshe, 1994.

Lu Xiaoman and Xu Zhimo. *Bian Kungang* 卞昆岡 (Bian Kungang). Shanghai: Xinyue shudian, 1928.

Ru Zhijuan

"A Promise Is Kept." In *Sowing the Clouds: A Collection of Chinese Short Stories*, 78–89. Peking: Foreign Language Press, 1961.

Caoyuan shang de xiaolu 草原上的小路 (Small road in the grasslands). Tianjin: Baihua wenyi chubanshe, 1982.

Gao gao de baiyangshu. 高高的白楊樹 (White poplars). Shanghai: Shanghai wenyi chubanshe, 1959.

"How I Came to Write 'Lilies on a Comforter.'" Tr. John Balcom. In Helen Siu, ed., *Furrows, Peasants, Intellectuals and the State: Stories and Histories from Modern China*, 297–303. Stanford: Stanford University Press, 1990.

Jingjing de chanyuan 靜靜的產院 (The quiet maternity ward). Beijing: Zhongguo qingnian chubanshe, 1962.

Lilies and Other Stories. Beijing: Panda Books, 1985.

Mantan wo de chuangzuo jingli 漫談我的創作經歷 (A casual discussion of my creative experience). Changsha: Hunan renmin chubanshe, 1983.

Su Qing

"Going Home" (1949). Tr. Janet Ng. In *May Fourth Women Writers: Memoirs*, 123–33. Hong Kong: Renditions Press, 1996.

Jiehun shinian 結婚十年 (Ten years of marriage). Shanghai: Sihai chubanshe, 1944.

Su Qing sanwen 蘇青散文 (Su Qing's essays). Yu Liqing, ed. Taibei: Wusi shudian, 1989.

Su Qing xiaoshuo ji 蘇青小說集 (Su Qing's fiction). Hefei: Anhui wenyi chubanshe, 1996.

Su Qing wenji 蘇青文集 (Collected works of Su Qing). 2 vols. Shanghai: Shanghai shudian, 1994.

Tao 濤 (Waves). Hong Kong: Lili chubanshe, 1952.

Xu jiehun shinian 續結婚十年 (Sequel to *Ten years of marriage*). Shanghai: Sihai chubanshe, 1947.

Xie Bingying

Congjun riji 從軍日記 (War diary) (1928). In *Xie Bingying wenji*, vol 1, 287–308. Hefei: Anhui wenyi chubanshe, 1998.

"Gei S-mei de yifeng xin" 給 S- 妹的一封信 (A letter to S—) (1929). In *Xie Bingying zuopinxuan*, 553–69. Changsha: Hunan renmin chubanshe, 1985.

Girl Rebel: The Autobiography of Hsieh Pingying, with Extracts from Her New War Diaries.
Tr. Adet and Anor Lin, intro. by Lin Yutang. New York: Da Capo Press, 1975.

"Guanyu *Nübing zizhuan*" 關於女兵自傳 (About *Autobiography of a woman soldier*).
In *Nübing zizhuan*, 1–10. Sichuan: Wenyi chubanshe, 1985.

Lihun 離婚 (Divorce, 1947). In *Wutiji* 無題集 (Untitled). Zhao Qingge, ed. Shanghai: n.p., 1947.

Nübing zizhuan 女兵自傳 (Autobiography of a woman soldier) (1936). In *Xie Bingying wenji*, vol. 1, 3–283. Hefei: Anhui wenyi chubanshe, 1998.

"Paoqi" 拋棄 (Abandoned, 1936). In *Xie Bingying daibiaozuo*, 323–63. Beijing: Huaxia
chubanshe, 1999.

A Woman Soldier's Own Story: The Autobiography of Xie Bingying. Trans. Lily Chia
Brissman and Barry Brissman. New York: Columbia University Press, 2001.

Xie Bingying sanwen xuanji 謝冰瑩散文集 (The selected essays of Xie Bingying). De-
min Fu, ed. Tianjin: Baihua wenyi chubanshe, 1992.

Xie Bingying wenji 謝冰瑩文集 (Collected works of Xie Bingying). 3 vols. Hefei: Anhui wenyi chubanshe, 1998.

Xie Bingying zuopin xuan 謝冰瑩作品選 (Selected works of Xie Bingying). Changsha:
Hunan renmin chubanshe, 1985.

Yang Gang

Daughter. Beijing: Foreign Languages Press, 1988.

Huan Xiu waizhuan 桓秀外傳 (An unofficial biography of Huan Xiu). Shanghai:
Wenhua shenghuo shudian, 1941.

Meiguo zhaji 美國札記 (Notes from America). Beijing: Shijie zhishi she, 1951.

Tiaozhan 挑戰 (Throwing down the gauntlet). Beijing: Renmin wenxue chubanshe,
1988.

Yang Gang xiaoshuo: Huan Xiu waizhuan 楊剛小說: 桓秀外傳 (Yang Gang's fiction:
The unofficial biography of Huan Xiu). Shanghai: Guji chubanshe, 1999.

Yang Gang wenji 楊剛文集 (Collected works of Yang Gang). Beijing: Renmin wenxue
chubanshe, 1984.

"Yige nianqing de Zhongguo gongchangdangyuan de zizhuan" 一個年輕的中國共
產黨員的自傳 (Autobiography of a young Chinese communist) (1931). In *Yang
Gang wenji* 楊剛文集 (Collected works of Yang Gang). Beijing: Renmin wenxue
chubanshe, 1984.

Yang Jiang

"The Art of Listening." In David Pollard, ed., *The Chinese Essay*, 260–264. New York:
Columbia University Press, 2000.

Chenxin Ruyi 稱心如意 (As you desire). Beijing: Shijie shuju, 1943. Reprinted in *Yang
Jiang zuopinji*, 247–344. Beijing: Zhongguo shehui kexue chubanshe, 1993.

"Cloak of Invisibility." In David Pollard, ed., *The Chinese Essay*, 264–269. New York:
Columbia University Press, 2000.

Nongzhen chengjia 弄真成假 (Forging the truth). Shanghai: Shijie shuju, 1944. Reprinted in *Yang Jiang zuopinji,* 345–430. Beijing: Zhongguo shehui kexue chubanshe, 1993.

Six Chapters from My Life "Down Under" (1981). Tr. Howard Goldblatt. Seattle: University of Washington Press, 1988.

Yang Jiang zuopinji 楊絳作品集 (Collected works of Yang Jiang). 3 vols. Beijing: Zhongguo shehui kexue chubanshe, 1993.

"Windswept Blossoms" (1946). Tr. Edward Gunn. In Edward Gunn, ed. *Twentieth-Century Chinese Drama, An Anthology,* 228–275. Bloomington: Indiana University Press, 1983.

Women sa 我們仨 (We three). Beijing: Sanlian shudian, 2003.

Xizao 洗澡 (Taking a bath). Beijing: Sanlian shudian, 1988.

Zong Pu

"The Back Door." In Hugh Anderson, ed., *A Wind Across the Grass,* 89–98. Ascot Vale, Victoria: Red Rooster Press, 1985.

"The Call of the Ruins." Tr. David Pollard. In David Pollard, ed., *The Chinese Essay,* 317–20. New York: Columbia University Press, 2000.

The Everlasting Rock. Tr. Aimee Lykes. Boulder: Lynne Rienner, 1997.

"Lu Lu." In Hugh Anderson, ed., *A Wind Across the Grass,* 105–16. Ascot Vale, Victoria: Red Rooster Press, 1985.

"The Marriage of Late Sister." Tr. Sidney Shapiro. *Chinese Literature* 1 (1964): 3–21.

"Melody in Dreams." Tr. Song Shouquan. *Chinese Literature* 8 (1979): 78–99.

"The Tragedy of the Walnut Tree." Tr. Zhu Hong. In Zhu Hong, ed., *The Serenity of Whiteness: Stories by and About Women in Contemporary China,* 282–300. New York: Ballantine, 1991.

"Who Am I?" In Hugh Anderson, ed., *A Wind Across the Grass,* 99–104. Ascot Vale, Victoria: Red Rooster Press, 1985.

Translators

GEREMIE R. BARMÉ is a professor of Chinese history at the Australian National University, as well as a writer, translator, and filmmaker whose recent works include the two-hour documentary film *Morning Sun* (co-director and co-writer), the Web site www.morningsun.org, and *An Artistic Exile: A Life of Feng Zikai (1898–1975)* (University of California Press).

AMY D. DOOLING is associate professor of Chinese literature at Connecticut College. She is the coeditor, with Kristina M. Torgeson, of *Writing Women in Modern China: An Anthology of Women's Literature from the Early Twentieth Century* (Columbia University Press, 1998) and the author of *Women's Literary Feminism in Twentieth-Century China* (Palgrave Macmillan, 2005).

HOWARD GOLDBLATT, Research Professor at the University of Notre Dame, is best known for his translations of modern and contemporary fiction from China and Hong Kong.

MINGLIANG HU, Ph.D. in linguistics from the University of Florida (1991), has taught Chinese at Bowdoin College and Connecticut College. He is now professor of English and linguistics at Shanxi University, China. He has published articles on linguistics, translation, and contrastive studies of English and Chinese.

ANN HUSS is assistant professor of modern Chinese literature, cinema, and language at Wellesley College.

DEIRDRE SABINA KNIGHT, assistant professor of Chinese and comparative literature at Smith College, is completing a book manuscript titled *The Heart of Time: Moral Agency in Twentieth-Century Chinese Fiction*.

YUNZHONG SHU teaches Chinese and Chinese literature at Queens College, CUNY. He is the author of *Buglers on the Home Front: The Wartime Practice of the Qiyue School* (Albany: SUNY Press, 2000) and is engaged in research on modern and contemporary Chinese literature.

CATHY SILBER has been teaching and translating Chinese literature for several years, most recently at Hamilton College.

ROBIN VISSER, assistant professor of Chinese language and modern literature at the University of North Carolina at Chapel Hill, is completing a book manuscript titled *The Urban Subject in the Cultural Imagination of Post–Mao China*.